ISSUES AND PARTIES
IN LEGISLATIVE VOTING

Harper's American Political Behavior Series
Under the Editorship of DAVID J. DANELSKI

HARPER & ROW, PUBLISHERS
New York, Evanston, and London

ISSUES AND PARTIES
IN LEGISLATIVE VOTING

METHODS OF STATISTICAL ANALYSIS

DUNCAN MACRAE, Jr.

University of Chicago

ISSUES AND PARTIES IN LEGISLATIVE VOTING:
Methods of Statistical Analysis

Library of Congress Catalog Card Number: 72-96231

To my parents

CONTENTS

PART II
PARTIES AND FACTIONS

PREFACE

LTHOUGH statistical analysis of legislative votes is being used increasingly in political and historical studies, its methodological foundations are still insecure. Some researchers use advanced statistical techniques, programmed for computers, without sufficient scrutiny of the conditions for their application to particular problems. And general concepts such as "party loyalty" are often identified with particular measures in a way that hinders research by slowing the search for better measures. Such problems, especially in political science, may have resulted from an artificial consensus among behavioral researchers defending their innovations against criticism based on a more traditional approach to politics. But the practice of natural scientists reminds us that it is absurd to leave the criticism of research methods to those who do not fully understand them; a lively and penetrating criticism, leveled by specialists at one another, is one condition for the rapid improvement of methods and concepts. I hope that my own contributions will be viewed in this way, and that as criticism develops, abler mathematical minds will be drawn to participate in it.

The relations between concepts and measurement can be usefully illustrated by an account of the various indices that have been developed for the analysis of legislative votes. In this volume I shall illustrate some general points about concept formation in social science—including shortcomings as well as advantages of prevalent methods. The limitation of our subject matter to legislative votes, however, makes the treatment of methods appear less general than the broad issues that the materials illustrate. Unlike a general textbook on research methods, this book deals with methods of measurement and classification related to *particular concepts*. This restriction emphasizes certain general points: that concepts and hypotheses guide the choice of methods; that there is a continual interplay between measurements and concepts; and that multiple operational definitions of a given concept are not always clearly distinguishable from indicators of a multiplicity of distinct concepts.

Our choice of concepts and methods is also constrained by the practical facilities for carrying out certain operations at a particular time. The importance of research technology is well known in the natural sciences. In social science, survey analysis and computer applications have been among the most important developments of this kind in recent decades. Yet there is a continual concern that the availability of such methods will improperly affect our choice of problems. Without rejecting this concern, I have deliberately chosen methods here that can be used with reasonable economy for large data matrices such as those provided by the votes of the U.S. House of Representatives. In doing so, I note simply that choices of research strategy and tactics, like all other choices, involve the comparison of alternatives; and the advantages of particular methods and techniques ought to be weighted in the balance together with other considerations, rather than ignored.

One consequence of these practical limitations is that I have used methods perhaps less elegant than some that are now available for smaller data matrices. The work of Guttman and Lingoes on nonmetric multidimensional scaling, of Coombs on multidimensional unfolding, and Lazarsfeld on latent structure analysis, all exemplify models that make fewer assumptions about the operations that can be performed on data of this type. Eventually one or more of these methods may prove useful for the problems treated here. But the computer programs in which they are now embodied do not even approach the capacity of 150 roll calls and 450 legislators, which we need. Since I wish to study legislatures rather than to develop general measurement models, I have chosen other alternatives.

It is tempting, and perhaps more conventional, to present this material in a more general perspective, relating to dichotomous variables generally rather than simply to legislative roll calls. But I have resisted this temptation, because no matter how general and inter-disciplinary the methods treated here may seem, their evaluation repeatedly draws us back to the specifically political and legislative problems which we have to consider in choosing alternative methods. The nonexperimental nature of the data, the difficulty of assigning polarities automatically, the importance of actual social groups and formal organizations (legislative parties) whose members consult about the responses we are analyzing, and the publicly known identities and statements of the legislators—these features distinguish our particular sort of data from other data to which similar methods have been applied in the study of attitudes and psychological tests. Psychologists who read this book may also reflect on the fact that the generality of the arguments used to introduce factor analysis has often been limited by a perspective peculiar to psychology. General texts on factor analysis often contain references to the presumed nature of personality, the structure of which may not be the same as that of legislative issues. And Thurstone's notion of "simple structure" seems unduly restricted in comparison with the criteria we need to reveal the existence of parties and partisanship by rotation of axes. Thus even if my perspective here is narrowly restricted to legislative analysis, it can serve as a corrective to other perspectives, also nar-rower than they appear, and perhaps advance the development of a more general one when a variety of data and substantive contexts are systematically explored.

There is, nevertheless, a greater generality in my treatment than one often finds in the literature of political science. Unfortunately, different methods have been used in the study of state legislatures, Congress, the Supreme Court, and the United Nations General As-sembly; and the problems of method encountered in each of these substantive fields have not been sufficiently considered in the others. Thus while there is some virtue in social scientists' concentration on problems of application to particular contexts, this should not blind them to the more general implications of their work for theory and method.

In at least two respects, the argument presented here must be considered part of a more extended one that will continue beyond this volume. First, the contention that I am measuring issue positions and partisanship requires support from extensive tests of hypotheses connecting these variables with others. Second, my emphasis on specific concepts, rather than blind empiricism or content-free methods, can be carried further than I have carried it here. Specific models of legislators' decision processes might be introduced prior to an effort to measure general attitude variables; these models might be concerned with events that occur during the time interval in which a legislator arrives at his position on a bill. The models toward which I am implicitly working involve the interrelations between changes in legislators' positions, constituency variables, and careers over time intervals of one or more years; the corresponding measurement procedures thus conceal and summarize changes that take place over shorter intervals. Evaluation of the relative merits of these two approaches, and their synthesis, are tasks that must be left to the future.

The level of mathematical treatment also deserves some explanation. Political science has been among the most backward of the social sciences in its students' mathematical preparation. The level of expectation in this respect in the not-too-distant past was shown by Key's *Primer of Statistics for Political Scientists,* which assumed only high-school algebra. The same level of preparation has typically been assumed in introductory statistics courses for political scientists. But mathematical knowledge among students of politics is increasing rapidly, as is its relevance to research and theory formulation. Moreover, we cannot be sure that the best path to competence in this area is through a conventional social statistics course. Calculus and matrix algebra may come to be universal features of undergraduate preparation in the social sciences. We cannot assume at present that standard courses of this sort exist, but one of my tasks here is to indicate how that gap might be filled. For this reason I present elementary derivations making use of calculus, so that those readers who know it may use it. But in the longer run this approach may well be superseded by genuine courses in mathematics.

Social scientists who are accustomed to reading books passively should note that the derivations are often condensed, and that one can get more from them by reading with paper and pencil at hand. Full understanding of the numerical and algebraic materials requires that the reader be able to carry through all the exercises indicated in the text.

Because the mathematical materials I have drawn on are not common knowledge among political scientists, I have tried to keep them to a minimum necessary for the understanding of the argument. Thus the treatment of statistical inference, or of communalities and oblique axes in factor analysis, has been sharply restricted. While the reader will become acquainted with scaling, cluster analysis, regression, and factor analysis, he should recognize that a more complete coverage of each of these topics can be found elsewhere.

A number of technical terms that occur in the text, relating either to mathematics or to roll-call analysis, are defined in the Glossary at the end of the book. The footnotes throughout the book provide abbreviated citations to published sources; the complete citations are given in the Bibliography at the end of the book.

I am indebted to the National Science Foundation for supporting the research in which some of these methods were developed or tested. For valuable insights into the legislative process in Congress, I am indebted to a grant from the Rockefeller Foundation which enabled me to spend several months in Washington in 1965, to The Brookings Institution for its hospitality at that time, and to the congressmen and informed observers who shared their experience with me. While much of this book will seem remote from the day-to-day workings of Congress, that experience was essential in convincing me of the importance of measuring partisanship, and in providing valuable qualitative data against which various measures might be checked.

I have been aided by a number of conscientious research assistants —David H. Johns, Paul A. Epstein, A. Stephen Boyan, Tetsuya Kataoka, Jeanne Hahn, Daniel R. Graves, Brian F. Sherry, Susan B. Schwarz, Erik Jensen, and Jonathan Still. Helpful suggestions have been made by several persons who have read all or part of the manuscript in various drafts—Jonathan Pool, Herbert Weisberg, Robert Beckman, Terrance A. Nosanchuk, John L. McCarthy, David J. Danelski, Gerald Kramer, and Harold J. Spaeth. The students in my course on legislative voting behavior have given me useful reactions over the years in which this material has taken shape. The remaining errors are, of course, mine. Dwythea Banks typed the manuscript with care.

Edith K. MacRae, in addition to providing wifely encouragement, has continually reminded me by her own work of the procedures followed in the more rigorous sciences, which I have taken in large measure as a model.

Duncan MacRae, Jr.

ISSUES AND PARTIES
IN LEGISLATIVE VOTING

1.
LEGISLATURES, CONCEPTS, AND MEASUREMENT

THE recorded divisions in legislative bodies provide valuable information about the larger political systems in which those bodies function. The external relations of legislatures to other branches of government, and to influential groups in the society, tell much about how policies are formed and where power lies.[1] Their internal relations tend to obey regularities of their own, as de Jouvenel recognized when he observed:

There is less difference between two deputies, one of whom is a revolutionary and the other is not, than between two revolutionaries, one of whom is a deputy and the other is not.[2]

And for the study of the specific problems of how particular laws come into existence—or fail to do so—the study of legislatures is essential.

The general inferences that we can make about legislatures and political systems from divisions of the vote can also be made about other bodies and groups that resemble legislatures. Not only national, state, and local governing bodies, but also multimember courts, political party conventions, international assemblies, constitutional conventions, and other collegial

[1]See MacRae, "The Sociology of Legislatures." For a complete citation for this and all other sources mentioned in the footnotes, see the Bibliography at the end of this book.

[2]*La République des camarades*, p. 17.

bodies convened for various purposes can be studied by similar methods.[3] Indeed, the work of any group concerned with common issues, and recording disagreements about them, involves processes and data similar to those of legislatures. Thus the attitudes of the public at large or segments of it are also amenable to the techniques we shall consider, many of which were first developed in attitude and opinion research.

We shall be concerned primarily with identifying issues and group alignments from legislative votes or related data.[4] This concern may seem narrow compared with broader questions to which we have alluded. But the precise study of many of these broad questions depends on accurate indicators for variables related to issues and factions. Moreover, merely to compare two measures of a concept with each other we need to consider their relative efficacy in demonstrating propositions or answering questions that connect the concept measured with other concepts.

A scientific proposition is normally expressed as a relation between certain words or symbols. These words or symbols stand for concepts or general notions that can be defined in abstract terms. Alternatively, a concept may be given an operational definition which puts it into correspondence with a procedure of measurement.[5] But this is a one-to-many correspondence, for normally a concept may be operationally defined in various ways, each corresponding to a distinct procedure. Some of these operational definitions may correspond with one another to a high degree of accuracy (especially in natural science) and be practically interchangeable; others may be better or poorer manifestations of the general concept. Whether one operational definition is better than another is a question with which we shall be frequently concerned.

Many sources of information can be used to test propositions about legislative bodies. Recent studies in the U.S. Congress, for example, have included close observation of the workings of House and Senate; systematic interviews of legislators about their attitudes, decisions,

[3]Schubert, The Judicial Mind; Munger and Blackhurst, "Factionalism in the National Conventions"; Alker and Russett, World Politics in the General Assembly; Canon, "The Case of the FCC."

[4]See MacRae, "Some Underlying Variables in Legislative Roll-Call Votes."

[5]See Kaplan, The Conduct of Inquiry, pp. 39–42; Mellor, "Inexactness and Explanation."

and roles; and careful reading and analysis of the voluminous printed record produced by these bodies.[6] A similar variety of methods has been used in the study of other legislative bodies.[7]

These different sources of information correspond to multiple possible operational definitions of various concepts. We shall be particularly concerned with operational definitions of one type—those that derive from the written record. This record provides a kind of information that interviews and contemporary observation cannot: a series of comparable data covering in some cases more than a century.[8] And while contemporary researches have obvious practical relevance, historical and comparative studies set the limits to our generalizations. In scientific work we must try not only to generalize, but also to seek out the limits within which our generalizations hold. A scientific proposition consists not merely of a relation between concepts, but also of a set of conditions under which that relation holds. Research involves a constant effort to push generalizations to their limits, in order both to know these limits and to replace the generalizations by new ones when they are challenged at their limits. The changes in political and social institutions that have taken place over the time span of recorded legislative votes are different from, and sometimes broader than, the variations that we can observe within or between contemporary societies. Moreover, the study of historical series permits the control of formal institutional variables in a way that cross-national comparisons do not.

Among the written records available in historical series we make a further selection by concentrating our attention on roll-call votes and similar data.[9] These have the further advantage of having been grouped

---

[6]See, for example, Peabody and Polsby (eds.), *New Perspectives on the House of Representatives;* Miller and Stokes, "Constituency Influence in Congress"; Rosenau, "Senate Attitudes Toward a Secretary of State."

[7]See Wahlke, Eulau, Buchanan, and Ferguson, *The Legislative System;* Barber, *The Lawmakers;* Prewitt, *The Recruitment of Political Leaders.*

[8]Some historical researches using legislative votes are Aydelotte, "Voting Patterns in the British House of Commons in the 1840's"; Silbey, *The Shrine of Party;* and Alexander, *Sectional Stress and Party Strength.* Other written records are of course also used by historians, and some provide useful time series over long periods.

[9]Other types of data that are formally similar include the names on members' petitions, such as discharge petitions in Congress or Early Day Motions in the British House of Commons (see Finer, Berrington, and Bartholomew, *Backbench Opinion in the House of Commons 1955–59);* whip polls, as used in Froman and

into simple categories—yea and nay—by the legislators themselves. Without the classifying operations of content analysis, they are immediately adapted to statistical analyses that allow comparison of one historical period with another. With this sort of comparison, we can study aspects of the functioning of a party system, the leadership of the executive branch, or the career patterns of legislators in relation to their positions on issues. Roll-call votes are not the only such pre-classified data; legislators' committee memberships, the votes polled for legislators within their constituencies, and the progress of bills through the necessary legislative stages, for example, are equally amenable to statistical analysis.

Computer programs for processing legislative votes, and archives including extensive series of such votes in form suitable for computer input, now permit repeated tests of numerous hypotheses about legislative processes. We can delineate the bases of division within a given legislative body and within its parties, examine the changes of these divisions over time, and relate these bases of division to party control of the executive and legislative branches. In addition, we can discover the ordering of legislators in relation to these bases of division and correlate their individual positions with party, constituency, and biography. The sensitivity of legislators' votes to influences measured in these ways can be related to their electoral security, their seniority and positions of legislative leadership, their party's majority or minority status, and their ambitions. Provided that legislators differ sufficiently from one another in their votes, and not simply along party lines, systematic study of their votes can throw new light on questions of this sort.

Before detailed consideration of methods of analysis of roll-call votes, we should consider the possible shortcomings of these data as well as their advantages. What they gain in historical depth, they may lose by being only indirect indicators and resultants of various factors that can be examined separately and directly in studies of contemporary legislatures. Interviews, debates, and legislative documents may be both more directly relevant to legislative processes and more detailed. Roll-call data are selective—some important

---

Ripley, "Conditions for Party Leadership"; and lists of names corresponding to joint sponsorship of bills (in the U.S. Senate) or joint questions (in the Indian Lok Sabha).

legislative decisions never reach this stage. And they are joint products or resultants of numerous influences; unless we can separate these influences, purer indications of the legislator's private attitudes or of the influences of his constituency may be available from other sources. Insofar as these disadvantages obtain, other methods should be used. Some of these other methods, however, are subjective as well as selective, and often require the objectivity of supplemental statistical analysis. For this purpose, even when other sources of data are available, roll-call analysis still has much to offer.

Some of the problems involved in evaluating roll-call votes as research data are illustrated by two recent articles on the measurement of legislative partisanship. One simple and widely used measure of the degree of partisanship on a roll call in a two-party legislature is Rice's index of difference—the absolute difference between the percentages voting "yea" in the two parties. This is one possible operational definition of "partisanship" as applied to roll calls.[10] Crane, in a study of the Wisconsin legislature, compared it with the legislators' own explanations for their votes, given in interviews.[11] For each of 20 selected roll calls, the percentage of legislators citing partisan reasons for their votes was calculated. This percentage correlated +.50 with the index of difference.

This correlation describes the relation between two possible operational definitions of "partisanship" or "party pressure," for it seems reasonable that legislators should be aware of party influence. In Crane's interpretation, this was far less than perfect, and showed that the index of difference—or perhaps roll-call analysis in general—could not adequately reveal the partisan influences involved on these bills. But from another viewpoint, .50 might be considered a high association. And in a reply to Crane, Greenstein and Jackson pointed out that either of the two operational definitions might be at fault.[12] They suggested alternative definitions of "party influence" such that this influence could occur even without legislators' reporting partisan reasons for their votes.

[10]The general problem of measuring partisanship, and alternative indices for this purpose, will be considered in Part II.

[11]Crane, "A Caveat on Roll-Call Studies of Party Voting." The presentation of Crane's findings is modified here for simplicity of exposition.

[12]Greenstein and Jackson, "A Second Look at the Validity of Roll-Call Analysis."

The general lesson to be drawn from this interchange is that while certain indices derived from roll calls may diverge to some extent from other measures of the same variables or concepts, the source of this disparity may not lie exclusively in the use of roll calls. Either of the alternative measures or operational definitions may in principle be criticized; and it may also be found that the conceptual definitions underlying the two measures are not precisely the same. This necessity to question both concepts and definitions complicates the evaluation of methods, yet continually confronts us as we compare procedures even within roll-call analysis alone. We shall show in Part II, for example, that there are many possible ways of treating roll-call votes so as to measure partisanship, and that consideration of the index of difference is merely a beginning of this subject.

ISSUES AND PARTIES

The major conceptual distinction with which this book is concerned is that between legislative issues and factions; the chief factions that we shall consider are the two legislative parties in Congress. To explain the division on a roll call, or to generalize about a number of similar divisions, we may look to the issues at stake or to the interrelations of the legislators grouped on each side. Each of these perspectives leads us to seek a corresponding type of information with which to supplement and interpret the votes. First, we may consider the substance of the matter on which the vote was taken: the wording of the bill, its expected effects, the arguments that interpret it in terms of general justifying principles. Alternatively, we may consider the groupings of legislators who are typically allied or opposed—their group ties and channels of communication, their strategic and tactical calculations, their political ambitions.

These two considerations, of issues and factions, are related. The effect of a bill may impinge directly on groups represented in the legislature—parties, factions, or their constituent interests. Conversely, the very existence of parties or factions may depend on their having common ideological principles that relate the substance of bills to the group's existence and cohesion.

Nevertheless, the concepts are not identical and must be distinguished. They have been unnecessarily combined and confused in legislative analysis, especially roll-call analysis. The same data, used in similarly computed and highly correlated indices, have been used by different authors to infer legislators' "liberalism–conservatism" and "partisanship." The conditions under which one or the other use of such data is permissible have not been adequately explored.

Moreover, each of these two general concepts can profitably be subdivided; the same procedures of clarification that help to separate one from the other can also be used in the internal subdivision of each. When we deal with issues we need to specify for particular roll calls just which issues are involved and to what degree. In distinguishing one issue from another we properly begin by reading and interpreting the title of a bill, its text, the committee hearings and debates, interview material, and the commentary of the press. But we soon find it necessary to sort out and correct the multiple and contradictory impressions thus gained. And looking for the broader picture amid the hundred or more roll calls in a legislative session, we need time-saving devices that will automatically classify them into approximately similar subsets. The interplay between these subsets and various issue concepts defines the scope of Part I of this book.

On the other hand, as we look for significant groupings of legislators—i.e., interacting social groups and not just categories of ideological resemblance—we may introduce concepts corresponding to particular types of groups. In the congressional material with which we shall deal, our concern will be largely with the two American legislative parties. But even here, as we shall see in Chapter 8, the possible interpretations of "party" are multiple rather than unitary. The reasoning that leads to this conclusion, and its embodiment in specific procedures of measurement, occupies Part II of this book.

PART I
ISSUES

2.
SCALE ANALYSIS

W E shall now analyze two main problems: the identification of issues and of factions. We shall initially consider each separately, and not combine them until we have covered methods complex enough to show how they are related.

We define an issue as a characteristic that distinguishes certain roll calls from others in terms of their substance or content.[1] Thus if we say that certain roll calls involve foreign policy and others domestic policy, we have separated them according to two issue categories. Such categories may be more or less specific: within domestic policy we might speak, for example, of agricultural and tax policy.

Characteristics defining issues may be either categories into which each roll call may be placed, or they may be variables to which a given roll call is more or less related. The distinction between categories and variables corresponds to a difference in methods of analysis that will be discussed later.

Although an observer may categorize roll calls in many different ways—by their date of occurrence, degree of partisanship, the committee reporting the bill, and so on—we imply a

---

[1] Issues are also clearly involved in campaigns, discussions, and many other situations; we limit the definition here for simplicity. When we relate an issue to a set of roll calls, we consider the latter to involve not only lists of names, but extensive processes of opinion and attitude formation associated with these lists.

double restriction in categorizing them in terms of issues. First, as the definition implies, it is the substance of the bill or motion at hand that must provide the basis of the classification. Second, the classification must be useful in formulating general statements about the legislative body under study.

These two requirements may be connected if we assume that the most useful categories for our analysis are those entertained by the participants themselves. We therefore seek a common frame of reference shared by legislators and others who participate in legislative decisions—a frame of reference that the participants recognize and can formulate in words. The fact that two or more roll calls share a common issue is to be inferred not only from the votes themselves, but also from the words that the participants use in justifying their votes or describing the matters at stake. The notion that issues are related to the participants' perceptions of the questions being considered is analogous to Crane's requirement for indices of partisanship, discussed above: that the legislators be aware that party is involved.

We shall be concerned mainly with inferences from roll-call votes rather than from legislators' reports, but cross-checking and comparison of independent indicators of the same concept is important. The more diverse and independent these indicators are, the greater is our assurance that our results do not depend on the particular context—such as the survey interview or the roll call—within which the data are generated.[2] And just as the diverse measures of a given concept, if empirically concordant, render it more useful, so too do the diverse relations of this concept with others in a network of empirically verified hypotheses.

But the hypotheses used may affect the relevant classifications. This is shown by another classification that we might call one of "issue-types." Lowi has distinguished among redistributive, regulative, and distributive issues.[3] The first of these three categories corresponds most nearly to "issues" as we have considered them so far: these issues tend to involve many roll calls on which the same arguments and forces are repeatedly marshalled; they engender considerable

[2]See Webb, Campbell, Schwartz, and Sechrest, *Unobtrusive Measures,* pp. 3–5; Campbell and Fiske, "Convergent and Discriminant Validation by the Multitrait-Multimethod Matrix."

[3]Lowi, "American Business, Public Policy, Case-Studies, and Political Theory."

debate both on the floor of Congress and in the press; and the executive tends to be more involved on this type of measure than on others. At the other extreme (distributive) is the type of bill that attracts little public attention except among narrow beneficiary groups, is little contested on the floor because its details have been worked out in committee, and, on statistical analysis, seems to elicit different divisions within the parties on different roll calls. The divisions that occur on measures of this sort tend to be neglected by factor analysis or scale analysis because of their diversity and uniqueness; but they share a use of certain legislative procedures, a characteristic distribution of power in the House, and other features that make it useful to group them together. Categories that are useful for one purpose may be less so for another. But this multiplicity of concepts is an unavoidable price we pay for the multiple relations into which roll calls enter.

We cannot at this point use Lowi's distributive category, because the roll calls in it are not revealed by similarity of votes. It is quite conceivable that legislators, or students of legislative bodies, may classify roll calls alike even though the divisions of the vote on them do not resemble one another at all. Our task is therefore further limited: we seek those categories into which roll calls with similar voting patterns can be placed.[4]

Even with this restriction, one might imagine that we could classify roll calls according to issues by examining the words used to describe them in debates or other references—perhaps even the words in the bills or amendments themselves. Alternatively, we could allow informed participants to make the classification—the ADA, the Farm Bureau, the AFL–CIO, Americans for Constitutional Action, or legislative committees. Particularly if the group in question is an influential one, the legislature will be forced to consider alike those bills that the group considers alike. On this basis a number of "a priori indices" have been constructed. Legislators' scores on them have been published or used not only by groups such as those cited, but by periodicals, and by historians or commentators on the political scene.

Each of these indices is based on a selected set of roll calls; our problem is how such sets of roll calls should be chosen. Those using such indices then go on to calculate the proportion of roll calls in the

[4]Possible precise meanings of "similarity" will be considered in Chapter 3.

chosen set on which each legislator voted "favorably." Consideration of this step, of scoring or ranking legislators on issues, will also lead us toward the problem of identifying factions.

Such a priori indices are not satisfactory because the categories on which they are based may be neither objective nor significant for our understanding of the legislature. The researcher may want to know whether legislators view different roll calls as embodying different issues, or the same issues in different degrees. On occasion roll calls are classified in terms of the ideological categories of the classifiers rather than of the legislators generally. Such a classification may be important for reform but not for an understanding of the legislature as it operates.

This seems to have been the case with the *New Republic*. It has long considered advocacy of foreign aid, support of the under-privileged, and federal action for social welfare, as positions sharing a common characteristic of "liberalism." But Gage and Shimberg, as well as others, have shown that the patterns of voting on foreign and domestic questions were quite different in several Congresses following World War II.[5] The chief method used for this purpose was cumulative or Guttman scaling.

Thus if a set of roll calls are to be placed in the same issue category, we require that their vote divisions resemble one another. We begin by focusing attention exclusively on the identification of similar vote divisions. Once we identify them, we can then return to the substance of the bills, and the debate over them, to test the validity of our categories and to specify their meaning more precisely.

If we work with only the yeas and nays on each roll call (and assume for simplicity that there are no absences[6]) the data may be presented in the form of a matrix—a rectangular array with columns corresponding to roll calls, rows to legislators, and individual entries

[5]Gage and Shimberg, "Measuring Senatorial Progressivism."

[6]Another type of research would concern itself precisely with the analysis of absences. Not merely the type of differences in congressional attendance that is mentioned in campaigns, but also the cyclical absences of the "Tuesday–Thursday club" with their development over time and their relation to special types of legislation, might be studied by computer processing of roll-call data.

Certain legislatures also provide for declarations other than yea and nay on roll calls, such as abstention; these other positions can be treated by including them in dichotomies, or conceivably by models analyzing ordered polytomies directly.

to yeas and nays.[7] The operations described here for calculation of various indices based on roll-call votes may be considered as operations on this data matrix.

The task of organizing and simplifying the data matrix in terms of issues may be defined in two alternative ways, corresponding to distinct methods of analysis. One way is to ask that a given set of roll calls be sorted into subsets or categories so that the roll calls in any one subset all deal with the same issue, while those in different sets deal with different issues. The subsets found in this way need not exhaust the initial set. Alternatively, the problem can be phrased in quantitative rather than qualitative terms. In this phrasing, an issue may be involved to a greater or lesser degree in a given roll call. This second phrasing corresponds to the model of factor analysis.

But before using either of these methods, we confront a prior question: Should we start with the entire data matrix, or part of it corresponding only to a particular set of legislators? This problem can be illustrated by a finding concerning a roll call in the French National Assembly, which was considered by members of one party to involve economic questions, but by another to involve the Algerian controversy. Similarly, there is reason to believe that the structuring of issues is not always the same within the two congressional parties in the United States.[8]

In Part I, when we look for issues, we shall deal exclusively with the votes cast by a single party at a time. Although this decision is not fully justified until Part II, we call attention to it at this point.

CUMULATIVE SCALING

We begin with cumulative scaling, a method that was initially developed for analysis of questionnaire responses and later adapted for roll-call studies. Described concisely, this method aims at simplifying a data matrix by three operations:

1 *Polarity adjustment* (transformation of yea and nay into + and −) This is not normally a problem with questionnaire items,

[7]This arrangement of rows and columns is conventional in psychological research. The mathematical properties of matrices will be introduced in Chapter 4.

[8]MacRae, *Parliament, Parties and Society in France 1946–1958*, pp. 169, 173, 180; MacRae, "A Method for Identifying Issues and Factions." The prevailing practice in roll-call studies by other researchers, however, has been to combine the parties.

which are constructed so that a response in one sense, e.g., "agree" or "disagree," will be known in advance to correspond to a positive or negative tendency on the variable being measured.

2 *Rearrangement.* The order of columns (and later of rows) in the matrix may be altered to reveal the pattern that is sought.

3 *Selection.* Items (roll calls) may be omitted if they do not fit the desired pattern closely enough.[9] We thus create a single subset that is expected to be more homogeneous in issue content.

This method is based on a particular model that defines "simplicity"; we must first describe this model, for it is not the only one that can be entertained for our data. If an underlying continuum or ranking existed, on which both legislators and roll calls could be located, then this assumed model would lead to the particular simple configurations of votes that cumulative scaling seeks.

Cumulative scaling was developed by Louis Guttman during World War II for the analysis of responses on attitude questionnaires.[10] Guttman has since pioneered in developing more sophisticated techniques using more advanced mathematics and computer programs. But this particular technique has the advantages of yielding considerable clarification with few mathematical requisites.

The initial step in this procedure, as it is generally used, is to decide just what variable (dimension, concept) is to be measured. For attitude questionnaires, this decision is necessary to the design of the questions, which are considered to be chosen from a "universe of content" corresponding to the attitude under consideration. The scaling technique serves (like item analysis and related methods) to sort out, within such a universe of content, the questions that jointly fit the model from those that do not. But the initial conceptual decision gives basic guidance to the procedure which selects questions related to the initial concept and orders respondents by means of them.

Let us suppose we are trying to measure liberalism and we ask Congressmen several questions (similar to those that they ask themselves on roll calls):

a *Do you favor continuing the poverty program?*

---

[9]It is not customary to select legislators, or respondents, in this way; we shall consider below the reasons for this asymmetry in the treatment of the data matrix.

[10]See Stouffer *et al.*, *Measurement and Prediction*, chaps. 1–6.

b Do you favor expanding it by at least 10 percent?
c Do you favor expanding it by at least 30 percent?
d Do you favor expanding it by at least 50 percent?
e Do you favor home rule for the District of Columbia?

Certain obvious problems arise as to the relations between these questions and the concept "liberalism." The range of questions may be too narrow; the set of questions may not be homogeneous; and the phrases used may be ambiguous. Examination of the wording is relevant to these problems; but we may also throw light on them by studying the responses themselves in order to decide whether the questions measure the same variable.

The wording of questions a-b-c-d was chosen so as to imply that anyone answering "yes" to a lower question on the list would also say "yes" to those above it. This relationship can be represented graphically if we imagine legislators to be arrayed along a horizontal line, as in Table 2.1, and the four questions to correspond to points on this same line. They are known as "cutting points," for we further assume that each point corresponding to a question cuts the line segment into two parts, the legislators in the left-hand part voting negatively and those on the right positively. Under these assumptions the votes of the legislators in each of the five segments of the line (designated 0, 1, 2, 3, 4) will display the "perfect-scale" pattern of answers (votes) shown in Table 2.1. We can therefore identify each segment with the corresponding number of positive responses; these are in fact the designations we have given for the segments, for those

Table 2.1 Continuum with cutting points and corresponding response patterns

| | | Question | | |
	a Continue	b 10%	c 30%	d 50%
Segment	0 1	2	3	4

Responses by legislator in segment	a Continue	b 10%	c 30%	d 50%
(−)				(+)
0:	−	−	−	−
1:	+	−	−	−
2:	+	+	−	−
3:	+	+	+	−
4:	+	+	+	+

in segment 0 have no positive responses, and so on. Moreover, this number determines exactly which questions will be answered positively and negatively by legislators in that segment. The patterns of response have a cumulative property, i.e., the item answered positively by legislators in segment 1 is also answered positively by those in segment 2, whose response patterns thus cumulate.

Now suppose question e is also included. Two things might happen: it might conform to this pattern, by having a definite location on the line, or it might not. If it did conform, would we say that it measured the same variable? Perhaps, but this requires clarification of "liberalism." If it did not, would we say that it measured something different? Guttman's initial treatment gives heavy weight to conceptual considerations here; but in the study of roll calls it may be harder to do so, because we have less control over the items and their correspondence with the concepts.

The triangular pattern of pluses and minuses that we have shown to correspond to a cumulative relation between votes on individual roll calls is the configuration at which cumulative-scaling procedures aim. It is taken to be an approximate indication of the common issue content of the various roll calls that constitute it.[11] By finding sets of roll calls displaying this pattern, students of legislative processes have thrown light on the issues involved.[12]

An illustration of how such a pattern may be arrived at from roll-call data may be provided by the votes of the Republican members of the U.S. Senate on four roll-call votes in 1961, as shown in Table 2.2. The 36 Senators' votes form a matrix of 36 rows and 4 columns. The four roll calls were chosen because of their patterns of votes, not because they embodied a clearly specifiable issue concept. They are arranged in chronological order.

The votes presented in the table have no obvious relation to the

[11]Approximate, because other factors such as partisanship or group allegiance may be combined with issues and affect the result; because two or more issues may combine and elicit the same legislative divisions, through the action of parties or factions; and because the cumulative relation, while it can be produced by a set of roll calls embodying the same issue, can also derive from a cumulative relation among factions in coalitions.

[12]Two of the earliest studies of this kind by political scientists were Belknap, "A Method for Analyzing Legislative Behavior," and Farris, "A Method of Determining Ideological Groupings in the Congress."

Table 2.2 Votes of Republican Senators on four selected roll calls, 1961

Senator	Roll-call number 11	47	78	130
Aiken	N	N	N	Y
Allott	O	Y	N	Y
Beall	Y	N	Y	Y
Bennett	N	Y	Y	Y
Boggs	Y	N	Y	N
Bridges	N	Y	Y	Y
Bush	Y	N	Y	N
Butler	N	N	Y	O
Capehart	N	Y	N	Y
Carlson	Y	O	N	Y
Case (N.J.)	Y	N	O	N
Case (S.D.)	N	N	N	Y
Cooper	Y	N	N	N
Cotton	N	N	Y	Y
Curtis	N	Y	Y	Y
Dirksen	N	N	Y	Y
Dworshak	N	N	N	Y
Fong	Y	N	Y	Y
Goldwater	N	Y	Y	Y
Hickenlooper	N	N	Y	Y
Hruska	N	Y	Y	Y
Javits	Y	N	Y	N
Keating	Y	N	Y	N
Kuchel	N	N	N	Y
Miller	N	N	Y	Y
Morton	Y	N	N	N
Mundt	N	N	N	Y
Prouty	O	N	N	N
Saltonstall	Y	N	N	N
Schoeppel	N	Y	N	Y
Scott	Y	N	N	N
Smith (Me.)	Y	N	N	Y
Tower	O	O	Y	Y
Wiley	Y	O	O	N
Williams (Del.)	N	N	Y	Y
Young (N.D.)	Y	N	N	Y

NOTES:
   Y = voted, paired, or announced Yea.
   N = voted, paired, or announced Nay.
   O = Other—absent, general pair, etc.
The roll calls concerned the following bills (designated by *Congressional Quarterly* number):
   11: Area Redevelopment Act (depressed areas), passage.
   47: School Assistance Act: Goldwater substitute on tax relief.
   78: Agriculture Department authorization: Douglas amendment, reduce conservation payments.
   130: Foreign Assistance Act: Byrd amendment, require annual appropriation for Development Loan Fund.

simple pattern of pluses and minuses shown in Table 2.1. We wish to rearrange the columns (and perhaps the rows) of the matrix, and to consider eliminating one or more roll calls, in order to attain a pattern like that of the perfect scale. A necessary first step is to find out which vote on each roll call (yea or nay) should be considered positive. This is a relative decision only, since the uniform interchange of $+$ and $-$ leaves a scale essentially unaffected.

In the table as given, our task in choosing a mutually consistent set of polarities for the roll calls is facilitated by our knowledge of the subject matter of the roll calls and the identities of the Senators. (We shall show in Chapter 3, however, that polarities can be chosen on the basis of the votes alone.) Inspection of the subject matter reveals that while all four bills involve positive legislative action proposed by the Kennedy administration, the last three actually concern amendments curtailing the effects of this legislation. Two of the amendments were proposed by well-known conservatives, Goldwater and Byrd, suggesting clearly that their intention was the opposite of President Kennedy's; in the remaining case (roll call #78), the amendment was proposed by the liberal Senator Douglas, and classification of the vote on it is thus less certain.

Another clue to the polarities of the roll calls comes from the identities of the Senators who voted in particular patterns. The votes of Goldwater were N, Y, Y, Y; those of Javits, a liberal Republican, were Y, N, Y, N. On all but the third roll call they disagreed. The polarities of their votes could be made consistent by reversing the first relative to the second and fourth, e.g., by letting $N = +$ and $Y = -$ on #11. As for the third, even though the information we have on it is inconclusive, let us simply leave its polarity unaltered (let $Y = +$ and $N = -$) and proceed with the analysis.

The fact that we *can* choose the polarities of roll calls should be contrasted with the impropriety of a similar procedure for legislators —a contrast that will be important for us in Chapter 7. We can easily imagine another roll call that is the mirror image of a given roll call, with yeas and nays interchanged; such a relation between two roll calls is often created by the tactical alternation of favorable and unfavorable motions on a bill. But such an alteration of all of a legislator's votes cannot so easily be imagined, for the result would be the creation of a new and distinct legislator, opposed to the first. This asymmetry between the ways in which roll calls and legislators may be treated results from the fact that a roll call is, in one sense, simply a partition of the legislators into two subsets, unordered with respect to one another. A legislator, in contrast, cannot so easily be considered a partition of the set of roll calls being studied.

Once we convert a matrix of yeas and nays into pluses and minuses, our next step is to rearrange the matrix to approximate the cumulative model. We shall consider the fit to be perfect if the columns can be arranged so that no − precedes a + in any row. In order to make such a rearrangement, we often begin with a summary score, the number of positive responses on each roll call; a corresponding summary score can also be formed for each legislator.[13] We start by forming summary scores for roll calls, and rearranging roll calls first, because we customarily eliminate roll calls rather than legislators to improve the response patterns. As we eliminate roll calls, the summary scores of some legislators will change, while the ordering of the remaining roll calls will be unaltered.

For the four roll calls in the sequence of Table 2.2, with N considered as the positive vote on #11 and Y on each of the others, the respective proportions of positive votes (p_+) are .55, .24, .53, and .69. If we have chosen the polarity of the third roll call (#78) erroneously, then its value of p_+ will be .45 instead. Thus if we wish to arrange the columns of the table in an order that will most nearly reproduce the cumulative scale pattern, i.e., in decreasing order of p_+, we place them in the sequence: #130, #11, #78, #47, from left to right.[14] The result of rearranging the columns in this way, and changing the polarities to convert Y and N to + and − as indicated, can be discovered by the reader by making these changes in Table 2.2. (Exercise: do this.) The modified data are shown in Table 2.3, in which those Senators with identical vote patterns are grouped together and the groups arranged vertically in sequence.

The upper part of Table 2.3 consists of a "dictionary" ordering of response configurations for Senators who voted on all four roll calls; response patterns are arranged with − coming above + and left-hand

[13]This approach is used in item analysis; see Goode and Hatt, *Methods in Social Research*, pp. 275–276. It is also used in Guttman, "The Cornell Technique for Scale and Intensity Analysis"; and, together with a mathematical model, in Rasch, *Probabilistic Models for Some Intelligence and Attainment Tests*, chaps. 5, 6.

[14]With experience it becomes apparent that the sequence can equally well be followed from right to left, and that + and − can be interchanged for convenience.

Table 2.3 Republican Senators' 1961 votes, with polarities chosen and columns
and rows rearranged

Senators	Roll-call number				Scale score (without #78)
	130	11	78	47	
			p_+		
	.69	.55	.53	.24	
Without missing votes:					
Cooper, Morton, Saltonstall, Scott	−	−	−	−	0
Boggs, Bush, Javits, Keating	−	−	+	−	0
Smith (Me.), Young (N.D.)	+	−	−	−	1
Beall, Fong	+	−	+	−	1
Aiken, Case (S.D.), Dworshak, Kuchel, Mundt	+	+	−	−	2
Capehart, Schoeppel	+	+	−	+	3
Cotton, Dirksen, Hickenlooper, Miller, Williams (Del.)	+	+	+	−	2
Bennett, Bridges, Curtis, Goldwater, Hruska	+	+	+	+	3
With missing votes:					
Allott	+	0	−	+	3
Butler	0	+	+	−	2
Carlson	+	−	−	0	1
Case (N.J.)	−	−	0	−	0
Prouty	−	0	−	−	0
Tower	+	0	+	0	1, 2, 3
Wiley	−	−	0	0	0

responses taking precedence over those to the right. Of the logically possible 2^4 or 16 patterns, only 8 appear; clearly some nonrandom structure limits the response patterns on these 4 roll calls. Furthermore, if we examine the patterns of response for sources of error in one or another item, we find that all errors can be eliminated by the removal of #78; and that this situation will still remain even if the polarity on #78 is reversed. Thus the ambiguity about the polarity of #78, which we found in examining the content of the roll calls and the known positions of their sponsors and of the Senators voting, is confirmed by study of the response patterns themselves. The example was chosen to demonstrate this point, but similar findings have emerged from many other sets of data.

By eliminating roll calls, such as #78, we identify a subset of roll calls that fit the scale model better and perhaps define an issue more precisely. But as long as the initial set of roll calls are chosen to exemplify a common issue, the statistical procedure is a corrective at best and is not expected to alter the original issue concept appreciably. Thus the main function of scaling is to arrange legislators in rank order with greater accuracy than the entire initial set of roll calls would afford.

If we eliminate #78, we find that the top eight lines of the table fit perfect scale patterns, and can be assigned scale scores equal to the corresponding numbers of positive responses, 0 to 3.[15] Moreover, if we consider the lower seven patterns, involving zeros or instances of nonvoting, we can assign scale scores by modifying the zeros in ways that will fit scale patterns. (Exercise: do this.) For all of these seven but Tower, unique scale scores are assignable in this way. The resulting scores can not rigorously be treated as providing cardinal measures of distance between Senators, however, as they provide only an ordered set of categories in which Senators are placed.

In analysis of actual data (rather than selected roll calls such as we have considered), we must be concerned with relations that come near the perfect scale model, but depart from it to some extent; we cannot expect a perfect fit. Various criteria have been used to assess the extent of error or departure from the model; one of the earliest was the coefficient of reproducibility, which expressed the proportion of all responses in the final matrix that conformed with the scale pattern.[16] The difference between this coefficient and unity then measured the proportion of responses that had to be altered in order to achieve a perfect scale pattern. For the 29 Senators in the upper part of Table 2.3, the total number of responses is $29 \times 4 = 116$. The patterns of eight Senators contain one error each; thus for the four items, the coefficient of reproducibility would be $1 - (8/116) = .931$. But as we have seen, all the errors can be eliminated by removing #78 (and thereby achieving a reproducibility of 1.0), and this coefficient should not be considered as reflecting a satisfactory scale.

Other measures of the adequacy of a scale have been proposed, taking into account various criteria initially mentioned by Guttman as

---

[15]Note that the "dictionary" ordering, based on responses *including* #78, places the sixth and seventh lines in the wrong order. The further rearrangement of rows after elimination of a column resembles the procedure followed on the scalogram board; see Stouffer *et al., op. cit.,* chap. 4.

[16]See Stouffer *et al., op. cit.,* pp. 77–80; the coefficient was intended to be used with other criteria.

important but not included in the coefficient of reproducibility.[17] We shall not dwell on these, because they have not occupied a central place in legislative analysis, and because in discussing cluster analysis (Chapter 3) we shall propose still another measure that is of more importance in the studies we present.

The Senate votes that we have considered, even though selected for simplicity, illustrate some additional problems of scale construction. We left it to the reader to examine Table 2.3 and decide just why roll call #78 should be eliminated.[18] If one tries to carry out this selection procedure, he will realize that the attribution of error responses to one roll call or another is not always clear, since a nonscale pattern can often be converted into a scale pattern in more than one way. This problem becomes more acute if the data matrix contains many roll calls that do not fit together into a single scale, since the elimination of columns that produce errors depends on a signal–noise or figure–ground relation. Methods such as item analysis, which depend on comparison of each roll call with a summary score based on the entire matrix, lose their efficiency as the entire matrix ceases to reflect a single dimension or principle of legislative division.

The initial step that reduces the seriousness of these problems in attitude scaling is the construction of items by the investigator in view of a concept he has in mind. The corresponding step in legislative scaling would be the preliminary selection of sets of roll calls believed by the researcher to have issue content in common. In Guttman's treatment of attitude scaling this content category was called "the universe of attributes," and in roll-call analysis a similar category gives rise to a "preliminary universe of content."[19]

These procedures were in fact followed by Belknap and Farris.[20] Universes of content were the bases of their analyses. Different rank-

---

[17]Menzel, "A New Coefficient for Scale Analysis"; Borgatta, "An Error Ratio for Scalogram Analysis"; Green, "A Method of Scalogram Analysis Using Summary Statistics." Other coefficients, and statistical tests for them, are discussed in Goodman, "Simple Statistical Tests for Scalogram Analysis." A recent summary of this literature is Chilton, "A Review and Comparison."

[18]Criteria for selection of roll calls will be reconsidered more systematically in Chapter 3.

[19]See Stouffer et al., op. cit., pp. 80–88; MacRae, Dimensions of Congressional Voting, pp. 220–221.

[20]See Belknap, op. cit.; Farris, op. cit.

ings on different issues resulted, and multiple scales permitted Farris to classify congressmen into ideological groupings. But it is possible that the breadth or narrowness of initial concepts, depending on the researchers' judgment, prevented such studies from being completely comparable.

Another procedure for selecting scale items, which has greater flexibility for legislative analysis, compares each item not with a combination of all the others, but with each other separately. This procedure was proposed by Toby and Toby.[21] In one respect it is more complicated, since in place of n indices of adequacy for n items, it gives rise to $n(n-1)/2$. But its compensating advantage is that this larger number of comparisons are no longer confounded by the heterogeneity of the overall collection of items.

To compare the votes on one roll call with those on another, we cross-tabulate the two. If we consider only yea and nay (or positive and negative) responses, the result will be a fourfold table. If the yeas and nays are transformed into $+$ and $-$ responses as before, and the fourfold table is arranged so that the roll call with the larger p_+ corresponds to the columns of the table, then the upper-right cell will be empty if the two items have a perfect scale relation with one another. The reason for this is that this cell corresponds to a negative response on the item with the larger p_+. In a perfect cumulative scale, such a conjunction of responses cannot occur, since it would correspond to a $(-+)$ sequence if the items are arranged in decreasing order of p_+. Several of the fourfold tables in Table 2.4 illustrate this perfect scale relation; if we designate the four cells in such a table as

a	b
c	d

then in the center table of the top row in Table 2.4 these values are 7, 0, 11, and 13 respectively, and $b = 0$.

A set of roll calls can then be examined for their mutual scalability by preparation of a matrix of such fourfold tables. Such a matrix is presented in Table 2.4 for the same votes considered in the two pre-

[21]See Toby and Toby, "A Method of Selecting Dichotomous Items by Cross-Tabulation " pp. 339–355. The method described there was suggested by S. A. Stouffer.

			Roll call number 47			78			−11			130		
			.24			.53		p_+	.55			.69		
		Total	+	−	0	+	−	0	+	−	0	+	−	0
47	+	8				5	3	—	7	—	1	8	—	—
	−	25				12	12	1	11	13	1	14	10	1
	0	3				1	1	1	—	2	1	2	1	—
78	+	18							11	6	1	13	4	1
	−	16							7	7	2	11	5	—
	0	2							—	2	—	—	2	—
−11	+	18										17	—	1
	−	15										5	10	—
	0	3										2	1	—
130	+													
	−													
	0													
	Total					18	16	2	18	15	3	24	11	1

vious Tables. Here the roll calls are arranged in ascending order of p_+. Three by three tables are presented in order to show an important principle in hand tabulation of data: all cases should be accounted for in order to provide checks against errors of various kinds. If this procedure is followed, the overall total and the individual row and column totals can be used for checking. Alternatively, they can be used for rapid calculation by counting only certain cells and determining the others by subtraction.[22] Of the full square matrix that might have been shown, only an upper triangle of six tables is needed; the self-comparisons of the roll calls are of no interest, and the lower triangle would duplicate the information in the upper.

Inspection of the six fourfold tables in Table 2.4 shows that three perfectly fulfill the scale criterion and three do not. All of the latter type include roll call #78, which is therefore a clear candidate for exclusion.

[22]Such checking is important for human tabulation but unnecessary on computers once the programs are free of error.

So far, we have set the polarities on the basis of information external to the votes themselves—our knowledge of the ideological positions of Senators, or the content of bills. It is also possible, however, to make the polarity decisions without this information. We shall see in Chapter 3 that when the scalability of a fourfold table is measured by an index of association, then polarity is relatively easy to set on this basis.

We have assumed so far, as a matter of convention, that the selection we make is among roll calls rather than legislators. One reason for this may be that the rationale of scaling concerns general attitude continua, which may be represented by one or another roll call, but which need not be represented by any particular one. In this perspective, as long as we are interested in general rather than particular issues, the loss of a particular roll call is not necessarily a disadvantage. But it is harder for us to restrict our attention to a subset of legislators who "stand for" certain general tendencies; legislators are known as public figures, they represent constituencies that are of interest, and they are usually not so numerous that we can afford a substantial reduction of our sample.

Yet it is reasonable to ask why we treat legislators and roll calls asymmetrically, and this question will recur throughout the book. In the particular case of selection for the improvement of scale patterns, we do occasionally perform a type of selection of legislators. When a legislator's votes depart so far from the scale pattern that the assignment of a scale score is likely to be imprecise, he is conventionally not assigned any score and thus deleted from subsequent analyses. And more important, just as we separate sets of roll calls dealing with different issues, we also find it convenient to analyze legislative parties separately, because more general orderings often are found within a single party than in a combination of parties.[23] More generally, a test as to whether subsets of legislators should be analyzed separately is that these subsets should have conceptual significance or relation to independently defined variables (e.g., sociometric linkages); in principle, this is the same criterion we should like to use in selecting subsets of roll calls.

[23]See Chapter 8. Occasionally two parties may be combined as well; see MacRae, *Parliament, Parties and Society,* chaps. 4–7.

THE ASSIGNMENT OF SCALE POSITIONS

The construction of a scale begins with the selection of certain roll calls that fit together in a cumulative pattern, and the elimination of others. But the cumulative model is a ranking of roll calls and legislators together, and thus also provides an indication of the positions of legislators relative to one another. Those legislators who fall into perfect scale patterns may be placed in a set of ranked categories corresponding to the numbers of + responses among their votes. When the patterns depart somewhat from perfection, various methods have been proposed for assigning approximate scale scores, or for rejecting certain response patterns as not reliably assignable to any scale category.[24]

But the designation of a set of ranked categories does not make full use of the information in the legislators' responses, nor does it easily permit certain types of analysis comparing the positions of legislators at different times. For while these categories are a ranking, and not a set of cardinal numbers, the scale scores tell us nothing about how many legislators are in each category, or how the categories compare in size.

One way to compensate for the possible inequality of categories in size was recommended by Guttman: select items, among those that might constitute a scale, which have their positive proportions (p_+ or marginals) as nearly as possible equally spaced along the continuum of p_+ from 0 to 1. A modification of this technique, for assignment of scale scores on scales with large numbers of items, is to arrange those items in sequence of p_+ and then group them into *contrived* items that are approximately equidistant from one another.[25]

This modified procedure, which will be used in the next chapter, may be illustrated with the responses of Republican congressman Van Zandt (Pa.) on a set of eight roll calls selected by cluster analysis (see also Table 3.4). The values of p_+, and the congressman's responses on the corresponding roll calls, are as follows:

[24]See MacRae, *ibid.*, Appendix B, for one such procedure. An example of this method is given in Chapter 3.

[25]*Ibid.*; and MacRae, "A Method for Identifying Issues and Factions."

p_+		.63		.41	.41	.40	.39	.36		.13	.09
Response		+		−	+	+	−	−		−	−

If each roll call was considered a separate cutting point, the response pattern would contain one error, regardless of the order in which the two roll calls with $p_+ = .41$ were arranged. The procedure used is to group the eight roll calls into three items, as indicated by the spacing above, on the basis of the separation of the values of p_+. The congressman is then assigned the preponderant vote on each such item: + on the first roll call, − on the middle group of five, and − on the last group of two. For this three-item scale he is then assigned a score of 1, since he has only one positive response on the three resulting items.

This procedure is objective, in that it can be specified in such a way as not to depend on the investigator's judgment, and it has been used extensively by the author. However, it discards information that might permit more precise location of legislators on the continuum. For example, another legislator who voted "−" on all five of the roll calls in the middle item would be assigned the same score as Van Zandt; perhaps a more refined procedure would assign them slightly different scores. The optimal use of this information has attracted little attention in attitude studies, because attitude data are considered to have a substantial random or error component. However, the greater precision of roll-call data may justify improving the method.

The assignment of quantitative indices of scale position has taken two directions. One approach, used by Schubert in the analysis of Supreme Court decisions, defines the distance between justices as proportional to the number of decisions that separate them.[26] In a nine-man court, ties in position between justices are less likely than in legislative bodies, and the only interesting departure from a simple one-to-nine ranking would come from counting decisions. In comparison with the second approach to be discussed, this corresponds to placing roll calls, rather than legislators, at equal intervals on the continuum being scaled. We shall see in Chapter 7 that the use of

[26]Schubert, *The Judicial Mind*, pp. 104–112, defines "scale positions" by counting cases or decisions; at p. 78, the "scale score" is defined as a linear function of the scale position, ranging between −1 and +1.

factor scores for placement of legislators also has this property of separating them farther when they differ on a larger number of roll calls.

Another approach, used by Kesselman and Bogue, has been to assign each legislator a score corresponding to his rank order among the legislators being studied.[27] It is conventional in the assignment of ranks to use the median (or average) rank in a given category, if legislators are tied; and this procedure was used by these writers. For simplicity in the treatment that follows, let us assume that a legislator's rank is indicated by the value of p_+ for a roll call at the same point on the continuum. If the continuum is considered to be divided into as many unit intervals as there are legislators, then this point will be the midpoint of that legislator's unit interval; and p_+ will be the proportion of all legislators who vote more positively than that legislator, with his own interval being divided into two halves, one on either side of the point. A legislator with a high value of p_+ will then be one with a low proportion of positive votes.

For the data in Table 2.3, for example, the numbers of Senators in categories 0, 1, 2, 3 are 11, 5, 11, and 8 (omitting Tower). We assign ranks 1–11 to category 0, 12–16 to 1, 17–27 to 2, and 28–35 to 3. The average ranks are then 6.0, 14.0, 22.0, and 31.5. These values could be assigned to Senators in the corresponding groups. Or we could assign values of p_+; the three cutting points are at .69, .55, and .24, and the midpoints of the intervals are thus at .845, .62, .395, and .12. These correspond closely to the average ranks (minus ½), expressed as proportions of the 35 Senators, the differences being due to absences and to the omission of Tower.

This procedure is shown graphically in Figure 2.1, using Kesselman's (unpublished) data. The 351 congressmen who sat in both 86th and 87th Congresses were scored on a foreign-policy scale in each. Assigning average ranks to scale categories equates the interval for each scale score to the number of legislators in it. Thus the six horizontal categories, and the four vertical ones, correspond to intervals of different length. Legislators are placed at the midpoints of these intervals; for two scales jointly, this corresponds to placing them at the centers of rectangles, as a rectangular array of points.

[27]Kesselman, "Presidential Leadership in Congress on Foreign Policy"; Bogue, "Bloc and Party in the United States Senate, 1861–1863," p. 229, where "mean percentile positions" are used.

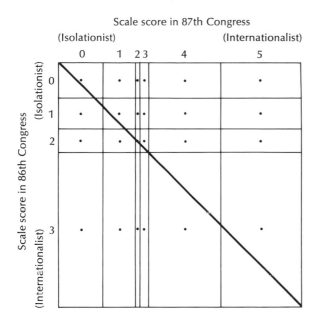

FIGURE 2.1. Conversion of Scale Scores into Average Ranks (Kesselman Data on U.S. House of Representatives, 86th and 87th Congresses). Distances in the figure are proportional to numbers of congressmen in the corresponding scale types. The diagonal line corresponds to equal ranking on both scales among the 351 congressmen in question.

If each legislator maintained the same rank position on the two scales, and the categories were small enough to place each precisely, all legislators' points would fall on the diagonal line. The distance from that line to a legislator's point then gives an estimate of his change in rank from one Congress to the other. By choosing those rectangles whose center points were farther from the line than a specified distance, Kesselman distinguished large from small shifts in position, in a way that depends less on the distribution of cutting points than do conventional scale scores. He thus showed that the legislators at the upper right with substantial shifts toward internationalism tended to be Democrats, those at the lower left Republicans; those belonging to the party holding the presidency tended to be more internationalist.

The procedure followed here has not ordinarily been necessary in survey research on attitudes; for if the researcher is able to reinterview or retest the same respondent population, he can also use the same measuring instrument again.

In this example, the difference between the two scales in number of cutting points, or of categories, would by itself prevent direct comparison of the numerical scale scores between the two. The nonuniform distribution of cutting points on both scales accentuates the problem. Even if there were denser distributions of cutting points on the two scales, although this would render the scale placements more accurate, it would not necessarily make them comparable between the two scales if the density of cutting points were variable. We are thus seeking a description of a legislator's position that is invariant with respect to a change in density of cutting points, which could occur because of duplication or near-duplication of roll calls.

This example is one of the few we shall use in Part I in which both congressional parties are combined for analysis. The data were treated in this way in order to show that partisanship, reflecting presidential leadership, entered into congressmen's positions on foreign policy. But this very demonstration of partisanship suggests that group allegiances, as well as the substance of the policy in question, may be involved. Thus the example does not involve issues in their purest form. The method may be used, however, to compare the orderings of legislators within a single party as well.

The assignment of scale positions based on legislators' average ranks thus seems useful for the precise analysis of roll-call votes. When there are ties in scale position between legislators, it is useful for some purposes to take the size of these tied groups into account. As we shall see below, this approach also provides for fuller use of the information provided in roll-call votes, as we suggested above in considering the example of Van Zandt's votes; and while it has not been widely used, it promises to be useful. Moreover, the repetition or duplication of a roll call on a given issue seems to introduce undesirable artifacts into scale scores, at least in legislative analysis, and this second approach permits us to minimize such effects.

We wish then to assign each legislator a "best" scale score in terms of rank or p_+, on the basis of his response pattern. We do this by considering what assigned score will produce the fewest rank reversals of his position relative to other legislators, summing over

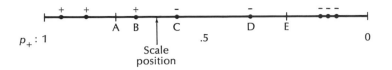

FIGURE 2.2. Assignment of Rank Scores for a Perfect Scale. Equal distances correspond to equal numbers of legislators. The response to each item is plotted at the corresponding value of p_+.

all roll calls in the scale.[28] Let us first examine the result for a perfect scale, which will be seen to be identical with the ranking customarily assigned.

In the case of a perfect scale with no absences, we can assume at the start that we know the locations of all cutting points on the continuum of p_+ from 1 to 0; these are given by the initial values of p_+ of the roll calls. For a given legislator, each response may then be located on the continuum at the point corresponding to that roll call's p_+. Such a location of responses, for a perfect scale, is shown in Figure 2.2. All the $-$'s are to the right of all the $+$'s. Now if we were to assign the legislator to position A, we should find a number of rank reversals corresponding to the interval AB; for the item at B, a $+$, would be to the right of the assigned position. Similarly, if we considered assigning the position E, we should find a number of rank reversals corresponding to interval CE for the item at C, and in addition a number corresponding to the interval DE for the item at D. In general, rank reversals in this sense correspond to the presence either of $+$ responses to the right of the assigned position, or of $-$ responses to the left.

In the example in Figure 2.2, it is clear that there will be *no* rank

[28]Alternative criteria are possible. For example, a score may be obtained by simply summing positive responses; or a response pattern may be assigned to the perfect scale configuration which differs from it in fewest responses. We shall apply our rank-reversal criterion by first deciding on the rank order of the roll calls, then assigning each legislator a "best" category. But another more general procedure might be to try to find, at the same time, an ordering of roll calls and a categorization of legislators which would jointly minimize the number of rank reversals. Such a procedure would be analogous to Guttman's solution for "the principal components of scale analysis," but might yield a simpler solution for a perfect scale. See Stouffer *et al., op. cit.,* chap. 9.

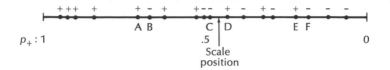

FIGURE 2.3. Assignment of Rank Scores for a Pattern Containing Errors.

reversals for any assigned position in the interval BC; we therefore assign the midpoint of this interval, consistent with the convention of assigning average ranks.

Now let us extend this reasoning to the case of response patterns including errors but no absences. Such patterns may well arise when we have large numbers of items in a scale; and yet in spite of "error" responses they may permit placing legislators with considerable precision. A pattern of responses containing some errors is shown in Figure 2.3. In this figure, although we indicate distances along the p_+ continuum, they are not given simply by the p_+ values for the roll calls. Rather, the legislators are placed in ranked intervals separated by the roll calls, and the resulting distribution of legislators is used to define the distances between the cutting points, to which the values of p_+ are only an approximation. To carry out this operation we need assume at the start only that we know the ordering of the roll calls. For a set of roll calls nearly fitting the scale model, it seems plausible that the ordering of p_+ values can be used for this purpose.

We can first see that the assigned scale position for this pattern must be in the interval AF, for a position chosen to the left of A would unnecessarily add rank reversals due to the + at A, and to the right of F would add them due to the − at F. We thus restrict our attention to the AF interval, which in general is defined by the rightmost of the sequence of + responses at the left, and the leftmost of the converse sequence of −'s at the right. If such sequences cannot be found, then we simply substitute the interval (1, 0).

This restriction of our attention has the advantage of making the scale rank assignment independent of duplicated items outside the interval in question. For a perfect scale pattern, of course, the assignment of rank position is entirely independent of duplicated roll calls;

but in the present scoring procedure it is only partially so. Within the interval AF, it is sensitive to duplicated responses only if they are errors.

The interval on which we focus our attention includes more than half the larger interval (1, 0), and might be considered so large that a scale position should not be assigned; in such cases, we can specify additional rules as to when no rank score shall be assigned. But the example shown may also be considered simply a magnification of the problem that occurs when a scale has many items, with the errors concentrated within a narrow range of p_+, and we might feel fully justified in assigning a score provided that we could specify a determinate and optimal procedure for doing so.

Although it would be possible to program a computer to calculate the number of rank reversals corresponding to any position on the continuum, there is an easier procedure for finding the position corresponding to the minimum number of rank reversals. This involves considering not the total number of rank reversals, but the way in which that total changes as we move along the horizontal continuum from one possible rank-score position to another. (The principle is that of finding a zero derivative.) As we move to the right from A toward B, all the rank reversals are due to the five +'s to the right of the position under consideration; and since we are moving toward all of them, the number of rank reversals is being reduced in proportion to five times the distance (i.e., to five times the number of ranks) traversed. It is clearly an improvement to move from A to B. Immediately to the right of B, by moving to the right we are still decreasing these same rank reversals at a ratio of five times the distance traversed, but we are now also increasing the number of rank reversals with respect to B, corresponding to a − now on our left. The net rate of decrease of rank reversals is thus now only four times the distance traversed. Conversely, in moving from E to F we would increase the number of rank reversals at a rate five times the distance traversed, because of the five −'s to the left; but if we were just to the left of E and moving toward it, the number of rank reversals would increase with a ratio of only four.

The principle implied by these considerations is that if we chose a point having the same number of −'s to the left as +'s to the right, we should be neither increasing nor decreasing the number of rank reversals as we moved in the vicinity of such a point, as long as we did not pass the p_+ value of any item response. In Figure 2.2, the interval CD has such a zero derivative, and we locate the assigned rank score at its center. This principle is a general one, for whenever the number of $-$'s to the left equals the number of $+$'s to the right, the rate of change will be zero. Moreover, since a move past one roll call to the left will always increase the balance of the right errors over the left, and a move to the right will have the converse effect, the interval that balances the two types of errors equally will always be one of minimum error.

The interval CD, which we have chosen, is not, however, the one that will minimize the number of errors in the conventional sense. This interval gives rise to six errors, three on each side; if, however, we moved to the left past two roll-call points, we could reduce the number of left-hand errors to one. Our rank-reversal criterion does not count such a move as an improvement, because it weights errors by distance along the line, and this move would increase the number of rank reversals for the three $+$'s on the right.

The interval defined in this way can easily be identified if each interval between adjacent cutting points is assigned a number equal to the number of cutting points on its left. The intervals will then be numbered from 0 to n, the total number of roll calls considered; and the interval to which a legislator is assigned (his scale score) will be given simply by the number of his $+$ responses.

We now pass to the more general case including absences. Here we can no longer use p_+ with the same confidence as an indicator of the ordering of roll calls on the continuum. For if two roll calls are being compared, and if absences on one correspond largely (e.g.) to $+$'s on the other, their proper ordering will not necessarily be the order of their p_+'s. Rather we must now begin by establishing a rank order of roll calls. Starting with an ordering based on the p_+ of each roll call, we check the consistency of this ordering by examining the pairwise cross-tabulations of roll calls as to whether the off-diagonal cells b and c of the fourfold tables have consistent orderings. For a set of consistently ordered roll calls, if the item to be located toward the higher-p_+ end of the continuum corresponds to the columns of the fourfold table, as in Table 2.4, then c will exceed b. This test may require the rearrangement of rank ordering of some roll calls if the absences are numerous and distributed in certain ways. Conceivably, too, a triadic relation among three roll calls may be inconsistent; in this case, we assume that enough roll calls are to be eliminated to remove all such inconsistencies and permit a consistent ordering.[29] The procedures described above can then be followed to assign each legislator to an *interval,* but we do not yet know its midpoint. Rather, after assigning all legislators to the set of ranked intervals defined by the roll calls, we simply use the distribution of legislators in these intervals to convert the ranked categories to average ranks. This is the same procedure that would be followed in converting a conventional set of cumulative scale scores into average ranks.

If in these terms we wish to assess the scalability of a set of items, or the departure from scalability of a particular legislator's responses, we can again use the notion of rank reversal to do so. For we can specify the number of rank reversals for each legislator, in comparison with the number of consistent rankings. Individually this can be a measure of the accuracy of a legislator's score assignment and, averaged over legislators, it can measure the scalability of a set of data.[30]

We shall return at various points to compare other methods of roll-call analysis with cumulative scaling. Chapter 3 will continue to follow the general logic of scale scoring outlined here, though we shall there use the more conventional and less precise method. We shall also adhere throughout Chapters 3–5 to the definition of "similarity" between roll calls that corresponds to the cumulative-scale

[29]A detailed procedure for this step has not yet been specified, but the situation is believed to be extremely rare. The more general problem of which this is a special case is that of combining a number of individual rankings into a collective ranking; see Arrow, *Social Choice and Individual Values;* and Kemeny and Snell, *Mathematical Models in the Social Sciences,* chap. 2. In this special case, each roll call constitutes an ordering of the legislators, and we wish to combine a set of selected roll calls to form a best overall ranking of the legislators. By assuming that the roll calls have consistent polarities, and that they can be ordered in terms of p_+, we simplify the problem considerably.

[30]If we have defined scale clusters by a threshold value of an index of association such as Q (Chapter 3), then that threshold value provides an indication of the quality of the scale, and further indices of scalability are less necessary. The measurement of scale quality in terms of rank reversals is related to several measures proposed in Davis, "On Criteria for Scale Relationships."

model, preferring it to certain widely used alternatives. In Chapter 7, when we consider the computation of factor scores, we shall again point out the advantage of the scale model in that it is not so dependent on duplication of roll calls. At that point, we shall also discuss the problems of extending this type of reasoning to multidimensional scales, and contrast its properties with those of factor scores.

3.
CLUSTER ANALYSIS
OF ROLL CALLS

ALTHOUGH the cumulative-scale model appears to be a good one for the issue continua related to roll calls, the conventional procedures for identifying data which fit that model are not. These procedures typically thin out a set of attitude items that were created by the investigator to measure a particular concept. The attitude or issue continua manifested in roll calls, however, are not so obvious. The matters being voted on are typically extensive texts, some parts of which are far more important to the legislators than others. Just which parts are important depends not merely on the text itself, but on the legislative strategies followed by proponents and opponents, often designed to stress a particular aspect of a bill that will be to their advantage. For this reason, even if the investigator chooses roll calls that he believes to share issue content, it is desirable to have a corrective on his judgment. We therefore need an objective procedure for selecting sets of similar roll calls, independently of investigators' judgment of their content. The participants' judgment would of course be relevant; but in addition, a statistical procedure that permits the discovery of scalable subsets without preliminary judgment of content would be helpful.

The Toby procedure for scale analysis by pairwise comparisons permits a step away from the conventional Guttman procedure, toward a more empirical approach. For while the elimination of items (by procedures such as the scalogram board) depends on an initial choice of the universe of content such that most of the roll calls (or questions) do in fact scale, pairwise comparison does not require this. And if the Toby criterion for assessing the fourfold tables is replaced by other coefficients, a variety of other methods of cluster and factor analysis become relevant.

Moreover, the degree of interrelation among a set of roll calls that have been chosen on some a priori ground can be used as an indication of the degree of structure of that set, and thus as a test of relevant hypotheses. This approach was followed in an earlier study to show a higher structuring of votes in the race-relations or civil-rights area among Democrats than among Republicans.[1] But an even more interesting hypothesis is that of Lowi and Roos, concerning the interrelation of roll calls in the "arenas of power" that Lowi has called redistributive, regulative, and distributive.[2] For this purpose, the use of an index of association than can measure either high or low degrees of interrelation, rather than simply the high degrees important in cumulative scaling, has advantages.

The general class of methods to be considered in this chapter are those that start with a matrix of measures of pairwise relations between roll calls, and from this produce lists or subsets of similar roll calls.[3] This division into discrete subsets distinguishes these methods from factor analysis, which will be discussed in Chapter 4. But as we shall see, certain methods that generate quantitative rather than discrete outputs can also be treated discretely; in particular, nonmetric multidimensional scaling will be treated in this way.

Methods of this type are probably most familiar to political scientists in connection with the cluster-bloc analysis which has been used to identify blocs of legislators rather than roll calls. They are appropriate for this purpose, though with some limitations which will be discussed in detail when problems of bloc analysis are treated in Chapter 7. They have also been used for various other purposes including biological taxonomy, analysis of psychological tests, and the typology of

[1]MacRae, *Dimensions of Congressional Voting*, pp. 233–235.

[2]Unpublished research by Theodore J. Lowi and L. John Roos shows that the average association between roll calls differs systematically among these three types of issues.

[3]An alternative procedure, also aimed at producing sets of cumulative scales through empirical analysis of data of this type, is described in Lingoes, "Multiple Scalogram Analysis."

mental illnesses. We shall draw on this other literature for assistance and contrast.

We shall be concerned primarily with the empirical search for clusters (subsets) of similar roll calls on the basis of the votes cast. We shall first consider the indices that may be used to assess the relationship between the votes on two roll calls, as revealed by a fourfold table. Then we shall treat procedures for analyzing a matrix of such indices, and the substantive findings that permit us to test (at least approximately) whether the "issues" thus discovered are validly distinguished.

Our search for empirical clusters of roll calls, however, unrestricted by preliminary universes of content, creates a problem with respect to concepts and operational definitions. We cannot identify every empirical similarity between roll calls with a similarity in issues. We must try to specify those conditions under which this empirical similarity is a better or poorer indicator of issue similarity. We have already suggested one: when our study is restricted to the internal divisions of a party or group that has extensive internal communication and thus forms collective classifications of legislative matters and of its members. We approximate this condition in Congress by analyzing one party at a time in the search for issue divisions.

A second condition, to be suggested later, is that roll calls with extreme divisions of the vote (small minorities in opposition) are less reliable definers of issues, and provide less information about issue similarity, than do roll calls that divide the legislators in question more evenly.

A purely empirical approach, therefore, cannot suffice to tell us the conditions under which our inferences from roll calls are to be interpreted in terms of issues or factions. The distinction between these two concepts and between their measures, which depends on an interplay between statistical procedures and substantive consideration of the functioning of legislatures, is a continuing theme of this book.

MEASURES OF THE RELATION
BETWEEN TWO ROLL CALLS

To express the relation between votes on two roll calls, we shall assume that only two categories matter on each vote, and that the relation between any two votes is thus completely described by a fourfold table. We shall then compare various methods of identifying issues, based on particular indices of pairwise similarity. Such an index can be characterized as a function of the numbers in the cells, i.e., as $f(a, b, c, d)$.

We first set aside those measures that depend on the actual numerical values of the cell frequencies, rather than their relative or proportional values. These numerical values are relevant if we wish to make statistical inferences, including tests of significance, on the table in question, but not if we wish simply to measure the degree of association. One measure of this type is the chi-square statistic, which was used by Turner to measure the association between roll-call votes and party. A second is the difference between the frequencies in cells c and b, cited by Davis as a criterion for the significance of the difference in location between two items on a scale.[4]

If we set aside measures of this type, then we need to know only the relative frequencies in the table, and not the actual numerical values. Thus the indices that we discuss below will be unchanged if we consider a, b, c, and d as proportions, rather than frequencies, with the sum of the cell frequencies $(a + b + c + d = N)$ as the denominator.

Proportion in the "zero box"

The Toby procedure included a criterion for scalability of a fourfold table: that the proportion of cases in the "zero box" (b/N) not exceed 10 percent. This was consistent with the conventional standard proposed by Guttman that the reproducibility of a scale should be at least .90.[5] But because this criterion produced undesirable results when the items in question had extreme marginal frequencies, another auxiliary criterion was added: it was necessary for scalability that the cell entries a and d each be at least twice b. Moreover, Toby and Toby pointed out that when this criterion was applied to a pair of items whose marginal frequencies were widely separated, it could be satisfied without the items being associated.[6] Thus it was suggested that the search for sets of items, all of whose pairs met the criterion, was often equivalent to building a chain in which the links between

[4]Turner, *Party and Constitutency*, pp. 31, 40–68; Davis, "On Criteria for Scale Relationships."

[5]See Stouffer *et. al.*, *Measurement and Prediction*, p. 77.

[6]Riley, Riley, and Toby, *Sociological Studies in Scale Analysis*, pp. 347–348.

items adjacent in the sequence of p_+ were most crucial. But if the pairs in adjacent links are associated, this suggests a comparison between this criterion and that of an index of association, which we shall consider below.

This criterion has been used by Aydelotte in a study of voting in the British House of Commons in the 1840's, with a threshold of 6 rather than 10 percent.[7]

If the criterion is applied in hand tabulation, there is usually no ambiguity as to which cell is b, the "zero box." In computer data processing, it is necessary first to set the polarities of items automatically or to specify them by inspection; then this proportion can be specified as [min $(b, c)]/N$, the proportion of cases in the lesser of two off-diagonal cells.

Proportion of similar responses or agreements

A second criterion, used more often in comparing pairs of legislators than pairs of roll calls, is based on the proportion of responses in the fourfold table that are identical $(a + d)$ in relation to those that are different $(b + c)$ or in relation to the total (N). This index can take several forms; two are the total agreement $(a + d)/N$, and the net agreement $[(a + d) - (b + c)]/N$, the latter being simply a linear function of the former. If we designate them as I_1 and I_2 respectively, then $I_2 = 2I_1 - 1$. (Exercise: prove this.) A third equivalent form is $(b + c)/N$, equal to $1 - I_1$. This form is generated if the positive and negative rows and columns of the fourfold table are assigned the values 1 and 0 respectively, and a measure of "squared distance" (D^2) is computed between the two roll calls; $D^2 = (b + c)$, or $N(1 - I_1)$. Like the proportion in the "zero box," the index I_1 has no well-defined zero point, and is not an index of association.[8] Variations of this index will be discussed in Chapter 7.

The percentage difference: An asymmetric measure

In survey analysis it is customary to compare two variables by computing percentages down the rows or across the columns of a con-

[7]Aydelotte, "Voting Patterns in the British House of Commons in the 1840's."

[8]If this index were used to compare roll calls, it would permit two unanimous roll calls to be judged perfectly similar—a judgment that is impossible with indices of association.

tingency table, with each row or column total corresponding to 100 percent. If column percentages are computed, then the resulting percentages are compared across rows to see the extent to which the variables are associated. In the case of the fourfold table, the top-row proportions corresponding to column percentage computation are $a/(a + c)$ and $b/(b + d)$. Their difference is $(ad - bc)/(a + c)(b + d)$. (Exercise: derive this.) Conceivably this difference might be used as an index of the scalability between two roll calls. However it fails one important criterion; unlike the two preceding indices or functions, it is not independent of the order in which the two roll calls are considered, i.e., of which corresponds to the rows and which to the columns in the table. If, however, we computed this index for rows as well, and took the geometric mean (square root of the product) of the two indexes, the result would be the correlation coefficient or ϕ, to be discussed below.[9]

All the indices to be discussed below satisfy this condition of *symmetry* with respect to interchange of the rows with the columns. In addition, they satisfy the criterion of vanishing in the case of *independence;* i.e., if the percentage difference is zero, the index is also zero. This is equivalent to the condition that the index must be zero if $ad = bc$, or $a/b = c/d$, or $a/c = b/d$. When this relation obtains, knowledge of one of the variables is useless in predicting the corresponding value of the other. If the variables are positively associated, $(ad - bc) > 0$.

We can now see that the "zero box" criterion does not insure that

---

[9]The percentage difference is a special case of asymmetric index, d_{yx}, proposed by Somers in "A New Asymmetric Measure for Association of Ordinal Variables." The geometric–mean relationship is also demonstrated in this article. The percentage difference and several of the other indices we consider are described in Alker, *Mathematics and Politics,* chap. 4.

Our requirement of symmetry is a case of a general condition for indices: "independence of irrelevant alternatives." This condition was used in Arrow, *Social Choice and Individual Values,* pp. 26–28. It has been widely used in the evaluation of indices, though not always under this name; we shall refer to it in Part II in evaluating indices of agreement between legislators. For an application of this and other considerations to the choice of indices, see Edwards, "The Measure of Association in a 2 × 2 Table."

The interchange of rows and columns is "irrelevant," however, only within the patricular perspective we have chosen—the search for multiple measures of what is presumed to be one variable, with the subsequent aim of condensing or summarizing them. If, on the other hand, we should find that a set of roll calls at time *1* could be considered a causal or antecedent variable for another set at time *2* then this symmetry might no longer obtain.

the two dichotomies in question are positively associated; for if b is small (e.g., .1 as a proportion of N), a small value of a or d can still make $(ad - bc)$ zero or negative. The auxiliary condition in the Toby criterion, that a/b and d/b each be at least 2, if barely satisfied together with $b/N = 0.1$, would still lead to a negative association: $(ad - bc) = (.2)(.2) - (.1)(.5) = -.1$.

An additional condition is also satisfied by all the following indices: if either the columns or the rows of the fourfold table are interchanged, the index is altered in sign only. This may be called the condition of *reversibility*. Most of the indices to be treated below can be seen to satisfy this criterion if they have in their numerators either $(ad - bc)$ or $[g(ad) - g(bc)]$, where g is the same function in both terms; for interchange of the rows or of the columns transforms ad into bc and vice versa, and only the sign changes. The denominator must then remain unchanged. This requirement relates to the fact that roll calls of reversed polarity but similar political significance often occur. For other data formally similar to roll calls, however, this condition need not obtain, and the requirement of reversibility may seem unreasonable.[10]

The cross-product

The simplest expression satisfying all the above conditions is $(ad - bc)/N^2$, or simply $(ad - bc)$ if cell entries are expressed as proportions of N. This has been used by Lazarsfeld in the algebra of latent-structure analysis, and by Coleman as an indicator of social polarization in attitude structure.[11] We shall see in Chapter 7 that this emerges from one version of direct factor analysis of dichotomous roll-call data. But as a basis for cluster analysis, it has a serious disadvantage: its

[10]The condition of symmetry may be expressed $f(a, b, c, d) = f(a, c, b, d)$. That of reversibility is expressed $f(a, b, c, d) = -f(c, d, a, b) = -f(b, a, d, c)$. A number of indices that do not meet the condition of reversibility are listed in Sokal and Sneath, *Principles of Numerical Taxonomy*, pp. 129–130. The comparison of biological specimens for taxonomic purposes apparently poses different requirements from the comparison of roll calls, and these authors explicitly reject the use for this purpose of indices that assume particular values, such as zero, in the case when two dichotomies are statistically independent (p. 128). And in fact we shall define one index similar to theirs in Chapter 7, used to analyze joint questions in the Indian Lok Sabha; for joint questions, or joint memberships, partition a legislature into subsets that are not so interchangeable conceptually.

[11]See Lazarsfeld, *Mathematical Thinking in the Social Sciences*, p. 367; Coleman, *Introduction to Mathematical Sociology*, chap. 12.

maximum value, attained when $b = 0$, varies greatly with the marginal proportions (p_+) of the roll calls. In a sense, the difficulty with the cross-product for cluster analysis places it at the opposite extreme from the Toby criterion (b/N), for whereas that criterion easily tolerates items with disparate values of p_+, the cross-product is greatly reduced by such a disparity; and if we should set a threshold for scalability in terms of the cross-product, items with disparate values of p_+ would be unlikely to be considered scalable.

The cross-product is also equal to the covariance of the two dichotomous variables corresponding to the rows and columns of the table, if each dichotomy is assigned numerical values of 0 and 1.

An increasing function of the cross-product which has also been used to characterize association in a fourfold table is the cross-product ratio $J = (ad/bc)$. The logarithm of this ratio is equal to zero when there is no association in the table.[12]

The fourfold point correlation coefficient (ϕ)

The coefficient most commonly used for assessing fourfold tables in factor analysis of legislative votes is the fourfold point correlation coefficient, phi (ϕ), a special case of the well-known Pearson or product–moment correlation coefficient. This equivalence may be shown easily. The product–moment correlation coefficient is invariant under positive linear transformations of X and Y, i.e., its value is unchanged if a constant is added or subtracted from X or Y, or if either is multiplied by a positive constant. We may therefore assign convenient numerical values to the rows and columns of the fourfold table for the proof; we let the first row and column be unity, the second row and column zero. Then the familiar computational formula for the correlation coefficient becomes:

$$r = \frac{N\Sigma XY - (\Sigma X)(\Sigma Y)}{\sqrt{[N\Sigma X^2 - (\Sigma X)^2][N\Sigma Y^2 - (\Sigma Y)^2]}}$$

$$= \frac{Na - (a + c)(a + b)}{\sqrt{[N(a + c) - (a + c)^2][N(a + b) - (a + b)^2]}}$$

$$= \frac{ad - bc}{\sqrt{(a + c)(b + d)(a + b)(c + d)}} = \phi \qquad (3.1)$$

[12]This ratio is discussed in Mosteller, "Association and Estimation in Contingency Tables," p. 4; and in Stone, Dunphy, Smith, and Ogilvie, *The General Inquirer*, p. 128.

(Exercise: carry out the intermediate steps of this proof.) The last expression, with rearrangement of the terms in the denominator, is the conventional expression for ϕ. Its numerator is the same as that of the cross-product; its denominator, if considered in terms of proportions of N, is equal to $(p_1q_1p_2q_2)^{1/2}$, where p designates the positive proportion in the margin of the fourfold table (row or column total) and q its complement, $(1 - p)$. N times the square of ϕ is also equal to chi-square, and ϕ is also equal to tau-b, Kendall's rank correlation coefficient corrected for ties, in the special case of the fourfold table.[13]

For testing the conformity of a pair of roll calls to the cumulative scale model, however, ϕ has a serious disadvantage. It attains its maximum value of unity not for every cumulative relationship ($b = 0$), but only for the case in which the two dichotomies being compared are identical ($b = 0$ and $c = 0$). When $b = 0$, substitution in (3.1) shows that

$$\phi_{max} = \sqrt{\frac{ad}{(a + c)(c + d)}} = \sqrt{\frac{p_2q_1}{p_1q_2}} \qquad (3.2)$$

where the subscript 1 refers to the columns of the fourfold table, 2 to the rows. (Exercise: show this.) Guttman uses this result to show that a perfect cumulative scale cannot yield a single-factor solution in factor analysis.[14]

Corrected ϕ (ϕ/ϕ_{max})

Because of this difficulty, it has been suggested that ϕ might be corrected by division by the maximum value that it can attain, for given marginals.[15] In the case $b = 0$, this maximum value is given by the right-hand expression in (3.2). Expressing this in terms of the cell entries (a, b, c, d) and dividing ϕ by the resulting expression gives

$$\frac{\phi}{\phi_{max}} = \frac{ad - bc}{(a + b)(b + d)}$$

[13]See Alker, op. cit., pp. 80–84. For the relation to tau-b see Somers, op. cit., 804.

[14]See Stouffer et al., op. cit., p. 203. A perfect scale actually corresponds to a simplex in the ϕ-matrix. See Guttman, "A New Approach to Factor Analysis: The Radex," p. 274; Horst, Factor Analysis of Data Matrices, chap. 22; and Gibson, "A Latent Structure for the Simplex."

[15]Cureton, "Note on ϕ/ϕ_{max}."

or more generally, when either b or c may be the lesser off-diagonal cell,

$$\frac{\phi}{\phi_{\text{max}}} = \frac{ad - bc}{[a + \min(b, c)][d + \min(b, c)]}$$

This corrected coefficient has sometimes been used in factor analysis, and could also be used for the identification of clusters of items satisfying the cumulative scale relationship.

This is the first index of association we have considered that can also function as an indicator of a cumulative scale relation between two roll calls. But for this and other similar indices of association, it is the term bc that measures the departure from a perfect cumulative relation. The proportion of errors, b, is thus multiplied by a weighting coefficient, c, which is approximately equal to the difference in p_+ between the two roll calls being compared.

The tetrachoric correlation coefficient

Another approach to the problem of recovering a coefficient of 1.0 when a cell such as b is zero, was proposed early in the development of correlation analysis. Both Yule and Pearson considered the problem of estimating the product–moment correlation in a bivariate normal distribution, if such a distribution were cut by two perpendicular lines and only the proportions of cases in the resulting four parts were known.[16] This "reconstructed" correlation, computed from a given fourfold, is known as the tetrachoric correlation coefficient (r_t). Among several approximations proposed by Pearson, one simple equation which is a considerable improvement on Yule's Q for this purpose is

$$r_t = \sin 90° \left[\frac{\sqrt{ad} - \sqrt{bc}}{\sqrt{ad} + \sqrt{bc}} \right] = \cos 180° \left[\frac{\sqrt{bc}}{\sqrt{ad} + \sqrt{bc}} \right] \quad (3.3)$$

Numerical methods have also been used to estimate the underlying product–moment correlation from a fourfold table.[17]

The resulting estimate also attains unity for a perfect cumulative-scale relationship. It has not been used widely, probably because of

[16]Yule, "On the Association of Attributes in Statistics," 275–276; Pearson, "On the Correlation of Characters Not Quantitatively Measurable," 1–17. The problem of approximation to r_t is also discussed in Walker and Lev, *Statistical Inference*, p. 274.

[17]Chesire, Saffir, and Thurstone, *Computing Diagrams for the Tetrachoric Correlation Coefficient*.

the laborious operations necessary for calculating it in the precomputer era, and more recently, because of the apparently unduly restrictive assumption of an underlying normal distribution. As Guttman has pointed out, the use of this coefficient can lead to inconsistencies in the correlation matrix, in that one item can have associations of 1.0 with two others, and yet these others need not themselves have a perfect association.[18] This difficulty exists, in fact, for any $f(a, b, c, d)$ that attains unity for a perfect scale relationship, as scale relationships are not necessarily transitive in the logical sense unless the items are considered in the proper order of p_+.

Regardless of whether the tetrachoric coefficient is justifiable by a presumed underlying normality of distributions, we can still investigate its properties in comparison with the other indices discussed here.

Yule's Q

Another coefficient that attains its maximum value for a perfect scale relationship, but one derived from reasoning based on pairwise rankings rather than products or normal distributions, is Yule's Q, given by the expression

$$Q = \frac{ad - bc}{ad + bc} \tag{3.4}$$

Proposed by Yule, this is a special case of the Goodman-Kruskal gamma coefficient, the latter being defined for contingency tables of any size.[19] This coefficient satisfies all the conditions mentioned above for indices of scalability. (Exercise: prove this.) It will also be used extensively in our subsequent treatments of cluster analysis. It has the disadvantage for factor analysis, however, that a matrix of Q coefficients is not necessarily positive semidefinite, a condition customarily required in principal component analysis.[20]

Yule's Y and other variants of Q

The indices we have discussed so far have numerical values, and can presumably be treated as cardinal numbers, e.g., in averaging. But for many of the applications we shall consider, only weaker assumptions

[18]See Stouffer et al., op. cit., pp. 195–199.

[19]See Yule, op. cit., 271–273; Yule, Introduction to the Theory of Statistics, p. 38; and Goodman and Kruskal, "Measures of Association for Cross Classifications" (I).

[20]See Chapter 5.

will be made—for example, that only the rank ordering of various values of such an index will be considered. If the assumptions are weakened in this way, then a set of indices may be equivalent to one another as regards the order in which they rank particular fourfold tables even though their numerical values are not identical. An example of such an index providing a ranking identical with Q is $1 + Q = 2ad/(ad + bc)$. This particular index, though having no practical use, illustrates that addition of a constant is one way to produce an identical ranking. The cross-product ratio, mentioned above, also gives rise to the same ranking as Q. This can be shown by the fact that twice the reciprocal of the previous index, $2/(1 + Q)$, is equal to $1 + (1/J)$. Since the reciprocal of the previous index provides a ranking inverse to that index, inverse to Q, and inverse to J, then J provides a ranking identical to that of Q, i.e., one is an increasing function of the other.

But whereas none of the three indices we have just considered shares with Q all the properties of reversibility, boundedness and attainment of the upper limit in the case of a perfect scale relationship, there are others that do. A set of such indices may be generated by the expression $[(ad)^x - (bc)^x]/[(ad)^x + (bc)^x]$ where x is a positive real number. The special case $x = \frac{1}{2}$ is of particular interest, as it gives rise to Yule's "index of colligation,"[21]

$$Y = \frac{\sqrt{ad} - \sqrt{bc}}{\sqrt{ad} + \sqrt{bc}} \tag{3.5}$$

This index will be of interest to us below, for while it appears that no index will both measure scalability and satisfy all the conditions customary for factor analysis, Y may provide one of the closest approximations in certain respects. This is because Y is equivalent to the value of ϕ that would be obtained if the fourfold table were transformed so that its horizontal and vertical marginal proportions were each one-half.[22]

The approximation to the tetrachoric coefficient given by (3.3) can also be shown to be an increasing function of Q. For in the first expression given there, it is simply $\sin(90° \cdot Y)$; and since Y is an in-

[21]See M. G. Kendall and Stuart, *The Advanced Theory of Statistics*, vol. 2, p. 539.

[22]This is proved in Yule, "On the Methods of Measuring the Association Between Two Attributes." See also Goodman and Kruskal, "Measures of Association for Cross Classifications. II: Further Discussion and References," p. 125.

creasing function of Q, and the sine function in this interval is an increasing one, the relation also holds between Q and the tetrachoric approximation.

An index based on information or uncertainty

Proceeding from an entirely different line of reasoning, Gerson and Kassan have proposed an index of association in contingency tables, based on uncertainty or information.[23] This index ranges from 0 to +1 and characterizes the amount of information provided by the cell entries, over and above that provided by the marginals. Presumably it could be given a positive or negative sign according to the sign of $(ad - bc)$, and thus made to meet the requirements we have considered. Although this index has not been used extensively, it might be worthy of comparison with the other indices we have discussed.

CLUSTER ANALYSIS
AND ITS VARIATIONS

The measures of relation between pairs of roll calls, discussed above, exemplify a restriction on the methods to be treated in this chapter: they deal with matrices of pairwise relations as data. Pairwise relations are by no means the only form in which the information in the initial roll-call votes could be summarized for analysis. The matrix of votes contains much more information; and higher-order relations among three or more roll calls are considered, for example, in latent-structure analysis.[24] One type of roll call that cannot easily be detected by pairwise comparisons is the alliance of both extremes against the middle on a compromise proposal. However, a three-way tabulation can in some cases reveal such a relation, even without advance knowledge of the legislators and issues involved. In such a case, it might still be meaningful to say that only a single underlying dimension was involved, but that the roll calls did not all fit it in a cumulative fashion.[25]

[23]Gerson and Kassan, "A Measure of Association Based on Analysis of Uncertainty." Additional references to this approach are given in Goodman and Kruskal, "Measures of Association for Cross Classifications. II," 147.

[24]See Lazarsfeld and Henry, Latent Structure Analysis.

[25]It is also possible that an entire set of roll calls are related to one another by a process in which legislators agree only with proposals near their own positions on a

A second restriction on the methods we are considering in this chapter is that we are seeking a number of discrete subsets of the initial list of roll calls, each composed of roll calls that resemble one another in terms of a selected measure of similarity. These procedures thus differ from factor analysis, which produces quantitative measures of the relation between roll calls and factors. The results of factor analysis, however, can be used to produce clusters; and at least one method of cluster analysis depends on the mathematics of factor analysis, and is therefore considered in Chapter 4.

Use of cluster analysis has also sometimes been justified on the ground that its results are nearer to the data than those of factor analysis. A *cluster* is a set of roll calls, and not a hypothesized variable defined by a set of numbers relating it to particular roll calls. We might also contend that the clusters we find, as discrete sets of roll calls, are a more appropriate description of the categories in which legislators place particular measures than quantitative mixtures of factors would be. This second argument might indeed have some force, if we could be sure that every cluster we found corresponded to a category perceived by the legislators. But there are, in fact, various models or hypotheses that can be reasonably entertained as to the processes giving rise to clusters. In addition to perceptual categories, there are also the combined influences of interest groups and multiple roles, which might better be described in terms of factor loadings. And alternatively, as we shall see in Chapter 8, parties and blocs of legislators may perhaps best be discerned by a third and different type of clustering of legislator points in the factor-score space.

One useful property of cluster analysis with coefficients of association is that it permits setting the polarities of roll calls by means of the matrix itself. With Q we can show how a single divergent polarity can be seen and corrected. This property is shared by all indices that are reversible. Consider the data presented in Table 2.4, on fourfold tables of association between pairs of four roll calls for the Republican Senators in 1961. Had we simply considered the four roll calls in temporal order (the order of their serial numbers), and not reversed any polarities, we would have obtained a Q-matrix such as shown in

---

continuum. This process leads to "proximity scaling" in contrast with "dominance scaling," a distinction made in Weisberg, "Dimensional Analysis of Legislative Roll Calls " chap. 3.

Table 3.1 Q-matrix for four selected roll calls, Republican Senators, 1961

Roll-call number	Roll-call number			
	11	47	78	130
11	X	−1.00	−.29	−1.00
47	−1.00	X	+.25	+1.00
78	−.29	+.25	X	+.19
130	−1.00	+1.00	+.19	X

Table 3.1. (Exercise: calculate the values of Q.) It will be seen, first, that if the polarity of #11 is reversed, all signs in the matrix then become positive; and second, that the three remaining associations less than unity are all in the row and column corresponding to #78. These last two judgments are facilitated, for the beginner, by our inclusion of the symmetric entries below as well as above the diagonal X's in Table 3.1. The diagonal X's are substitutes for the self-associations of +1.0 that would otherwise appear there, but which would provide us with no new information. In some later presentations of tables of this type, the associations below the diagonal will be omitted, but the reader may fill them in using paper and pencil.

Thus these four roll calls provide a simple example of how the Q-matrix (or a matrix based on any coefficient with similar properties to Q) can be used for both polarity assignment and selection of roll calls, without the use of any information other than the votes themselves.

In larger matrices we can set polarities in several ways. First, we can use preliminary information (such as the association of votes with party) to yield an approximate polarity assignment, and then correct the few remaining errors by inspection, as we have just indicated. If no simple criterion such as legislators' party affiliation is available, we can assign polarities on the basis of the substance of the vote. And if we wish to rely on the data alone for this purpose, if they are sufficiently homogeneous we can use the sign of the first principal component as a polarity indicator.[26]

Given a matrix of coefficients of one of the types we have discussed,

---

[26]The association of vote with party is a useful guide to approximate polarity settings for congressional votes. In a multiparty system such as that of France, an automatic procedure of this sort is harder to devise. One systematic procedure is described in Carroll and Levin, "A Method for Determining the Polarity of Behavior Items." We will consider principal-component analysis in Chapters 4 and 5.

we may use any of various methods to select clusters or subsets of similar roll calls. This general approach is known as cluster analysis, and has received extensive and increasing treatment in the literature of disciplines other than political science. The procedure followed by Toby and Toby is one particular type of cluster analysis; but a more general perspective is supplied in articles by Bonner, McQuitty, Cattell, and Coulter.[27] We shall proceed now to present a systematic treatment of some currently available procedures for cluster analysis that seem applicable to roll-call studies.

One fundamental difference among methods of cluster analysis relates to the ways in which the individual coefficients of similarity or association are treated. Each of the coefficients we have considered is expressed as a number, and each is obtained by performing arithmetic operations on the cell entries $a, b, c,$ and d. Nevertheless, there are numerous methods of analysis that treat these coefficients not as cardinal numbers, capable of addition and multiplication, but simply as rankings, or even as dichotomies. Each of the three procedures considered below corresponds to use of a different proportion of the information provided in the initial matrix of associations. In order to begin with the simplest procedures, we shall treat them in reverse order, considering first the "binary matrix" (in which the coefficients are reduced in effect to a matrix of 0's and 1's), then the "ranked matrix" (in which only their rank order is used), and finally the "cardinal matrix" in which the entries are treated as ordinary cardinal numbers.

Before presenting these methods, we will consider what we expect their comparative merits to be. One general principle of statistical analysis is that the information in our data should be used fully and efficiently—we should not, for example, collapse reliable quantitative variables into dichotomies. For, in so doing, we risk ignoring associations that more efficient use of our data would reveal, and we risk introducing additional "noise" variation into the deviations from an initial model, making the analysis of deviant cases less precise. In terms of this principle, the cardinal matrix would seem best to use.

[27]See Bonner, "On Some Clustering Techniques"; McQuitty, "Elementary Linkage Analysis for Isolating Orthogonal and Oblique Types and Typal Relevancies"; Cattell, "A Note on Correlation Clusters and Cluster Search Methods"; and Cattell and Coulter, "Principles of Behavioural Taxonomy and the Mathematical Basis of the Taxonome Computer Program."

Yet the very multiplicity of indices we have presented suggests another problem: *which* cardinal matrix should be used? We have shown that several different indices (such as Q, Y, and an approximation to the tetrachoric coefficient) are increasing functions of one another, and provide completely equivalent rankings. Perhaps if we wished to leave open the question as to which of these was best, and to obtain results equally valid for all of them, we should use a method that depends only on the ranking of coefficients in the matrix. Such methods have been extensively developed in the past few years, and need to be tried and evaluated for roll-call analysis. They were originally devised, however, for social-science data such as cumulative-scale rankings or judgments of similarity—"weaker" data than the coefficients we are using. We shall see that for at least some of these methods, the use of only rankings of coefficients in the matrix omits valuable information—the values of 1 and 0, corresponding to perfect scalability and to independence in the fourfold table.

Treating the matrix of coefficients as a binary matrix is the simplest, but perhaps the least efficient, of the three methods. This approach does have a superficial congruence with the goal of cluster analysis, which is the identification of discrete sets of roll calls; but this goal can also be attained by methods that give rise to quantitative results (e.g., factor loadings or spatial coordinates) or rankings, which can then be reduced in various ways to categories if desired. The use of a binary matrix also has some precedent in the Toby and Toby procedure, in which each fourfold table is classed simply as "scalable" or not. More generally, if we wish to generate scales and place legislators on them, we must normally insist on a minimum degree of similarity between pairs of roll calls, below which the proliferation of errors would render the conventional scale-scoring procedures increasingly difficult. It still does not follow, however, that one and the same threshold value is appropriate for all sets of data. An obvious adjustment would be to create several binary matrices by means of different cutting points or thresholds, and compare the results. But even this does not fully justify the use of the binary matrix in preference to the ranked or the cardinal. We shall, indeed, consider analyses of the cardinal matrix (factor analysis) at length in later chapters. The methods currently available for analyzing the ranked matrix are either difficult to implement (in terms of computer time), or appear to involve questionable assumptions, or are simply less prevalent in roll-call analysis than those of the binary matrix. For these reasons we present first the latter procedure.

THE BINARY MATRIX

The analysis of a matrix of similarity coefficients assumes its simplest form if we require that each such coefficient have only one of two values, e.g., 1 and 0 for "similar" and "dissimilar." To reach this situation we might start with a matrix of numerical coefficients, and by setting a threshold value convert all matrix values that attain or exceed that value into 1's, all below it into 0's. We thus convert the variable $f(a, b, c, d)$ in the initial matrix into a binary variable or a dichotomy. In this new matrix (produced by either rewriting or marking up the initial matrix), we then ask that every pair of roll calls within a cluster be related by at least the threshold level of the coefficient. This line of reasoning is susceptible of various modifications, such as computation of a "squared" matrix each of whose elements is a summary index of the degree of similarity between two rows or columns in the initial binary matrix, and the repetition of this procedure.

The results of such a procedure clearly depend on the threshold value chosen. If that value is set to 0, then all positive coefficients in the initial matrix will be represented by 1's in the binary matrix, and the resulting clusters will reveal nothing more than the polarities of of the roll calls. For some data, on the other hand, a threshold of 1 will leave the entire binary matrix blank, i.e., consisting of 0's, and no clusters will be found. Moreover, when matrices for several parties or several periods of time are being compared, a threshold suitable for one may produce one of these extreme results for another, and deprive us of useful clusters.

It is also clear that if several indices of similarity are increasing functions of one another, i.e., produce identical rankings, then a given threshold value for one index has an equivalent threshold value for each other corresponding index. Consequently, the binary matrix formed from a matrix of values of one such index may be recreated identically from values of another corresponding index, simply by the choice of a corresponding threshold. Conversion of the Q-matrix at a threshold of .8, for example, produces the identical binary matrix as conversion of the Y-matrix at .5. (Exercise: show this equivalence.)

We shall deal primarily with one widely used procedure for clustering the binary matrix. In this procedure we look first for the largest cluster such that every element of the cluster has an association above the threshold (a value of 1 in the binary matrix) with every other. Once such a cluster is found, we eliminate its elements from the overall matrix and repeat the procedure. This process is continued until no further clusters having at least a specified minimum number of elements are found. Clusters of this type may be built up by the successive addition of elements, with the requirement that each new element must have a relation of 1 with each former element. For small matrices, or those with few 1's, this procedure may be carried out by hand. For larger and more complex matrices, it has been programmed for computer solution, but risks being quite time-consuming.[28]

The assumptions involved in the above procedure are not, however, the only ones that could be chosen. At the start, one alternative is to choose a central or "pivot" item (or a pair of items defined by a matrix element) and to add to it other items that have specified relations to it. A second is to permit the building of chains of items, such that each is linked by 1's in the matrix to others, but not necessarily to all elements of its cluster. A third is to use substantive classifications of roll calls as an additional basis of cluster definition.

After the first cluster is found, subsequent clusters might be required to be "different" from the first; thus a low proportion of associations between a prospective new cluster and previous clusters might be taken to count in favor of the new one, or items similar to previous clusters might be eliminated. Subsequent clusters might also be allowed to overlap earlier ones. When we consider the clustering of the ranked or cardinal matrix, we shall also see that clustering can proceed by stages: one cluster (e.g., a pair) may be formed, and then this cluster may be combined and treated for subsequent analysis as a single contrived element. Thus after forming a trial subset, instead of first enlarging it we might look for higher-order relations between this and other subsets.

The clustering procedure we shall follow requires proper choice of

---

[28]Programs for this purpose have been written at the University of Chicago by Frank K. Bamberger and by Robert Axelrod. A faster program, based not on the largest cluster but on a "pivot item," has been written by David H. Klassen.

roll-call polarities, for a high negative coefficient will be treated similarly to a zero value. In the design of computer printouts, selection for printing can be based on the absolute value of the coefficient, to permit correction of polarity errors.

Two interesting features of binary-matrix analysis are that it discards information—as is always done when a quantitative variable is converted to a dichotomy—and that it performs a type of data-smoothing function. This is especially true for large clusters, where the requirement that an additional item have coefficients above the threshold with *all* previous items prevents a few fortuitous high values from defining an element of a cluster. Thus the 1.0 values, for Q and similar coefficients, that arise unreliably from tables with extreme marginals are prevented from exercising a determinative effect on cluster membership.[29] Or as Toby and Toby observed, if the coefficient imposes more stringent conditions for some fourfold tables than for others (e.g., in relation to the separation of the component items in their p_+), then clusters will in effect be formed on the basis of a subset of pairwise relationships for which the criterion is more stringent. If, within this subset of matrix cells (e.g., relations between roll calls near one another in p_+), the corresponding binary values are similar to those that are found for another index of similarity, then clusters formed from matrices using different types of coefficients might be more similar than would otherwise be expected.

The clustering technique with which we are mainly concerned is illustrated in Table 3.2. This table presents a Q-matrix for a selected subset of roll calls for the Republicans in the U.S. House of Representatives in the 84th Congress.

Entries below .8 (the chosen threshold value) are left blank. The matrix presented is thus equivalent to a binary matrix in which each blank entry would be replaced by a 0 and each nonblank entry by a 1. The threshold value was chosen after comparative study of a large number of such matrices for Congress and the French National Assembly, with the aim of making these analyses comparable and revealing the greatest possible amount of information in them.[30] An

[29]We shall encounter this problem later in the present chapter in connection with clustering based on Kruskal's MDSCAL. It was noted early by Yule, in "On the Association of Attributes in Statistics," p. 276.

[30]See MacRae, "A Method for Identifying Issues and Factions"; and MacRae, *Parliament, Parties and Society in France 1946–1958*.

earlier trial value of .7 was revised after comparison of clustering with other methods of analysis showed that the clusters at this level were unnecessarily heterogeneous in subject matter.[31] Even with the choice of .8, some Q-matrices for the Democrats in the House might well have been studied at higher thresholds to resolve closely correlated clusters on foreign and domestic affairs; and some for the French Socialist party required lower thresholds to reveal their underlying divisions clearly. The general relation between cluster structures found at different threshold levels is analogous to that of a relief map portrayed by various contour lines. As Cattell once put it,

A matrix which yields, in a certain area, two distinct clusters when a high level of correlation is demanded may yield only one large cluster when the level is lowered, as two islands become one when the tidal level falls.[32]

The entire square matrix is presented, rather than simply the upper diagonal, to show the pattern of rows and columns in which the associations fall if they satisfy the cluster criterion. With practice, this pattern may easily be imagined in analysis of a matrix including only one of the two symmetric diagonal parts. Table 3.2 shows six clusters of four or more roll calls, found by application of a set of fixed rules to a larger (102×102) Q-matrix which included all roll calls in 1955–1956 on which the Republicans had at least 7 percent dissidence. The process of finding these clusters is simplified by the fact that none of the Q's presented in the table is negative, since suitable polarity changes made them all positive. Of the polarities set by the association of votes with party, only four of those for the roll calls in Table 3.2 needed further modification for this purpose; these roll calls are indicated there by superscripts. This possibility of making all associations positive is slightly exaggerated in Table 3.2, since the roll calls in it were selected as belonging to clusters; but even without such selection the number of irremovable negative signs is usually extremely small.

The first step in identifying the clusters is to find the largest cluster, i.e., the one containing the most roll calls. We might begin our search, for example, with the cluster of five roll calls at the upper left. We can then see whether others may be added to this cluster, by looking

[31]The study that showed this was MacRae, "Cluster Analysis of Congressional Votes with the BC TRY System."

[32]"A Note on Correlation Clusters and Cluster Search Methods," p. 181.

Table 3.2 **Q-matrix for Republicans, U.S. House of Representatives, 84th Congress (selected roll calls)**

CQ number:	1955: 6	7	8	9	10	15	22	23	24	27	28	29	30	42	43	47
1955: 6	X	9	9	9	9										10	
7	9	X	9	8	9									10	9	
8	9	9	X	9	9									10	10	
9	9	8	9	X	10									10	10	
10	9	9	9	10	X										10	
15						X									9	8
22							X	10	10			10	10			
23							10	X	9			9	9			
24							10	9	X			9	9			
27										10	X					
28										X	10					
29							10	9	9			X	10			
30							10	9	9			10	X			
42			10	10	10									X		8
43	10	9	10	10	10	9									X	
47						8								8		X
50	8	8	9	8	9	8								8	9	8
52ᵃ						10	10									8
57						9									8	9
59						9									8	9
60						9									8	9
72								8						10		
76								8				8	8			
1956: 13										10	10					
14										10	10					
16										9	9					
23										10	10					
29										10	10					
30														10		
32						8									8	9
42ᵃ							10									
48																
52						8									8	9
59ᵃ															8	
60ᵃ															8	
Cluster		←————3————→				←1→	←——4——→			←—2—→		←—4—→	←6→	←3→	←1→	

Table 3.2 (Continued)

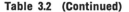

							1956:										
50	52[a]	57	59	60	72	76	13	14	16	23	29	30	32	42[a]	48	52	59[a] 60[a]

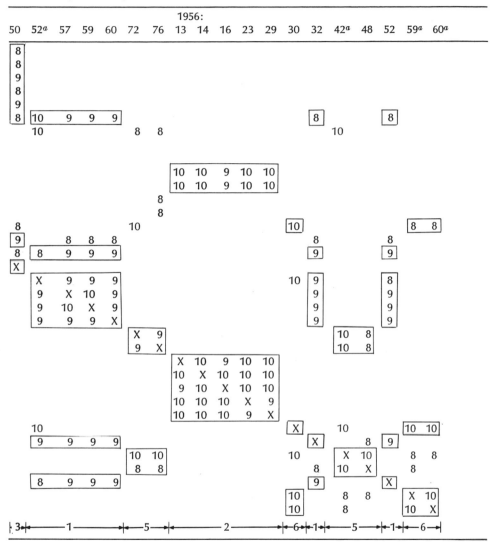

```
8
8
9
8
9
8  |10   9   9   9|              8         8
   10                  8   8              10
                  |10  10   9  10  10|
                  |10  10   9  10  10|
                           8
                           8
8               10          |10|          |8   8|
|9|      8   8   8            8            8
|8| |8   9   9   9|          |9|           |9|
|X|
   |X   9   9   9|        10 |9|           |8|
   |9   X  10   9|           |9|           |9|
   |9  10   X   9|           |9|           |9|
   |9   9   9   X|           |9|           |9|
              |X   9|               |10  8|
              |9   X|               |10  8|
                  |X  10   9  10  10|
                  |10   X  10  10  10|
                  |9  10   X  10  10|
                  |10  10  10   X   9|
                  |10  10  10   9   X|
   10                    |X|    10    |10  10|
  |9   9   9   9|        |X|    8  |9|
              |10  10|   10  |X  10|   8   8
              | 8   8|       |10   X|  8
  |8   9   9   9|        8   |X|
                         |9|           |X|
                        |10|    8   8  |X  10|
                        |10|    8      |10   X|
| 3→|←——1——→|←—5—→|←——2——→|←6→|←1→|←—5—→|←1→|←6→|
```

[a] Polarity reversed relative to that chosen from the association of vote with party.

NOTE: Of the 102 roll calls on which the party had at least 7 percent dissidence, this table retains only the 35 that were members of scale clusters at $Q_{min} = .8$. Table entries are $10Q$, unrounded, for $Q \geqslant .8$.

horizontally or vertically for groups of five Q's of at least .8. Two additional groups of associations appear—those of roll calls 5–43 and 5–50 (the first number being the last digit of the year in question). We thus have a seven-item cluster to which no further items can be added without losing more of the existing cluster in return.

This seven-item cluster may not be the largest, however, even though it is easiest to see at first. Another seven-item cluster can be seen, centering about an adjacent set of five items near the lower right of the diagram. If these two were indeed the largest, and if they had shared an item that might have fitted either one, then we would have resolved the tie by computation of the average Q for the alternative clusters.[33]

Further inspection of Table 3.2 will reveal that neither of these two seven-item clusters is the largest. An eight-item cluster can be found, including a set of four adjacent items near the center of the table: 5–52, 57, 59, and 60. This is therefore designated as cluster #1, and the items in it are eliminated before a second cluster is sought. This procedure was repeated until no further clusters containing as many as four items could be found, and the items in the resulting clusters are those selected for presentation in the table. Because of the distinctness of issues among the Republicans, the overlap of clusters was small, and procedures for choosing among alternative overlapping clusters were not required except for the clusters of size four. The relatively low proportion of the roll calls in the initial matrix, which entered the largest cluster, also indicates the multiple divisions of the party.

While it is feasible to find clusters of this type by means of computer programs, programs for this particular clustering procedure have proved so time-consuming that we shall discuss here means of clustering by the human brain, aided by visual inspection and paper and pencil. Table 3.2 reveals a symmetry that is a useful clue to the existence of clusters in which each member of a cluster has a specified relation with each other. If we include the association of each item with itself, corresponding to the diagonal X in its row and column

[33]This tie-breaking criterion departs from the strict assumption that only a binary matrix is being considered. It is also considered in Sokal and Sneath, *op. cit.,* p. 181. After the first cluster is found, one alternative procedure is to eliminate not only its elements, but also other items highly associated with it; see Lorr, *Explorations in Typing Psychotics,* p. 26.

in Table 3.2, we can then see that every item in a given cluster has the same set of items as associates. If we enclose every such association in a rectangular box, the rows or columns of such boxes are identical for all items in a given cluster. Cluster membership is indicated at the foot of the corresponding columns in Table 3.2, and the similarity of configurations of columns (or rows) within each cluster may be seen. The visibility of these configurations is enhanced by blanking out entries below the threshold value, and by the clumps of associations corresponding to roll calls in contiguous sequences. The latter effect may be heightened by re-printing the matrix with rows and columns rearranged and thinned out.

The subject matter of the roll calls in the clusters is shown in Table 3.3. Each cluster is there referred to as a "scale," as it will be subsequently used in this way. In the first cluster, all but one of the items deal with foreign aid, and the cluster is titled correspondingly. The one item that apparently does not conform in subject matter will be shown later to be improperly placed in this cluster, when we compare this method with more complex clustering procedures that use more of the information in the Q-matrix. In the second cluster (Scale 2), all the items deal with agricultural policy. In the third, all items but one deal with a reciprocal trade bill, and the remaining item concerns the simplification of customs procedures—a clearly related matter. In the fourth cluster, all items deal with a bill on the pay of postal employees. Up to this point, the subject matter of the roll calls provides ample support of the basic hypothesis that roll calls linked by high values of Q also resemble one another in the issues they involve, and that distinct clusters reflect distinct issues.

The fifth and sixth clusters are less distinct both conceptually and empirically. Both appear to deal with general liberal–conservative matters, and the particular roll calls included in the two cannot easily be separated conceptually. The orderings of legislators which they provide are closely associated with one another, as indicated by the association of $\gamma = .74$ between them (to be discussed below). And in fact, great care was required to identify these two sets of four roll calls, among several overlapping four-item clusters; only consideration of values of Q accurate to two digits permitted a clear choice of these two to be made.

This lack of clarity of the issues in the last two scales appears, however, to be a feature of the data rather than of the method. Another

Table 3.3　84th Congress, House, Republicans; Roll calls in scale clusters

Cluster	CQ number	p_+ (x100)	Issue	Associations (γ) with clusters					
				1	2	3	4	5	6
Scale 1. Foreign aid	5–15	63	Supplemental appropriation, UN aid funds						
	5–47	13	Congressional delegation, NATO						
	5–52[a]	09	Debt limit						
	5–57	41	Mutual Security Act of 1955, passage						
	5–59	40	Mutual Security Act of 1955, conference report						
	5–60	41	Mutual Security, appropriation						
	6–32	39	Mutual Security, passage						
	6–52	36	Foreign aid appropriation, passage	X	–.28	.54	.05	.41	.36
Scale 2. Agriculture	5–27	90	Price supports, recommit						
	5–28	88	Price supports, passage						
	6–13	86	Price supports, recommit						
	6–14	75	Price supports, conference report						
	6–16	89	Price supports, pass over veto						
	6–23	34	Soil bank, passage						
	6–29	26	Revised farm bill, conference report	–.28	X	–.03	–.07	–.20	–.13
Scale 3. Reciprocal trade	5– 6	63	Reciprocal trade extension						
	5– 7	64	Reciprocal trade extension						
	5– 8	60	Reciprocal trade extension						
	5– 9	64	Reciprocal trade extension						
	5–10	42	Reciprocal trade extension						
	5–43	20	Reciprocal trade extension, conference report						
	5–50	51	Customs simplification	.54	–.03	X	–.20	.17	.33

Scale 4. Postal pay	5–22	88	Postal pay, raise rates					
	5–23	63	Postal pay, recommit					
	5–24	43	Postal pay, passage					
	5–29	64	Postal pay, return to conference					
	5–30	37	Postal pay, adopt conference report	.05	–.07	–.20	X	.59	.42
Scale 5. Welfare state	5–72	80	Housing Act of 1955, eliminate public housing					
	5–76	79	Housing Act of 1955, conference report					
	6–42[a]	10	School construction, open rule					
	6–48	60	School construction, passage	.41	–.20	.17	.59	X	.74
Scale 6. Extreme blocs	5–42	07	Inter-American highway, appropriation					
	6–30	90	Crow Indians, Yellowtail Dam					
	6–59[a]	15	Civil rights bill, recommit					
	6–60[a]	13	Civil rights bill, recommit	.36	–.13	.33	.42	.74	X

[a]Polarity reversed relative to that chosen from the association of vote with party.

NOTE: The year, corresponding to the volume of the *Congressional Quarterly Almanac* in which a roll call appears, is indicated by its last digit (5 or 6) preceding the roll call number.

study of these same data indicated that general domestic liberal–conservative issues in these data had a much looser structure than did the issues revealed in the preceding scales.[34] Thus although the results of the method are less clear for the last two clusters, they are not necessarily less valid if interpreted correctly.

A clustering operation such as that of Table 3.2 permits us not only to identify sets of similar roll calls, but also to locate legislators in relation to the issues or principles of division corresponding to these sets. One need only treat each cluster as a possible cumulative scale, and assign scale scores by one of the methods appropriate for such scales. The assignment of such scores not only allows us to investigate the differences among legislators in their votes, but also permits a more precise statement of the relations among the clusters. In Table 3.3, for example, we specify indices of association (γ) between all pairs of scales.[35] These indices are based on the sets of ranked categories in which the Republican congressmen may be placed on each corresponding scale. The cutting points (p_+) that divide these categories from one another may be distributed nonuniformly in the interval between 0 and 1; this is an inconvenience if compared with the requirements of the original attitude-scale model, but it may afford some information about blocs and coalitions among the legislators under study.[36]

The associations (γ) between the scales in Table 3.3 can be used to group together those scales that order the legislators similarly. One way to do this follows our clustering procedure for the binary matrix; if we set a threshold, say, of .7, only the association between Scales 5 and 6 exceeds it. At a threshold of .5, γ_{45} and γ_{13} would be added.

[34]MacRae, "Cluster Analysis of Congressional Votes."

[35]These indices are defined in Goodman and Kruskal, "Measures of Association for Cross Classifications" (I), The scale scores on which these associations are based were assigned by a procedure described below; it is also described in MacRae, *Parliament, Parties and Society*, Appendix B, and in "A Method for Identifying Issues and Factions." An alternative measure of the relation between two clusters would be the average index of association between their respective elements.

[36]Inferences about coalitions from the distribution of values of p_+ are discussed in MacRae, "A Method. . . ." Even aside from these inferences, there are various ways in which the information afforded by a cumulative scale can be assessed. Some scales give little information about the ranking of legislators, but what they do give is highly consistent; others the converse. See Davis, "On Criteria for Scale Relationships," p. 376.

Congressman	5–15	5–60	5–57	5–59	6–32	6–52	5–47	5–52a	Scale score
	.63	.41	.41	.40 p_+	.39	.36	.13	.09	
Halleck (Ind.)	−	−	−	0	−	−	−	−	0
Arends (Ill.)	+	−	−	−	−	−	−	−	1
McCulloch (Ohio)	+	+	+	+	+	+	−	−	2
O'Konski (Wis.)	+	+	+	+	+	+	+	0	3
Van Zandt (Pa.)	+	−	+	+	−	−	−	−	1
Coon (Ore.)	−	+	+	+	+	+	−	−	1a
Reed (N.Y.)	+	0	0	0	+	+	0	0	2b
Poff (Va.)	+	−	−	−	−	−	−	+	X
Johansen (Mich.)	0			+	+	+	+	−	2b

a Contains an error response.
b Contains ambiguous vote.
NOTE: 0 = absent or general pair.

Another way to interpret these associations, which we shall discuss below in connection with the ranked matrix, is to look for the highest associations of *each scale*, and by implication to use a different threshold or criterion for each. With this approach, we should again join scales 4–5–6 together, and join the pair 1–3. The last pair deals with foreign aid and foreign trade.

Scale 2, dealing with agriculture, has uniformly low associations with the others. Moreover, these associations are negative; the polarities chosen for these roll calls on the basis of the parties' positions do not accurately indicate which segment within the Republican party took the more liberal position. This is because conservative rural Republicans tended more to vote with the Democrats, for aid to the farmer, than did their otherwise liberal urban colleagues. For this reason we shall reverse the polarity of Scale 2 in further analysis below.

The procedure used to assign scale scores is illustrated for Scale 1 in Table 3.4.[37] The roll calls in the scale cluster are first arranged in descending order of p_+, and the columns of the table appear in this order from left to right. For roll call 5–52, polarities were inverted

[37]We use here an earlier and less precise scaling procedure than the one proposed in Chapter 2; the values of gamma are not greatly affected by this choice.

relative to the sense defined by the relation of vote to party, and the original apparent p_+ (.91) was subtracted from unity to yield the value of .09 shown. The sequence of p_+ was then divided into segments corresponding to "contrived items"—sets of adjacent roll calls to be combined and treated as single hypothetical roll calls in scoring. Since the intervals between .63 and .41, and between .36 and .13, each exceeded a criterion value of .1, divisions between cutting points were made there. None of the remaining contiguous sequences of p_+ spanned an interval more than .15, and therefore according to our conventions none was subdivided further.

The first four rows of scores in Table 3.4 show assignments of perfect scale scores to four well-known Republicans, ranging from Halleck (who supported Eisenhower's foreign aid program) to O'Konski (who opposed it). Occasional absences among these men's votes do not prevent us from assigning them to scale categories, because the use of more than one roll call as a cutting point allows another roll call in the same contrived item to define the congressman's position on that cutting point. The overwhelming majority of the scale scores could be placed unambiguously in this way.

The next five rows in Table 3.4 illustrate the variations occasionally necessary in order to place certain legislators. On the middle cutting point, Van Zandt had three $-$'s and two $+$'s. The predominant vote determines the response on this cutting point, and the resulting $-$ assigns Van Zandt to scale category 1. Coon had a response pattern of $- + -$ on the three cutting points, a nonscale pattern which we assign by convention to category 1, adding a superscript a to indicate that it contained an error response. Daniel Reed, absent on five of the eight roll calls in this cluster, had an equivalent response pattern of $+ + 0$, corresponding to a scale score of 2 or 3. Again by convention we assign this ambiguous type to category 2, changing the ambiguous vote (on 5–47 and 5–52) to the negative vote that prevailed among Reed's party colleagues; we indicate this type of assignment by a superscript b following the scale score. In the cases of Poff and Johansen, the contrived-item response on the rightmost item is a tie, composed of one plus and one minus. We break this by giving additional weight to the item with higher average Q in the cluster, in this case 5–52. The result for Poff is a response pattern of $+ - +$, but having attained this nonscale pattern only after breaking a tie, we assign no scale category, indicating this by the symbol X. Johansen, however, now has the pattern $0 + -$, and is assigned the score of 2. Scale scores have been assigned in this way for clusters containing as many as 60 roll calls, and can be used to examine the interrelations among clusters.

Once we carry out the clustering procedure—or any procedure for identifying issues from such matrices—we must then ask whether the results are valid or are artifacts of the method. Among the practical problems revealed by this example are those relating to classification of borderline roll calls in one cluster or another. The difficulty experienced by the analyst when a roll call barely fails to meet the conditions for inclusion in a cluster, may perhaps be lessened by the use of "powered" matrices, in which the rows or columns of the matrix of agreement are examined in pairs to give rise to indices of *their* agreement.[38] Or this problem may be answered in part in several ways:

1 Valid assignment of roll calls to categories may be important if it is the particular roll call that interests us; but if we need only a general measure of a variable, such measures may not be greatly affected by the inclusion or exclusion of borderline cases from a large cluster. Variations in the composition of a large cluster may not greatly affect our judgment of its issue content, or the corresponding placement of legislators. And those roll calls barely eliminated from a cluster may still be characterized by their association with it.

2 Sometimes in the analysis of a single matrix multiple clusters are found that overlap in content and rank the legislators quite similarly. If no rational basis for distinguishing them can be found, the smaller of such a pair of scales may be regarded as a "shadow" of the larger, not as an indicator of a distinct issue concept. The finding of such shadow or artificial scales generally depends on the placement of borderline roll calls, which might equally well have been placed in two or more clusters were it not for the sequence in which clusters were formed and set aside. But such clusters can also be detected by their high associations with others.

When several similar or hightly associated scales are found, there may also arise the problem of choosing among them that scale that

---

[38]See Bonner, *op. cit.;* and for another measure of profile similarity, see equation (3.7) below.

is most useful for further analysis or which most clearly represents a particular issue concept. Questions of this sort may be investigated by examination of the interrelations between legislators' rankings on different scales. For example, Clausen selected for particular attention those scales that showed closest association with scales found in other Congresses.[39] Another procedure that has been used extensively to clarify the conceptual meaning of scales is to examine the names of the legislators who are placed differently on otherwise similar scales—the ideological "deviant cases." Knowledge of the legislators' political positions, and study of their speeches, provides information about the differences in meaning between the two scales on which their positions differed.

We shall use these clusters for comparison of various other methods, and for this reason it will be useful to examine the selective processes that have led us to the particular clusters we have found.[40] The choice of a particular Congress and of the Republican party are of course important; a multiply divided congressional party, and a weak President representing the moderate wing of the Republican party, contributed to the distinctness of the issue clusters we have found. Among the Democrats, a single internal factional division has been more dominant in recent years.[41]

But even within the 84th Congress, our findings represent various sorts of selective processes. By investigating only those roll calls on which the party had at least 7 percent dissidence, we have omitted roll calls on which the Republicans were united, either alone or together with the Democrats. The former—partisan roll calls—were few in that Congress, and included such matters as the election of the Speaker, the farm program, and public works. Nearly unanimous roll calls, on the other hand, were far more numerous and included anticommunist measures (the HUAC appropriation), defense legislation, aid for widespread and popular interest groups (postal employees' pay, the school milk program), and votes on final passage of certain measures distributing federal money (payment for highways, for sur-

[39]Clausen, "Measurement Identity in the Longitudinal Analysis of Legislative Voting."

[40]Such comparisons have been made in MacRae, "A Method . . . ," and "Cluster Analysis of Congressional Votes"; and in MacRae and Schwartz, "Identifying Congressional Issues by Multidimensional Models."

[41]MacRae, "A Method . . . ," p. 923.

plus agricultural commodities; tax reduction). Votes of this sort furnish valuable information about the temper of Congress and its appraisal of public opinion, even though they do not distinguish many Congressmen from one another. In a sense, those matters on which a legislative chamber deems it important to spend a substantial amount of its time in recording a unanimous roll call are worthy of as much attention as the more divisive issues.

We also make another important type of selection when we choose roll calls that enter into large clusters. We favor those types of legislation that see more floor action; those whose fate is decided in committee, and which pass the stage of floor action more quietly and routinely, are disadvantaged. This could presumably be remedied by choosing for analysis only one representative roll call on a bill, rather than including amendments, rules action, conference reports, and final passage. Such a choice could be reflected simply in the count that we used to measure the size of a cluster.

Related to this choice is a second type of selection, intrinsic in the search for general and repetitive alignments. We omit by this procedure the bills that produce unique divisions of a party, or those whose basis of division is some mixture or combination of the purer issues reflected in the clusters. The latter omission is perhaps not serious, if the clusters have indeed identified the issues that are so combined; but the unique or rare divisions may still be worthy of analysis. They may deal with local matters or legislation serving particular limited groups, both of which may constitute important resources for exchange and power within the chamber. These lower-key measures may also be important sources of support for legislators, party, or regime.[42] Or occasionally a single unique division in a highly disciplined party may reflect an important ideological issue.[43] In recalling that our methods are limited in this way, we see again that they are useful for specific substantive purposes, and have been chosen to serve those purposes.

The validity of the results of this clustering technique can be illustrated by comparison of scales found for the Republicans in five dif-

[42]The conceptual distinction between authorities and regime is that of Easton in *A Systems Analysis of Political Life*.

[43]The votes of the French Socialists illustrate this point; see MacRae, *Parliament, Parties, and Society*, pp. 208–211.

ferent Congresses over the period 1947–1962. We again compare the rankings of legislators on different scales by the gamma coefficient. For any two Congresses, we base this coefficient only on the legislators who served in both. The coefficients are shown in Table 3.5.

Several previous studies have shown continuity over time in congressmen's roll-call voting, but most have used only a single index

Table 3.5 Temporal continuity of scale positions in U.S. House of Representatives
A. Republicans' association coefficients ($\gamma \times 100$)

		Foreign aid					Rural–urban					Domestic				
		Scale					Scale					Scale				
		1	3	1	1	1	3	6	5	2	5	5	1	3	5	2
		Congress number														
		80	81	83	84	87	80	81	83	84	87	80	81	83	84	87
Foreign aid	80	X	82	83	67	56	53	15	13	35	27	71	52	70	27	21
	81		X	85	68	78	69	16	30	43	34	58	63	74	33	31
	83			X	86	73	57	26	30	45	40	61	54	62	43	18
	84				X	69	44	20	23	28	26	58	37	35	31	16
	87					X	54	10	-01	25	0	62	29	73	20	46
Rural–urban	80						X	51	58	60	35	59	36	78	51	74
	81							X	71	81	68	24	03	45	-02	06
	83								X	78	49	31	06	04	-31	14
	84									X	70	53	32	33	0	-12
	87										X	49	45	18	-30	-17
Domestic	80											X	45	63	52	46
	81												X	100	72	39
	83													X	93	74
	84														X	89
	87															X

B. Democrats' dominant association coefficients ($\gamma \times 100$) over a wide variety of issues

Congress	80	81	83	84	87
80	X	93	85	82	91
81		X	88	91	91
83			X	93	90
84				X	90
87					X

NOTES: Scale numbers refer to scales identified in MacRae, "A Method for Identifying Issues and Factions from Legislative Votes," pp. 920–921. Table entries ($\gamma \times 100$) are based on scale scores of representatives who served in two or more of the selected Congresses; thus intra-Congress associations are slightly different from those reported in *loc. cit.* Italic values of gamma (for the Republicans) are those at least .70 in magnitude. The polarity of all rural—urban scales has been reversed from the value initially set by partisan alignment.

of these votes in a particular comparison.[44] By cluster analysis, we claim to identify distinct issues that may persist beyond a particular Congress. If we find such issues, they should be demonstrably similar over time but distinct from one another, and an indicator of congressmen's positions on one issue should be more similar to subsequent measures of the same issue than to measures of others. Without denying that issues and their interrelations can change, we shall examine three relatively lasting issues—foreign aid, rural–urban issues including agricultural policy, and other domestic liberal–conservative matters, over an extended period. We choose five Congresses in which all possible combinations of party control of Presidency and Congress obtained: the 80th (D President, R Congress), 81st (D, D), 83rd (R, R), 84th (R, D), and 87th (D, D). In each Congress we choose three scale clusters that appear to reflect these issues.[45] Scale clusters on a given subject in all five Congresses are grouped together in Table 3.5. The highest associations are within a given subject area, rather than across subjects or within years, as can be seen from examination of the highest associations (those at least .7) in Table 3.5 (in italics). The three triangular sections of the matrix near the diagonal contain the 30 associations between scales of like content, and 15 (50 percent) of these are .7 or higher. The three rectangular blocks off the diagonal contain the 75 associations across different content areas, and only six (8 percent) of these are .70 or higher. This demonstration of continuity of distinct issues over time cannot, however, be made for the Democrats in the same Congresses; in each Congress their dominant scale reflected the North–South division and included a wider variety of issues than did any comparable scale for the Republicans. These dominant scales showed continuity in ordering the Democrats, as Table 3.5B shows.

A secondary tendency shown by the Republicans' scales is an increasing divergence among the three in their ordering of the party's congressmen. The association between two different scale areas in a given Congress is shown by a corresponding entry on the main

---

[44]An early study of this kind was Brimhall and Otis, "Consistency of Voting in Our Congressmen." Differential consistency of legislators relative to districts has been studied in Froman, *Congressmen and Their Constituencies,* chap. 8; and Anderson, "Individuality of Voting In Congress" (dealing with domestic and foreign issues). Various indices relating to domestic issues are compared over time in Clausen, *op. cit.*

[45]For the 84th Congress we used clusters 1, 2, and 5.

diagonal of the rectangular array comparing the two issues. For foreign aid and rural–urban issues, these associations (γ) are .53, .16, .30, .28, .0; for foreign aid and domestic issues, .71, .63, .62, .31, and .46; for rural–urban issues and other domestic issues, .59, .03, .03, .0, −.17. In each case the highest association was that for the 80th Congress. A similar decline in the association between domestic and international issues over the period 1939–1958 has been shown by Rieselbach.[46] While such changes may result from a redefinition of apparently similar issues, they may also reflect secular changes in the cohesion of legislative parties.[47] Analyses of this kind show that validation of particular measures blends imperceptibly into their use to test substantive hypotheses.

The presence of a single dominant scale for the Democrats calls attention to that fact that cluster analysis need not yield distinct clusters for conceptually distinct issues. Issues—which we recognize by their substantive content—may be joined together by a controversy between factions or parties, in which the two sides tend to assume opposing positions on a variety of particular questions.[48] We cannot say automatically, therefore, that a cluster is the operational definition of one and only one issue. Rather, it is an indicator of some basis of legislative division—often an issue, for the Republicans in this period —but a basis that requires examination in the light of other information, as to whether it represents an issue or a factional antagonism.

The fact that clusters of similar votes can reflect coalitions is also shown by the concentration of state delegations in particular scale categories. Several scales for the 81st Congress showed this property. And in addition, the substance of roll calls at one end of a scale continuum (e.g., with high p_+) may be recognizably different from those at the other. This property of clusters again requires analysis in terms of the specific legislative processes that give rise to it, rather than the simple assimilation of findings to a model developed to measure attitude continua.[49]

[46]Rieselbach, *The Roots of Isolationism,* p. 37.

[47]These changes will be discussed in more detail in Chapter 6.

[48]This fusion of issues, as it occurs in public opinion formation, is discussed in Coleman, *Community Conflict.* In the period we are examining, such fusion seems to have been declining both within the Republican party and between the parties, but increasing within the Democratic party.

[49]See MacRae, *Dimensions of Congressional Voting,* pp. 269–270, 274–276, 310–311, 328.

THE RANKED MATRIX

While useful results can be obtained with the binary matrix, the particular threshold chosen for the index of association sometimes needs to be varied from one problem to another. The degree of closeness of resemblance among roll calls for one issue, or one party, may differ from that for another. Clusters of a more general type may arise when the threshold is set low, more specific ones when it is high. To cope with these problems we can either repeat the analysis of a binary matrix with different values of the threshold,[50] or look for other methods that use more of the information in the initial matrix of associations.

The next step toward using more of this information corresponds to making use of the ranking of the coefficients in it. It is sometimes considered inappropriate to treat social data as cardinal numbers, and this concern can be obviated by considering only their rank order. Moreover, certain coefficients which can be converted into one another by an order-preserving transformation (e.g., Q, Y, and the like) will lead to identical results if clusters or groupings are found that depend only on the rank order of the coefficients in the matrix.

The methods that treat the matrix in this way range from the quite simple techniques of McQuitty (which do not introduce cardinal numbers) to the more complex models involved in nonmetric multidimensional scaling (Kruskal) or smallest-space analysis (Guttman, Lingoes). But even these latter models not only make fewer assumptions than factor analysis, but require less mathematical preparation for their understanding.

When we use this additional information about the ranking or ordering of coefficients in the matrix, we shall ordinarily be able to say more about the roll calls than that they belong in certain distinct subsets. We may, for example, arrange them in a tree-like diagram indicating those which are grouped at various levels of similarity. Or we may construct a new metric space, characterized by coordinates that are cardinal numbers. In either case we shall have gone beyond cluster analysis as it was defined at the start of this chapter.

---

[50]An example of this procedure is given in Lijphart, "The Analysis of Bloc Voting in the General Assembly," pp. 913 ff. Note that the specification of numerical threshold values provides information not available for the ranked matrix.

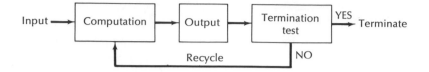

FIGURE 3.1. General Block Diagram for Recycling Program.

Our excuse for treating these methods here—together with some methods for the cardinal matrix—is that these more complex representations of the matrix can, or sometimes must, be simplified again for better understanding, and this simplification often takes the form of specifying clusters or categories.

Several of the methods used in analyzing the ranked matrix (as well as some for the binary and cardinal matrices) are particularly suited for implementation by computer programs, because they perform essentially the same operation repeatedly until some desired condition is attained. The general form which a computer program will assume for this type of operation is indicated in Figure 3.1. An initial set of data (in this case, the matrix of associations transformed into ranks) is input; and computations are performed on them, resulting in an output consisting, for example, of one or more clusters or a set of parameters. This output is compared with a criterion which determines whether the operation is completed. The criterion may be one of exhaustion of the data (no more clusters can be found) or of convergence (the parameters resulting from cycle $i+1$ are within a specified degree similar to those of cycle i). If the criterion is not met, then the computation operation is repeated with some modification of its inputs, e.g., either new values of the parameters or elimination of part of the data matrix. This recycling procedure is continued until the criterion is met. It is assumed that a theoretical analysis guarantees that the criterion will be met eventually.

A matrix of associations may be converted to ranks in more than one way. One approach, used in the work of McQuitty, ranks the entries in each column of the matrix, thereby judging each column in terms of its own characteristic level of association. Rows or columns that then have high ranks with each other are permitted to become members of clusters or types. This method, known as *rank order typal analysis,* "defines a type as a category of people of such a nature that everyone in the category is more like everyone else in the category than he is like anyone in any other category."[51] The phrase "he is" distinguishes this method from those that impose a common threshold or standard of association on all elements in the matrix. This approach would give results differing from those of the binary matrix, in that a roll call whose column elements in the initial matrix were all low could still be added to a cluster if its own highest associations were consistently distributed. But in the absence of a fixed threshold for pairwise association, the resulting clusters could not be expected to provide scale scores with predictable degrees of error.

A second approach is to consider all the $n(n-1)/2$ entries in the initial matrix in a single overall rank order. This has also been incorporated in a procedure of McQuitty's, known as hierarchical syndrome analysis, and a related method has been presented by Johnson.[52] In one version of this procedure, the investigator starts by considering the highest association in the matrix. The two items (rows or columns) connected by this association are then joined together and their rows (columns) replaced by a single row (column). The elements of this single row are the associations of the combined item with each other item in the matrix; they are chosen by picking the lower of the associations of the two joined items with the other item in question. The procedure is then repeated. At each repetition cycle, a new combination is made at a new and lower level of the index of association. The result may be pictured as a tree in which the definition of branches starts at the top with a large number of branches; as we move downward, pairs of branches are joined to form new branches at successively lower levels, until the last junction defines the trunk at the bottom. In principle, only ranks need be used to describe this

[51]McQuitty, "Multiple Rank Order Typal Analysis for the Isolation of Independent Types," p. 4, and "A Conjunction of Rank Order Typal Analysis and Item Selection." The approach of ranking a subset of matrix entries separately is also followed in Kossack, "Statistical Analysis, the Computer, and Political Science Research," pp. 84–86. McQuitty has proposed various methods for cluster analysis; another, known as "elementary linkage analysis," has been used to identify issue clusters in VanDerSlik, "Constituencies and Roll Call Voting," p. 174 n., and blocs of Supreme Court justices in Ulmer, "Toward a Theory of Sub-Group Formation in the United States Supreme Court."

[52]For cardinal treatment see the following section. An alternative method is presented in McQuitty, "Improved Hierarchical Syndrome Analysis of Discrete and Continuous Data." See also Johnson, "Hierarchical Clustering Schemes."

operation, though the actual numerical values at which junction occurs (the "heights") are often specified in methods of this sort.

An example of this type of procedure may be given with the gamma coefficients between scales from Table 3.3:

	1	2	3	4	5	6
1	X	.28	.54	.05	.41	.36
2	.28	X	.03	.07	.20	.13
3	.54	.03	X	−.20	.17	.33
4	.05	.07	−.20	X	.59	.42
5	.41	.20	.17	.59	X	.74
6	.36	.13	.33	.42	.74	X

The polarity of Scale 2 has been reversed in order to make as many associations positive as possible.

We begin with the highest value in the table, $\gamma_{56} = .74$, and combine these two. If we use the lower of their associations with each other item as the corresponding element of their combined row or column, these elements will be .36, .13, .17, and .42. This combination rule causes the second highest association, .59, to disappear, and the next highest value remaining in the matrix is $\gamma_{13} = .54$. Items 1 and 3 are then combined and the next highest association in the matrix is .42, between items 4 and 5–6. (Exercise: verify this.)

The process could be continued, but the remaining associations are all .17 or lower. The higher-order clusters we have found so far are 1–3, dealing with foreign aid and reciprocal trade; 5–6 with 4 joined to it, dealing with largely domestic liberal–conservative issues; and Scale 2, dealing with agriculture, remains by itself. These are essentially the same results we described in the discussion of Table 3.3, though by less precise reasoning. Another example of this type of tree analysis will be presented in Figure 7.2.

Numerous variations on this procedure are possible, some making use of the cardinal values in the matrix of similarities and others restricted to the ranked matrix; among them are some proposed by McQuitty. The method we have described is limited in a way that makes it inappropriate for analysis of Q-matrices containing high associations; for not only are there typically many Q's tied for highest, but initial pairings made on the basis of Q's of 1.0 are fixed, perhaps erroneously, for the remainder of the tree-clustering process.

A much more general approach to the problem has been proposed recently by Hartigan.[53] He considers a wider variety of possible tree-type structures that can be matched to a given matrix of similarities, and iterative methods that will maximize a measure of goodness of fit. Links or nodes once formed can be broken in this procedure, and groupings of more than two members can be made. This approach permits different types of solutions, but because of computational difficulties it proceeds iteratively from a given starting point and does not in fact consider all possible solutions.

Another way of using the $n(n-1)/2$ ranked entries of the initial matrix is exemplified by computer procedures developed by Kruskal (MDSCAL) and by Guttman and Lingoes.[54] This is to look for coordinates of points in a multidimensional space, such that the interpoint distances will reproduce in their ranking the ranking of the coefficients of association. This approach is equally applicable to measures of similarity or of dissimilarity, the only difference being an inversion of the order in which the $n(n-1)/2$ coefficients in the initial matrix are considered.

The Kruskal version of this approach may be described with reference to Figure 3.1. The input consists of the initial matrix, converted to an overall ranking, together with some set of starting coordinates for the n points in a space of specified dimensionality. An optimum number of dimensions may often be found by repeating this procedure with different numbers of dimensions, and examining the improvement in goodness of fit that results from increasing the number of dimensions.

The first computational step involves finding interpoint distances based on the starting coordinates, and comparing their ranks with those of the matrix entries. These two sets of ranks are compared, with the aid of the numerical values of the interpoint distances, in a parameter known as the "stress." The disparity between the two rankings is measured by comparing the interpoint distances d_{ij} with a re-

---

[53]Hartigan, "Representation of Similarity Matrices by Trees."

[54]J. B. Kruskal, "Multidimensional Scaling by Optimizing Goodness of Fit to a Nonmetric Hypothesis," and "Nonmetric Multidimensional Scaling: A Numerical Method"; Lingoes, "New Computer Developments in Pattern Analysis and Nonmetric Techniques"; Guttman, "A General Nonmetric Technique for Finding the Smallest Coordinate Space for a Configuration of Points." A critique of these methods is given in Spaeth and Guthery, "The Use and Utility of the Monotone Criterion in Multidimensional Scaling."

lated sequence of numbers $\hat{d}_{ij}$, the latter varying in monotonic sequence with the ranking of the initial coefficients of association. The stress is defined by

$$S = \sqrt{\frac{\Sigma(d_{ij} - \hat{d}_{ij})^2}{\Sigma d_{ij}^2}} \qquad (3.6)$$

In the above expression, for any configuration of points in multidimensional space, the d_{ij} are fixed. Then "the values of $\hat{d}_{ij}$ are those numbers which minimize S subject to the constraint that the $\hat{d}_{ij}$ have the same rank order as the [coefficients of association]."[55]

The output of this computation is then a value of the stress, at the first cycle. On the second and successive cycles, the starting coordinates are modified so as to reduce the stress, and the output then consists of the new coordinate values as well as the stress. When the stress changes less than a specified amount between one cycle and the next, the computation is terminated.

The operations carried out by a computer on each cycle can be illustrated with a simple numerical example. We consider only four points in two dimensions—so small a number that the solution is not completely determinate, but a number for which the computations can be carried out by hand.

We begin with the four points A, B, C, D, as shown in the upper diagram of Figure 3.2. The distances between these four points are then ranked, and this ranking constitutes the *only* source of input data for the problem. In order from shortest to longest, the distances are AB, CD, BC, AC, BD, AD. Had we begun with a matrix of associations, all the $n(n-1)/2$ entries would have been ranked similarly. There are also provisions for treatment of ties in the analysis of such rankings, but we ignore them in this example.

Starting only with this ranking of distances (or similarities), we wish to find a set of numerical coordinates that reproduces that ranking as nearly as possible. The degree of recovery of the rankings will depend only on the *relative* positions of the points—not on the scale of the graph, or on any rotation or translation of the axes. We may do this by starting with arbitrary coordinates (such as those of A', B', C', D' in the lower graph), and moving these points so as to improve

[55]Kruskal, "Nonmetric Multidimentional Scaling," p. 115. In the numerical examples below, the four middle values of d_{ij} are in reverse order, and their average is assigned to all the corresponding values of d_{ij}.

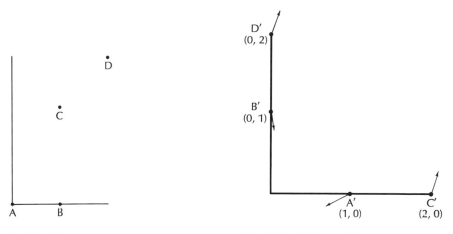

| Configuration Used to Produce Ranked Distances | Trial Coordinates and Changes on First Iteration |

FIGURE 3.2. Numerical Example of MDSCAL Procedure.

the fit between them and the desired ranking of the interpoint distances.[56]

The principle on which the program operates is to evaluate the partial derivatives of the stress with respect to the eight coordinates of the four points. These numbers measure the change in stress that would occur for a small unit change in the corresponding coordinate. Each coordinate is then changed a small amount, proportional to this derivative but in the opposite direction, so as to decrease the stress.

Without following all the steps in the compuation, we can indicate how we find the directions in which the points A', B', C', and D' are to be moved. Suppose we compare the desired ranking of distances (as in A, B, C, D) with the corresponding distances derived from the trial positions of A', B', C', D':

Desired ranking (in increasing order):	AB	CD	BC	AC	BD	AD
Distances based on A', B', C', D':	1.41	2.83	2.24	1.00	1.00	2.24

[56]The initial configuration can also be chosen by principal-component analysis, to reduce the number of iterations; this has been done in later versions of the Kruskal program, and in the Guttman-Lingoes procedure.

If A', B', C', D' were a good solution, the distances between them would increase when arranged in the desired order. Actually, the fit is quite poor, the initial stress being .34; but if we wished to improve it we might try to decrease the distances A'B', C'D', and B'C', while increasing A'C' and B'D'. We might not, of course, be able to make all these changes consistently at once.

The arrows in the lower diagram of Figure 3.2, which result from the computation of partial derivatives, show the directions in which the changes would be made. The two shortest distances, A'C' and B'D', which should be high in the rank order, will both be increased as the corresponding points move apart. A'B' will be decreased, C'D' and B'C' left relatively unchanged. Presumably not all the desired changes could be made at the same time.[57]

After the four points are moved in one iteration, their coordinates are standardized (means set to zero, overall sums of squares set to unity times the number of points), the stress is computed, and the procedure is repeated. After the stress reaches a satisfactory value, or fails to improve appreciably, or after a specified number of iterations, computations are terminated and the resulting coordinates are output.

An example of the type of output that results is shown in Figure 3.3, for a different set of data—part of the Q-matrix for the Republicans in the 84th Congress, corresponding to 25 roll calls in 3 clusters found at a threshold of $Q = .7$. These clusters dealt with agriculture, foreign aid, and general domestic welfare-state issues. The roll calls in the first two of these clusters were nearly the same as those listed for corresponding clusters in Table 3.3. The last cluster was more inclusive at the threshold of .7, and contained roll calls appearing in Table 3.3 in both the postal pay and welfare state clusters, as well as others. Two dimensions were specified for this computation; the values of stress for 2, 3, and 4 dimensions respectively were .122, .097, and .082. The MDSCAL plot clearly separated the three input clusters. It may also reveal finer details of their interrelation, since the loca-

---

[57]The exact formula for the derivatives, which was used to compute the positions of the arrows in Figure 3.2, is given in Kruskal, "Nonmetric Multidimensional Scaling," p. 126. The lengths of the arrows are set numerically equal to the (negative) derivatives, divided by the stress, so that the reader may check the computations numerically. The actual movement of the points made by the program was nearly seven times the distance indicated by the corresponding arrow.

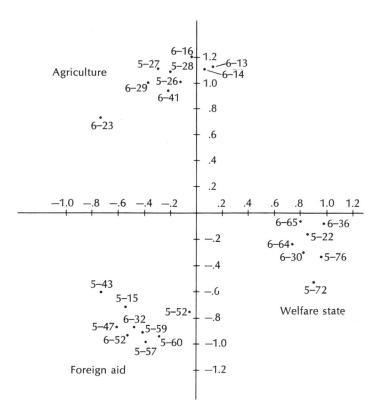

FIGURE 3.3. Two-Dimensional MDSCAL Output for 25 Selected Roll Calls for Republicans in 84th House, Based on Q-Matrix.

tions of the points provide more information than cluster analysis, as a procedure for classification, can provide.

The multidimensional space produced by the Kruskal procedure (and presumably that from the Guttman-Lingoes method as well) has properties different from the space produced by factor analysis. Its origin, its identity relation, and inverse relation are not defined in the ways that persons accustomed to factor space would expect. But trials of the Kruskal procedure indicate that for the data we have considered (Republicans in the 84th Congress) it reproduces the clusters we have found, and smoothes the data to eliminate some of the apparently random fluctuations in the Q-matrix.

We next consider a six-dimensional MDSCAL solution for a larger number of roll calls in the 84th Congress. A Q-matrix for 70 roll calls, based on the Republicans' votes, was analyzed with six dimensions specified.[58] For results of this kind, two-dimensional plots are clearly less helpful. For this reason the resulting set of coordinates in six dimensions was converted to a form independent of rotation of the axes, by computing the $n(n-1)/2$ distances between pairs of points. These distances corresponded approximately in their rank order to the (inverse) rank order of the entries in the Q-matrix, but with an imposed consistency resulting from the spatial model. The matrix of distances was treated as a binary matrix for comparison with results of clustering the 70×70 Q-matrix. The threshold that defined this binary matrix was set so as to define the same number of "near" distances as there had previously been high Q's, first at the level of 1.0 ($N = 84$) and then at .9 ($N = 144$). The resulting clusters, and their differences from those of the Q-matrix at these threshold values, are shown in Table 3.6.

The main result of this comparison is that the clusters are quite similar between the Q-matrix at the .9 level and the distance matrix based on MDSCAL, but that the Q-matrix clusters at the 1.0 level are far inferior to the corresponding MDSCAL clusters. The 84 Q's of 1.0 in the initial Q-matrix included a high proportion of pairs that did not fit consistently into larger clusters. Of the clusters in Table 3.3, only Scale 2 would have been reproduced at the threshold of 1.0, with two items eliminated. The corresponding number of shortest distances reproduced Scales 1, 2, and 3 fairly closely. One cause of this may have been a higher sampling variability of Q's for pairs of items in which one or both had extreme marginals. The resulting high Q's appear, therefore, to contribute less consistent information than those between .90 and .99. The closer agreement between the clusters found in the Q-matrix at a threshold of .90, and the corresponding 144 shortest distances, is shown in Table 3.6. And while this deficiency of the Q-matrix at the "perfect scale" level seems to cause no difficulty if a threshold of .9 or .8 is used, it might well produce artifacts if the Q-matrix were analyzed by methods that placed a heavy weight

[58]Further details are reported in MacRae and Schwarz, "Identifying Congressional Issues." The 70 roll calls were those, out of the initial 102 that produced Table 3.2, with highest communalities based on six principal components. They included all members of the scale clusters shown in Table 3.3.

Table 3.6 Distance clusters based on six-dimensional MDSCAL output

Cluster	Roll call number	Changes relative to Q-matrix clusters at .9 Additions	Changes relative to Q-matrix clusters at .9 Deletions
Scale 1. Foreign aid	5–15, 5–57, 5–59, 5–60, 6–32, 6–52	5–15 (UN aid funds)	5–47 (Congress delegation to NATO)
Scale 2. Agriculture	5–26, 5–27, 5–28, 6–13, 6–16	5–26 (Farm price supports)	6–14, 6–23, 6–29 (Farm bills)
Scale 3. Foreign trade	5–6, 5–7, 5–8, 5–9, 5–10	5–7 (Reciprocal trade)	5–43 (Reciprocal trade)
Scale 4. Postal pay	5–23[a], 5–24, 5–29, 5–30		5–22 (Postal pay)
Scale 5. Welfare state	5–64[a], 5–72, 5–76, 6–48[z]	—[c]	
Scale 6. Extreme blocs	—[b]	—[b]	

[a] Indicates roll calls that were added to clusters on the basis of the 144 shortest distances, but did not enter when the lowest 84 were used.
[b] Fails to appear in either method; exists only at $Q_{min} = .8$.
[c] Did not appear in Q-matrix at .9.

on the highest Q's and made irrevocable pairings on this basis, as some of the tree-clustering methods do.

THE CARDINAL MATRIX

If we assume that the entries in the matrix of pairwise relations are susceptible to addition, subtraction, multiplication, and division, we may consider another family of procedures for analysis. Best known among these, at least in political science and sociology, is factor analysis, which will be treated in the next chapter. But there are other, simpler, clustering procedures that we shall consider first.

An earlier version of McQuitty's hierarchical syndrome analysis made use of averages of coefficients in the matrix, and thus falls in this category. As in the version described above, it proceeds by picking the highest coefficient in the matrix and combining the corresponding rows and columns into a new one. Instead of replacing two entries with the lower of the two, it is also possible to replace them with their average.[59] Alternatively, a weighted combination of the previous coefficients might be used, depending on such variables as the number of rows or columns already aggregated in the combinations existing at a given step; and other functions may be used to determine which pair of items shall be combined and how their new matrix entries shall be calculated.[60] The form of the output from either of these methods is a tree-like structure with two branches at each junction, constructed from the smallest branches down toward the trunk.

This method does not seem appropriate for use with the Q-matrix —not only because so many Q's are tied at 1.0, but also because (as we have seen) a number of the high Q's represent inconsistent and random variation. Because this method joins a pair of items irrevocably when they have $Q = 1.0$, it would be more useful if a preliminary data smoothing were performed on the Q-matrix.

Tree-like structures of this kind can also be constructed by working from the trunk up to the smallest branches. To do so requires some

[59]McQuitty, *A Method of Pattern Analysis for Isolating Typological and Dimensional Constructs.*

[60]See King, "Step-Wise Clustering Procedures," p. 87–91; Ward, "Hierarchical Grouping to Optimize an Objective Function."

criterion function that can be maximized with respect to various possible divisions of the initial set of roll calls. The general reasoning followed in these methods is to use as this criterion function some measure of the difference or separation between two prospective groups, in comparison with the similarity within groups. All possible two-way divisions of the larger group must then be searched, requiring more computer time than the combination of pairs corresponding to small branches of the tree.[61]

The tree-like structure is often reported by arrangement of the items thus linked together along one axis of a table, with the corresponding coefficients of association, at which branches are joined, plotted along the other. Such a plot, by its unidimensional ordering on the first axis, may imply a constraint that is not strictly required by the data. For example, if it were done with roll calls, it might imply a unidimensional ordering of the roll calls. Such an ordering might be imagined in terms of p_+; but many other types of ordering are possible, including nearness in multiple dimensions, or Guttman's "circumplex"; consequently, for the most general usage we should regard this method of presentation with the same skepticism as the one- or two-dimensional sociogram.[62]

A second simple method for clustering the cardinal matrix is based on Holzinger and Harman's B-coefficient, the ratio of the average intercorrelation among variables in a cluster, to their correlation with variables outside.[63] Initial location of clusters is facilitated by ranking coefficients down the columns of the matrix, and by comparing profiles of coefficients with one another graphically. Once a cluster has been started in this way, additional items are considered for addition to it. Each possible addition is evaluated for its eligibility in terms of the B-coefficient. A threshold for B defines the stopping point.

[61]This approach has been used in King, *op. cit.*, pp. 91–99; and in Edwards and Cavalli-Sforza, "A Method for Cluster Analysis." A related approach is that of Mattson and Dammann in "A Technique for Determining and Coding Subclasses in Pattern Recognition Problems." These methods, while still falling within the category of cluster analysis, require more advanced mathematics than those that start at the smaller branches of the tree. An extensive literature also exists on the problem of partitioning a set of items with respect to a quantitative criterion function.

[62]See Coleman and MacRae, "Electronic Processing of Sociometric Data for Groups up to 1,000 in Size"; and MacRae, "Direct Factor Analysis of Sociometric Data."

[63]See Harman, *Modern Factor Analysis*, pp. 119–121; Fruchter, *Introduction to Factor Analysis*, chap. 2.

After one cluster is found, the variables in it are eliminated, and the process is repeated.

A third method for the cardinal matrix, which involves some features of factor analysis but is less complicated, has been proposed by Tryon.[64] The initial matrix (whose elements we designate as r_{ij}) is searched for a suitable pivot variable, about which the first cluster may be centered. For this purpose, the computer program calculates the variance of r^2 for each row (or column) in the matrix, and considers the variable with the highest variance as a possible pivot variable. If the program can find at least one other variable sufficiently similar to the first, it allows this group of two or more to form a cluster.

Similarity between two variables is judged in terms of their patterns of association with all other variables in the matrix. It is measured by an index analogous to the square of the product–moment correlation, differing only in that moments between two rows in the matrix are computed about zero. This *index of collinearity* is[65]

$$P_{ab}^2 = \frac{(\Sigma r_{ai} r_{bi})^2}{\Sigma r_{ai}^2 \Sigma r_{bi}^2} \tag{3.7}$$

For a pivot variable to be chosen, it must have one or more other variables related to it by values of P^2 of at least .4. If the trial pivot variable fails to pick up any partners, the variable with the next highest variance of r^2 is tried; after four unsuccessful tries, computations are terminated.

Up to this point, the logic is similar to that of the types of cluster analysis we have considered previously. We are working with a ranking of the variances in the r-matrix (to pick the initial pivot variable), and with the P^2-matrix as a binary matrix with the threshold of .4. Conceivably we could eliminate the first cluster from consideration and repeat the procedure. If we did so, we should have no need to consider any new mathematical details.[66]

After the first cluster, however, the Tryon procedure involves subsequent clustering operations with residuals rather than with the initial matrix of associations. The notion of a residual, essential to

[64]See MacRae, "Cluster Analysis of Congressional Votes"; Tryon and Bailey, *Cluster Analysis*.

[65]Tryon, "Domain Sampling Formulation of Cluster and Factor Analysis."

[66]One way in which this could be done is suggested in Lorr, *op. cit.*, pp. 25–27; he also reviews clustering methods generally.

factor analysis, has not yet been introduced in our treatment of cluster analysis. It will be described more precisely in the next chapter where discussion of this technique is continued.

STATISTICAL INFERENCE

The identification of clusters, like all the decisions we must make in identifying issues and factions, may be made erroneously. One source of such errors which we customarily try to estimate in social research is that of sampling variation. Whether we wish to compare our findings with a null hypothesis, to estimate the values of parameters that characterize the universe from which our data arise, or simply to make decisions in view of the available information, we must be concerned with statistical inference.

This book will not emphasize the random models that characterize sampling distributions, because of the complexity of the problems involved. Nevertheless we may point to some efforts to carry out analyses of this type with respect to clustering procedures. One such effort is that of Fortier and Solomon, applied to clustering of measures of social class.[67] Another is a test proposed for this purpose by Bonner, which goes back to the original (roll-call) data and examines whether the means of these data differ significantly between the cluster and the larger set from which it was drawn.[68] Applied to roll-call data, this approach might correspond to examining whether the values of p_+ in a cluster differed from others. This might be of some value, but it is by no means clear that differences in p_+ are the only or the most important criterion for distinctness of clusters. Clusters may be distinguished by the ways in which items interact as well as by their inclusion of predominantly positive or negative responses. Indeed, if items were initially chosen so as to have marginals in a limited range, this would militate against a significant result on such a test, yet not preclude the existence of meaningful and distinct clusters.

Probably more valid, in the terms of our analysis, would be the comparison of values of association within clusters and between clusters, or between a cluster and items that did not enter into any cluster. As to the former of these comparisons, we have implied that

[67]Fortier and Solomon, "Clustering Procedures."

[68]Bonner, op. cit., p. 27.

a value of gamma between two clusters, which is far less than the threshold value of Q required to constitute the clusters, provides supporting evidence that the clusters correspond to distinct issues. The latter comparison might also be relevant if the initial matrix of associations contained a high proportion of entries that exceeded a threshold value; in this case, it is conceivable that the external associations of a given cluster would be nearly as high as those within the cluster. Alternatively, one might consider taking a large cluster and attempting to subdivide it, using more stringent criteria of association; a test of significance in this case would be expected to indicate the stage at which such subdivision failed to produce results differing significantly from those of a random model.

Our examples have also implied that the validity of cluster definition is greater for large clusters than for small (for a given degree of association with items not in the cluster). This distinction would certainly be brought out by a test of significance, since the probability of finding a new item associated to a specified threshold degree with n others, on the basis of a random drawing from a universe with a fixed probability less than unity of attaining the threshold, decreases as n increases.

Though our examples are based on large numbers of legislators, additional problems may arise in the study of small legislatures or judicial bodies. In such bodies, alteration in the votes of a single member can clearly have a larger effect on the definition of issue clusters.

While systematic statistical tests are desirable, the very fact that we are dealing with matrices of association suggests the difficulty that the entries in such a matrix are not fully independent. Simple tests as to whether the mean value of association was greater within a cluster than between items inside and outside the cluster would therefore be misleading; statistical tests for this purpose would have to take into account the interrelations among elements of the matrix.

The examples we shall consider for Congress will involve nonrandom or 100 percent samples of the roll calls during a given period; but in the study of some other legislative bodies, random samples from a large universe of roll calls may be used, and statistical inference may have additional relevance.

We conclude that more precise procedures of statistical inference ought to be developed (and we do not wish to derogate them by lack of emphasis) but that they are beyond the scope of this book.

4.
FACTOR ANALYSIS:
INTRODUCTION

AMONG the various procedures for analyzing the cardinal matrix of associations, the best known is factor analysis. While this method requires more mathematical introduction than others, it is most closely related to standard courses of statistical instruction, including notions of variance, product–moment correlation, and regression. We shall present a condensed introduction to these topics for the reader who has had some college mathematics but not statistics. After an exposition of some aspects of factor analysis, we can then treat other related methods, such as the BC TRY system of cluster analysis, which depend on the computation of residuals and on other mathematical operations used in factor analysis.

The present chapter will deal primarily with the mathematical preliminaries to factor analysis; the next will be concerned with principal-component analysis and problems of applying it to roll calls.

Factor analysis, like cluster analysis, aims at simplifying the data matrix and expressing important aspects of it in terms of a smaller number of underlying variables. But unlike a cluster, a factor is a *quantitative* variable, which may enter in various degrees into particular roll calls. We may find, for example, that the votes on a given roll call are explainable in terms of a combination of rural–urban conflicts and partisanship; that the votes on another relate to a combination of isolationism–internationalism and partisanship; and a third roll call may

Table 4.1 Hypothetical matrix of associations corresponding to a single underlying factor

Roll calls	A	B	C	D	E
A		.63	.45	.27	.18
B	.63		.35	.21	.14
C	.45	.35		.15	.10
D	.27	.21	.15		.06
E	.18	.14	.10	.06	

involve the same variables in different proportions. There is nevertheless usually a close correspondence between the results of factor analysis and those of cluster analysis, since quantitative variables can always be classified into categories. We performed such a classification in Chapter 3 in clustering the distance matrix based on MDSCAL coordinates.

Table 4.1 shows a fictitious matrix of associations that would correspond to a single underlying factor. The coefficients in this table are low in comparison with those we considered for cluster analysis. It is their quantitative relation to one another, rather than their magnitude, that determines the simplicity of the description provided by factor analysis. Inspection will reveal that the entries in one row or column have a constant ratio to corresponding entries in another—a feature that corresponds to the simple factorial structure we shall discuss below.

The coefficients in a matrix of associations to be factor analyzed are usually product–moment correlation coefficients. Factor analysis seeks underlying variables or factors that are related to the observed items and will account for their correlations. It expresses this relation in terms of another set of correlation coefficients (factor loadings) between the items and the underlying factors. The extent to which each factor accounts for a given item (e.g., votes on a given roll call) is then indicated by the loading of that item on that factor.

When one variable accounts for or predicts another in terms of a correlation coefficient, the proportion of the sum of squares for which it accounts is r^2, the square of the correlation coefficient. Thus the factor loadings also account for proportions of sum of squares in the items, equal to the squares of the factor loadings. If the conditions for this model are met, then for a given item the sum of these squares cannot exceed unity.

Because factor analysis depends so much on the properties of correlation coefficients, we shall next show that correlation coefficients have the necessary properties.

THE CORRELATION COEFFICIENT

In order to show that the square of the conventional Pearson (product–moment) correlation coefficient measures the proportion of variance accounted for by a corresponding linear prediction, we must relate it to linear regression, which concerns the optimum prediction of one quantitative variable from another by a linear equation. We wish to show the properties of correlation coefficients in order to deal both with the relations between roll calls, and with the relations between roll calls and factors. While factors are quantitative variables, roll calls are dichotomies. But we can consider dichotomies as a special case of quantitative variables, by assigning numerical values such as 0 and 1 to the two values of a dichotomy.[1] We begin by deriving the expression for the regression line, to which the correlation coefficient is closely related.

Given a set of observed values of two quantitative variables, X and Y, for a set of N cases, the problem of simple regression is to find the straight line

$$Y = a + bX \tag{4.1}$$

which will best predict the values of Y from those of X. "Best" is understood in the least-squares sense, i.e., the best line is considered to be that for which the deviations of the Y's from their predicted values on the line have the least sum of squares. This criterion is widely used because of its convenient properties, some of which will be shown below.[2] We distinguish henceforth between the predicted value $\hat{Y}$ given by

$$\hat{Y} = a + bX \tag{4.2}$$

and the observed value, written simply Y.

[1] We shall show below that the value of the correlation coefficient is unaffected by our choice of these numerical values, as long as the two are not identical and as the polarity is preserved. The derivations we shall present for linear regression and correlation thus apply to dichotomous variables such as roll calls.

[2] An alternative derivation of these results, based on the maximum-likelihood criterion and assuming a normal distribution, is given in Mood and Graybill, *Introduction to the Theory of Statistics*, pp. 229–231.

The sum of squares (S) that we wish to minimize is

$$S = \sum_i (Y_i - \hat{Y}_i)^2 = \sum_i (Y_i - a - bX_i)^2$$

In this summation we indicate the case number (e.g., the legislator) by the index i, running from 1 to N. Those symbols that represent variables, having different values for different values of i, are shown with i as a subscript; the constants have no such subscript. In many of the derivations that follow we shall omit this subscript; with this omission the above equation becomes

$$S = \sum (Y - \hat{Y})^2 = \sum (Y - a - bX)^2 \tag{4.3}$$

To minimize the sum of squares we take the partial derivative of S with respect to a and b, since it is these parameters that we wish to determine. Each of these partial derivatives is set to zero:

$$\frac{\partial S}{\partial a} = -2\sum(Y - a - bX) = 0 \tag{4.4}$$

$$\frac{\partial S}{\partial b} = -2\sum X(Y - a - bX) = 0 \tag{4.5}$$

A considerable simplification can be obtained by examining the consequences of (4.4). If we divide its central summation by $(-2N)$, it becomes

$$\bar{Y} - a - b\bar{X} = 0, \quad \text{or} \quad \bar{Y} = a + b\bar{X} \tag{4.6}$$

where $\bar{X} = X/N$ and $\bar{Y} = Y/N$. In its form, (4.6) is the same as (4.1) or (4.2), except that X and Y have been replaced by their mean values $\bar{X}$ and $\bar{Y}$. In other words, the line we seek (to be called the *regression line*) passes through the point $(\bar{X}, \bar{Y})$. We can thus simplify our treatment by measuring X and Y from their respective means, defining the deviations from those means as

$$x = X - \bar{X} \quad \text{and} \quad y = Y - \bar{Y} \tag{4.7}$$

When this is done the means of the new variables x and y are both zero, and the equation of the straight line becomes simply

$$\hat{y} = bx \tag{4.8}$$

(Exercise: show this.) Equations (4.3) to (4.5) now hold with $a = 0$ and x, y substituted for X, Y. Thus equation (4.5) becomes

$$-2 \sum x(y - bx) = 0 \tag{4.9}$$

Performing the summations in (4.9) and omitting the coefficient (-2),

$$\Sigma xy - b\Sigma x^2 = 0, \quad \text{or} \quad b = \frac{\Sigma xy}{\Sigma x^2} \qquad (4.10)$$

We have thus solved for the slope b of the regression line, and can calculate both b and a by means of the standard formulas given in statistics textbooks. If we substitute for x and y the defining expressions of (4.7), and replace the means $\bar{X}$ and $\bar{Y}$ by their defining expressions, then with some simplification we obtain

$$b = \frac{N\,\Sigma XY - (\Sigma X)(\Sigma Y)}{N\,\Sigma X^2 - (\Sigma X)^2} \qquad (4.11)$$

(Exercise: show this.) We can then solve for a by substituting in (4.6).

The relation between X and Y can also be expressed in another way. In addition to finding the best straight line for predicting Y from X, we can measure the success of that line in predicting Y from X. This provides us with one definition of the correlation coefficient.

Our task in predicting Y may be viewed as that of accounting for the variation in Y. This variation is conventionally measured about $\bar{Y}$ as a sum of squares

$$\Sigma(Y - \bar{Y})^2 = \Sigma y^2 \qquad (4.12)$$

We shall see that if we express the variation in this way, it can be divided into two parts: a part which is accounted for by the regression line, and the variation of residuals about the regression line. For simplicity, let us again use the notation involving x and y. In these symbols, we can define three sums corresponding to various aspects of the variation:

$\Sigma y^2 = $ total variation

$\Sigma(bx)^2 = $ variation of the predicted values $\hat{y} = (\hat{Y} - \bar{Y})$

$\Sigma(y - bx)^2 = $ variation (sum of squares) of residuals from the regression line

The interesting relation among these three summations is that the lower two may be added to give the upper one. To prove this, we express the sum

$$\Sigma(bx)^2 + \Sigma(y - bx)^2 = \Sigma(bx)^2 + \Sigma y^2 - 2b\Sigma xy + \Sigma(bx)^2$$
$$= 2b^2\,\Sigma x^2 - 2b\,\Sigma xy + \Sigma y^2 \qquad (4.13)$$

This sum is simply equal to Σy^2; for in the last expression in (4.13), the first two terms are equal in magnitude and cancel one another. This can be shown by substituting (4.10) for b: each of these two terms then equals $2(\Sigma xy)^2/(\Sigma x^2)$. Consequently, we can say that the variation Σy^2 is divisible into two parts: a part accounted for by the regression line and the variation of residuals about the regression line. If we divide each term by N, a corresponding division of the total sample variance $s_y^2 = \Sigma y^2/N$ can be made.[3]

The proportion of the sum of squares, or of the variance, accounted for by the regression line may then be expressed as $\Sigma(bx)^2/\Sigma y^2$, and is equal to the square of the correlation coefficient, r.

$$r^2 = \frac{(\Sigma xy)^2}{\Sigma x^2 \, \Sigma y^2} \tag{4.14}$$

We can thus write for the sum of squares

$$\Sigma y^2 = \Sigma \hat{y}^2 + \Sigma(y - \hat{y})^2 \tag{4.15}$$

The left-hand side of (4.15) is the total variation in y; the two terms on the right correspond respectively to the variation accounted for by the regression line, and the variation about the line, i.e., not accounted for by it. The proportion of the total variation accounted for by the regression line is r^2, and the proportion not accounted for is $(1 - r^2)$.

This partitioning of variation or variance is a very useful property of the conventional least-squares approach and its corresponding indices of regression and correlation, b and r; it will be used in factor analysis. The correlation coefficient is the square root of (4.14)

$$r = \frac{\Sigma xy}{\sqrt{\Sigma x^2 \, \Sigma y^2}} \tag{4.16}$$

(Exercise: using the numerator of [4.16], show that the residual $[y - \hat{y}]$ has zero correlation with x.)

In the preceding treatment we arrived at the expression for r from a type of reasoning that relates to partition of variation. But there is another line of reasoning that leads to the same equation and explains why r is called the product–moment correlation coefficient.

Suppose we use a scatter diagram to express graphically the rela-

---

[3]Our use of s_y to denote the sample standard deviation, rather than an unbiased estimate of the universe value, follows Harman, *Modern Factor Analysis*, p. 12.

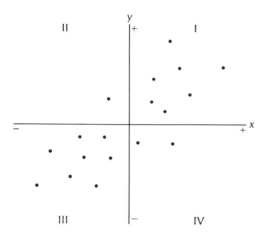

FIGURE 4.1. Scatter Diagram with Points Distributed in Four Quadrants.

tion between X and Y. Let us again center it at $\bar{X}$, $\bar{Y}$ and measure the coordinates from this point, making them x, y. The problem we now pose is to measure the intensity of association between x and y irrespective of the scales of measurement in which the data are given.

The notion of a product–moment can be clarified with the aid of the scatter diagram in Figure 4.1. We wish to count in favor of the association (positively) the contribution of all points in the first and third quadrants (I, III) and negatively that of points in the second and fourth (II, IV). This can be done by multiplying the values of x and y for each point; for this product xy will be positive for points in the first and third quadrants, negative in the second and fourth. Moreover, the distance of the point from the origin, as well as its coordinates, will affect the size of that point's contribution. This acts in a similar way to a *moment* of force, in which the distance of a force from the fulcrum affects its leverage. The product xy in (4.16) has this effect.

It will be convenient if the value of the resulting sum of products, as in (4.16), is not only independent of the units of measurement of x and y, but is also constrained to vary only between -1 and $+1$. Since the closest possible association between x and y corresponds to their lying on a straight line through the origin, $y = bx$, the sum of products Σxy can attain a maximum value proportional to Σx^2 or to

Σy^2. Consequently, it will be appropriate to use these summations to adjust the units of measurement of x and y.

A conventional procedure for adjusting scale factors is to calculate *standard scores,* rendering the result invariant under positive linear transformations:

$$z_x = \frac{x}{\sqrt{\dfrac{\Sigma x^2}{N}}} \quad \text{and} \quad z_y = \frac{y}{\sqrt{\dfrac{\Sigma y^2}{N}}} \qquad (4.17)$$

The denominator in each case is the sample standard deviation s_x or s_y of x or y, i.e., the square root of the sample variance of x or y respectively. This is of the same dimensionality as x or y, i.e., it can be represented by a distance along the x- or y-axis. If we then define r as the average product–moment of the standard scores z_x and z_y, we have another derivation of (4.16):

$$r = \frac{\Sigma z_x z_y}{N} = \frac{\Sigma xy}{N \sqrt{\dfrac{\Sigma x^2}{N} \dfrac{\Sigma y^2}{N}}} = \frac{\Sigma xy}{\sqrt{\Sigma x^2 \, \Sigma y^2}}$$

ACCOUNTING FOR THE RELATION BETWEEN TWO VARIABLES IN TERMS OF A THIRD

Factor analysis aims at accounting for the association between two observed variables (roll calls) in terms of a third, an underlying factor that they may have in common. The principle of accounting for the relation between two variables in terms of a third is far more general than its application in factor analysis, and enters into numerous procedures of data analysis in research. It has been outlined in a number of publications by Lazarsfeld and Kendall, and constitutes the basis for the reasoning of latent-structure analysis.[4]

In this reasoning, the association between two dichotomous variables x and y is denoted by the symbol [xy]. The relation between x and y is considered for two subsets of cases that differ on a third or "test" variable t (also dichotomous); the associations within these two

[4]P. L. Kendall and Lazarsfeld, "Problems of Survey Analysis"; Hyman, *Survey Design and Analysis,* chaps. 6, 7; Lazarsfeld, "Interpretation of Statistical Relations as a Research Operation," pp. 115–125, esp. p. 118.

subsets are denoted by $[xy;t]'$ and $[xy;t]''$. The relation between these various associations is expressed

$$[xy] = [xy;t]' \oplus [xy;t]'' \oplus [xt][ty] \qquad (4.18)$$

The circles around the plus signs on the right signify that the relation is one not of exact addition, but of weighted addition; the terms on the right are added, but with coefficients that may differ from unity, to give $[xy]$.[5] The last term on the right of (4.18) indicates the contribution made by the direct associations between the initial variables (x, y) separately and t. These are known as *marginal relationships;* we shall show below that they relate to marginal frequencies in fourfold tables. The two associations containing $;t$ are known as *partial relationships,* in that the variable t is controlled or held constant at one of its values when the measure of each relationship is calculated.

A relationship between x and y may therefore be explainable in various ways when its dependence on t is examined. If t were unrelated to x or y, or to their association, then the right-hand term $[xt]$ $[ty]$ would be expected to be zero, and the combination of the first two terms on the right of (4.18) would simply tell us that the associations between x and y for the two values of t were the same and were equal to the initial association $[xy]$. It is also possible that one value of t ($'$ or $''$) corresponds to a higher association between x and y than the other; if this condition is found, the analysis is said to have *specified* the relation, by stating a condition (a value of t) under which the relation is more pronounced.

For our purposes, however, the most interesting type of explanation that can be introduced in this way is that in which the right-hand term of (4.18) makes the main contribution. An example of this is the relation between two roll calls in the 84th Congress, considered first for all members of the House and then for Republicans and Democrats separately, shown in Table 4.2. The roll calls in question took place in 1955, and appeared in Tables 3.2 and 3.3 in the preceding chapter. The first roll call, #9, was on a motion opposing the extension of reciprocal trade; the overall vote was 199–206 (Republicans, 119–66; Democrats, 80–140). The second roll call, #27, was on a motion to recommit a bill for agricultural price supports;

[5]The exact relation is given in M. G. Kendall and Stuart, *The Advanced Theory of Statistics,* vol. 2, p. 543. The general reasoning of (4.18) can also be extended to polytomous test variables.

Table 4.2 Association between two roll calls, controlling on party

		Overall association				Republicans				Democrats		
		[xy] 27				[xy; t]′ 27				[xy; t]″ 27		
		+	−			+	−			+	−	
	9 +	119	82	201	9 +	108	11	119	9 +	11	71	82
	9 −	80	135	215	9 −	62	7	69	9 −	18	128	146
		199	217	416		170	18	188		29	199	228
ad		16065				756				1408		
bc		6560				682				1278		
$(ad-bc)/N^2$		.055				.002				.0025		
$r\ (=\phi)$		.22				.015				.015		
Q		.42				.05				.05		
Y		.22				.01				.02		

Associations of roll calls with party

		[ty]				[xt]		
		R	D			R	D	
	9 +	119	82	201	27 +	170	29	199
	9 −	69	146	215	27 −	18	199	217
		188	228	416		188	228	416
ad		17374				33830		
bc		5658				522		
$(ad-bc)/N^2$		.068				.193		
$r\ (=\phi)$		.27				.77		
Q		.51				.94		
Y		.28				.78		

NOTE: Roll calls are identified by *Congressional Quarterly* numbers for 1955.

the vote on this was 199–212 (Republicans, 175–19; Democrats, 24–193). These official vote figures differ somewhat from those shown in Table 4.2 because of the inclusion there of paired and announced votes, and the omission from the table of votes of congressmen who could not be thus classified on both roll calls. On both roll calls a yea was a conservative or positive vote; both motions were closely contested but unsuccessful attempts to defeat legislation that was supported primarily by the Democrats. Both were partisan, but the second was considerably more partisan than the first.

The salient feature of Table 4.2 is the dominant role of party in accounting for the association between the two roll calls. Regardless of which index of association (the cross-product, ϕ, Q, or Y) is considered, the overall association between the two roll calls for both parties together is very large compared to the associations within the two parties. The overall association is due almost entirely to the marginal frequencies in the tables for Republicans and Democrats; these marginal associations are shown in the two lower fourfold tables in the diagram. We are led to interpret the overall association as due to the relations of roll calls #9 and #27 with party, rather than to an intrinsic relation between the issues they embodied.

The general type of explanation that these data illustrate (at least approximately) is one in which we can find a test variable such that for any fixed value of this variable, the association between the first two vanishes. Such a relation can exist for quantitative as well as dichotomous variables; it corresponds to the more general condition that if a third variable is controlled, the association between the first two vanishes. Finding such test variables often gives us the feeling that we have penetrated nearer the heart of the matter; and if we were able, by controlling such a variable, to cause a great many other associations to vanish, we should have reason to feel quite successful in explaining or understanding these associations.

Factor analysis is aimed at this same sort of explanation. Unlike the process described above, however, it does not aim directly at finding actual measurable test variables (such as party affiliation), but constructs a simple set of test variables or factors from the given data themselves, without requiring new measurements, at least at this stage. It is an effort, then, to find an underlying structure in a given set of data, by producing a new smaller set of variables that will reproduce certain aspects of the original data more economically.

The data of Table 4.2 also demonstrate a quantitative relation between $[xy]$ and the product $[xt][ty]$, which exists for the correlation coefficient (r or ϕ). For that coefficient, these terms are respectively .22 and $.77 \times .27 = .21$—identical within the range of the small partial associations (.015). This identity holds exactly for ϕ when the partials are zero; but it fails to hold for either the cross product, $(ad - bc)/N^2$, or Q. However, it does hold numerically in this case for Y, whose values are nearly the same as those of ϕ. This latter relationship suggests that under some conditions Y might serve both as an indicator of scalability in the Guttman sense and as an index having some of the useful properties of ϕ.

The relationship $[xy] = [xt][ty]$, when the partial terms on the right-hand side of (4.18) vanish, is central to factor analysis, and we shall now demonstrate that it holds in general when the measure of association used is the correlation coefficient (ϕ). The demonstration will take the form of derivation of the expression for the partial correlation coefficient.[6]

Our line of reasoning will be to derive an expression for the partial correlation coefficient, i.e., the term corresponding to [xy;t]' and [xy;t]'' in (4.18). Then by equating this to zero, we shall show that the desired relation between [xy] and [xt][ty] obtains.

Let the variables x_j, x_k, t be quantitative variables, like x and y in the earlier derivations concerning the correlation coefficient. We wish to express the relation between x_j and x_k when t is held constant. To control a quantitative variable or to hold it constant, we use it as the predictor in a regression equation, and consider only the residuals from that equation. This is in one sense a more general procedure than that of allowing a dichotomous variable to assume first one and then another of its two values, but we may treat a dichotomous variable as a special case of a quantitative one. The partial association that results is then a weighted average of the associations within the two groups defined by the dichotomous test variable.

To simplify the derivation, we shall work with the corresponding standard scores z_j, z_k, and z_t. In these terms, $r_{jt} = b_{jt}$, since $\Sigma z_t^2 = N$, a result that follows from (4.17). The corresponding residuals are computed with respect to the regression lines $\hat{z}_j = r_{jt}z_t$ and $\hat{z}_k = r_{kt}z_t$, and are equal to $(z_j - r_{jt}z_t)$ and $(z_k - r_{kt}z_t)$ respectively. We then compute the correlation between these two residuals by substituting the expressions for the residuals in (4.16). The partial correlation is then

$$r_{jk \cdot t} = \frac{\Sigma(z_j - r_{jt}z_t)(z_k - r_{kt}z_t)}{\sqrt{\Sigma(z_j - r_{jt}z_t)^2 \; \Sigma(z_k - r_{kt}z_t)^2}}$$

Expansion of the numerator produces four terms each of which includes a summed product of z's. These sums can be replaced by r's by means of the relation $r_{jk} = \Sigma z_j z_k / N$. A similar substitution is possible in each of the two parts of the denominator, after expansion, leading to

[6]This line of reasoning is used in Du Bois, *Multivariate Correlational Analysis*, pp. 55, 88; Solomon, "A Survey of Mathematical Models in Factor Analysis," p. 279; and Kenney, *Mathematics of Statistics*, pt. 2, pp. 94–95. A more general and more conventional treatment is given in Harman, *op. cit.*, chap. 2.

$$r_{jk \cdot t} = \frac{N(r_{jk} - r_{jt}r_{kt} - r_{jt}r_{kt} + r_{jt}r_{kt})}{\sqrt{N(1 - 2r_{jt}^2 + r_{jt}^2)N(1 - 2r_{kt}^2 + r_{kt}^2)}}$$

$$= \frac{r_{jk} - r_{jt}r_{kt}}{\sqrt{(1 - r_{jt}^2)(1 - r_{kt}^2)}} \tag{4.19}$$

(Exercise: complete this derivation.) The right-hand expression in (4.19) is the conventional expression for the partial correlation coefficient. It may be restated in words:

$$\text{partial correlation} = \frac{\text{(total correlation)} - \text{("marginal" correlation)}}{\text{(geometric mean of residual proportions of variance)}}$$

If it is zero—i.e., if the residuals of x_j and x_k are uncorrelated after the effects of t are set aside by regression—then its numerator, $r_{jk} - r_{jt}r_{kt}$, is zero. Thus if the correlation between variables x_j and x_k results only from the "marginal" influence of t, then

$$r_{jk} = r_{jt}r_{kt} \tag{4.20}$$

This relation, which held approximately for the data of Table 4.2, holds in general if ϕ is used as the measure of association and if the partial correlation is zero. While it also holds approximately for Y in Table 4.2, it does not hold for Y in general, but depends on the particular conditions that obtain in the example.

DEFINING FACTORS
BY GROUPS OF VARIABLES

If $r_{jk} - r_{jt}r_{kt} = 0$ when there is no partial association, then we may assume that a nonzero value of this difference reflects an association independent of t. If we know r_{jt} and r_{kt} we can then proceed to examine this difference, or residual—or the entire matrix of $n(n-1)/2$ residuals—for other sources of variation, as when we analyze individual deviant cases by the corresponding residuals from a regression equation.

But before we can do this we must find the numerical values of r_{jt} and r_{kt}. When t is a known dichotomous variable, we can simply divide the sample according to the two values of t (for example, party in Table 4.2) and examine the association between x_j and x_k for each of the two subsets. If we wished to obtain a measure of the partial or residual association averaged over both groups, we might compute it for each group separately and combine the two results in a weighted average.[7]

When t is a known quantitative variable, it would seem equally reasonable simply to compute the correlations between t and x_j, and between t and x_k, and use these values as r_{jt} and r_{kt} respectively. But a problem arises if we try to use one of the variables in the correlation matrix for this purpose, as we can show with the aid of the associations in Table 4.1. The associations in that table were computed artificially on the assumption that they could all be accounted for by a single underlying t, and the values of r_{jt} assumed for $j = A, B, C, D, E$ respectively were .9, .7, .5, .3, and .2. It will be seen that all the entries in Table 4.1 can be accounted for by multiplication of the appropriate values of $r_{jt}r_{kt}$. (Exercise: carry out this operation.)

If we try to use one of the variables in the table ($A, B, C, D,$ or E) as t, however, to supply the correlation r_{jt} directly, we cannot easily recover the simple relations between the r's in the table. For suppose we used A in this way. We should then expect $r_{BC} = r_{AB}r_{AC}$; but r_{BC} is .35, and the product $r_{AB}r_{AC}$ is $.63 \times .45 = .2835$. A repetition of this attempt to account for the correlations between other variables in terms of their correlations with A would reveal that the result was in each case only .81 times the value in Table 4.1. The reason for the discrepancy is that the variable t assumed in construction of the table is not identical with A, but is rather another variable with which A has a correlation of .9. This discrepancy is clear for the artificial data we have used, but the problem would remain for real data as well. The use of one of the variables in the matrix as t might fail to account for simple relations among the observed correlations.[8] We therefore need procedures to solve for, or estimate, the values of $r_{jt}, r_{kt},$ etc., from the correlation matrix. We shall discuss simple procedures in this section and a more powerful one in Chapter 5.

In the perfect one-factor case, such as that of Table 4.1, it is possible to solve for the values of r_{jt} from the correlations in the table,

[7]See Goodman, "Partial Tests for Partial Taus"; Davis, "A Partial Coefficient for Goodman and Kruskal's Gamma."

[8]It is possible to take variable A as t, in the square-root method of factor analysis; but the results depend on knowledge of the diagonal values in the correlation matrix. See Harman, op. cit., pp. 101–103. A single variable has also been used as an approximation to a factor in McQuitty, "Elementary Factor Analysis."

since the data provide ten equations of the form of (4.20) for only five unknowns, the values of r_{jt} for $j = A, B, C, D, E$. One solution is the "method of triads," which leads to the equation[9]

$$r_{jt} = \sqrt{r_{jk}r_{jl}/r_{kl}}$$

The same underlying simplicity of relations among the r's in the table, which permits solutions of this type, also provides ways of recognizing whether a correlation matrix conforms to the one-factor model. If the correlations between a set of variables were explainable in terms of a single test variable t, all these correlations would vanish when t was controlled, and (4.20) would hold for all of them ($r_{jk} = r_{jt}r_{kt}$). If this were true, any two correlations such as r_{j1} and r_{j2} involving the variable x_j would have in common the term r_{jt}, and would therefore stand in the ratio ($r_{j1}/r_{j2} = r_{1t}/r_{2t}$). This ratio would have the same value regardless of j, and would thus be expressed in relations such as $r_{31}/r_{32} = r_{41}/r_{42} = r_{51}/r_{52}$, etc. Relations of this type hold for all such 2×2 submatrices in Table 4.1, since the data in this table were constructed in this way; e.g., $.45/.35 = .27/.21 = .18/.14$. If empirical data approximate this derivability from a single factor, then relations of this sort provide a test of that fact from inspection of the correlation matrix.[10]

In actual problems of factor analysis the number of expected factors normally exceeds one, and we cannot then take any triad indiscriminately for the estimation of factor loadings. It is nevertheless possible to estimate factor loadings by using a cluster of variables that have high correlations with one another or similar correlations with other variables. If we do this, and if we wish to estimate the correlations between the factor defined by this cluster and variables not in the cluster, an alternative method can be used. We shall illustrate it with the data of Table 4.1, even though this involves using an approximation on data that afford an exact solution. We consider using a combination of the variables A and B in the data matrix to make inferences about t.

Just as in our previous attempt to let A correspond to t, we cannot

---

[9]See Harman, *op. cit.*, p. 115; Du Bois, p. 88. The reader can verify the equation by substituting (4.20) with appropriate changes of subscripts. (Exercise: carry out this substitution.)

[10]This test corresponds to Spearman's early criterion of tetrad differences; see Harman, *op. cit.*, pp. 73–74.

simply equate the average correlations of A and B with another variable to those of t with that variable. We should find the average correlations of A and B, on the one hand, with C, D, and E, on the other, for example, to be uniformly too small. These averages, for C, D, and E respectively, are .40, .24, and .16, and according to this assumption would be set equal to r_{Ct}, r_{Dt}, and r_{Et}. We can then test whether this plausible assumption is correct, by calculating the expected values of r_{CD}, r_{CE}, and r_{DE}—.096, .064, and .0384. In comparison with the actual values in Table 4.1 (.15, .10, and .06), each is too low, being only .64 times the value in the table. If we divided each factor loading by .8, then each product $r_{jt}r_{kt}$ would be divided by .64.

One way to estimate this multiplicative constant (.64) from the data is to approximate it by the correlation r_{AB}, which in this case is .63. If this correlation were due entirely to t, it would be equal to $r_{At}r_{Bt}$; and if r_{At} and r_{Bt} were similar in magnitude, the square root of their product would approximate their average (in this case the average of .9 and .7).[11] This approximation is available only if more than one item is used in estimation. If three or more items are used, we should then use the average of all their intercorrelations.[12] The result is an estimate of factor loadings on t, though the values of t itself are not known. The factor loadings r_{jt} are thus calculated as

$$r_{jt} = \frac{\text{(average correlation of variable } j \text{ with those in cluster)}}{\sqrt{\text{(average correlation of variables in cluster with one another)}}}$$

The advantage of this method is that it can be used, not only when the entire correlation matrix approximates one-factor structure, but also when part of the matrix has that property. Thus loadings on a first factor can be defined which will account for that part of the matrix, reducing the corresponding residuals to low values. Other parts of the matrix not accounted for by the first factor will then stand out in the residual matrix, and subsequent factors can be defined so as to reduce them in turn.

The method we have just described is also used in one of the BC

---

[11] In the single-factor model, $\mathrm{av}(r_{AC}, r_{BC}) = r_{Ct}\,\mathrm{av}(r_{At}, r_{Bt})$.

[12] A more rigorous treatment of a similar procedure is given in Harman, *op. cit.*, pp. 236–238; another similar method is described in Horst, *Factor Analysis of Data Matrices*, pp. 138 ff.

TRY cluster analysis techniques.[13] In this procedure an initial pivot variable is chosen as the variable with the greatest variance or r^2, and one or more others are added on the basis of their values of the index of collinearity P^2 with it, provided one can be found whose value exceeds a specified threshold.[14] This group of two or more variables is then related to t in the same way as the average of A and B above, and the factor loadings r_{jt} are computed by means of the above expression.

For every entry in the correlation matrix, the residual is then calculated, i.e., $r_{jk} - r_{jt}r_{kt}$. The matrix of residuals is then treated in exactly the same way as the initial correlation matrix. Another cluster is found in it, if one can be found which meets the criteria; factor loadings on the corresponding second factor are computed, and second residuals are found. The procedure is repeated either until the clustering criterion fails to be met, or until the number of clusters set by the investigator has been computed.

For clusters after the first, there are two alternatives for assessing the relation between individual variables (e.g., roll calls) and the test variable defined by a cluster. One is to use only the residual matrices, and define this relation by residuals. The other is to return to the initial correlation matrix after having defined the second or later cluster, to assess the relations of individual roll calls to the cluster. The second approach is closer to the data and easier to interpret; but if it is used, then the correlations between particular roll calls and those in (say) the second cluster will in general involve contributions that are also attributable in part to the first cluster. In terms that we shall develop below, correlations with clusters as defined by the initial correlation matrix are no longer independent of one another; in this sense clusters define variables that are oblique, not orthogonal, to one another.

This procedure was carried out with the Q-matrix for the 102 roll calls for the Republicans in 84th Congress—the same matrix used to produce the clusters shown in Tables 3.2 and 3.3. To use a procedure involving residuals with a Q-matrix is not strictly permissible, since equation (4.20) does not hold for Q; we should therefore be con-

[13]This particular variant is "noncommunality cluster analysis," which proceeds without estimation of the diagonal entries of the correlation matrix. See Tryon, *Theory of the BC TRY System: Statistical Theory*, pp. 31, 58–78. A closely related method is presented in Overall, "Cluster Oriented Factor Solutions."

[14]The coefficient P^2 was defined in equation (3.7).

Table 4.3 Clusters of roll calls resulting from BC TRY noncommunality cluster analysis (Republicans, 84th Congress, House of Representatives, Q-matrix)

Defining variables	Other variables with average Q ≥ .7 in relation to defining variables
Cluster 1	
5–22 Postal pay, amendment	5–63 Social security, extend
5–21 Independent offices appropriation	5–29 Postal pay, return to conference
6–36 Water pollution act, recommit	5–76 Housing act of 1955, conference report
5–23 Postal pay, recommit	5–30 Postal pay, adopt conference report
	5–72 Housing act of 1955, omit public housing
	6–37 Water pollution act, pass
	5–24 Postal pay, pass
	5–16 Postal pay raise
	6–40 Liberalize veterans' pensions, pass
Cluster 2	
6–16 Farm program, pass over veto	5–44 Regulate bank holding companies, pass
5–28 Farm price supports, pass	6–14 Farm program, conference report
6–13 Farm program, recommit conference report	6–23 Agriculture act of 1956 (soil bank), pass
5–27 Farm price supports, recommit	6–29 Revised farm bill, conference report
	5–26 Farm price supports, amendment (peanuts)
	6–41 Defense production act, dispersion of industry
	6–72 Block southwest power-rate increases
	6–71 Block southwest power-rate increases
	6–18 Upgrade positions in Immigration Department
	6–38 Extend D.C. daylight saving time
	5–35 D.C. judges' pay raise, pass
	5– 5 Pay raise for Congress and other officers

Table 4.3 (Continued)

Defining variables	Other variables with average $Q \geq .7$ in relation to defining variables
Cluster 3	
5–43 Reciprocal trade extension, conference report	5– 9 Reciprocal trade extension
	5– 6 Reciprocal trade extension
5–10 Reciprocal trade extension, pass	5– 7 Reciprocal trade extension
5–50 Customs simplification, recommit	5–42 Inter-American highway
5– 8 Reciprocal trade extension, closed rule	5–15 Supplemental appropriation, restore UN aid funds
	5–47 Congressional delegation to NATO parliament conference
	5–60 Mutual security appropriation
	5–65 Reserve forces, conference report
	5–57 Mutual security act of 1955, pass

NOTE: Roll calls are identified by the last digit of the year (5 or 6) followed by the *Congressional Quarterly Almanac* number. After the defining variables, others are listed in decreasing order of correlation.

cerned that residuals involve some contribution from the previous clusters as well as exclusively new sources of variation. Our reason for violating this assumption is that those coefficients that do satisfy (4.20), such as ϕ, are sensitive to the marginals (p_+), and do not reproduce cumulative scales in the clusters or factors that they yield. The result of this procedure is a compromise which has to be viewed critically, but which nevertheless has clear advantages with respect to the more orthodox coefficient (ϕ) in the interpretation of roll-call data.

Three such clusters were defined, each by four roll calls, before the process was automatically terminated. The program then computed the average association between the roll calls in each cluster and each other roll call, and ranked the other roll calls in descending order of association with each cluster.[15] Table 4.3 shows the sets of roll calls that resulted for average associations down to .7.

The lists of roll calls in Table 4.3 are recognizably similar to those in the clusters of Table 3.3, but with some exceptions. Cluster 1 includes all five items in Scale 4 (postal pay) as well as two in Scale 5

[15]For Clusters 2 and 3, these average associations (Q's) were based on the initial Q-matrix rather than residuals.

(welfare state), these two scales having been closely associated before. A general domestic left–right dimension seems to be involved. Cluster 2 includes all the items in the previous Scale 2 (agriculture). Cluster 3 has as its first seven items those composing the previous Scale 3 (reciprocal trade), but also includes four items of the eight that were in Scale 1 (foreign aid). Scales 1 and 3 were also moderately closely associated previously. That cluster 3 is closer to former Scale 3 is also indicated by a sharp drop in the average Q with the four defining items (from .9 to .8) after the first seven items.

Thus approximately the same clusters have been found, but they are not defined in precisely the same way, and individual clusters that were separate in the earlier analysis have been combined by the BC TRY procedure. The reason for this, as we shall see below, is that the process of computing residuals describes the data in terms of a space of few dimensions, and the number of dimensions may be fewer than the number of clusters found previously. Those clusters that were closely associated with one another before, here tend to be combined, though with different degrees of association with the defining items.

In interpreting the clusters of Table 4.3, we begin to see some problems that were not encountered in clustering the binary matrix, problems that are especially important in interpreting factor loadings. The variables in the right-hand column differ in their strengths of association with the defining variables in each cluster. If we were dealing only with these clusters, and had to name the concepts or issues they represented without reference to our previous results, we should wish to take these different strengths of association into account. We should then give greater weight to the subject matter of some members of a cluster than to others in inferring the common issue that the cluster represented.

THE PROBLEM OF ROTATION OF AXES

In the BC TRY cluster analysis procedure described above, factors after the first were defined in terms of a matrix of residual correlations. This sequential procedure of computing loadings on one factor, finding residuals by subtraction, and then repeating the initial procedure on the residual matrix, is common to a variety of methods of factor analysis. We must now consider this procedure for finding residuals and computing successive factors from them in more detail.

If nonzero residuals remain after introduction of the first test variable or factor, and if we wish to proceed to account for them by a second factor, we may continue the analysis with the residuals

$$_1r_{jk} = r_{jk} - r_{j1}r_{k1}$$

where we now use the subscript 1 rather than t to indicate the first of a series of test variables or factors.[16]

If we succeed in accounting for the residual correlation between variables x_j and x_k exactly by means of a second factor, the correlation r_{jk} will then be attributable to contributions from both factors:

$$r_{jk} = r_{j1}r_{k1} + r_{j2}r_{k2} \qquad (4.21)$$

where 2 denotes the second factor or test variable. It is conventional in factor analysis to reserve the symbol r for the input correlations, and to designate the correlations between factors and data variables (factor loadings) by the symbol a. Moreover, in general the reproduced correlation $\hat{r}_{jk}$ is not identical with the observed r_{jk}. In this symbolism (4.21) becomes

$$\hat{r}_{jk} = a_{j1}a_{k1} + a_{j2}a_{k2} \qquad (4.22)$$

Equation (4.22), relating the factor loadings a and the reproduced correlation coefficients $\hat{r}_{jk}$, can also be expressed geometrically. If we consider a pair of Cartesian coordinate axes, and let one correspond to loadings on factor 1, and the second to loadings on factor 2, then each pair of factor loadings corresponding to one of the variables (roll calls) may be plotted as a point in this two-dimensional space. Such a plot of two points is shown in Figure 4.2. It can be shown with the aid of this figure that equation (4.22) is equivalent to another formulation that is independent of the coordinate axes, and depends only on the positions of the two points relative to the origin. Equation (4.22) can be rewritten in terms of the radial distances to the points j and k from the origin (h_j and h_k respectively), and the angles that these radial lines make with the x-axis, θ_j and θ_k.

---

[16]We do not divide by the square-root term that would appear in the denominator of the partial correlation coefficient, because we are now expressing only the total covariation explained by each factor. Conceivably partial correlations could be factored, but they would not have the additive relations between the contributions of successive factors, which we shall discuss below.

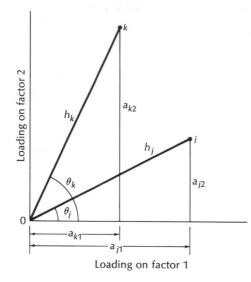

FIGURE 4.2. Factor Loadings of Two
Variables Plotted in Two Dimensions.

For

$$a_{j1} = h_j \cos \theta_j$$
$$a_{j2} = h_j \sin \theta_j$$

$$a_{k1} = h_k \cos \theta_k$$
$$a_{k2} = h_k \sin \theta_k$$

Substituting in (4.22),

$$\hat{r}_{jk} = h_j h_k (\cos \theta_j \cos \theta_k + \sin \theta_j \sin \theta_k) = h_j h_k \cos(\theta_k - \theta_j) \quad (4.23)$$

The final form of (4.23) obtains because of the trigonometric identity for the cosine of the difference between two angles. But in this form the coordinates on axes 1 and 2 are no longer present, and the correlation coefficient is expressed in terms of the lengths of the two radial lines and the angle between them. This result can be extended to multidimensional space as well.

The fact that the correlation can equally well be expressed in this way implies that if we drew any other pair of perpendicular axes through the origin in Figure 4.2, found the coordinates of points x_j and x_k on them, and recomputed the correlation from (4.22), the result would be the same. There are thus an infinite number of alternative solutions, corresponding to alternative sets of factors, that would reproduce the correlation coefficients in the matrix identically with the one particular solution of this kind that we may have. This multiplicity of solutions, convertible into one another by rotation of the coordinate axes, gives rise to one of the major problems of factor analysis: Is there a best or preferred solution? And while we have shown this problem only in the case of two dimensions or factors, it exists in more general form for any number of factors that may be found.

Several general procedures have been proposed for resolving this ambiguity. They include a preference for those axes that account for the largest sums of squares in the correlation matrix or data matrix (principal components); a preference for those axes that lead to especially simple configurations of the x-points in the space (simple structure); the presentation of the data in coordinate-free form (e.g., a distance matrix); and the use of substantive or conceptual criteria of selection. We shall discuss these possibilities below.

FACTOR SCORES, RESIDUALS, AND ORTHOGONALITY

So far we have discussed the test variable or factor t as though all we knew of it were its correlations with the observed variables. For many purposes these are all that are needed; and if our analysis begins with a matrix of coefficients of association, without reference to the data values on which they are based, they are all that can be found. But if we know the values in the data matrix as well, we can then compute estimates of the *factor scores*—the values of t for individual legislators. Procedures for computing factor scores will be considered in Chapter 5; here we shall deal with their mathematical relations.

Our distinction between these two cases is an unconventional one, and derives from our intention later to factor-analyze matrices of coefficients such as Q, which do not have such simple relations to the data matrix as does r or ϕ. But we now return to a line of reasoning closer to the conventional basis of factor analysis, in which factor scores are considered from the start.

The fundamental equation (4.20), $r_{jk} = r_{jt}r_{kt}$, can also be derived from assumptions about regression equations involving the variables

x_j, x_k, and t. It is conventional, and simplifies the treatment, to deal only with standard scores for these variables. The relation between the standard scores z_{ij} and z_{it} can be written analogously to (4.8):

$$\hat{z}_{ij} = r_{jt}z_{it} \tag{4.24}$$

where $\hat{z}_{ij}$ is the predicted value of the standard score of z_j for legislator i, the vertical coordinate of a point on the regression line. The slope of the regression line is again indicated by r_{jt} because the correlation coefficient is equal to the regression slope when only standard scores are considered.

But we can also express (4.24) as a relation between z_{it} and the observed z_{ij}, if we introduce into the equation a term for the residual or error. In these terms, the corresponding equations for z_{ij} and z_{ik} are

$$z_{ij} = r_{jt}z_{it} + e_{ij} \quad \text{and} \quad z_{ik} = r_{kt}z_{it} + e_{ik} \tag{4.25}$$

Each of these equations, considered separately, depends on no further assumption than that it is a regression equation. But jointly, they also require the assumption that e_{ij} and e_{ik} are uncorrelated, in order that the correlation r_{jk} be exactly reproduced by the single factor t. If the two error terms were correlated, then more than one factor would be required to account exactly for r_{jk}. Subject to these assumptions, the total variance of each variable (z_j or z_k) can then be expressed as a sum of two terms:

$$\frac{\Sigma z_{ij}^2}{N} = \text{var}(z_j) = 1 = r_{jt}^2 + \frac{\Sigma e_{ij}^2}{N}$$

$$\frac{\Sigma z_{ik}^2}{N} = \text{var}(z_k) = 1 = r_{kt}^2 + \frac{\Sigma e_{ik}^2}{N}$$

The correlation between x_j and x_k is

$$r_{jk} = \frac{\Sigma z_{ij}z_{ik}}{N} \quad \frac{\Sigma(r_{jt}r_{kt}z_{it}^2 + r_{jt}z_{it}e_{ik} + r_{kt}z_{it}e_{ij} + e_{ij}e_{ik})}{N} = r_{jt}r_{kt}$$

since $\Sigma z_{it}^2 = N$; since equations (4.25) are regression equations whose residuals are uncorrelated with the predictor t; and since the error or residual terms are assumed to be uncorrelated with one another ($\Sigma e_{ij}e_{ik} = 0$), as in partial correlation. We have thus derived (4.20) again.

The proportional contribution of the common factor t to the variance of x_j is r_{jt}^2. If x_j and x_k are correlated with one another, but only because of correlations with t which are similar in magnitude, then the element r_{jk} in the correlation matrix provides an estimate of r_{jt}^2. This type of estimate was used above in our combination of variables A and B, and in the BC TRY method of cluster analysis.

A similar derivation of (4.22), accounting for r_{jk} in terms of two underlying factors, may also be carried out in terms of standard scores on the two factors. We introduce for this purpose more of the conventional notation of factor analysis. In writing (4.22) we represented the correlations between the underlying factors as a_{j1}, a_{k1}, a_{j2} and a_{k2}. We now also substitute the symbol F_{i1} for z_{i1}, the standard score (factor score) of individual i on factor 1, and F_{i2} for z_{i2}. We then generalize (4.25) to the case of two factors, at the same time reversing the order of terms in multiplication, for later matrix treatment:

$$z_{ij} = F_{i1}a_{j1} + F_{i2}a_{j2} + e_{ij}$$
$$z_{ik} = F_{i1}a_{k1} + F_{i2}a_{k2} + e_{ik}$$

$$(4.26)$$

The error terms e_{ij} and e_{ik} in (4.26) are now residuals after two predictor variables, F_{i1} and F_{i2}, have been used in predicting the z's.

In this model, each individual (i) may be characterized by two standardized factor scores, F_{i1} on factor 1 and F_{i2} on factor 2. His reproduced standard scores on the observed variables, z_{ij} on x_j and z_{ik} on x_k, may be calculated from these factor scores by weighted addition, the weights being the loadings of the variable in question on the two factors (the a's).

We assume in (4.26) that factors 1 and 2 account for the correlation r_{jk} exactly, extending the similar assumption made in connection with (4.25). This implies that the residuals e_{ij} and e_{ik} are uncorrelated with one another, a relation we shall use in simplifying (4.28) below. If the second factor has been computed from residual correlations after the computation of the first, then the error terms e_{ij} and e_{ik} are uncorrelated with F_{i2}, for the same reason that the residuals were independent of the factor scores in (4.25); the reasoning indicated there can be repeated but applied to the residual correlations and the residuals of the standard scores z_{ij} and z_{ik} after the first factor is removed.

It is also customary to assume that the two factor scores F_{i1} and F_{i2} are independent of, or *orthogonal* to, one another. This relation does not hold automatically for any choice of the second factor in

(4.26), but does obtain when the residual correlations are used to estimate the second factor. For the residuals after the first factor are uncorrelated with the first factor, and their correlations cannot then involve any contribution from the first factor. We can thus assume that

$$\sum_i F_{i1}F_{i2} = 0$$

It follows from this assumption that the error terms e_{ij} and e_{ik} are uncorrelated with F_{i1}. For we know from the reasoning concerning the first factor that if a_{j1} is a correlation coefficient, it enters into the regression equation

$$z_{ij} = a_{j1}F_{i1} + (F_{i2}a_{j2} + e_{ij}) \tag{4.27}$$

a reordered form of the first equation of (4.26) showing the regression slope a_{j1} and the residual $(F_{i1}a_{j2} + e_{ij})$. Since the residual is uncorrelated with the predictor, we can write, using the notation $r_{xy} = r(x, y)$,

$$r(F_{i1}, F_{i2}a_{j2} + e_{ij}) = 0$$

And since $r(F_{i1}, F_{i2}) = 0$, and the expression above is a linear combination of $r(F_{i1}, F_{i2})$ and $r(F_{i1}, e_{ij})$, then the latter is also zero.[17]

Subject to these assumptions, equation (4.22) can be derived from (4.26), with the observed correlation r_{jk} substituted for the reproduced correlation on the left-hand side of (4.22). This follows from a derivation analogous to that following equation (4.25). The corresponding expansion is

$$r_{jk} = \frac{\sum z_{ij}z_{ik}}{N} = \frac{\sum (F_{i1}a_{j1} + F_{i2}a_{j2} + e_{ij})(F_{i1}a_{k1} + F_{i2}a_{k2} + e_{ik})}{N} \tag{4.28}$$

We first eliminate the product terms involving the e's, for the same reasons as in the derivations following equations (4.25). Since the F's are standard scores, $\sum F_{i1}^2 = \sum F_{i2}^2 = N$, and the two terms that include these summations reduce to $a_{j1}a_{k1} + a_{j2}a_{k2}$, as in (4.22). The terms in $F_{i1}F_{i2}$ vanish because

$$\sum_i F_{i1}F_{i2} = 0$$

[17]The correlation between the sum of two variables, and a third variable w is given by

$$r(x + y, w) = \frac{s_x}{s_{x+y}} r_{xw} + \frac{s_y}{s_{x+y}} r_{yw}$$

as can be shown by substitution in (4.16). (Exercise: Carry out this substitution.)

The result is another derivation of (4.22): subject to the assumptions stated, $r_{jk} = a_{j1}a_{j2} + a_{k1}a_{k2}$.

In carrying out this derivation we have shown that if the second factor is based on residuals, its factor scores are independent of those on the first factor. This result holds for multiple dimensions as well. It applies, but only approximately and by analogy, to our analysis of the Q-matrix with the BC TRY system. While there is no precise parallel to factor scores for Q, which is not related to regression coefficients, the scale scores based on Q-clusters are analogous to factor scores. Thus we expect the scale scores corresponding to different BC TRY clusters in Table 4.3 to have low associations with one another, and this is generally confirmed by the values of γ in Table 3.3. The analogy is imperfect not only because of the use of Q, however, but also because the associations in Table 3.3 are based on actual votes rather than on residuals. Nevertheless, by forcing the choice of the second and third clusters to be made on the basis of residuals, the BC TRY procedure gives precedence to pivot variables that are uncorrelated with those in the first cluster.

Not all types of factors may properly be plotted in a space of perpendicular (orthogonal) axes, but those that are computed by successive residuals in the matrix of associations may be, as in Figure 4.2. If factors are also based on residuals in the data, the sum

$$\sum_i F_{i1}F_{i2} = 0$$

as we have shown after (4.26). It is not in general true in these cases that

$$\sum_j a_{1j}a_{2j} = 0$$

This latter relation, involving a summation over roll calls rather than individuals, holds in principal component analysis, which we shall discuss in the next chapter.

If this relation between the factor scores holds, i.e., if the values of individuals (legislators) on two factors are uncorrelated with one another, we say the factors are *orthogonal* to one another; the above reasoning following (4.26) then justifies our plotting the factor loadings along orthogonal coordinate axes and treating the reproduced correlations accordingly. It is the definition of factor loadings by *residual* correlations that insures orthogonality of factors; if (as in

Table 4.3) roll calls are characterized by their associations with clusters in the original matrix, we should not expect these associations to have the properties that (4.22) implies for factor loadings.

A further important property of the factor scores F_{i1} and F_{i2} is that their orthogonality is preserved by rotations of the type discussed above.[18] This property will be discussed below after matrix operations have been considered.

OPERATIONS ON MATRICES[19]

Several of the relations we have introduced can be treated much more concisely, especially as the number of variables, legislators, and factors increases, by means of a set of conventions for operating on large rectangular arrays of numbers, or matrices. Among these are: $r = \Sigma z_x z_y / N$ and $\hat{r}_{jk} = a_{j1} a_{k1} + a_{j2} a_{k2}$ and the equations that correspond to the rotation of one coordinate system to change it into another. For this reason we now introduce the rules for matrix multiplication. We must first define a matrix and its transpose.

A *matrix* is a rectangular array of numbers in rows and columns, subject to certain rules and operations. The *elements* in a matrix may be indicated by subscripts, the first indicating the row number and the second the column number. Thus in the matrix **A** below, there are three rows and two columns—we thus refer to it as a 3×2 matrix—and $a_{32} = 10$.

$$\mathbf{A} = \begin{bmatrix} 3. & 40 \\ .01 & 1 \\ 0. & 10 \end{bmatrix} = \begin{bmatrix} a_{11} & a_{12} \\ a_{21} & a_{22} \\ a_{31} & a_{32} \end{bmatrix}$$

In illustrating this convention for referring to rows and columns, we have also made use of two other properties of matrices: the rectangular array is conventionally enclosed by brackets (or double vertical lines) to indicate that it is to be treated as a matrix; and two matrices are equal to another if every element in one is equal to the corresponding element in the other. It is also conventional to designate an entire matrix by a single symbol, and for this purpose we use a **bold-**

[18]This is proved in Horst, *op. cit.*, pp. 406–407.

[19]Introductory sections on matrix operations are given in Harman, *op. cit.*, chap. 3, and Horst, *op. cit.*, chaps. 2–4. Many mathematical introductions to matrix algebra are also available.

face capital letter; the corresponding lower-case *italic* letter, with subscripts, is then used to designate an element of the matrix.

We often wish to deal with the modification of a given matrix that results from interchanging its rows and columns. This is known as the *transpose* of the initial matrix, and is indicated by the symbol of the initial matrix followed by a prime ('). Thus for the matrix above,

$$\mathbf{A}' = \begin{bmatrix} 3 & .01 & 0 \\ 40 & 1. & 10 \end{bmatrix}$$

The transposition of a matrix takes the element that was originally in the ith row and jth column, into the jth row and ith column of the transpose. The operation of transposition, performed twice on a given matrix, brings us back to the original matrix. $(\mathbf{A}')' = \mathbf{A}$.

One type of matrix that we have already encountered in the *square* matrix, which has the same number of rows as columns. The number of rows or columns of such a matrix is known as the *order* of the matrix. The Q-matrix, the correlation matrix, and any matrix whose elements are indices of pairwise relationships between all members of a set of roll calls or legislators, are square.

For the indices of relation between pairs of roll calls that we have considered, almost all fulfilled the condition of symmetry, $f_{ij}(a, b, c, d) = f_{ji}(a, c, b, d)$; interchange of the rows and columns of the four-fold table interchanges b and c, but leaves the value of the index unchanged. When this condition is satisfied, the matrix of indices is not only square but also *symmetric*. For any matrix **A**, if $a_{ij} = a_{ji}$, then **A** is symmetric. It follows from our definition of the transpose that the transpose of a symmetric matrix is the same as the initial matrix: $\mathbf{A} = \mathbf{A}'$ for a symmetric matrix, and conversely.

The principal operation that we shall perform with matrices, and the one whose convenience justifies our introducing matrix notation, is matrix *multiplication*. It may be applied in several of the operations we have discussed which involve matching two sequences of numbers, multiplying the corresponding numbers in each matched pair, and adding the resulting products to produce an overall sum. The computation of the correlation coefficient is an example; the summation of $x_{ij}x_{ik}$, or of $z_{ij}z_{ik}$, illustrates this process of matching, multiplying, and summing. Similarly, equation (4.22), which expresses the reproduced correlation coefficient as a sum of products of factor loadings, is of this type:

$$\hat{r}_{jk} = a_{j1}a_{k1} + a_{j2}a_{k2} \tag{4.22}$$

Although we are summing only two such products for each reproduced correlation $\hat{r}_{jk}$, more products would be summed if there were more than two factors.

The rules of matrix multiplication involve this same matching, multiplying, and summing, and thus summarize concisely the operations we have just described. If the product **AB** of two matrices, **A** and **B,** is to be calculated, the matching takes place between the rows of the matrix on the left (**A**) and the columns of that on the right (**B**). Each row of the left-hand matrix must have the same number of elements as each column of the right-hand matrix; that is, the number of columns of the left matrix must equal the number of rows of the right matrix. An example of two matrices that can be multiplied, and their product, is the following:

$$\begin{bmatrix} 8 & 4 \\ 2 & -7 \\ 3 & 6 \\ 6 & -2 \end{bmatrix} \begin{bmatrix} 1 & -4 & 0 \\ -2 & 3 & -1 \end{bmatrix} = \begin{bmatrix} 0 & -20 & -4 \\ 16 & -29 & 7 \\ -9 & 6 & -6 \\ 10 & -30 & 2 \end{bmatrix}$$

(Exercise: carry out the multiplication.) The two matrices on the left can be multiplied by one another because the first has two columns and the second has two rows. Thus any row of the first can be matched, element for element, with any column of the second.

After the matching is made, we perform the multiplication, add the products, and place the overall sum in the product matrix on the right. It is placed in the row of the product matrix corresponding to the row of the left-hand matrix being multiplied, and the column of the product matrix corresponding to the column of the right-hand matrix being multiplied. For example, the second row on the left $(2, -7)$ is matched with the third column on the right $(0, -1)$ to yield the element in the second row and third column of the product: $2 \times 0 + (-7) \times (-1) = 7$.

More generally, if we designate the matrices being multiplied as **A** and **B,** and the product as **C,**

$$\sum_k a_{ik}b_{kj} = c_{ij} \tag{4.29}$$

This example illustrates a number of properties of matrix multiplication:

1   Not every two matrices have a product; the number of columns

of the matrix on the left must match the number of rows of the matrix on the right in order for a product to be defined.

2 The number of rows of the product is equal to that of the left multiplier, and the number of columns of the product is equal to that of the right multiplier.

3 The product of two matrices depends in general on the left–right sequence in which they are multiplied (matrix multiplication is not commutative). If this sequence is reversed, a product may not even be defined; or even if it is defined, it may be different from the product of the two matrices taken in the initial sequence. Thus to speak precisely about the product of two matrices in a given sequence (**AB**) we must speak of "*pre*-multiplying **B** by **A**" or "*post*-multiplying **A** by **B**." For the product **BA** (if it existed) we should use either of these phrases with **A** and **B** interchanged.

4 The ordinary rules of multiplication, which are used in multiplying individual elements, permit the elements in the multipliers or the product to be positive, negative, or zero.

5 Certain simple sets of elements in one of the matrices being multiplied produce correspondingly simple results in the product. Thus the presence of the third column $(0, -1)$ in the right-hand multiplier in the above example leads to the reproduction of the second column of the left multiplier $(4, -7, 6, -2)$ with reversed sign as the third column of the product $(-4, 7, -6, 2)$.

The transpose of the product of two matrices is given by the product of their transposes in reverse sequence: if $\mathbf{AB} = \mathbf{C}$, then $(\mathbf{AB})' = \mathbf{C}' = \mathbf{B}'\mathbf{A}'$. The reader may show this numerically for the above example. The proof of this relation results from (4.29). First we note that the number of columns of **B'** (former rows) still matches the number of rows of **A'** (former columns), since the same numbers are being matched together. To carry out the operations of (4.29) on the transposed matrices, in reverse order, we should then calculate

$$\sum_k (b')_{ik}(a')_{kj} = \sum_k b_{ki}a_{jk} = \sum_k a_{jk}b_{ki} = c_{ji}$$

the corresponding element of **C** but with row and column indices interchanged. Thus the product matrix, composed of these elements, is **C'**.

If **A** and **B** are symmetric matrices, $\mathbf{AB} = \mathbf{A}'\mathbf{B}' = (\mathbf{BA})'$. But even when **A** and **B** are symmetric, **AB** is not necessarily symmetric.

It is also possible to multiply three or more matrices, forming a product such as **ABC.** The sequence in which the two multiplications are performed is immaterial, i.e., $(AB)C = A(BC)$, and matrix multiplication is associative. This property can be demonstrated by successive application of (4.29); the result will be that any element of **ABC** consists of a double summation, but it does not matter which of the two summations is performed first. Alternatively, the reader may convince himself of this property by carrying out the operations $(AB)C$ and $A(BC)$ on numerical examples.

If a square matrix is multiplied by itself a number of times, the result may be referred to as a *power* of the original matrix, e.g., A^n.

An important special case of a symmetric matrix is the *diagonal* matrix, all of whose elements off the main diagonal (all other than the elements a_{ii}) are zero. An example of a diagonal matrix is

$$\begin{bmatrix} 3 & 0 & 0 & 0 \\ 0 & 2 & 0 & 0 \\ 0 & 0 & -1 & 0 \\ 0 & 0 & 0 & -5 \end{bmatrix}$$

Postmultiplication of a matrix by a diagonal matrix multiplies every column entry by a corresponding constant; premultiplication by a diagonal matrix multiplies every row by a corresponding constant. The instance shown above, in the numerical example of matrix multiplication, where one column of the left multiplier matrix was reproduced in the product with signs reversed, illustrates how this works. The reader may demonstrate it by constructing numerical examples.

A diagonal matrix all of whose diagonal elements are the same multiplies every element of the initial matrix by that same number. This operation has the same result regardless of whether pre- or postmultiplication is performed, although the size (order) of the diagonal matrix may be different in the two cases. This multiplication of all elements of a matrix by a constant may also be written as multiplication of the matrix by that constant. An ordinary number is known in this context as a *scalar,* in distinction to a matrix. Multiplication by a scalar can be indicated interchangeably as either pre- or postmultiplication.

A special case of multiplication by a scalar constant is multiplication by unity. An *identity* matrix (designated **I**) is a diagonal matrix all of whose diagonal elements are unity. Either pre- or postmultiplication of a matrix by an identity matrix leaves its elements unchanged.

MATRIX APPLICATIONS
IN FACTOR ANALYSIS

We can now express the computation of the correlation matrix, with its $n(n-1)/2$ entries on either side of the diagonal, as a single matrix equation. Let us start with a matrix of standard scores for roll-call votes, with rows corresponding to legislators and columns to roll calls. The entry in row i ($i = 1, 2, \ldots, N$) and column j ($j = 1, 2, \ldots, n$) will be z_{ij} and the matrix as a whole will be denoted by $\mathbf{Z}$. This matrix can be considered to have been derived from a vote matrix $\mathbf{M}$ by subtraction of the column means and division of the elements in each column by the corresponding standard deviation. The initial values in $\mathbf{M}$ might have been $+1$ for "yea," -1 for "nay," and 0 for "no vote," or a linear transformation of these values.[20] Our treatment, holds, however, for any data matrix $\mathbf{M}$ and not simply for roll calls.

Since $r_{jk} = \Sigma z_{ij}z_{ik}/N$, we can consider r_{jk} to be one entry in a matrix $\mathbf{R}$, in which it occupies row j and column k. We thus write

$$\mathbf{R} = \frac{\mathbf{Z'Z}}{N} \tag{4.30}$$

making use of the operations of transposition, matrix multiplication, multiplication by a scalar $(1/N)$, and equation of two matrices, which we have discussed above. A diagram showing the operations of (4.30), with matrices as rectangles, is given in Figure 4.3 below. If there are more legislators than roll calls, $\mathbf{Z}$ will be a rectangular array with its long side vertical, and $\mathbf{Z'}$ an array with its long side horizontal, as in Figure 4.3. Any element in the product $\mathbf{Z'Z}$ will result from matching together the two standard scores corresponding to legislator i, multiplying them, and summing the products over all legislators. The diagonal elements of $\mathbf{R}$ in (4.30) will each be 1.0, the correlation of a variable with itself.[21]

[20]It has been pointed out, however, that the assignment of "no vote" to the mean value between yea and nay is a gratuitous assumption; see Brams and O'Leary, "An Axiomatic Model of Voting Bodies."

[21]We do not treat here the estimation of communalities as diagonal elements. We also depart from the notation of Harman (*op. cit.*, pp. 25, 27), in which, letting rows be variables, he writes $\mathbf{R} = \mathbf{ZZ'}/N$. Our notation resembles that of Horst, *op. cit.*, p. 110.

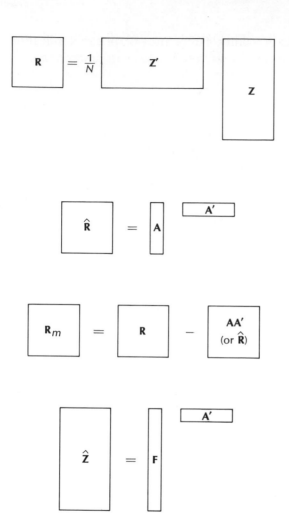

FIGURE 4.3. Representation of Matrix Equations in Factor Analysis by Rectangles.
Computation of the Correlation Matrix,
$$\mathbf{R} = \mathbf{Z'Z}/N \quad \text{(Eq. 4.30)}$$
Reproduction of **R** from the Factor Loadings,
$$\mathbf{R} = \mathbf{AA'} \quad \text{(Eq. 4.32)}$$
Computation of Residuals, $\mathbf{R}_m = \mathbf{R} - \mathbf{AA'}$
$$\text{(Eq. 4.34)}$$
The Factor Model, $\mathbf{Z} = \mathbf{FA'}$ (Eq. 4.35)

Note that the product $\mathbf{Z'Z}$ is symmetric; for $(\mathbf{Z'Z})' = \mathbf{Z'Z}$ by the rules considered above. This result holds for the product of any matrix by its transpose. But $\mathbf{ZZ'}$, which is also symmetric, is *not* the same as $\mathbf{Z'Z}$; we shall discuss the analysis of $\mathbf{ZZ'}$ in Chapter 7, as its elements are measures of similarity between legislators and may be used in the identification of blocs or factions.

The correlation matrix $\mathbf{R}$, in addition to being calculated from the matrix $\mathbf{Z}$ of standard scores, can also be reproduced from the matrix $\mathbf{A}$ of factor loadings. Using the same notation as for regression, we denote the matrix of reproduced correlations as $\hat{\mathbf{R}}$. Then if we rewrite (4.22), generalizing it to the case of m factors, we obtain

$$\hat{r}_{jk} = a_{j1}a_{k1} + a_{j2}a_{k2} + \ldots + a_{jm}a_{km} \tag{4.31}$$

With these conventions, the matrix of reproduced correlations is given by the matrix equation

$$\hat{\mathbf{R}} = \mathbf{AA'} \tag{4.32}$$

This operation is also shown in Figure 4.3. The matrix $\mathbf{R}$, as reproduced in this way from the factor-loading matrix $\mathbf{A}$, has as its off-diagonal elements the approximations to the initial correlations r_{jk}. Its diagonal elements are sums of squares of factor loadings, known as the *communalities* and denoted by the symbol h^2:

$$h_j^2 = a_{j1}^2 + a_{j2}^2 + \ldots + a_{jm}^2 \tag{4.33}$$

In (4.33), h_j^2 is equivalent to the squared distance of the point j from the origin in an m-dimensional space. It was because of this convention that the distances of the points j and k from the origin in Figure 4.2 were designated h_j and h_k. The communality measures the proportion of variance of a variable that is accounted for by the factors that have been computed, and is normally less than unity.[22]

We can now express the computation of residuals by introducing the operation of matrix subtraction. *Addition* and *subtraction* of matrices are defined as addition and subtraction of corresponding elements, the results becoming corresponding elements of the sum or

---

[22]When ordinary correlation coefficients are used, h^2 never exceeds unity except in the "Heywood case" where an artificially lower rank can be obtained by higher h^2; see Harman, *op. cit.*, pp. 117–118. But for coefficients such as Q, this assumption is violated more often.

difference. Thus two matrices can be added or subtracted only if they have the same number of rows and the same number of columns. Addition of matrices, like addition of ordinary numbers, is commutative. In these terms, the residual after m factors can be expressed as

$$\mathbf{R}_m = \mathbf{R} - \hat{\mathbf{R}}_m = \mathbf{R} - \mathbf{AA}' \qquad (4.34)$$

where $\hat{\mathbf{R}}_m$ denotes the reproduced matrix after m factors, and the elements of $\hat{\mathbf{R}}_m$ are $_m\hat{r}_{jk}$. The distribution of residuals after m factors has sometimes been used as a criterion as to how many factors should be computed.

The matrix operations of (4.30), (4.32), and (4.34) can be visualized more clearly if the matrices involved are shown as rectangles, as in Figure 4.3.

In addition, equations (4.26) above are special cases of another matrix equation, which can be expressed in terms of the reproduced standard scores $\hat{z}_{ij}$ instead of the observed standard scores:

$$\hat{\mathbf{Z}} = \mathbf{FA}' \qquad (4.35)$$

where $\hat{\mathbf{Z}}$ is the reproduced matrix of standard scores and $\mathbf{F}$ is the matrix of factor scores for individual legislators.[23] Equation (4.35) is also represented in Figure 4.3. In the figure, we assume the largest dimension to correspond to the number of legislators, N (say, 200); the next largest, the number of roll calls, n (say, 100); and the smallest, the number of factors, m (say, 25).

A third application of matrix multiplication is to the rotation that transforms one system of coordinates (factor loadings) into another. We have seen in (4.23) that the reproduced correlation coefficient can be expressed in a form that depends only on the distances of two points in the factor space from the origin (the h's) and the angle between the two corresponding lines from the origin. This implies that if a new set of rectangular coordinates were defined with the same origin as that from which the initial factor loadings were plotted, the loadings or coordinates in the new system would give rise to the same reproduced correlation coefficients as before.

The computation of such new coordinates (rotated factor loadings) must be carried out if new rotated coordinates are preferred to the

---

[23]The form of this equation differs from that in Harman (*op. cit.*, p. 25), because we have let the rows of the data matrix correspond to legislators rather than roll calls.

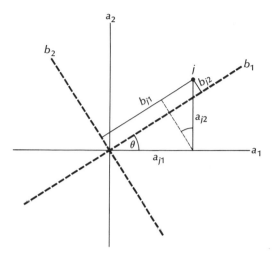

FIGURE 4.4. Orthogonal Rotation of Factorial Axes.

old.[24] The procedure can be shown in two dimensions with the aid of trigonometric functions. In Figure 4.4, the horizontal and vertical axes represent the initial factors 1 and 2, and the dashed axes represent a new pair of axes, also perpendicular (orthogonal) to one another but rotated counter-clockwise relative to the initial axes 1 and 2 by an angle θ. We denote the initial axes by a_1 and a_2, the transformed matrix of factor loadings by **B**, and the rotated axes by b_1 and b_2. In this notation

$$b_{j1} = a_{j1}\cos \theta + a_{j2}\sin \theta \quad \text{and} \quad b_{j2} = -a_{j1}\sin \theta + a_{j2}\cos \theta$$

$$(4.36)$$

Equations (4.36) define the projections of point j on axes b_1 and b_2. If we let the index j vary, each point corresponding to a value of j has its coordinates transformed by the same equations. If we then consider the $n \times 2$ matrix **A**, we can express its conversion into another $n \times 2$ matrix **B** by the matrix equation

$$\mathbf{B} = \mathbf{AT} \qquad (4.37)$$

[24]The most frequently used criterion for coordinate rotation is Kaiser's Varimax criterion; see Harman, *op. cit.*, pp. 304–313. We shall consider coordinate rotation again in Chapter 8.

where a typical row of **B** is (b_{j1}, b_{j2}), the corresponding row of **A** is (a_{j1}, a_{j2}), and the transformation matrix **T** is

$$\begin{bmatrix} \cos\theta & -\sin\theta \\ \sin\theta & \cos\theta \end{bmatrix}$$

This expression can also be generalized to multiple dimensions. In this general case, the transformation defined by the matrix **T** preserves distances, angles, and reproduced correlations, and is said to be *orthogonal,* if **T'T** = **I,** the identity matrix. This condition is equivalent to **TT'** = **I**.[25] Other transformation matrices that do not preserve angles will nevertheless preserve straight lines; we shall discuss them in Chapters 7 and 8, as *shearing* transformations.

After an initial set of factor loadings has been computed, transformation procedures such as those represented by (4.36) and (4.37) may be used to compute loadings on a new set of preferred axes, rotated with respect to the initial ones. It is possible, of course, that the initial procedure for computing factor loadings may lead directly to the preferred axes. The method of principal components (discussed in the next chapter) gives rise to a set of axes that successively account for greatest sums of squares in the data; if this is the criterion of preference, no further rotation is needed from this solution. Cluster analysis procedures such as the BC TRY procedures described above also lead to axes that may not require further rotation, as they are chosen so as to pass through clusters of points lying close to one another in the factor space, and thus clustering is another possible criterion of preference for axes.[26] Procedures that circumvent the problem of rotation, such as clustering the distance matrix from the factor space, also render rotation unnecessary.[27]

But the most common procedure in the social sciences is first to compute factor loadings based on principal components, and then rotate them in order to produce variables that can be interpreted more easily in conceptual or theoretical terms. Such rotation can be done by direct introduction of information based on concepts or hy-

[25]On the preservation of distances see Harman, *op. cit.,* pp. 54–55. On the equivalence to **TT'** = *I*, see Mac Lane and Birkhoff, *Algebra,* pp. 400–401.

[26]The multiple-group procedure for factor analysis also has this property; see Harman, *op. cit.,* chap. 11.

[27]See Tables 3.6 and 5.4.

potheses, but it is more common to attempt a rotation of coordinates based only on the numerical properties of the factor loadings. One method in widespread use for this purpose is Kaiser's Varimax procedure, which performs a succession of two-dimensional rotations on the factors until a certain criterion function is maximized. This function relates to the distribution of factor loadings in the matrix **A**. Before the procedure is carried out, the rows of **A** are first normalized, i.e., multiplied by respective constants to make the sum of squares of factor loadings in each row equal to unity. Then the distributions of loadings in the columns, for each factor, are considered. The variance of the squared factor loadings is computed for each factor, and the sum of these variances is then maximized. The result is that after rotation each factor tends to have some high loadings and some near-zero loadings, and a greater parsimony is attained in the description of the variables (roll calls).[28]

The reasoning underlying the Varimax criterion, and others related to it, relates to an earlier criterion proposed by Thurstone—that of "simple structure." In the precomputer era, rotation was done graphically and depended on subjective judgments by the researcher. One of the major criteria of these procedures was to obtain axes or rotated factors that described the data more simply than the initial factors, i.e., had as many as possible near-zero entries in the factor-loading matrix. A special case of such a criterion would correspond to a factor which was also a cluster, i.e., one on which certain roll calls had high loadings, these roll calls also having near-zero loadings on all other factors. This special case was not ordinarily sought in the Thurstone procedure, nor will it appear generally as a result of the Varimax procedure; it depends on the presence of clusters in the data and their correspondence to the dimensional model used, both in orthogonality and in number of dimensions.[29]

The Varimax criterion and others like it provide not only an objective counterpart for the formerly subjective rotation procedures, but also a measure of the simplicity of structure obtained (the final value of the criterion function), so that the simplicity of one rotated configuration can be compared with that of another.

[28]We have described the "normal Varimax" version, which is most commonly used. After rotation the row sums of squares are returned to their initial values, the communalities. See Harman, *op. cit.*, pp. 304 ff.

[29]See Chapter 5, section on "Clustering Roll Calls in the Factor Space."

These procedures, developed largely in psychometrics, define simplicity of structure solely by the configuration of points in the factor-loading space. But as we shall see, the factor-score space corresponds in its dimensions to the factor-loading space, and provides additional information for choosing preferred coordinates. In particular, we shall find the factor-score space important for the investigation of party differences and partisanship (in Chapter 8).

So far we have discussed rotation only in relation to factor loadings. But to anticipate our discussion in Chapter 8 of factor scores, we may present the necessary matrix relations here. Consider first equation (4.35), $\hat{Z} = FA'$, as it is affected by rotation. If we introduce a rotation matrix T producing a new factor-loading matrix B according to the equation $B = AT$ (4.37), what changes in F will be necessary if we are again to account for Z as before the rotation? We can show that if F is rotated in exactly the same way, the reproduced matrix $\hat{Z}$ will be the same. For

$$FT(AT)' = FT(T'A') = F(TT')A' = FIA' = FA' = \hat{Z} \qquad (4.38)$$

as before.

A similar proof will show that the orthogonality relation between the factor scores is invariant under rotation of this type. This relation may be expressed by the equation

$$\frac{F'F}{N} = I \qquad (4.39)$$

as reference to Figure 4.3 will remind us that this product sums over the longer (legislator) dimension of F and produces a small $m \times m$ identity matrix. The zeros off the main diagonal of this matrix reflect the fact that factor scores on different factors are independent of one another, subject to the conditions of the derivation following (4.27). The values of unity on the diagonal of I reflect the fact that the factor scores (columns of F) are standard scores, as stated when the notation of F was introduced at (4.26).

If F is transformed by a rotation matrix into FT, then the product $F'F/N$ will become

$$\frac{(FT)'FT}{N} = \frac{(T'F')FT}{N} = T'IT = T'T = I$$

as before.

5.
PRINCIPAL-COMPONENT ANALYSIS
AND ROLL-CALL DATA

WE shall now introduce one of the most frequently used methods of computing factor loadings, making use of the matrix operations treated in the preceding chapter. This method—principal-component analysis—will first be introduced briefly as a means of analyzing the correlation matrix. Then we shall go back one step, to the data matrix, and show that the method can be derived from operations on that matrix as well. This will lead us to the computation of factor scores (legislator scores on the factors). Finally, we shall consider the problems involved in applying this method to roll-call data, whose dichotomous character gives rise to certain compromises of technique that depart from the initial assumptions of principal component analysis.

PRINCIPAL-COMPONENT ANALYSIS[1]

Most of the results we have presented so far are valid for a wide variety of choices of the initial and subsequent factors.

[1]Harman distinguishes this from "principal factor analysis," which uses estimates of communality instead of unity as diagonal elements of **R** (*Modern Factor Analysis*, pp. 136–137). We omit the problems of estimating communality, both for simplicity of exposition and because the diagonal elements do not appreciably affect our results when large data matrices are used, few factors are computed, and factor loadings are high.

We have also implied that the adequacy of a solution—a matrix **A** of factor loadings—is unaffected by orthogonal rotations of the coordinate axes, which substitute one set of factor loadings for another. There is, however, a sense in which we can ask that the first factor we compute be the best possible, and each subsequent one also be the best possible at that stage. This is the least-squares sense, in that each factor may be chosen so that its factor loadings make a maximum contribution to the total communality, i.e., to the sum of squares that the factor accounts for in the data.[2] This requirement gives rise to definite sets of loadings on successive factors, each set corresponding to an *eigenvector* or *principal component*. The name "eigenvector" derives from the definition of a vector, which we must now give.

In relation to our treatment of matrices, a vector can be most simply defined as a one-row or one-column matrix. To indicate this similarity, we shall denote vectors by lower-case boldface letters, e.g., the vector **v**. Vectors can be added, subtracted, and multiplied according to the rules for matrices. We speak of a $1 \times n$ matrix as a *row vector* and an $n \times 1$ matrix as a *column vector*.

A set of n numbers constituting a vector may be considered geometrically as well as in matrix terms, for it defines the position of a point in n-dimensional space. We have already interpreted the rows in the factor-loading matrix **A** in this fashion, in considering the problem of rotation in a space whose dimensions corresponded to factors. A column of a matrix may also be interpreted as a vector, though the number of dimensions will in general be different for columns and for rows. But in either case, a vector has another property that we have not so far considered in connection with matrices: the distance of the point it defines from the origin. This distance is the square root of the sum of squares of the components or elements of the vector:

$$|\mathbf{v}| = (v_1{}^2 + v_2{}^2 + \ldots + v_n{}^2)^{1/2}$$

This distance is known as the *magnitude* or norm of the vector. In Figure 4.2, the distances h_j and h_k, the square roots of the communali-

---

[2]This criterion has three variants. The best known, principal-component analysis, maximizes the sum of squares accounted for in the data *and* in the correlation matrix. The variant we shall use later, involving factoring of the Q-matrix, has no direct relation to the data matrix. Third, the "minres" solution has been proposed to minimize the residual sum of squares in the correlation matrix, but only for off-diagonal elements; see Harman, *op. cit.,* chap. 9.

ties, were the magnitudes of the vectors **j** and **k.** We shall make use of this feature of vectors in the next section.

Any square matrix has a set of *characteristic vectors* (in German, *Eigenvektoren*) which correspond to fundamental features of the matrix; a substantial mathematical literature exists concerning their properties.[3] We state without proof at this point that these are the factors that are best in the least-squares sense, and we now define them more precisely and present a procedure for computing them.

If a square matrix is premultiplied by a vector of the appropriate dimensionality, the result will be another vector of the same dimensionality. A defining feature of an eigenvector of a matrix is that if it is used in this multiplication, the result will be another vector proportional in each of its elements to the initial vector, i.e.,

$$\mathbf{v}_p\mathbf{S} = \lambda_p\mathbf{v}_p \tag{5.1}$$

where

S — any square matrix,

$\mathbf{v}_p$ = a row vector, the pth eigenvector of **S** satisfying (5.1), and

λ_p = the corresponding multiplicative constant, known as the pth *eigenvalue*, characteristic root, or latent root of the matrix.

We have assumed $\mathbf{v}_p$ to be a row vector, but a column vector $\mathbf{u}_p$ can also satisfy the equation $\mathbf{S}\mathbf{u}_p = \lambda_p\mathbf{u}_p$, with the set of λ_p the same as in (5.1) but $\mathbf{u} \neq \mathbf{v}$ in general unless **S** is symmetric. The number of eigenvalues or eigenvectors cannot exceed the order (number of rows or columns) of **S**.

If **S** is multiplied by itself to yield a new matrix denoted by $\mathbf{S}^2$, the eigenvectors and eigenvalues of $\mathbf{S}^2$ bear a simple relation to those of **S.** For (5.1) implies that if **v** is an eigenvector of **S**

$$\mathbf{v}\mathbf{S}^2 = (\mathbf{v}\mathbf{S})\mathbf{S} = (\lambda\mathbf{v})\mathbf{S} = \lambda(\mathbf{v}\mathbf{S}) = \lambda(\lambda\mathbf{v}) = \lambda^2\mathbf{v} \tag{5.2}$$

Hence any **v** which was an eigenvector of **S** is also an eigenvector of $\mathbf{S}^2$; and the corresponding eigenvalue of $\mathbf{S}^2$ is the square of the eigenvalue of **S.** We shall use this result below.

If **S** is a symmetric matrix (as it is for the indices of association we shall consider), then **u** and **v** will be the same (one will be the trans-

[3]See, for example, Mac Lane and Birkhoff, *Algebra,* pp. 290–293; Halmos, *Finite-Dimensional Vector Spaces,* pp. 102, 105; Stewart, *Introduction to Linear Algebra,* pp. 214–217; Bodewig, *Matrix Calculus.*

pose of the other) and there will be no difference between the eigen-vectors found by pre- and postmultiplication. Moreover, if **S** is sym-metric, all values of λ_p will be real (nonimaginary); and if **S** is pro-duced by multiplying a matrix (e.g., a data matrix) by its transpose, they will be nonnegative. This last property may also be expressed by saying that **S** is Gramian or positive semidefinite.[4] If **S** is the correla-tion matrix **R**, with unities on its diagonal, then none of its λ's will be negative.

The eigenvectors are usually computed in descending order of λ_p. One method of computing them is to start with any row vector of the appropriate number of elements, postmultiply it by the (symmetric) matrix **S**, and repeat the process over and over with the resulting vectors. This iterative procedure can be expressed

$$\mathbf{v}_k\mathbf{S} = \mathbf{v}_{k+1} \tag{5.3}$$

where the subscript now indicates the number of the repetition or iteration of the process. It can be shown that ordinarily the result will eventually be the first eigenvector, i.e., the one with largest λ. If **S** is the correlation matrix, the value of λ also measures the contribu-tion of the eigenvector to the overall communality, and thus the first eigenvector is also best in the least-squares sense.[5]

The matrices of associations with which we shall deal in analyzing roll-call data will ordinarily have of the order of 100 rows or columns, and thus can have an equally large number of eigenvectors. In prin-ciple some of the eigenvalues may be zero, but with actual data the question is usually how many are sufficiently important to analyze. We shall usually interpret only a few.

The vector $\mathbf{v}_p$ in (5.1) is still undefined within a multiplicative con-stant, for both sides of (5.1) may be multiplied by such a constant. If, however, the sum of squares of the elements of $\mathbf{v}_p$ is set equal to λ_p, the elements will be properly adjusted to correspond to factor load-

[4]This property of correlation matrices is referred to by Guttman in Stouffer et al., *Measurement and Prediction, passim.* See also Nering, *Linear Algebra and Matrix Theory*, p. 150; and Harman, *op. cit.*, p. 62.

[5]If the initial vector $\mathbf{v}_1$ is nonzero and is not a subsequent eigenvector of **S**, then it can be shown that the iterative procedure will converge to the first eigenvector; see Harman, *op. cit.*, p. 144. For the relation to sums of squares, see *ibid.*, pp. 137–141, and the following section of this chapter.

ings, and the vector thus adjusted in scale may be referred to as $\mathbf{a}_p$ (which is customarily treated as a column vector). This adjustment will be justified by a proof below at (5.12).

Once the multiplicative constant of $\mathbf{v}_p$ is adjusted in this way, this vector can be considered as a set of factor loadings $\mathbf{a}_p$ (i.e., as a column of $\mathbf{A}$). It may be used to compute the reproduced correlations, and residuals can be found as before. If the same computational procedure is repeated on the residual matrix, the result will be the next eigenvector (i.e., the one with the next highest λ) of the original matrix.[6]

The sets of factor loadings, or vectors, computed in this way have another important property: for any two such vectors

$$\sum_j a_{jp}a_{jq} = 0 \quad \text{if } p \neq q$$

Two vectors having this property are said to be *orthogonal* to one another.[7] Thus the product $\mathbf{A'A}$ is a diagonal matrix with the λ's on its principal diagonal and zeros elsewhere. This relation is peculiar to the principal-component solution, and can be destroyed by rotation of coordinates.

The fact that the eigenvectors are best in a least-squares sense has led statisticians to prefer them. However, these factor loadings may be used for further rotation as well, and they may be calculated initially simply in order to account for a maximum proportion of variance for a given number of factors computed. The values of λ have also been used as a basis of decisions as to how many factors should be computed before stopping factoring.[8]

We now present a numerical example of principal-component analysis of a correlation matrix. (Exercise: carry out the indicated numerical operations.) The matrix with which we start is a hypothetical 3×3 correlation matrix $\mathbf{R}$ whose elements can be described in terms of a single factor; to attain this simplicity we use the equivalent of communalities, rather than unities, on the diagonal.

[6]Harman, *op. cit.*, pp. 142–143.

[7]This relation should not be confused, however, with the analogous relation between factor *scores*, in terms of which factor solutions are classified as "orthogonal" or "oblique." The principal-component solution is not the only orthogonal solution, in the latter sense.

[8]Harman, *op. cit.*, pp. 167–169.

Let

$$\mathbf{R} = \begin{bmatrix} .64 & .48 & .32 \\ .48 & .36 & .24 \\ .32 & .24 & .16 \end{bmatrix}$$

and let

$$\mathbf{v}_1 = [1 \ 1 \ 1]$$

then

$$\mathbf{v}_1\mathbf{R} = \mathbf{v}_2 = [1.44 \quad 1.08 \quad .72]$$

The row vector of ones is chosen simply as a convenient starting point. In the centroid method of factoring, which became obsolete with the advent of computers, a vector of ones (with plus or minus signs) was used in this way for one iteration only, and the resulting $\mathbf{v}_2$ was used for the first factor.[9]

Since the elements of $\mathbf{v}_2$ are not related to those of $\mathbf{v}_1$ by a constant ratio, (5.1) is not yet satisfied, and $\mathbf{v}_1$ is not an eigenvector of $\mathbf{R}$. We thus continue by forming the product $\mathbf{v}_2\mathbf{R}$; but before doing so, we can adjust $\mathbf{v}_2$ by a multiplicative constant for convenience. One method, used by Hotelling when he initially proposed this iterative procedure, is to divide by the largest element of $\mathbf{v}_2$.[10] This leads to

$$\mathbf{v}_2/1.44 = [1.00 \quad .75 \quad .50]$$

If we rename the resulting vector $\mathbf{v}_2$ and postmultiply it by $\mathbf{R}$, we obtain

$$\mathbf{v}_2\mathbf{R} = [1.00 \quad .75 \quad .50] \begin{bmatrix} .64 & .48 & .32 \\ .48 & .36 & .24 \\ .32 & .24 & .16 \end{bmatrix} = [1.16 \quad .87 \quad .58] = \mathbf{v}_3 = 1.16\mathbf{v}_2$$

Since $\mathbf{v}_3$ is equal to a constant, 1.16, times $\mathbf{v}_2$, we have found the first eigenvector and eigenvalue of $\mathbf{R}$. The process usually requires much more computation, but computers make such calculations possible routinely.

We then set the multiplicative constant to transform $\mathbf{v}$ into $\mathbf{a}_1$ (whose subscript is now the number of the factor, rather than the iteration). To do this, let the desired vector equal $k\mathbf{v}_2$ and solve for k.

[9]See for example Fruchter, *Introduction to Factor Analysis*, chap. 5.

[10]Hotelling, "Analysis of a Complex of Statistical Variables into Principal Components," p. 432.

(The resulting vector would be the same if we started with any constant times v_2.) The sum of squares of the elements of the vector is

$$k^2(1.00) + k^2(.5625) + k^2(.25) = 1.16$$

Hence

$$k^2(1.8125) = 1.16$$

$$k^2 = .64$$

and

$$k = .8$$

Multiplying by the values of v_2, we obtain the solution

$$\mathbf{a}_1 = \begin{bmatrix} .8 \\ .6 \\ .4 \end{bmatrix}$$

which reproduces the values of $\mathbf{R}$ exactly. (Note that $\mathbf{a}$ is conventionally shown as a column vector.) Since the residuals are zero, the remaining eigenvalues are zero and of no interest. The alternative solution, $k = -.8$, would give rise to a set of factor loadings inverted in sign from $\mathbf{a}_1$, which would also have reproduced $\mathbf{R}$ exactly; this corresponds to a 180° rotation, and except for the convenience of positive signs, is completely equivalent to $\mathbf{a}_1$. In subsequent examples, we shall sometimes invert the signs of all loadings on a given factor, knowing that no important properties are altered.

Note also that in the preceding example, the value λ was just equal to the sum of the diagonal elements of the initial matrix $\mathbf{R}$: $.64 + .36 + .16 = 1.16$. This is a special case of a general property of the eigenvalues of a matrix: the sum of all the eigenvalues must equal the sum of the diagonal elements of the matrix, this sum being known as the *trace* of the matrix.

A further example will show an elementary two-factor case. Suppose the 3×3 matrix we have just analyzed is augmented by two additional rows and columns to form the matrix

$$\begin{bmatrix} .64 & .48 & .32 & 0 & 0 \\ .48 & .36 & .24 & 0 & 0 \\ .32 & .24 & .16 & 0 & 0 \\ 0 & 0 & 0 & .36 & .36 \\ 0 & 0 & 0 & .36 & .36 \end{bmatrix}$$

The first eigenvector of this matrix will be $(.8, .6, .4, 0, 0)$. This may be verified by substituting it as v_1 in (5.1). (Exercise: perform this verification.) Numerous iterations would be required, however, to produce it from an initial **v** consisting of a row of five 1's. If we then calculate the residuals, all that will be left other than 0's will be the four entries of .36 in the lower right-hand corner. The residual matrix will have the eigenvector (0, 0, 0, .6, .6), and the eigenvalue .72. (Exercise: verify this.) Since this eigenvalue is less than λ_1, which was 1.16, it will be obtained from the residual matrix, but not from the original unless a precise multiple of this vector is used in (5.1).

The sum of the two eigenvalues is again equal to the trace of the correlation matrix, 1.16 + .72. We can see in an approximate way that the eigenvalue measures the importance of the contribution of the corresponding eigenvector. It is roughly analogous to the proportion of all roll calls that enter a particular cluster—hence a possible measure of the importance of clusters such as we found in Chapter 3.[11]

FACTORING THE DATA MATRIX

The operations of principal-component analysis can also be derived by starting from the data matrix rather than the correlation matrix. If we approach them in this way, we shall also see the relation between factor loadings on roll calls and factor scores of legislators. The procedure we shall discuss has been referred to as "direct factor analysis,"[12] though it is considered in much of the factor-analysis literature as simply a convenient relation between factor loadings and factor scores that obtains for principal components of the correlation matrix.[13]

The following procedure is applicable to any data matrix. It is most

[11]See MacRae, "A Method for Identifying Issues and Factions from Legislative Votes," pp. 923–924.

[12]See MacRae, "Direct Factor Analysis of Sociometric Data"; MacRae and Meldrum, "Critical Elections in Illinois, 1888–1958"; Harman, *op. cit.,* p. 348; Horst, *Factor Analysis of Data Matrices,* chap. 12; Woodbury and Siler, "Factor Analysis with Missing Data"; Good, *The Estimation of Probabilities,* pp. 61–64.

[13]Principal components may also be defined, especially in the statistical literature, as optimal linear combinations of variables in the data matrix. See T. W. Anderson, *Introduction to Multivariate Statistical Analysis,* chap. 11; and M. G. Kendall, *A Course in Multivariate Statistical Analysis,* chap. 2.

closely related to our preceding treatment of principal-component analysis of the correlation matrix, however, if the data matrix with which we start is one of standard scores. For since $R = Z'Z/N$, we can define a new matrix $X = Z/\sqrt{N}$, so that $R = X'X$. We shall deal with a general data matrix X, which in this particular case gives rise to the correlation matrix. In Chapter 7, we shall consider alternative operations on the raw data matrix that give rise to various forms of X, and the consequences of these alternatives for factor analysis.

Given a data matrix X whose elements are indicated as x_{ij}, we seek a pair of vectors u (a column vector, for legislators) and v (a row vector, for roll calls), whose product uv will best approximate X in a least-squares sense.[14] The problem is analogous to a regression problem, and we can write

$$\hat{X} = uv \tag{5.4}$$

for the reproduced values in the matrix $\hat{X}$. A further aspect of the analogy is that we are not only minimizing the sum of squares of the residuals, but at the same time maximizing the sum of squares (or variance) accounted for.

Since u is a one-column vector and v a one-row vector, each element of $\hat{X}$ will be calculated as a single product rather than a sum of products. The same type of multiplication could have been used to express equation (4.20), $r_{jk} = r_{jt}r_{kt}$, where each correlation reproduced in this way was computed as a single product. Still more closely analogous is equation (4.35), $\hat{Z} = FA'$; the diagram of this multiplication in Figure 4.3 also illustrates (5.4) above.

The condition that (5.4) furnish a least-squares fit corresponds to minimizing the sum

$$\sum_i \sum_j (x_{ij} - \hat{x}_{ij})^2 = \sum_i \sum_j (x_{ij} - u_i v_j)^2$$

To minimize this sum of squares, we differentiate with respect to u_i and v_j and obtain two sets of equations. For the u_i we obtain N

---

[14]This derivation was given by W. Turanski at a lecture at the University of Chicago in 1957. Several treatments of an analogous problem have been given in the literature. See Guttman in Stouffer et al., op. cit., pp. 334–361; and Alker, "Statistics and Politics," Appendix. These latter treatments, however, characterize each category of an item (e.g., yea or nay) by a column in the data matrix.

equations corresponding to the rows of **X**, and for the v_j, n equations corresponding to the columns:

$$-2\Sigma_j v_j(x_{ij} - u_i v_j) = 0$$

$$-2\Sigma_i u_i(x_{ij} - u_i v_j) = 0 \tag{5.5}$$

Each of these sets of equations can be expressed as a matrix equation. We first recall our notation for the squared magnitudes of **u** and **v**:

$$\Sigma_i u_i^2 = |\mathbf{u}|^2 \qquad \Sigma_j v_j^2 = |\mathbf{v}|^2$$

In this notation, equations (5.5) reduce to

$$\frac{\mathbf{Xv'}}{|\mathbf{v}|^2} = \mathbf{u} \qquad \frac{\mathbf{u'X}}{|\mathbf{u}|^2} = \mathbf{v} \tag{5.6}$$

These equations define the vectors **u** and **v,** and lead to the multiple solutions of an eigenvector problem (as we shall see). They are also subject to an indeterminate multiplicative constant; for if **v** is multiplied by such a constant k, $|\mathbf{v}|^2$ is correspondingly multiplied by k^2, and **u** is divided by the same constant, the left-hand equation of (5.6) will still hold. The corresponding multiplication, maintaining the product **uv,** will also leave the right-hand equation of (5.6) unaltered.

Equations (5.6) can be combined to give two eigenvector equations. For if we transpose the left equation of (5.6) to give $\mathbf{u'} = \mathbf{vX'}/|\mathbf{v}|^2$, and substitute in the right equation, we obtain

$$\frac{\mathbf{vX'X}}{|\mathbf{u}|^2|\mathbf{v}|^2} = \mathbf{v} \qquad \text{or} \qquad \mathbf{vX'X} = |\mathbf{u}|^2|\mathbf{v}|^2\mathbf{v} \tag{5.7}$$

(Exercise: obtain [5.7] from [5.6] in this way.) Thus the desired **v** is an eigenvector of **X'X,** or in the particular case we have discussed, of **R.** The form of the right-hand equation in (5.7) parrallels that of (5.1), and it is for this reason that the eigenvector in (5.1) was symbolized as **v.**

We can also perform the opposite substitution, by transposing the right-hand equation of (5.6) to give $\mathbf{v'} = \mathbf{X'u}/|\mathbf{u}|^2$ and substituting in the left equation, obtaining

$$\mathbf{XX'u} = |\mathbf{u}|^2|\mathbf{v}|^2\mathbf{u} \tag{5.8}$$

This equation indicates that **u** is an eigenvector of another matrix product, **XX',** and the eigenvalues for (5.7) and (5.8) are the same, equal to $|\mathbf{u}|^2|\mathbf{v}|^2$, though we have not yet specified a procedure for calculating these numbers.

We can compute the eigenvectors $\mathbf{u}$ and $\mathbf{v}$ by an iterative procedure related to the one described in the preceding section in connection with (5.3). We begin with the matrix $\mathbf{X}$, and perform a set of iterative multiplications on it, alternately postmultiplying and premultiplying. We may start with a trial column vector, which might be a column of ones or a transposed row of $\mathbf{X}$:

$$\mathbf{X}\mathbf{v}_k' = \mathbf{u}_k \qquad \mathbf{u}_k'\mathbf{X} = \mathbf{v}_{k+1} \qquad (5.9)$$

The subscript index k denotes the iteration number, as in (5.3).

But instead of this alternating iterative procedure we can carry out two such procedures, each similar to (5.3). One of these is obtained by substituting the left-hand equation of (5.9) in the right, after transposing both sides of the left equation:

$$\mathbf{v}_k\mathbf{X}'\mathbf{X} = \mathbf{v}_{k+1} \qquad (5.10)$$

The other is obtained similarly, by incrementing the index in the left equation of (5.9), then substituting the right equation in it, after transposing both sides of the right equation:

$$\mathbf{X}\mathbf{X}'\mathbf{u}_k = \mathbf{u}_{k+1} \qquad (5.11)$$

Both (5.10) and (5.11) are of the form corresponding to the iterative procedure for finding the eigenvectors of a matrix. The iterations are expected to converge, and at convergence the vector $\mathbf{v}_{k+1}$ is equal to a constant times $\mathbf{v}_k$. The same is true for $\mathbf{u}_{k+1}$ and $\mathbf{u}_k$, and the constant for both is the eigenvalue, for we have shown in (5.7) and (5.8) that the same eigenvalue enters into both.

Equations (5.9) provide a procedure for finding $\mathbf{u}$ and $\mathbf{v}$, but they leave both undetermined by a multiplicative constant. We can solve for the eigenvalue of $\mathbf{X}'\mathbf{X}$ or $\mathbf{X}\mathbf{X}'$ by any of the available procedures for this purpose, including iteration, and we know from (5.7) and (5.8) that we must set

$$|\mathbf{u}|^2|\mathbf{v}|^2 = \lambda$$

for the solution to be a least-squares fit to $\mathbf{X}$.[15]

---

[15]This equation also shows that λ must be non-negative for $\mathbf{X}'\mathbf{X}$ or $\mathbf{X}\mathbf{X}'$. If the iterative procedure of (5.9) is used, the eigenvalue can also be found, at convergence, by use of the equation $\lambda = |\mathbf{u}_k|^2/|\mathbf{v}_k|^2$. (Exercise: prove this.)

If after solution the residual data matrix, $\mathbf{X} - \mathbf{uv}$, is factored in the same way, another pair of eigenvalues of $\mathbf{XX'}$ and $\mathbf{X'X}$ will be found.[16] Successive computation of these pairs of eigenvectors will yield all the eigenvectors of $\mathbf{XX'}$ and $\mathbf{X'X}$—a number that cannot exceed the smaller dimension of $\mathbf{X}$. The resulting matrices may be designated $\mathbf{U}$ and $\mathbf{V}$. Then the matrix equation $\hat{\mathbf{X}} = \mathbf{UV}$ is simply another form of equation (4.35) $\hat{\mathbf{Z}} = \mathbf{FA'}$, with $\mathbf{X} = \mathbf{Z}/\sqrt{N}$, $\mathbf{U} = \mathbf{F}/\sqrt{N}$, and $\mathbf{V} = \mathbf{A'}$. (See also Figure 4.3.)

Alternatively, we can factor the smaller matrix of the two ($\mathbf{XX'}$ or $\mathbf{X'X}$), and then obtain the other set of eigenvectors by using one of the equations (5.6). If $\mathbf{X} = \mathbf{Z}/\sqrt{N}$, $\mathbf{X'X} = \mathbf{R}$, and by setting $|\mathbf{v}|^2 = \lambda$ we can insure (as we shall show below at [5.12]) that the $\mathbf{v}$'s are proportional to factor loadings in the conventional sense. The $\mathbf{u}$'s will then be proportional to the corresponding factor scores, as $|\mathbf{u}|^2 = 1$ and the squared magnitude of a corresponding column of $\mathbf{F}$ is N.

Any of the various computer procedures for calculating eigenvectors and eigenvalues may be used here, and some are superior to the iterative procedure of (5.9); we describe only this procedure because its exposition involves the same operations as in the derivation in (5.5), which in turn follows reasoning parallel to that in regression analysis.

The correspondence we have noticed between the eigenvalues and eigenvectors of $\mathbf{XX'}$ and $\mathbf{X'X}$ relates to one of the major themes with which we shall be concerned. For while $\mathbf{X'X}$ corresponds to the matrix of correlations between roll calls according to the conventions we have used, $\mathbf{XX'}$ corresponds to a matrix of indices of agreement or similarity between legislators. Thus if we choose to measure similarity between legislators in this way, it will necessarily have close and precise relations to similarity between roll calls. One way to express this relation is to say that legislators' factor *scores* on the factors found from $\mathbf{X'X}$ will be proportional to their factor *loadings* as found from $\mathbf{XX'}$, and conversely. We are thus again reminded of the close interconnection between the study of issues and that of factions from roll-call votes; we shall clarify this further in Chapters 7 and 8.

---

[16]This general relation for square matrices is known as "deflation"; see Bodewig, *op. cit.* For residuals of the data matrix it can also be shown that if the residual is $\mathbf{X}_1 = \mathbf{X} - \mathbf{uv}$, then $\mathbf{X}_1'\mathbf{X}_1$ is also equal to the residual of $\mathbf{X'X}$, provided that $|\mathbf{v}|^2$ is set equal to λ.

FACTOR LOADINGS
AND FACTOR SCORES

So far we have found solutions for two vectors **u** and **v** which together account for the data matrix **X**. For the matrix product **uv** to correspond optimally to **X**, a constraint must be placed on the multiplicative constants of **u** and **v**. Neither **u** nor **v** need be exactly determined in this solution, but the product of their two multiplicative constants is so determined. This condition holds for each column of the matrix **U** and each corresponding row of the matrix **V**.

The solution we have found is proportional to that expressed by the basic model of factor analysis, in which the data matrix (of standard scores) is approximated by a matrix product of factor loadings and factor scores: $\hat{Z} = FA'$, equation (4.35). Yet in that model the factor loadings and factor scores are exactly determined. We shall now derive the additional condition necessary for the two solutions to coincide.

The basic requirement is that the correlation matrix **R** be accounted for optimally by the product **aa'** of a vector of factor loadings and its transpose—or by the matrix **A** of factor loadings, $\hat{R} = AA'$. To show the implications of this requirement, let us simply apply our analysis of the rectangular matrix **X** to a special case, the square symmetric matrix **R**. For this symmetric matrix we ask that $v' = u = a$, i.e., that the same set of column factor loadings serve also as row factor loadings. If we treat **R** as a special case of **X**, then the eigenvectors we find are those of **R'R** or **RR'**, each of which may be written simply as R^2. We have seen in (5.2) that these eigenvectors are the same as those of **R**, and the eigenvalues are the squares of the corresponding eigenvalues of **R**. The value of an eigenvalue is $|u|^2|v|^2$, and for a symmetric **X** this becomes $|v|^4$. If we designate λ as an eigenvalue of **R**, then the corresponding eigenvalue of R^2 is λ^2. Hence

$$\lambda^2 = |v|^4 \quad \text{and} \quad \lambda = |v|^2 \tag{5.12}$$

This is the customary condition for normalization of eigenvectors to produce factor loadings, stated without proof in the preceding section. If a matrix of other associations (e.g., of Q) is factored, the values of λ^2 will be nonnegative but some values of λ can be negative and thus cannot be set equal to $|v|^2$.

If we set the multiplicative constant for the **v** of a nonsymmetric **X** in this way, we must then require that $|\mathbf{u}|^2 = 1$, i.e., that factor scores have N as their sums of squares. This is consistent with the convention that they are standard scores; but this convention may be less appropriate in applications that are less clearly in the factor-analytic tradition.[17]

To return to the conventional factor-analytic model, if we set $|\mathbf{v}|^2 = \lambda$ in order to get $\mathbf{v} = \mathbf{a}'$, we also thus arrive at a further interpretation of λ. For this constant will be the sum of squares in a column of the matrix **A**, or the total sum of squares accounted for by the corresponding factor (eigenvector) in the variables under study. This sum of squares was to be maximized by our initial derivation in (5.5), and we have not only maximized it but also measured it by solving for λ. If our analysis satisfies the model of principal components, then all the λ's will be positive, and their sum will measure the total variance to be accounted for in the data (equal to n, the number of variables, each of which has a variance equal to unity). The proportion of this variance accounted for by the pth factor will then be λ_p/n. The distribution of values of λ_p over various values of p can then be a useful index of the structure of the set of variables under study. The votes of the Democrats in the House of Representatives in recent years, for example, normally show a predominant general factor (λ_1/n is relatively high); while for the Republicans the first eigenvalue is proportionally lower, reflecting division on a diversity of issues.

We can now specify the procedure for computation of the factor scores. If we have carried out the iterative procedure of (5.6) or (5.9), we shall have found them (as the elements of **u**) at the same time as the factor loadings, and we need only set their multiplicative constants so that for each factor $|\mathbf{u}|^2 = 1$. But it is also possible that we have factored the correlation matrix, or the matrix **X'X**, because this is smaller than the data matrix if there are fewer roll calls than legislators. In this case we can get the factor scores by applying the left-hand equation of (5.6), in the form $\mathbf{X}\mathbf{v}_p'/|\mathbf{v}|^2 = \mathbf{u}_p$.

Since we have set $|\mathbf{v}|^2 = \lambda$, for the particular case of factor analysis, this becomes

$$\frac{\mathbf{X}\mathbf{v}_p'}{\lambda_p} = \mathbf{u}_p \tag{5.13}$$

[17]For example, in MacRae ("Direct Factor Analysis") the convention $|\mathbf{u}|^2 = \lambda$ and $|\mathbf{v}|^2 = \lambda$ was followed, with the result that the relation $\mathbf{X} = \mathbf{u}\mathbf{v}$ failed to obtain.

This is the solution we are seeking for the pth column of $\mathbf{U}$; and it needs only to be multiplied by $\sqrt{N}$ to give the pth column of $\mathbf{F}$, or the factor scores on the pth factor. It may also be expressed in matrix form by means of a diagonal matrix whose diagonal elements are each $1/\lambda_p$.

Kaiser has given a matrix equation for computation of factor scores.[18] In our notation this becomes

$$\mathbf{F} = \mathbf{ZA(A'A)}^{-1} \tag{5.14}$$

The last expression on the right of (5.14), i.e., $\mathbf{(A'A)}^{-1}$, refers to the inverse of the matrix product $\mathbf{A'A}$. Although a general definition of inverses is not necessary for our argument, we may define the inverse of a diagonal matrix here, since the product $\mathbf{A'A}$ is diagonal. The inverse of a square diagonal matrix is another diagonal matrix which, when multiplied by the first, gives as product the identity matrix. Thus

$$\mathbf{A'A} = \begin{bmatrix} \lambda_1 & 0 & 0 & . & . & . & 0 \\ 0 & \lambda_2 & 0 & . & . & . & 0 \\ 0 & 0 & \lambda_3 & . & . & . & 0 \\ . & . & . & . & . & . & . \\ 0 & 0 & 0 & . & . & . & \lambda_n \end{bmatrix} \text{ and } \mathbf{(A'A)}^{-1} = \begin{bmatrix} 1/\lambda_1 & 0 & 0 & . & . & . & 0 \\ 0 & 1/\lambda_2 & 0 & . & . & . & 0 \\ 0 & 0 & 1/\lambda_3 & . & . & . & 0 \\ . & . & . & . & . & . & . \\ 0 & 0 & 0 & . & . & . & 1/\lambda_n \end{bmatrix}$$

The product of these two matrices (irrespective of their sequence) is $\mathbf{I}$, an identity matrix of the same order. The result of multiplying by $\mathbf{(A'A)}^{-1}$ in (5.14) is to divide each column of $\mathbf{V'}$ (i.e., of $\mathbf{A}$) by the corresponding eigenvalue, as in (5.13), making $|\mathbf{u}|^2 = 1$ for each column of $\mathbf{U}$, and the sum of squares equal to N for each column of $\mathbf{F}$.

If factor scores are computed by (5.14), and if all the factors of $\mathbf{R}$ are computed so that it is exactly reproduced by $\mathbf{R} = \mathbf{AA'}$, then we can show that the factor scores on the various factors are orthogonal, i.e., that $\mathbf{F'F} = N\mathbf{I}$. For by (5.14)

$$\mathbf{F'F} = \mathbf{(A'A)}^{-1}\mathbf{A'Z'ZA(A'A)}^{-1} = N\mathbf{(A'A)}^{-1}\mathbf{A'RA\,(A'A)}^{-1}$$
$$= N\mathbf{(A'A)}^{-1}\mathbf{A'(AA')A(A'A)}^{-1} = N\mathbf{I}$$

making use of the facts that $\mathbf{A'A}$ is symmetric, and that $\mathbf{Z'Z} = N\mathbf{R}$.

[18]Kaiser, "Formulas for Component Scores." This procedure is used in Alker and Russett, *World Politics in the General Assembly*, see p. 38 n. See also Horst, op. cit., p. 477. It is technically more correct to refer to the scores we compute as "component scores"; see Chester W. Harris, "On Factors and Factor Scores," pp. 371–372.

But if a matrix of values of some other index of association, such as Q, were factored, the relation $\mathbf{Z'Z} = N\mathbf{R}$ could no longer be used, and the factor scores would not be necessarily orthogonal.

NUMERICAL EXAMPLES

We shall now illustrate the operations involved in principal-component analysis of a data matrix, including the computation of factor scores. We begin with a simple matrix of dichotomous data of the sort that might be generated from roll calls. We consider five legislators and three roll calls in the vote matrix

$$
\mathbf{M} = \begin{bmatrix} 1 & 1 & 1 \\ 0 & 0 & 1 \\ 0 & 0 & 1 \\ 0 & 0 & 1 \\ 0 & 0 & 0 \end{bmatrix}
$$

Here we have assumed that there are no absences; that two of the three roll calls are identical (columns 1 and 2); that three of the legislators vote identically (rows 2, 3, and 4); and that the roll calls have a perfect cumulative scale relation. (Exercise: carry out all the numerical operations below on this example. Review relevant parts of Chapter 4 if necessary.)

Subtracting the column means (.2, .2, and .8), we obtain a matrix of deviation scores

$$
\begin{bmatrix} .8 & .8 & .2 \\ -.2 & -.2 & .2 \\ -.2 & -.2 & .2 \\ -.2 & -.2 & .2 \\ -.2 & -.2 & -.8 \end{bmatrix}
$$

Also, the standard deviation s of each column is $(.2 \times .8)^{1/2} = .4$. (Exercise: show this.) So we divide each entry by .4 to obtain the matrix of standard scores

$$
\mathbf{Z} = \begin{bmatrix} 2.0 & 2.0 & .5 \\ -.5 & -.5 & .5 \\ -.5 & -.5 & .5 \\ -.5 & -.5 & .5 \\ -.5 & -.5 & -2.0 \end{bmatrix}
$$

The correlation matrix is

$$\mathbf{R} = \mathbf{Z'Z}/5 = \begin{bmatrix} 1.00 & 1.00 & .25 \\ 1.00 & 1.00 & .25 \\ .25 & .25 & 1.00 \end{bmatrix}$$

The elements of $\mathbf{R}$ are r's or ϕ's. While the two identical roll calls have $r_{12} = 1.0$, and each roll call has $r_{ii} = 1.0$ for its self-correlation, two roll calls with different marginals have $r_{13} = r_{23} = .25$. In spite of being generated from a perfect cumulative scale, the matrix $\mathbf{R}$ will be accounted for in terms of two factors rather than one.

We shall factor the correlation matrix rather than the data matrix, as the results are equivalent and the operations are simpler on a 3×3 matrix.

The eigenvectors of $\mathbf{R}$, with multiplicative constants suitably set, will give the factor loadings. The first eigenvector can be obtained by the iterative procedure of (5.3), but the reader will find that more than six iterations are required to approximate the solution we shall give, which was in fact found by a different method.[19] We can, however, demonstrate that the eigenvector found $(9, 9, 4)$ is a solution to an adequate degree of accuracy. For if we substitute it in the eigenvector equation we obtain

$$\mathbf{v}_1\mathbf{R} = [9 \quad 9 \quad 4] \begin{bmatrix} 1.0 & 1.0 & .25 \\ 1.0 & 1.0 & .25 \\ .25 & .25 & 1.0 \end{bmatrix} = [19 \quad 19 \quad 8.5]$$

the ratios of the elements of this last vector to the corresponding elements of $\mathbf{v}_1$ being $(2.11, 2.11, 2.12)$. We assume (on the basis of a more exact solution) that $\lambda = 2.11$. Following the method shown above for setting the multiplicative constant k, we find for the factor loadings

$$\mathbf{a}_1 = \sqrt{\frac{2.11}{178}} \begin{bmatrix} 9 \\ 9 \\ 4 \end{bmatrix} = \begin{bmatrix} .98 \\ .98 \\ .44 \end{bmatrix}$$

We may now calculate the reproduced matrix $\hat{\mathbf{R}}$ and the residuals, given by

[19]For small matrices of this kind one can solve explicitly the polynomial equation defined by the determinant $|\mathbf{R} - \lambda\mathbf{I}| = 0$, an alternative and equivalent procedure for finding eigenvalues. In this example, the λ's are roots of a quadratic equation, and are equal to $(6 \pm \sqrt{6})/4$. See Harman, op. cit., p. 139.

$$\mathbf{R}_1 = \mathbf{R} - \hat{\mathbf{R}} = \mathbf{R} - \mathbf{A}\mathbf{A}' = \begin{bmatrix} 1.0 & 1.0 & .25 \\ 1.0 & 1.0 & .25 \\ .25 & .25 & 1.0 \end{bmatrix} - \begin{bmatrix} .96 & .96 & .43 \\ .96 & .96 & .43 \\ .43 & .43 & .19 \end{bmatrix}$$

$$= \begin{bmatrix} .04 & .04 & -.18 \\ .04 & .04 & -.18 \\ -.18 & -.18 & .81 \end{bmatrix}$$

The residual matrix $\mathbf{R}_1$ has the same simple relations between its row or its columns as did the 3×3 correlation matrix used in our earlier illustration of the iterative procedure for computing eigenvectors; it can be accounted for in terms of a single factor. We may demonstrate this by trying as the second eigenvector $(2, 2, -9)$:

$$\mathbf{v}_2\mathbf{R}_1 = [2 \quad 2 \quad -9] \begin{bmatrix} .04 & .04 & -.18 \\ .04 & .04 & -.18 \\ -.18 & -.18 & .81 \end{bmatrix} = [1.78 \quad 1.78 \quad -8.01]$$

$$= .89 \, [2 \quad 2 \quad -9]$$

Thus the second eigenvalue is .89. The second residual, $\mathbf{R}_2$, will consist of nine zeros in a 3×3 matrix, and no further analysis is necessary. The sum of the two eigenvalues is $2.11 + .89 = 3.00$, the total variance of the three standard scores to be accounted for. The first factor accounts for approximately 70 percent of this variance, the second for 30 percent, and none remains to be explained—a degree of exactness unattainable with two factors in any of the actual roll-call problems we shall consider. Yet the data involved only one cumulative scale, while two dimensions are required to represent the factor loadings.

The matrix of factor loadings is

$$\mathbf{A} = \begin{bmatrix} .98 & .20 \\ .98 & .20 \\ .44 & -.90 \end{bmatrix}$$

It can easily be verified that $\mathbf{A}\mathbf{A}' = \hat{\mathbf{R}} = \mathbf{R}$, by steps closely similar to those we have just followed to obtain the solution. It is also easy to show that

$$\mathbf{A}'\mathbf{A} = \begin{bmatrix} 2.11 & 0 \\ 0 & .89 \end{bmatrix} = \begin{bmatrix} \lambda_1 & 0 \\ 0 & \lambda_2 \end{bmatrix}$$

We can also calculate the matrix **F** of factor scores, by equation (5.14) above:

$$F = ZA(A'A)^{-1} = \begin{bmatrix} 2.0 & 2.0 & .5 \\ -.5 & -.5 & .5 \\ -.5 & -.5 & .5 \\ -.5 & -.5 & .5 \\ -.5 & -.5 & -2.0 \end{bmatrix} \begin{bmatrix} .98 & .20 \\ .98 & .20 \\ .44 & -.90 \end{bmatrix} \begin{bmatrix} \dfrac{1}{2.11} & 0 \\ 0 & \dfrac{1}{.89} \end{bmatrix}$$

$$= \begin{bmatrix} 1.96 & .39 \\ -.36 & -.73 \\ -.36 & -.73 \\ -.36 & -.73 \\ -.88 & 1.80 \end{bmatrix}$$

From these values it can be shown that

$$F'F = \begin{bmatrix} 5 & 0 \\ 0 & 5 \end{bmatrix}$$

within rounding error, as it should if the factor scores are standard scores and are independent of (orthogonal to) one another.

It would also have been possible, though less convenient, to factor the 5 × 5 matrix **ZZ′** and obtain equivalent results. The entries in this matrix would not have been correlation coefficients, but would in fact have been values of one type of index of agreement between legislators. This type of correspondence between roll-call factors and legislator factors will be treated in detail in Chapter 7, in the section on "Roll-Call—Legislator Duality."

It can also be verified numerically that **Z = FA′**, for

$$\begin{bmatrix} 2.00 & 2.00 & .50 \\ -.50 & -.50 & .50 \\ -.50 & -.50 & .50 \\ -.50 & -.50 & .50 \\ -.50 & -.50 & -2.00 \end{bmatrix} = \begin{bmatrix} 1.96 & .39 \\ -.36 & -.73 \\ -.36 & -.73 \\ -.36 & -.73 \\ -.88 & 1.80 \end{bmatrix} \begin{bmatrix} .98 & .98 & .44 \\ .20 & .20 & -.90 \end{bmatrix}$$

A second numerical example is shown in Table 5.1. The vote matrix **M** is arranged so that the vertical standard deviations assume simple values, and the reader can verify the computations up to the calculation of **R**. (Exercise: perform this verification.) Like the first, this example corresponds to a perfect cumulative scale. The matrix **R** has the form of a perfect simplex.[20] It gives rise to five factors (rather

[20]See Guttman, "A New Approach to Factor Analysis: The Radex," pp. 272–275.

Table 5.1 Numerical example: Factoring a perfect scale with five roll calls and ten legislators

$$M = \begin{bmatrix} 1 & 1 & 1 & 1 & 1 \\ 0 & 1 & 1 & 1 & 1 \\ 0 & 0 & 1 & 1 & 1 \\ 0 & 0 & 1 & 1 & 1 \\ 0 & 0 & 1 & 1 & 1 \\ 0 & 0 & 0 & 1 & 1 \\ 0 & 0 & 0 & 1 & 1 \\ 0 & 0 & 0 & 1 & 1 \\ 0 & 0 & 0 & 0 & 1 \\ 0 & 0 & 0 & 0 & 0 \end{bmatrix} \qquad Z = \frac{1}{6}\begin{bmatrix} 18 & 12 & 6 & 3 & 2 \\ -2 & 12 & 6 & 3 & 2 \\ -2 & -3 & 6 & 3 & 2 \\ -2 & -3 & 6 & 3 & 2 \\ -2 & -3 & 6 & 3 & 2 \\ -2 & -3 & -6 & 3 & 2 \\ -2 & -3 & -6 & 3 & 2 \\ -2 & -3 & -6 & 3 & 2 \\ -2 & -3 & -6 & -12 & 2 \\ -2 & -3 & -6 & -12 & -18 \end{bmatrix}$$

p: .1 .2 .5 .8 .9

$s = \sqrt{pq}$ .3 .4 .5 .4 .3

$$R = \frac{1}{36}\begin{bmatrix} 36 & 24 & 12 & 6 & 4 \\ 24 & 36 & 18 & 9 & 6 \\ 12 & 18 & 36 & 18 & 12 \\ 6 & 9 & 18 & 36 & 24 \\ 4 & 6 & 12 & 24 & 36 \end{bmatrix} = \begin{bmatrix} 1.00 & .67 & .33 & .17 & .11 \\ .67 & 1.00 & .50 & .25 & .17 \\ .33 & .50 & 1.00 & .50 & .33 \\ .17 & .25 & .50 & 1.00 & .67 \\ .11 & .17 & .33 & .67 & 1.00 \end{bmatrix}$$

$$A = \begin{bmatrix} .63 & .61 & -.34 & .24 & .20 \\ .74 & .53 & -.02 & -.30 & -.28 \\ .78 & .00 & .59 & .00 & .21 \\ .74 & -.53 & -.02 & .30 & -.28 \\ .63 & -.61 & -.34 & -.24 & .20 \end{bmatrix} \qquad \begin{matrix} 1.00 \\ 1.00 \\ h^2\text{: } 1.00 \\ 1.00 \\ 1.00 \end{matrix}$$

λ : 2.49 1.32 .58 .31 .29   5.00

than the single factor that would have resulted had a coefficient such as Q been used); these correspond to Guttman's "principal components of scale analysis."[21] Some efforts have been made to solve simplex matrices to reveal their underlying simplicity, by methods different from the factor-analytic model we have described.[22] The example in Table 5.1 shows the factorial complexity of the results of conventional factor analysis on such a ϕ-matrix, and a further example in the next section, using actual congressional votes, will demonstrate the difficulties of recovering issue-clusters when ϕ is used as the index of association in conventional factor analysis. For large matrices of

[21]Stouffer et al., op. cit., chap. 9; Guttman, "A Generalized Simplex for Factor Analysis."

[22]Guttman, ibid.; Kaiser, "Scaling a Simplex"; Gibson, "A Latent Structure for the Simplex." See also equation (3.2) above.

actual roll-call data, further technical developments will be necessary before multiple scale clusters can be discovered accurately from a ϕ-matrix.

The example of Table 5.1 will be analyzed further in Chapter 7 in connection with alternative indices of similarity between legislators.

PROBLEMS IN FACTOR ANALYSIS
OF DICHOTOMOUS VARIABLES

The two preceding numerical examples have shown that a set of roll-call data constituting a perfect cumulative scale do not necessarily yield a single factor in principal-component analysis. This results from the fact that ϕ does not attain unity for every cumulative relationship between a pair of items, but does so only when both b and c in the fourfold table are zero. For this reason, we made use of Q rather than ϕ in the examples shown in Chapter 3. But we have also seen that Q fails in general to fulfill the basic condition of factor analysis: $Q_{jk} \neq Q_{jt}Q_{kt}$.

It is nevertheless possible to carry out the operations of principal component analysis on a Q-matrix. If the input consists of a perfect cumulative scale, the matrix will have all entries equal to 1 and the result will be a single factor with all loadings equal to 1. This property holds for any of the indices that attain unity for a perfect scale relation, including Y, $\phi/\phi_{\max}$, and the tetrachoric correlation coefficient.[23] Unfortunately, none of these indices fulfills the basic condition in general either. Thus though a matrix consisting of any one of these coefficients would yield factors corresponding to cumulative scales in the perfect-scale case (all matrix entries 1), it would not yield the desired residuals in other cases.

The Q-matrix is normally not Gramian and cannot be generated by matrix operations from the data matrix **M.** If we perform principal-component analysis on it, we shall expect some negative eigenvalues. If we are to apply the mathematics developed earlier in this chapter, we must consider the matrix **Q** to correspond to **X,** and the squared eigenvalues λ^2 to measure the contributions of successive factors to approximating **Q,** rather than to approximating the data matrix. There

[23]The tetrachoric correlation coefficient was recommended by Thurstone in an early article on roll-call analysis, "Isolation of Blocs in a Legislative Body by the Voting Records of Its Members."

Table 5.2 Submatrices of ϕ for Q-clusters (Republicans, 84th Congress)

		5–15	5–47	5–52ᵃ	5–57	5–59	5–60	6–32	6–52	p_+
	5–15	X	13	09	44	38	43	41	39	63
	5–47		X	28	38	34	36	30	32	13
1.	5–52ᵃ			X	29	30	27	24	23	09
Foreign	5–57				X	93	92	79	82	41
Aid	5–59					X	87	78	82	40
	5–60					·	X	80	83	41
	6–32							X	91	39
	6–52								X	36

		5–27	5–28	6–13	6–14	6–16	6–23	6–29	p_+
	5–27	X	92	73	52	68	19	13	90
	5–28		X	80	57	72	21	16	88
2.	6–13			X	71	73	30	25	86
Agriculture	6–14				X	53	43	33	75
	6–16					X	21	18	89
	6–23						X	71	34
	6–29							X	26

		5–6	5–7	5–8	5–9	5–10	5–43	5–50	p_+
	5– 6	X	85	83	59	54	29	44	63
	5– 7		X	80	57	53	27	45	64
3.	5– 8			X	69	61	33	54	60
Reciprocal	5– 9				X	62	30	49	64
trade	5–10					X	49	60	42
	5–43						X	42	20
	5–50							X	51

		5–22	5–23	5–24	5–29	5–30	p_+
	5–22	X	47	31	49	28	88
4.	5–23		X	63	66	49	63
Postal	5–24			X	50	75	43
pay	5–29				X	56	64
	5–30					X	37

		5–72	5–76	6–42ᵃ	6–48	p_+
5.	5–72	X	86	15	42	80
Welfare	5–76		X	13	45	79
state	6–42ᵃ			X	27	10
	6–48				X	60

Table 5.2 (Continued)

		5–42	6–30	6–59^a	6–60^a	p_+
6. Extreme blocs	5–42	X	01	25	28	07
	6–30		X	05	05	90
	6–59^a			X	88	15
	6–60^a				X	13

^{a} Polarity reversed relative to that chosen from the association of vote with party.
NOTES: Values of ϕ and of p_+ are multiplied by 100. Clusters at the threshold value of $\phi_{min} = .7$ are enclosed in rectangular boxes.

remains the problem whether factor scores can be defined; we treat this in Chapter 7.

This departure of the Q-matrix from the underlying assumptions of principal-component analysis is not unprecedented in factor analysis. Another frequent procedure, which we have not discussed, is to replace the 1's on the diagonal of **R** with estimates of the communalities before computing eigenvalues. When this is done, some of the eigenvalues are ordinarily negative. The difference introduced by factoring the Q-matrix is that the negative eigenvalues tend to be larger in magnitude.[24]

The difference in results between factoring a ϕ-matrix and a Q-matrix for the same data may be illustrated with an example using Congressional votes. We again use the Republicans' votes in the 84th Congress (1955–1956) for comparison with the results in Chapters 3 and 4. The data are the 102 roll calls on which the Republicans had at least .07 dissidence, which were used to generate the Q-matrix whose clusters were shown in Tables 3.2 and 3.3.

We first compare the matrices of associations prior to factor analysis. Rather than examining the entire 102 × 102 matrices, we consider the submatrices corresponding to the clusters found earlier (Table 3.3), and present the corresponding submatrices of ϕ in Table 5.2. If these clusters were to be revealed identically in the ϕ matrix, these submatrices would contain uniformly high values of ϕ, as the corresponding Q-submatrices contain no values less than .8. It is clear, however, that they do not. Although close inspection of Table 5.2 will reveal much detail, its salient features are revealed by the clusters found

[24]An example in Harman, *op. cit.*, p. 168, based on ordinary correlations and communalities, shows eleven of twenty-four eigenvalues negative, but none more negative than −.27. The largest negative eigenvalue was ninth highest in magnitude. Corresponding data for Q-matrices will be given below.

within each submatrix by using our earlier clustering procedure at the threshold $\phi_{min} = .7$, and indicated by rectangular boxes in the table. In no case does such a cluster extend to the entire submatrix in question, nor could it be so extended without a drastic reduction in ϕ_{min}, such as might well link the cluster with irrelevant items outside. The main reason for the disparities in ϕ within the submatrices, of course, is the variation in p_+ among the items in each cluster; the items in each of the clusters enclosed in rectangles resemble one another closely in their values of p_+, but differ in p_+ from others in the submatrix.

The difference between Q and ϕ may be seen either empirically in the ϕ-submatrices, or theoretically, in that ϕ is dependent on the marginals of items and their differences. This dependency on marginals means ϕ is not simply uniformly depressed for an item with extreme marginals, but is nonuniformly depressed in relation to other items. This leads to multiple-factor loadings rather than a depressed single-factor loading for such an item. For example, in the agriculture cluster (#2) in Table 5.2, two subclusters in the ϕ's can be found at the threshold value of .7: among the three initial items, with values of p_+ from .86 to .90; and another between the last two items, with p_+ of .26 and .34. The maximum possible value of ϕ between two items with p_+ of .90 and .26 is given by equation (3.2) as

$$\sqrt{\frac{.26 \times .10}{.90 \times .74}} = .20$$

The actual ϕ, in the upper right corner of the agriculture submatrix, is .13—small in absolute terms but more substantial when compared with ϕ_{max}.

While we have demonstrated important differences between Q and ϕ for these data, we have not yet considered the associations outside the submatrices defined by the Q-clusters. These associations are taken into account in principal component analysis, and we shall now show the differences that result from principal component analysis of these two matrices, followed by Varimax rotation of the factor loadings. Table 5.3 shows the factor loadings that result, for the roll calls in the previous clusters, from applying this same procedure to the Q-matrix and the ϕ-matrix.[25] In each case the first six factors were considered, for comparison with the six clusters.

[25]The smallness of the differences resulting from the use of communalities, rather than unities, on the diagonal may be illustrated by comparison of these results with

The factor loadings obtained from the Q-matrix diverge in at least two respects from the assumptions we have listed above for principal component analysis. First, the ninth largest eigenvalue (in magnitude) is -4.4, a considerably larger negative value than commonly occurs in factor analysis. Second, the factor loadings are larger than those from the ϕ-matrix, and a number of the communalities exceed 1; this is probably due both to the properties of Q and to the large number of high Q's in matrices based on congressional votes.

In spite of these divergences, the factor loadings from the Q-matrix are very similar to one another for the items in a given cluster, particularly for clusters 1 through 4. One exception is roll call 5–52, which may have been misplaced in cluster 1 by the clustering procedure.

We should not expect each cluster to correspond exactly to a single rotated factor. In general, issues may be expected to correspond to oblique factors; there is no reason to expect votes on one issue always to be independent of votes on another. But for these data there is another problem in locating issues by means of rotated factors, which cannot be circumvented even by oblique rotation procedures.[26] The number of issue clusters in which we are interested here exceeds the number of dimensions, as the four major clusters are accounted for by three factors. This relationship appeared earlier in the BC TRY analysis of the same data. As a result, even an oblique rotation would reveal only three variables, and might fail to include as one of them an issue that we wished to trace over several Congresses.[27] For the purpose of identifying issues that are continuous over time, cluster analysis thus has the advantage of revealing more clusters than the corresponding number of factors.

---

a principal-factor analysis of the same Q-matrix, using communality estimates provided by the BC TRY system. None of the first six eigenvalues (which ranged from 30 to 6) differed by more than .4 between the computations. Moreover, none of the 408 loadings on the first four factors differed by more than .045 between the two analyses, most differences being far less. These discrepancies might be greater, however, for subsequent factors.

[26]Two oblique rotation procedures, Promax and binormamin, were tried on these data but did not circumvent this problem. See Hendrickson and White, "Promax: A Quick Method for Rotation to Oblique Simple Structure"; Warburton, "Analytic Methods of Factor Rotation"; Harman, op. cit., p. 326.

[27]For an example of this type of analysis, see Rieselbach, The Roots of Isolationism, esp. p. 37.

Table 5.3 Factor loadings from principal components and Varimax rotation of Q-matrix and φ-matrix (Republicans, 102 roll calls, 84th Congress)

Scale	Roll call	Q-Matrix factor 1	2	3	4	5	6	φ-Matrix factor 1	2	3	4	5	6
	5–15	82	−25	16	7	−29	18	36	−14	2	38	−2	17
	5–47	70	−57	13	−32	−18	34	31	−25	22	20	−18	−5
1.	5–52[a]	43	−33	27	−18	−14	94	20	−9	24	16	−17	−4
Foreign	5–57	72	−51	26	7	−26	17	83	−19	15	20	1	9
aid	5–59	69	−51	27	7	−27	17	82	−16	18	14	0	5
	5–60	73	−50	28	9	−26	21	81	−18	15	21	2	12
	6–32	68	−45	24	19	−24	29	82	−12	11	15	5	11
	6–52	69	−49	24	13	−28	13	84	−15	13	14	2	6
	5–27	−14	106	1	21	−8	−7	−6	78	−5	−4	3	3
	5–28	−4	109	1	16	−6	−6	−5	82	−2	1	0	0
	6–13	−2	109	−4	12	−7	−2	−10	84	−2	2	−10	−1
2.	6–14	−11	98	8	−18	5	2	−24	70	15	4	−17	−8
Agriculture	6–16	13	110	−4	1	−1	−42	−7	76	−4	7	−4	−7
	6–23	−14	82	−8	−33	−24	−26	−18	35	14	5	−48	−9
	6–29	−15	87	−10	−41	−36	−33	−21	30	7	10	−52	1
	5– 6	88	17	−23	−13	5	12	4	2	−17	83	−4	1
	5– 7	94	12	−21	−11	3	3	9	1	−16	81	−2	2
3.	5– 8	97	6	−9	−8	10	6	12	0	−9	86	4	4
Reciprocal	5– 9	90	8	−9	−4	10	−8	13	2	−5	71	8	−2
trade	5–10	95	−4	−5	−14	−6	0	34	−2	3	67	5	−2
	5–43	102	−2	−24	−10	−16	3	49	7	1	37	−12	−17
	5–50	92	1	8	−19	−3	11	29	0	12	65	−7	1

4. Postal pay													
5–22	−11	17	*107*	12	−18	16	1	11	30	−11	7	60
5–23	−18	−19	*83*	−5	−2	−10	−2	−7	*51*	−19	12	33
5–24	−13	−1	*78*	−23	9	−6	3	7	*70*	−21	5	8
5–29	−19	−23	*91*	−4	13	−9	−4	−11	*58*	−19	21	33
5–30	−16	−2	*89*	1	18	−10	0	6	*67*	−20	18	15
5. Welfare state													
5–72	33	−40	*89*	32	3	24	12	−12	20	9	35	*65*
5–76	13	−26	*97*	*40*	1	21	10	−6	23	−1	35	*69*
6–42ᵃ	*44*	0	*67*	−18	−8	*50*	−5	−3	32	20	−5	8
6–48	37	−26	*73*	26	−20	30	*40*	−2	32	3	12	*45*
6. Extreme blocs													
5–42	*86*	4	*52*	−45	13	−11	15	0	*43*	12	−8	−11
6–30	20	10	*76*	22	−27	4	−3	7	−4	−5	1	*42*
6–59ᵃ	*48*	−28	*59*	−21	0	7	9	−17	*50*	31	−3	4
6–60ᵃ	*56*	−23	*58*	−38	−10	2	11	−13	*52*	33	−10	1

ᵃ Polarity reversed relative to that chosen from the association of vote with party.

NOTE: Factor loadings are multiplied by 100. Signs of rotated factors have been reversed to make the large loadings positive. Sequence of factors from ϕ-matrix has been altered to procuce an approximate match with Q-matrix factors. Factor loadings of at least .40 in magnitude are shown in italic type.

If, however, we consider clusters 1 through 4 as revealed in factor loadings from the ϕ-matrix, we again see the confounding influence of the marginals. In each of these four clusters there is at least one item whose highest loading is on a factor other than that characteristic of the issue; and in each case the item or items in question diverge from the remainder of the cluster in their value of p_+, as comparison with Table 5.2 will show. The same effect can be noted in cluster 5, but here and particularly in cluster 6, even the factor loadings for the Q-matrix vary more among items in the cluster and are thus less useful for comparison.

We cannot, of course, deny that the factoring of the ϕ-matrix has revealed distinct issues corresponding to rotated factors. To some extent, the issues are even more distinct in the dimensions of the ϕ-matrix than in those of the Q-matrix. A number of studies have shown recognizable issues through factor analysis of ϕ-matrices.[28] The procedure also has ample precedent in psychological test analysis. But if one wishes to reveal a single underlying factor shared by roll calls (or test items) with diverse marginals, the ϕ-matrix cannot be relied on to do so.

In the psychological literature this problem has been treated in relation to so-called "difficulty factors"—possible factors related to p_+.[29] However, it seems more correct to say that the "difficulty" of an item influences its factor loadings, than to go further and expect individual rotated factors to reflect difficulty alone. Inspection of the divergent loadings of items with values of p_+ different from others in their clusters will reveal that these loadings do not simply group them with items that have similar marginals in other scales.

It is possible that careful comparison of the results of factor analyses

---

[28]See Lee F. Anderson, Watts, and Wilcox, *Legislative Roll-Call Analysis*, pp. 144–163, for an analysis of Senate votes in 1961 using this method; the spread of marginals may have been reduced by preliminary use of Riker's coefficient of significance for selecting roll calls. See also Marwell, "Party, Region, and Dimensions of Conflict in the House of Representatives." These studies will also be discussed in Chapter 8. An earlier study of this type was McMurray, "A Factor Method for Roll-Call Vote Studies."

[29]Some of this literature is reviewed in Horst, *op. cit.,* pp. 513–516; and in Weisberg, "Dimensional Analysis of Legislative Roll Calls." See also Borgatta, "Difficulty Factors and the Use of r_{phi}"; Henry and Borgatta, "A Consideration of Some Problems of Content Identification in Scaling"; and Coleman, *Introduction to Mathematical Sociology*, pp. 398 ff.

based on different coefficients may reveal a coefficient that more nearly approximates the conditions for principal component analysis, yet preserves a value of 1 for a perfect scale relation. Tests so far, however, have not revealed another coefficient superior in every respect to Q. The use of ϕ/ϕ_{max} seems to yield clearly inferior results; but Y and the tetrachoric approximation of (3.3) are generally comparable with Q.[30] We shall therefore continue to use Q for simplicity of exposition.

CLUSTERING ROLL CALLS
IN THE FACTOR SPACE

We have seen that factoring of the Q-matrix, in spite of its divergence from the model of principal component analysis, tends to assign a similar set of factor loadings to the roll calls in a given cluster. This may not be surprising, in view of the use of the Q-matrix to define the clusters initially; but it implies that the relation of cumulative-scale similarity between roll calls in a cluster is preserved by principal-component analysis, in spite of the failure of the conditions for residuals to hold exactly. This means, in effect, that if several roll calls are similar to one another, they will be assigned similar first-factor loadings and similar residuals, even though part of these residuals may be artificially due to the first factor. If, nevertheless, the relation of similarity is maintained, this can presumably be used to identify the original clusters again after principal-component analysis. At this point the accuracy of clustering may be even greater, in view of data

[30]For the 102 roll calls analyzed in Table 5.3, Y shows some improvement on Q: whereas it was the ninth largest eigenvalue of the Q-matrix that was negative, for the Y-matrix it was the eleventh—though its proportional relation to the highest eigenvalue was not improved. A second improvement was that while in the Q-matrix analysis 53 of 102 eigenvalues were negative, in the Y-matrix this figure was reduced to 32. Even the Y-matrix still seems quite distant in these respects from the comparable characteristics usually found in factor analysis.

Another comparative study was made for 113 roll calls in the House in 1962, on which one or more dissenting votes occurred. The results for ϕ/ϕ_{max} were clearly worst, with 56 percent of the eigenvalues negative, and the second largest eigenvalue negative. For the Q-matrix, the proportion was 50 percent and the fourth largest was negative; for the tetrachoric approximation, 47 percent and the fourth was negative; for Y, only 35 percent of the eigenvalues were negative, but these included the third largest.

smoothing such as we mentioned in connection with the MDSCAL procedure at Table 3.6.

Once the data are given as points in a multidimensional space, the clustering problem can be related to a substantial literature that was not relevant to the initial dichotomous roll-call matrix. The internal homogeneity of a cluster, and the distance between two clusters, may be given precise meanings in terms of sums of squares and properties of matrices.[31] We return, however, to a simpler procedure that permits direct comparison of results from the factor loadings with the clusters previously found.

The distribution of roll-call points in the multidimensional factor space may also be used for cluster analysis if we convert it into a matrix of interpoint distances as we did with the MDSCAL procedure in Chapter 3.[32] We first find clusters based on principal-component analysis of the Q-matrix. For comparison with the MDSCAL clustering we again use the Q-matrix based on the 70 roll calls with highest communalities chosen from the 102 for the Republicans in 1955–1956. We compute the first six principal components of this Q-matrix; if these are rotated according to the Varimax procedure, the results are generally similar to those presented for the full 102×102 matrix in the left-hand part of Table 5.3. Clusters 2, 3, and 4 correspond closely to rotated factors; cluster 1 (foreign aid) has a well-defined location in the factor space but combines two of the rotated factors.

We next construct a distance matrix based on the factor space, as we did for the MDSCAL space; and just as in that case, we expect a certain data smoothing to operate, insuring that the smallest distances (unlike the highest Q's of 1) give a great deal of accurate information about clusters. The validity of this procedure, however, now depends on our having excluded points near the origin, i.e., roll calls with low communalities.

To compare the clusters in the distance matrix based on principal components with those from the Q-matrix, we choose a set of shortest distances, equal in number to a set of highest Q's used to locate clusters in the Q-matrix. By doing this, we are effectively considering

[31]See, for example, Friedman and Rubin, "On Some Invariant Criteria for Grouping Data."

[32]This material is adapted from MacRae and Schwarz, "Identifying Congressional Issues by Multidimensional Models"; additional details are given there.

only the rank order of the distances, which is forced by the model (a six-dimensional space) to be more consistent than the rank order of the Q's. We consider first the 84 highest Q's, those of 1, in order to demonstrate a clear advantage of the distance matrix.

Among the 84 shortest distances in the principal-components-distance matrix, 55 (65 percent) correspond to pairs in the initial scale clusters, as against only 42 percent of the values of +1 in the Q-matrix. Moreover, the 84 values of Q = +1 in the Q-matrix themselves give rise to only one five-item cluster, dealing with agriculture, and no other of as many as four. The 84 shortest distances in the distance matrix, on the other hand, give rise to six-item clusters dealing with foreign aid and foreign trade, and four-item clusters dealing with agriculture and postal pay. These clusters are indicated in Table 5.4, by roll-call numbers without the superscript a.

If we extend the analysis of the distance matrix to include as many low distances as there were Q's, of .9 or greater (144), we find that four additional roll calls are added, and that a four-item cluster partly resembling the initial cluster 6 reappears. A comparison of roll calls added and deleted relative to the initial Q-matrix clusters (Table 5.4) suggests that the new roll calls added give rise to clusters that are slightly less homogeneous in content than those of the Q-matrix, but that the difference in content is small. Though the advantage of clustering the distance matrix is pronounced at the level of Q = 1, it is far less clear at the level of Q = .9. This is the same conclusion we reached in Chapter 3 for clusters based on the MDSCAL distance matrix.

It thus seems that either of these two methods of data smoothing, divergent though they are in their assumptions, leads to a distance matrix whose clusters are in some ways superior to those of the original Q-matrix. The feature they share is data smoothing which eliminates fluctuations manifested through Q's of 1 in the initial matrix.

While the procedure of clustering in the factor space appears promising from this example, additional work is required to test its general utility. In addition to other empirical examples, a theoretical justification would also be highly desirable. Criteria for the number of factors to be used are needed, and the precise nature of the data smoothing that takes place must be examined in comparison with other data smoothing methods.

An additional problem is that of placement of legislators—that is,

Table 5.4 Distance clusters based on six principal components of Q-matrix

Cluster	Roll call	Changes relative to Q-matrix clusters at .9 Additions	Deletions
Scale 1. Foreign aid	5–15, 5–57, 5–59, 5–60, 5–65[a], 6–32, 6–52	5–15 (UN aid funds) 5–65 (Reserve forces)	5–47 (Congress, delegation to NATO)
Scale 2. Agriculture	5–26[a], 5–27, 5–28, 6–13, 6–41	5–26 (Farm price supports)	6–14, 6–16, 6–23, 6–29 (Farm bills)
Scale 3. Foreign trade	5–6, 5–7, 5–8, 5–9, 5–10, 5–43[a], 5–50	5–7 (Reciprocal trade) 5–50 (Customs)	
Scale 4. Postal pay	5–21[a], 5–23, 5–24, 5–29, 5–30	5–21 (Independent offices appropriation)	5–22 (Postal pay)
Scale 5. Welfare state	—[b]		
Scale 6. Extreme blocs	5–48[a], 6–59[a], 6–60[a], 6–63[a]	—[c]	

[a] Indicates roll calls that were added to clusters on the basis of the 144 shortest distances, but did not enter when the lowest 84 were used.

[b] Fails to appear in either method; exists at $Q_{min} = .8$.

[c] Did not appear in Q-matrix at .9.

the generation of factor scores or the equivalent. One way to provide rankings of legislators would be to treat each cluster as a cumulative scale and assign scale scores according to the procedures indicated in Chapters 2 and 3. This method seems satisfactory as long as the cluster model applies, i.e., as long as roll calls may be grouped into discrete sets each of which has high internal and low external associations. The data we have used in most of our examples (Republican House votes in 1955–1956) fit this model well except for the diffuse and general welfare-state area, which may well involve two underlying dimensions in varying proportions.

For a multidimensional configuration that cannot easily be resolved into clusters, another possible approach might be to find principal components of the Q-matrix and then compute factor scores by an equation such as (5.14). But while these operations can be performed, they are of questionable validity unless they can be justified by a mathematical theory. One simple result may be noted, however: if a cumulative scale vote-matrix **M** is postmultiplied by a common vector with 1's corresponding to the roll calls in a given cluster, and 0's otherwise, the result will be a column vector of Guttman scale scores corresponding to the number of +'s in individual legislators' responses. (See the last section of Chapter 7.) This correspondence holds within a linear transformation and remains if a constant is added to the elements in each column of the vote matrix. It does not remain, however, for the standard-score matrix **Z.**

There remains another approach to the definition of legislators' positions. This is to form a matrix of indices of agreement between pairs of legislators and submit this to factor analysis or other techniques for generating a multidimensional legislator space. We shall discuss such approaches in Chapter 7 and relate them to the factor scores obtained by orthodox factor analysis.

COMPARISON OF METHODS FOR ARTIFICIAL DATA

Another approach to the computation of factor scores corresponding to scale clusters is to attempt to re-create assumed factor scores by analyzing hypothetical data. The general problem of defining the positions of individuals or objects in a multidimensional space is known as "multidimensional scaling," and we have considered one example, the Kruskal MDSCAL procedure. This term conventionally refers to the inference of positions of points in a multidimensional space from a matrix of pairwise interpoint relations.[33] But the present problem involves an additional step: the generation of interpoint-relation measures from dichotomous data. These data, in turn, are presumed to have been generated by the introduction of cutting surfaces in a multidimensional space, each surface dividing the space into two parts.[34]

When the dichotomous data in question are attitude data or legislative roll-call votes, the underlying multidimensional configuration is inferred, but not observed directly. When the data are judgments of preference between stimuli presented to a subject, the stimuli themselves may be considered by the experimenter, and a space defined by the experimenter in these terms may be compared with a space reconstructed from the subjects' responses. For roll calls, a similar analysis could be carried out with characteristics of the bills, the debates on them, or their political circumstances.[35]

To examine the adequacy of models of this sort in legislative analysis, we shall consider an array of points in a two-dimensional space, artificially constructed, divided by cutting lines to produce divisions similar to roll calls.[36] A graph of the points appears in Figure 5.1; the corresponding positive and negative votes were generated by assuming that the upper right of the diagram was positive and the lower left negative. These votes constitute a perfect two-dimensional cumulative scale by extension of the concepts of Chapter 2. This operation was carried out and the resulting "roll calls" were subjected to the procedure of factor analysis of the Q-matrix described above.

It might be imagined that the result of clustering matrices of similarity between roll calls should be a set of five perfect cumulative

---

[33]See Torgerson, *Theory and Methods of Scaling*, chap. 11.

[34]For an extensive treatment of this latter problem, see Coombs, *A Theory of Data*. The question whether such a space corresponds to observable psychological variables will be discussed in Chapter 8.

[35]Factor analysis of aspects of roll calls related to the content of the measures proposed and to the legislative situation has been carried out in Marvel, "The Nonpartisan Nebraska Unicameral," pp. 110–115.

[36]The configuration chosen will be reproduced fairly well by factor analysis of the Q-matrix. Not every set of artificial data has this property, however, and the conditions for useful application of factoring the Q-matrix remain to be specified precisely. This general strategy was followed for a related model in Coombs, *op. cit.*, chap. 8.

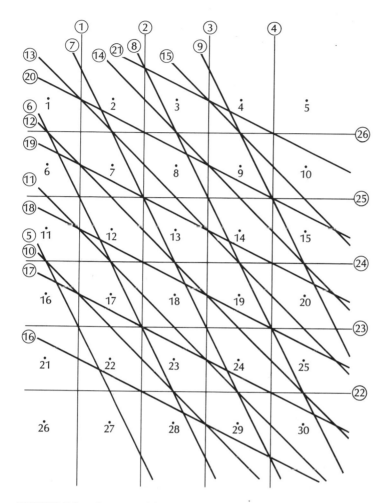

FIGURE 5.1. Thirty Artificial Data Points with Twenty-Six Cutting Lines.

scales corresponding to the five different slopes of parallel sets of cutting lines in the figure; 1 to 4, 5 to 9, 10 to 15, 16 to 21, and 22 to 26. But while these clusters do have perfect scale relations internally, the items in them also have perfect scale relations with items in other expected clusters, permitting alternative groupings or clusters that are perfectly scalable. In the third of these sets, for example, item 15 cuts off points 4, 5, and 10, a subset of those cut off by item

14; but item 9, in the second set, would do this equally well, and would therefore be an equally good candidate for membership in the third cluster. Similarly, item 14 could replace item 9 in the second set.

A more systematic examination of the possible scale relationships is permitted by constructing the Q-matrix among the items; if this is done, more possible perfect-scale clusters appear than might otherwise have been seen. The possible perfect pairwise relations are indicated in Table 5.5, a binary matrix produced from the Q-matrix at a threshold value of 1.

It can be seen from Table 5.5 that a variety of scale clusters are possible in these data. If the clustering method of Chapter 3 is followed, the largest cluster will contain nine items, but a cluster of this size can be found in eight different ways. We cannot resolve this tie by the method used previously, so we impose an additional criterion: priority will be given to those clusters having the largest *contiguous* sets of items. This criterion, applied repeatedly, leads to the clusters shown by rectangular boxes in Table 5.5. These clusters generally resemble the sets of parallel lines in Figure 5.1, though the resemblance has been increased by the contiguity condition. The sources of divergence between the parallel-line clusters and the matrix clusters are interesting, however; the matrix clusters pick up items with extreme marginal proportions from other parallel-line clusters. Thus the central parallel-line cluster, including items 10–15, adds items 9, 16, and 21, all of which have extreme marginals; the parallel-line cluster 16–21, thus bereft of two of its items, picks up item 5, and causes the initial cluster 5–9 to fall below the threshold of three items.

This clustering of perfect pairwise relationships reveals that the transformation of the spatial diagram into dichotomous votes, together with the use of a binary matrix, discarded much of the information implicit in the spatial coordinates of the points and the slopes of the cutting lines. It will be also noted, here and later, that the greatest discrepancies between the parallel-line clusters and the clusters retrieved from the artificial roll-call data tend to correspond to items with extreme values of p_+; these marginal values are shown at the bottom of Table 5.5.

We next factor analyze the Q-matrix for the 26 cutting lines and examine whether this form of data smoothing, together with its use of more of the information in the Q-matrix, provides a closer ap-

Table 5.5 Binary matrix for artificial data (26 cutting lines)[a]

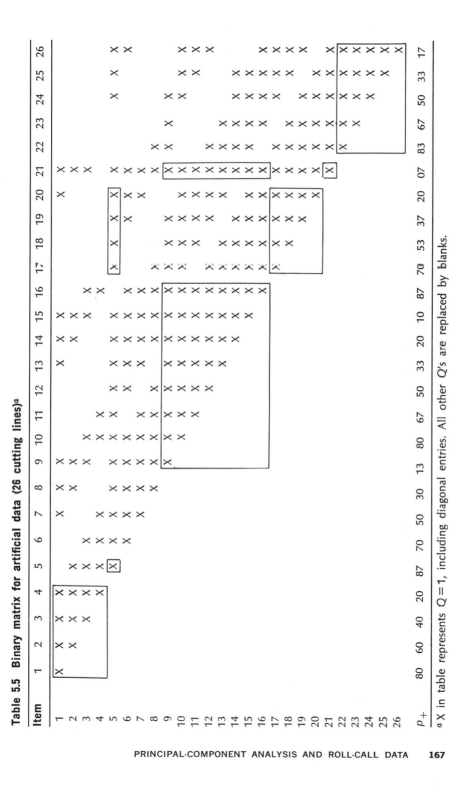

[a] X in table represents Q = 1, including diagonal entries. All other Q's are replaced by blanks.

proximation to the initial parallel-line clusters. The eigenvalues tend to indicate an underlying two-dimensional space; $\lambda_1 = 23.1$, $\lambda_2 = 5.0$, $\lambda_3 = 0.8$.[37] The loadings of the twenty-six "roll calls" on the first two factors of the Q-matrix are shown in Figure 5.2. For comparison with actual roll-call data in Chapter 8, two rotated axes, I' and II', are shown.

Inspection of Figure 5.2 suggests that there are three easily discernible clusters: items 1–4, items 22–26, and a large diffuse cluster in between. Within this central cluster, the items corresponding to lines with slopes nearest to 1–4 are also nearest to these items in the figure, and similarly for those nearest to 22–26.

A distance matrix was also computed on the basis of these two factors, and clusters based on it may be compared with those based on the Q-matrix. A threshold value of .1 will give approximately the same number of clusters as were obtained from the Q-matrix at $Q_{min} = 1$. The largest cluster at this threshold was 10-11-13-14-15-16-21. As Figure 5.2 shows, items 16 and 21 had factor loadings that placed them clearly in this cluster, even though the slope of the two corresponding lines (Figure 5.1) would have placed them in another cluster. Conversely, item 12 is omitted from this cluster, even though line 12 had the same slope as lines 10–15. Inspection of Figure 5.1 will show, however, that the points cut off by items 16 and 21 were subsets of those cut by the less extreme items in this cluster; their combination with the others in a perfect scale was also indicated in their entry into a common cluster at $Q_{min} = 1$ in the Q-matrix. Here, as in actual roll-call data, items with extreme values of p_+ can sometimes fit into various scales, and will be absorbed by the largest clusters if our procedure is followed.

The second and third largest clusters are now 22-23-24-25-26 and 1-2-3-4. They are no longer tied with other clusters of the same size,

[37]Half the eigenvalues are negative, the highest negative value being -1.19. When only the first 15 cutting lines were analyzed, factoring of the Y-matrix gave $\lambda_1 = 13.6$, $\lambda_2 = 1.8$, and the structure appeared more nearly one-dimensional. The data of Figure 5.1 were also analyzed by means of a ϕ-matrix. In this case the space was not clearly two-dimensional ($\lambda_1 = 11.5$, $\lambda_2 = 3.4$, $\lambda_3 = 3.3$), "difficulty factors" predominated, and the factor scores bore little resemblance to the initial configuration of points. Analyses of the data by means of matrices of r_t, Y, and ϕ/ϕ_{max} gave results inferior to Q, r_t being the best of these three as regards the predominance of the first two eigenvalues; but all three of these were far better than ϕ.

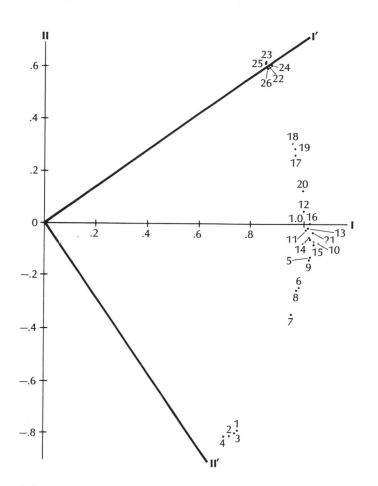

FIGURE 5.2. Factor Loadings of Twenty-Six Artificial Roll Calls, Based on First Two Principal Components of Q-Matrix.

and in this respect the factor-space clusters are superior to those from the Q-matrix in recovering the initial sets of parallel lines. These sets of five and four items are also distinct in Figure 5.2. The perfect recovery of these parallel-line clusters may be due to their extremeness in slope, or to their lack of highly extreme marginals. The remaining two clusters contain only three items each and would be ignored by our standard procedures: 6-7-8 and 17-18-19.

We find, therefore, that the use of the space defined by the first two factors has both advantages and disadvantages for the recovery of the set of parallel lines. The clusters based on it seem somewhat better than those based on the Q-matrix. However, some incorrect information is also introduced in the process. Those items that constituted perfect scales, as revealed by the Q-matrix, rarely had interpoint distances of exactly zero in the distance matrix; the most extreme example of this effect was the omission of item 12 from the first (largest) cluster. This results from the fact that the distances take into account not only the associations of items with each other, but the similarity of their associations with other items as well. These latter similarities add to our information, usually in a valid way, but sometimes in ways different from our expectations.

The two additional coordinate axes drawn in Figure 5.2 reveal another respect in which the factor loadings fail to reproduce the input data. The two clusters 1-2-3-4 and 22-23-24-25-26 were completely independent of one another and all Q's between items of one cluster and those of the other were zero. One would thus expect the two corresponding sets of points to define perpendicular axes. But if an axis is passed through the latter cluster, another axis perpendicular to it passes below the former. This distortion of the space will be considered again in Chapter 7 in connection with the resulting factor scores.

This example therefore shows some of the problems, as well as the advantages, of clustering in the factor space. It is by no means clear that the recovery of parallel-line clusters is a proper criterion for assessment of methods applied to data of this type, for the information defining parallelism is not necessarily incorporated in the artificial roll calls. One possible line of further development of this analysis is to consider a continuous set of points with a known distribution in the plane, and to use some measure of association between cutting lines which will measure the angle between them, under specified conditions (e.g., that they not intersect outside the distribution of points). This reasoning is akin to that involved in the tetrachoric correlation coefficient.[38]

---

[38]A more elegant method for treating data of this kind is the Lingoes multidimensional scaling procedure (MSA-II), which proceeds directly from the data matrix to find an optimal set of points for legislators, together with *two* points for the two alternatives of each dichotomy, in the same space. See Lingoes, "The Multivariate Analysis of Qualitative Data," and his prior paper, "New Computer Developments in Pattern Analysis and Nonmetric Techniques."

We shall continue the analysis of these artificial data in Chapter 7. We shall there develop a procedure for computing factor scores for legislators based on the factoring of the Q-matrix; and it will be seen that in spite of the shortcomings of factoring the Q-matrix, the configuration of points in Figure 5.1 can be reproduced in this way with a considerable degree of accuracy.

PART II
PARTIES AND FACTIONS

6.
THE COHESION OF
PARTIES AND FACTIONS

E turn now from the identification of issues to the study of parties and factions on the basis of legislative votes. In defining this problem, our first task is to enlarge the customary usage which separates "party" from "faction." For a general concept that embraces both we use the term "faction." By "faction" we shall refer to any subset or group of members in a legislative body who communicate with one another, show solidarity, and for this reason (and not simply because of prior similarity in attitudes) may be expected to vote alike. Examples of factions in this sense might include legislative parties, caucuses within a legislative party, state or regional delegations, or informal friendship groups. We thus extend the general scope of this part of the book to include collegial bodies that do not involve formal parties—the Supreme Court, the United Nations General Assembly, the conventions or congresses of individual parties—and the internal analysis of legislative parties themselves.

As in our analysis of issues, we wish to find measures of factional membership that are associated with other independently obtained measures of the same variables, or with measures of other variables. While the most frequently used indicator of factional membership has been official membership in a legislative party, other measures may sometimes be more appropriate and more valid. Several sociometric studies have been done on American state legislatures, and data of this type might be used to validate measures of factional membership.[1] Indeed, formal group membership is not very useful as a criterion in the study of one-party legislatures, intraparty factions, or nonpartisan bodies such as the United Nations General Assembly, where considerable ingenuity is required to validate measures of factional membership and cohesion.

This chapter will discuss those measures of factional cohesion that depend on prior knowledge of the formal membership of each faction being considered. This restriction will limit our attention largely to the analysis of legislative parties; but the analysis will be occasionally extended to other formally defined sets of legislators, such as the delegates of a party from a particular geographical area, that may also be analyzed in this way. We begin by assuming, therefore, that the bodies we deal with contain some subgroups whose membership is defined independently of the votes. We usually obtain lists of names of the members in these subgroups from official publications, such as the legislative journal or directory.

This emphasis on formally defined lists of legislators displays an asymmetry in the customary treatment of legislators and roll calls, for we scarcely considered the analogous procedures for roll calls. Conceivably one could carry out similar analyses of sets of roll calls that were similar in certain formal ways, such as those on bills reported by a given legislative committee.

After discussing those methods and indices that depend on prior lists of legislators in parties or other subgroups, we shall consider in Chapter 7 the more general question of identifying factions on the basis of roll-call votes alone. This question can arise if we wish to identify informally or privately defined factions, or if we are uncertain whether the formally defined parties really constitute the most important groupings in the legislature. Even an uncertainty about the proper placement of a few members, such as results from inadequate documentation on an earlier historical period, can lead us to consider these questions.

In Chapter 8 we shall use both these starting points—lists of party members and roll-call votes alone—as bases for placement of individual legislators in terms of their partisanship or party loyalty.

[1]These include Monsma, "Interpersonal Relations in the Legislative System"; Patterson, "Patterns of Interpersonal Relations in a State Legislative Group"; and Wahlke et al., The Legislative System.

THE COHESION OF INDIVIDUAL PARTIES

The simplest type of index that uses a formal listing of members of a faction to measure the cohesion of that faction is one that considers only one such faction at a time. The question is asked (usually of a legislative party), How cohesive is this faction on this roll call? Or, how cohesive is it over a specified series of roll calls? Whether an index of this type conforms to a conceptual definition of "cohesion" is a question that may properly be raised; but if we follow the conventional approach of considering each roll call separately, we have little choice among possible indices of cohesion.

One index of this kind was proposed by Lowell. In his classic analysis of legislative votes in England and America, he selected for particular attention those votes, for a given party, in which more than nine-tenths of the party's members voted on the same side of the question. The proportion of roll calls that fall into this category in a given period of time, or among those on a given issue, has been used by Lowell and others as an indicator of the corresponding degree of party cohesion or unity. It is particularly useful in the study of multiparty systems, where the indices of bipartisan opposition, to be discussed below, cannot be used.[2]

In evaluating this index, we confront a general question that affects other indices based on numbers or proportions of roll calls: How do the results depend on possible duplication or multiplication of roll calls on the same subject? If our results are affected by counting roll calls (as in determining cluster size), or by the proportion which roll calls of a given type constitute within a larger set, then the accidental duplication of a given roll call would seem to produce a change that was undesired because it was irrelevant to our purposes.

Our aim in constructing an index of this type is presumably to discover something about the motivations of the legislators. We may wish to measure how strongly they were motivated to vote together as a result of belonging to this particular group (the legislative party). Or we may wish to know whether other influences, such as similarity

[2]Lowell, "The Influence of Party upon Legislation in England and America." A few years earlier there had appeared Libby's "A Plea for the Study of Votes in Congress." Application to a multiparty system is made in MacRae, *Parliament, Parties and Society in France 1946–1958,* p. 56.

of constituency or of previous experiences in political careers, happened to coincide with party affiliation. In either case, we might be led to attach more importance to a roll call, or a vote, which better reflected this motivation.

In the contemporary U.S. House of Representatives, the need to consume half an hour or more in a roll call limits the number of frivolously duplicated votes. In the Senate, with its smaller membership and less stringent rules regarding amendments, tactical repetition of votes has been more frequent. Proxy voting in the Fourth French Republic, and perfunctory roll calls on unanimous votes in many American state legislatures, have made votes possible at less inconvenience to individual legislators, and thereby increased the probability of duplication. Electrical voting devices promise to heighten this problem for the analyst. One remedy may be the selection of "important" votes for study.[3]

A second general question that arises in connection with the Lowell classification is statistical rather than substantive. The choice of a 90 percent threshold for dichotomizing roll calls was an arbitrary one. Its use in the past is a reason for using it again, so that there may be comparability with the literature; but other considerations should also affect our choice. The choice of the best threshold level depends on the degree of division within the party being studied; if a dichotomy is to be created, then it will provide most information if the proportions in its two classes are as nearly equal as possible. This same problem arose in connection with the binary matrix in Chapter 3.

Regardless of what threshold level is chosen for a dichotomy, the results at this level need not agree with those at other levels. For example the French MRP (Christian Democratic party), when Campbell studied it, showed the lowest level of complete unanimity of any party in the National Assembly; but in votes with some dissidence but less than 5 percent, it was highest![4] The proportion of

---

[3]Lowell and others have omitted unanimous and near-unanimous votes from the base of percentages. Alexander, in *Sectional Stress and Party Strength*, analyzed selected subsets of votes in the smaller pre-Civil-War House; a political yearbook was used for sample selection in MacRae, *Parliament, Parties, and Society*, Appendix A; and Riker has proposed an index that may be used for such selection, in "A Method for Determining the Significance of Roll Calls in Voting Bodies."

[4]See Peter Campbell, "Discipline and Loyalty in the French Parliament During the Pinay Government," Table I.

votes on which the MRP exceeded a given threshold of unanimity would thus have ranked the party quite differently, depending on the threshold chosen. Such difficulties cannot be altogether avoided as long as we summarize an entire distribution in terms of a single number.

It is likely, however, that the data can be summarized more efficiently if each roll call is characterized by a quantitative index of party cohesion rather than a dichotomous classification. We have seen in connection with indices of association between roll calls (Chapter 3) that information is discarded when we change a quantitative variable into a ranking or a ranking into a dichotomy. A quantitative index, or the average of such an index over roll calls, will provide more information.[5]

An index of cohesion which uses more of the information available was proposed by Rice.[6] If we consider only those legislators who cast positive or negative votes, and let

N = the total number of legislators voting, in the group under consideration, and

p = the proportion voting yea,

then Rice's index of cohesion is $100|p - (1 - p)| = 100|2p - 1|$. Thus if 70 percent vote yea, the index is $70 - 30 = 40$. The same value will be obtained if 70 percent vote nay, since the absolute-value signs insure that the result will be positive. This index has been used extensively. If we wished to avoid absolute-value signs—a preference which is customary in least-squares analysis—we might also consider the index $(2p - 1)^2$ for this purpose. Since these indices are invariant under polarity change, it is immaterial whether p relates to yea or nay votes.

Another approach to measuring the cohesion of legislative groups has been proposed by Grumm.[7] He proposes an index of agreement

[5]The general problem involved is that of the relative efficiency of statistical tests. An example is the greater efficiency of the mean than the median as a measure of location, if the data are normally distributed; see Dixon and Massey, *Introduction to Statistical Analysis*, p. 72. The superiority of one index or statistic to another in this sense depends in general on the distribution of the universe from which the data are drawn.

[6]Rice, *Quantitative Methods in Politics*, chap. 15.

[7]Grumm, "The Means of Measuring Conflict and Cohesion in the Legislature."

(or cohesion) among a set of legislators on a set of roll calls, computed by averaging individual indices of agreement between all possible pairs of legislators in the set. Using this general notion but a different index of pairwise similarity, we can show that under certain conditions the same result is obtained by averaging either over legislator pairs or over roll calls.

In making this demonstration we shall assume for simplicity that there are no absences among the set of legislators with which we are dealing, on the roll calls under consideration. We consider first a single roll call, then aggregate over a number of roll calls. The first step is to express an index of agreement between legislators on a single roll call, based on summing the contributions made by the relations between particular pairs of legislators. One way to define this "increment of agreement" is to let it be +1 if the two legislators in question vote the same way on a roll call, and −1 if they disagree. The resulting algebraic sum will consist of one term for agreements minus another for disagreements. (This index will also be discussed in Chapter 7.)

We first derive a measure of the proportion of agreement on a single roll call in these terms: the proportion of possible pairs of legislators who vote alike. Let

n_+ = the number who vote positively (or yea) on the roll call $(= Np_+)$, and

n_- = the number who vote negatively (or nay) $(=Np_-)$.

Then the total number of agreeing pairs is

$$\frac{n_+(n_+ - 1)}{2} + \frac{n_-(n_- - 1)}{2}$$

the number of disagreeing pairs is n_+n_-, and the sum of these can shown to be $N(N - 1)/2$, where $N = n_+ + n_-$. (Exercise: show this.) In the limiting case when n_+, n_-, and N are very large relative to unity, the proportion of agreeing pairs among all possible pairs is

$$p_a = \frac{(n_+^2 + n_-^2)}{N^2}$$

This can also be expressed as

$$p_a = p_+^2 + (1 - p_+)^2 = 2p_+^2 - 2p_+ + 1 \tag{6.1}$$

If the proportions of agreements and disagreements are p_a and p_d respectively, and if there are no absences, $p_a + p_d = 1$. We have expressed p_a in (6.1); but if our index subtracts disagreements from agreements, we want $p_a - p_d = 2p_a - 1$. This is equal to $4p_+{}^2 - 4p_+ + 1$, or $(2p_+ - 1)^2$, the same index proposed above in our discussion of Rice's index of cohesion. The result so far is that, at least in the case of large N, we have gained greater generality of interpretation for our new index of cohesion by following conventional statistical practice rather than using absolute values.

Under this same assumption, it can be seen easily that the result of averaging over pairs of legislators and then averaging over roll calls is the same as that of first cumulating the contributions of various roll calls to the agreement of a given pair of legislators, then averaging over legislators. This result will hold for any index of interlegislator agreement, and any corresponding index of cohesion on a given roll call, that are computed by cumulating the individual contributions of legislator pairs; for we are simply performing a double summation—as in a matrix whose rows are the $N(N - 1)/2$ legislator pairs and whose columns are the n roll calls—and the order of summation is immaterial. This property, however, does not hold for all indices of cohesion (e.g., for Rice's index) or for all indices of interlegislator agreement.

A simple additive index does not tell us all that we might wish to know about the agreement and disagreement within a party or legislature. For it matters whether repeated disagreements separate the same or different sets of legislators. In the former case, we may have a stable structure of antagonistic blocs; in the latter, a set of shifting and cross-cutting factions. This distinction is well known in political sociology and corresponds to superimposed versus pluralistic cleavages respectively. However, indices that make this distinction for legislatures are rare.[8]

We may also wish to characterize an individual legislator's allegiance to his party. Although this type of index for individual legislators is

---

[8]The distinction is made in these terms in Dahrendorf, *Class and Class Conflict in Industrial Society*, pp. 215 ff. One approach to the measurement of superimposed cleavage derives from the study of cutting points in cumulative scales; see Silbey, *The Shrine of Party*, p. 63, where the proportion of legislators in the largest scale segment is used as a measure of party unity. Such a measure needs to be rendered independent of the number of roll calls in the scale, however.

most often calculated in relation either to an ideological criterion or to interparty opposition, it can also be done for a party considered alone. One simple way to do this would be to choose those roll calls on which the party attained a certain degree of cohesion (according to one of the indices considered above) and to count a legislator's deviations from the position of his party majority on those roll calls as a proportion of all roll calls of that type. If the threshold value of cohesion is set at zero and tie votes and absences are assumed not to occur, then an index of deviation from the party majority may be calculated, the average of which bears a simple relation to Rice's index of cohesion. For if we let $p_{min} = \min(p, 1 - p)$ then the sum of the values of this index for all legislators over a set of roll calls will be Σp_{min}. But Rice's index of cohesion can be written as $(1 - 2p_{min})$, and its average value over a series of roll calls will be one minus twice the average of this index of deviation from party.

Another measure of deviation from the party majority would be a weighted sum of deviations, each weighted by the index of cohesion of the party on the roll call in question, expressed as a proportion of the maximum value that such an index could attain (for a legislator who deviated from the majority position on every roll call considered). While these indices are not used often, they anticipate the type of reasoning that we shall use in considering indices in which loadings on a partisanship factor are used as weights—e.g., partisanship factor scores—in Chapter 8.

OPPOSITION IN TWO-PARTY SYSTEMS

Lowell also identified votes on which more than 90 percent of one party opposed more than 90 percent of the other, in the two-party legislatures he studied.[9] By expressing the number of these votes as a proportion of the total (omitting near-unanimous votes in which more than 90 percent of both parties were on the same side), he measured the general degree of partisanship in a legislature or a legislative session, and showed higher partisanship in England than America as well as fluctuations over time. This type of measure has been used in numerous studies of partisanship in Congress and American state

[9]Lowell, *op. cit.*, pp. 324, 348.

legislatures, though again with variation of thresholds among studies.[10] A vote meeting such a criterion is conventionally known as a *party vote*.[11] Similarly, the *Congressional Quarterly* classifies roll calls on which majorities of the two parties are opposed as *party unity votes*.

One might again ask, Why 90 percent? Conceivably one such threshold value may have particular significance in a legislative body. In an interview, the Republican whip of the Massachusetts House once stated that he counted his members' dissidence in precisely these terms, i.e., the number of times they voted against 90 percent of their party colleagues. But while this type of validation is relevant, the use of any single threshold value still discards information. A partial remedy is to use a quantitative measure of party opposition rather than a dichotomy.

Rice proposed two quantitative indices of party opposition (or of opposition between any two groups of legislators) which have been widely used. If we let

$p_{+1} =$ the proportion of positive votes among group 1 of legislators, and

$p_{+2} =$ the proportion of positive votes among group 2,

then the *index of difference* is defined as $100|p_{+1} - p_{+2}|$, and the *index of likeness* as $100(1 - |p_{+1} - p_{+2}|)$. The value of either if these indices is unchanged by the substitution of negative for positive votes as the basis of computation (as long as their sum is N), or by the reversal of the order in which groups 1 and 2 are considered.[12]

In calculating these indices, we are again working with a four-fold table relating two dichotomous variables—party and a particular roll call. Now, however, we are treating it asymmetrically, for Rice's index of difference is the absolute value of the (asymmetric) percentage difference, which we rejected earlier as an index for cluster-

[10]Lowell's 90 percent criterion was used in Turner, *Party and Constituency*. For a summary of studies using various criteria, see Jewell and Patterson, *The Legislative Process in the United States*, pp. 418–421.

[11]Lowell's use of the term to refer to 90 percent voting by a single party has not been retained.

[12]Rice, *op. cit.*, chap. 15. He used these indices to contrast not only parties, but also ideological groups within parties, and farm and labor members of legislatures.

ing. But the logical and conceptual relationship between party and vote may indeed be asymmetrical; party would seem antecedent, both temporally and causally; thus asymmetric indices are now appropriate even though the data again give rise to fourfold tables of the same form.

But as with the cohesion of a single party, it is desirable to consider indices that do not use the absolute-value sign. The analogous index of difference would be $(p_{+1} - p_{+2})^2$. This and other alternative indices, including some of those introduced in Chapter 3, will be discussed later in this chapter.

An additional problem in the use of this fourfold table is the possibility that independence between the two dichotomies is not conceptually equivalent to zero partisanship. We shall discuss this possibility in connection with Figure 6.4 below and in Chapter 8.

In studying opposition in two-party legislatures, we wish again to characterize the voting of individual legislators as well as of parties. The most frequently used index that purports to measure individual legislators' partisanship is the Congressional Quarterly's "party unity index," based on those roll calls in which majorities of Democrats and Republicans are opposed (party unity votes). The number of these roll calls in which a legislator deviates from his party's position is expressed as a proportion of the total number of such roll calls.[13] The result is to generate two indices for legislators of the two parties, one of which is essentially the negative of the other.

This index was used by Turner under the name "index of party loyalty," but it is questionable whether it measures loyalty to party as distinct from ideological position on issues.[14] The term "party loyalty score" has also been used by Mayhew for an index based on frequency of voting with one's party majority, but it seems open to the same criticism.[15] We shall discuss the distinction between group or party allegiance and ideological positions in detail in Chapter 8.

[13]Or to the number on which the legislator in question took a position.

[14]Turner, op. cit., pp. 78–79.

[15]Mayhew, Party Loyalty Among Congressmen, p. 10. His index, for a selected set of roll calls, is "the proportion of votes . . . cast in accordance with the positions of party majorities," and is thus the complement of an index of deviation from party, discussed above.

GRAPHICAL PRESENTATION OF
COHESION AND PARTISANSHIP

The conditions under which a roll call in a two-party legislature is judged to be partisan, according to the various measures we have considered, may be shown simply with the aid of a diagram. The data on which these indices are based can be reduced to two numbers: the proportion of legislators voting yea, for each of the two parties. In these terms, any roll call can be represented by a point in a square diagram such as that of Figure 6.1.[16] This graph is applicable only to a two-party legislature, but concevlably it can be generalized to a larger number of dimensions for a multiparty chamber.

Those votes on which individual parties have 90 percent or more of their legislators on the same side lie in regions bounded by parallel horizontal or vertical lines. Votes of party opposition (party votes or party unity votes) lie in squares at the upper-left and lower-right corners. A given value of the index of likeness or difference is represented by a diagonal line of 45° slope from lower left to upper right, together with the symmetrical line on the other side of the main diagonal. These same straight lines are also the loci of constant $(p_{yD} - p_{yR})^2$, the alternative index we have proposed, since if the square of a quantity is constant, that quantity $(p_{yD} - p_{yR})$ must also be constant. For the main diagonal, $p_{yD} = p_{yR}$.[17]

An additional interpretation of this type of diagram becomes possible if we can assign polarities (+ and −) to the roll calls under study and change the variables measured on the axes to p_{+D} and p_{+R}. Scale clusters such as we found in Chapter 3 provide one source of roll calls with definite (and usually consistent) polarities. Figure 6.2 shows the points corresponding to a number of roll calls in the House of Representatives in the 87th Congress (1961–1962).

The roll calls shown as points in Figure 6.2 are those that entered into the dominant scale for the Democrats and at the same time en-

---

[16]Such diagrams were proposed in Keefe, "Party Government and Lawmaking in Illinois General Assembly," 58 n., but have rarely been used since then.

[17]A line which is the locus of tie votes may also be shown on such a diagram: $N_D p_{yD} + N_R p_{yR} = (N_D + N_R)/2$.

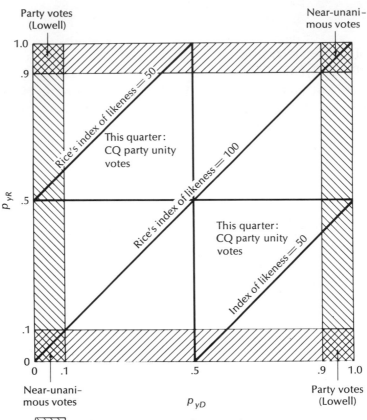

 Democrats vote with more than 90 percent on one side

 Republicans vote with more than 90 percent on one side

FIGURE 6.1. Graphical Classification of Party Votes in a Two-Party Legislature.

Definitions: p_{yD} = proportion of yeas among Democrats.
p_{yR} = proportion of yeas among Republicans.
Every roll call corresponds to a point within the square. Its horizontal distance from the left side is p_{yD}; its vertical distance from the bottom is p_{yR}.

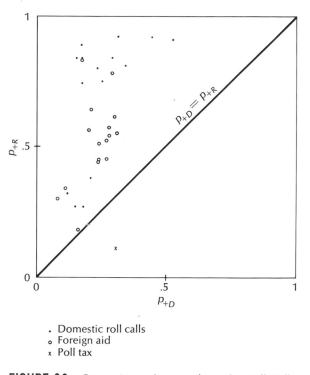

. Domestic roll calls
o Foreign aid
x Poll tax

FIGURE 6.2. Comparison of p_{+D} and p_{+R} for Roll Calls in Selected Scales, House of Representatives, 1961–1962.

tered into one of the five scales for the Republicans which shared a general left-right factor.[18] The positive polarity could be assigned without ambiguity to the conservative vote for each roll call. Since only roll calls with at least .07 dissidence were used, no points appear closer than .07 to the sides of the square.

The substantive features of the diagram stand out: its right-hand side and its lower triangle (below the line $p_{+D} = p_{+R}$) are nearly empty. The first of these features is due to the unity of the liberal Democrats, who tended to be united on the votes common to the scales of the

---

[18]The dominant scale for the Democrats included 41 percent of all the roll calls in their Q-matrix, while that for the Republicans, dealing with foreign aid, included only 12 percent. But five scales for the Republicans each included one or more items that were also in the Democrats' main scale, and these five scales had associations with one another of .47 or more; see MacRae, "A Method for Identifying Issues and Factions," pp. 921, 923.

two parties and were nearly equally united on all the votes in the Democrats' scale. The second feature reflects the generally greater liberalism (lesser conservatism) of Democrats than of Republicans, the only exception being a vote on the poll tax ($\times$ in the figure). This type of exception appeared in several Congresses, as the Republicans ("the party of Lincoln") often cast a higher proportion of their votes for civil rights than did the Democrats.

If a similar diagram were presented for one of the Eisenhower Congresses, more points would fall below the diagonal, since Eisenhower induced more of his party colleagues to support liberal measures at home and abroad—or failed to attract so many Democrats to their support.[19] The fact that the President's influence can sometimes run counter to the typical direction of ideological difference between the parties is a reminder that partisanship is logically distinct from ideology. Our use of the $p_{+D} - p_{+R}$ diagram allows us both to examine differences in partisanship among roll calls and to see at the same time whether they are in the direction of typical ideological difference.

Another difference between issues contrasts roll calls on foreign aid (circles in Figure 6.2) and those on domestic legislation (solid points). The Democrats had no more than 31 percent dissent on these votes on foreign aid while they approached 50 percent on some of the domestic votes. The Republicans tended to be evenly divided on foreign aid while they were more nearly unanimous, usually on the conservative side, on domestic votes. In general there was somewhat more partisan opposition on domestic affairs; imaginary lines corresponding to constant values of Rice's index of difference, parallel to the diagonal, would leave more of the solid points to the upper left.

Another way in which variation in partisanship among roll calls can affect scale clusters is shown in Figure 6.3. This figure is a graph of p_{+D} against p_{+R}, as before, but it is now based on scales from a single Q-matrix for Republicans and Democrats together. The entire membership of the House in the 87th Congress was treated as a single "party" and the 182 roll calls involving at least .07 overall dissidence were selected for the computation of a Q-matrix. The first two scale clusters, involving 63 and 35 roll calls respectively, are

[19]This same difference in voting between the parties was shown in another way in Kesselman's two articles on "Presidential Leadership in Congress on Foreign Policy." Variation in the degree and direction of partisanship in relation to party control of the Presidency were also shown in Turner, op. cit., chap. 3.

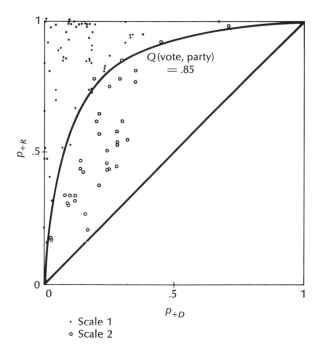

FIGURE 6.3. Comparison of p_{+D} and p_{+R} for Roll Calls in Two Scales for Democrats and Republicans Combined (87th House).

shown; roll calls in the first scale are plotted as solid points, those in the second as open circles. These two sets of points appear in generally separate regions of the figure, those in the first scale being mostly to the upper left. Individual points can now be located near the sides of the square, since the dissidence requirement can be satisfied by one party while the other is undivided, or by the interparty difference itself.

The roll calls in these two scales differ considerably in their degree of partisanship. They also happen to be somewhat distinct in subject matter, as more than half of the votes in the second scale concern foreign aid, while two at most in the first scale deal with this subject. Yet we hypothesize that it is differences in partisanship, rather than issues, that bring about this separation.[20]

[20]A similar difference in association between scales with party is reported in Clausen, "Measurement Identity in the Longitudinal Analysis of Legislative Voting," p. 1033.

The two regions of the graph in which the two scales fall cannot be cleanly separated by the loci of constant partisanship we have considered above; the diagonal lines corresponding to the Rice index of difference may fail to consider as highly partisan, for example, votes on which one party is unanimous and the other is deeply divided. The same problem arises, to a greater degree, for the party-vote type of classification with its corresponding squares at upper left and lower right. If, however, we measure partisanship by an index of association between party and vote (such as we shall discuss in the next section), we can obtain a curved line as a locus of constant partisanship. Such an "iso-Q line" for Q (vote, party) = .85 is shown in Figure 6.3 and separates the two clusters fairly successfully. (Exercise: plot such a line on graph paper. The equation of such lines is given in footnote 24 below.)

The result of scaling the parties together may thus be a set of scale clusters that differ from one another in the degree of partisan opposition they reflect, as well as in substantive issues. We saw in Table 4.2 that two roll calls might be associated with one another for the two parties combined, even though they were not associated within either party alone. This same general process seems to be operating in Figure 6.3; roll calls are grouped together in scale clusters because they share a particular degree of partisan opposition. If a particular issue, such as foreign aid, is associated with lesser partisan opposition, then it will tend to be manifested in a separate scale. But the separation of issues by scale clusters can be clearer in an individual party: the foreign-aid cluster for the Republicans in the 87th House had 95 percent of its items concerned with foreign aid, while the second scale for Republicans and Democrats combined had only 51 percent.

Combining the two parties may not only produce scales in which disparate issues are connected by partisanship; it may, conversely, separate issues from one another that combine in scales within the individual parties. While the internal ordering of legislators in each party may be quite constant over a large number of issues (especially for the Democrats), the two-party orderings may combine in characteristically different ways on different issues. One example is civil rights, which tends to fit into a general left–right division within each party, but on which the Republicans as a group have tended to vote more to the left. Another example showing a similar shift was foreign aid under Eisenhower. The possibility that an issue can form a scale within each party, yet not scale for the parties combined, may also be explained with reference to Figure 6.2; for unless the items have the same rank order of marginals (p_+) within both parties, some votes that fit the scale model within one party will become "errors" when the parties are combined.

For these reasons it is useful to distinguish the purposes for which scales should be constructed—some favoring the analysis of the parties separately, some the combination of parties. For identification of issues, it seems worthwhile to find scales for the parties separately, insofar as the parties constitute separate social groups with separate perspectives. We should expect Democrats in the U.S. House to have definite notions as to where they themselves stood with respect to their party colleagues on particular issues and Republicans to have similar views as to their relations to other Republicans; but because of the lesser communication across party lines,[21] and the variation among roll calls in degree of partisan opposition, we should expect the relative placement of a Democrat and a Republican to be less closely related to the attitude systems that we have in mind as "issues."

For the identification of partisanship and of the effects of presidential leadership, however, combination of the parties is essential. We have suggested that the degree of partisan opposition may be indicated by the proportion of all roll calls that fall into a leading or dominant scale for the parties combined. We shall also suggest in Chapter 8 that the differences in placement of legislators on two combined-party scales such as those of Figure 6.3 may tell us something about the partisanship of individual legislators. But if we combine the parties and look for issues in the resulting clusters, one of the resulting scales is likely simply to join end to end two scales for the individual parties; for a roll call to enter such a scale, one of the parties must be essentially undivided, and the dimension measured may well involve partisan opposition.[22]

Factor analysis of both parties together also tends to produce factors involving partisanship.[23] In several previous studies, however, an ana-

[21]See Clapp, The Congressman, p. 14.

[22]For the use of combined-party scales to measure partisan opposition, see MacRae, "A Method . . . ," p. 925. For scales linking parties end to end, see MacRae, "Roll Call Votes and Leadership," pp. 548–549, and Parliament, Parties and Society, p. 190.

[23]Factors involving partisanship have been found in Lee F. Anderson, Watts, and Wilcox, Legislative Roll-Call Analysis, p. 165; and in Marwell, "Party, Region, and Dimensions of Conflict in the House of Representatives."

lytic rotation procedure such as Varimax has been applied to the factor loadings, and certain of the resulting factors—usually the first rotated factor—interpreted in terms of partisanship. We shall argue in Chapter 8 that this procedure is inappropriate, but that with better rotation criteria, partisanship indices can be based on factor analysis.

ALTERNATIVE INDICES OF PARTISANSHIP OR BETWEEN-GROUP VARIATION

The preceding discussion has suggested that partisanship might be measured by an index of association, such as Q, between vote and party. The curves that are loci of constant Q can be shown to be hyperbolas passing through the points $(0, 0)$ and $(1, 1)$; one such curve is shown in Figure 6.3.[24] Other indices of association that attain unity for a scale relationship can also be used for this purpose; the corresponding curves may also pass through these points, since these indices permit high association to be measured even when substantial majorities of both parties vote on the same side. If ϕ is used, however, curves of constant but high ϕ will intersect the sides of the square; and for ϕ and some other indices, the curves will be altered by changes in the relative strengths of the parties.[25]

Whether an index of association is better than Rice's index of difference as a measure of partisanship, or whether one index of association is better than another, depends on our comparing the rival indices in terms of some external criterion. Such criteria may be logical (e.g., independence of irrelevant variables), empirical, or conceptual. We might examine which index gives rise to higher correlations with other indicators of partisanship, as Crane did with interview results in the research discussed in Chapter 1. Or we might consider their relation to our conceptual understanding of partisanship.

There is one hypothetical model of the behavior of social groups under external influences that would lead us to prefer an index of association, though whether this model applies to any particular

[24]If we let $x = p_{+D}$, $y = p_{+R}$, and $k = (1 + Q)/(1 - Q)$, then the equation of a line of constant Q is $kx - (k - 1)xy - y = 0$. (Exercise: demonstrate this.)

[25]Grumm (op. cit., p. 384) has proposed ϕ as a "coefficient of conflict" between groups.

legislative party is an empirical question. Let us assume that the legislators of the two parties can be assigned positions on an ideological or issue continuum, and that the distributions on this continuum for the two parties are similar but displaced from one another so that their central values or locations differ. Assume further that when group or partisan ties in the legislative parties are not mobilized, the central values are not identical, but differ by an amount reflecting the difference in distributions of individual members' ideologies between the parties. Finally, assume that when partisan ties are mobilized, the difference in location between the parties is changed—ordinarily, increased.

For any given degree of partisanship, or separation of the central values of the two distributions, we may imagine various roll calls to occur, corresponding to various cutting points on the continuum. The location of particular roll calls may depend on legislative strategy and tactics, the content of particular bills, or general fluctuations of public or legislative opinion—all without changes in the degree of partisanship involved. A proper index of partisanship would be one that had a constant value for all such cutting points, provided only that the difference of location between the distributions for the two parties remained the same. The reasoning involved in this model may be clarified with the aid of Figure 6.4.

The upper diagram in Figure 6.4 shows the model just described. The two legislative parties correspond to distributions along an ideological or issue continuum. Their separation is assumed to correspond to a particular degree of partisanship. Each of the two cutting points, A and B, generates a fourfold table of party versus vote. We assume that the difference between A and B is due to external influences not involving a change in partisanship and that the two corresponding fourfold tables should give rise to the same value of an index of partisanship. If such an index of partisanship could be found, a locus of constant value for this index would be a curved line on the $p_{+D} - p_{+R}$ diagram corresponding to a plot of the cumulative distribution for one party against that for the other. In shape this might resemble a curve of constant Q but would not be identical with it or with the curve for any other simple index of association; it would vary, depending on the distributions of the parties. If the parties' distributions were rectangular, the resulting curve would resemble a line of constant "index of difference." There is a question, of course,

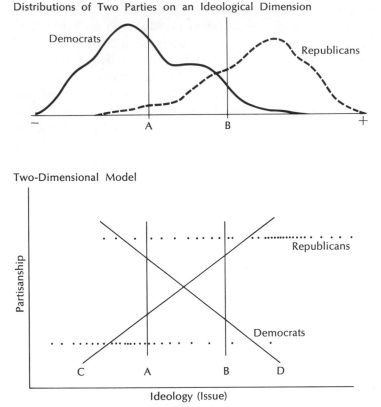

FIGURE 6.4. Two-Dimensional Model of Partisanship and Ideology.

whether such a measurable continuum has any operational counterpart, but we shall postpone that question for the following chapters.

The lower diagram in Figure 6.4 shows an elaboration on this model, in which the extent of partisanship is allowed to vary among roll calls while the distributions of legislators' ideological positions remain constant. The two cutting *lines* A and B again correspond to roll calls at a given constant degree of partisanship, but C now corresponds to a lower degree of partisanship, while D corresponds to a higher. An index of partisanship that conforms to the model should assign a higher value to D and to any roll call parallel to it, an intermediate value to A and B, and a low value to C and to any roll call parallel to it. The line C corresponds approximately to $Q = 0$, but in absolute terms this may correspond to *negative* partisanship as regards mobilization of the legislative party, for constituency and recruitment effects alone may give rise to a value of Q greater than zero.

We shall see in Chapter 8 that a two-dimensional distribution similar to that of the lower diagram emerges from a plot of factor scores based on congressional votes.

The roll call represented by D nearly separates the two parties from one another. If we imagine a set of lines parallel to D but shifted to right and left of it, they will generate a scale similar to Scale 1 in Figure 6.3. A set of lines parallel to A and B will generate a scale more like Scale 2 in that figure.[26]

This model directs us toward the use of measures of association as defining sets of roll calls having the same partisanship. It does not, however, tell us so easily how to define "zero" partisanship; for the separation of the two distributions in the upper diagram of Figure 6.4 would give rise to a nonzero value of any ordinary index of association, yet we have assumed this separation to result from individual ideologies rather than from group ties. This problem is a serious one to which we shall return in Chapter 8.

We have not yet considered in detail what "partisanship" or "party allegiance" means in substantive or conceptual terms. It might refer to the opposition of two solidarity groups, each internally cohesive, and thus correspond approximately to Coleman's model of community conflict.[27] In this case we should expect the leaders of the two groups to be more strongly opposed to one another than the rank and file. Or it might refer to responses to leadership by the Executive, involving cooptation of formal or alternative leaders in the legislative parties. As a third possibility, it might refer to allegiance to the legislative leaders within the chamber—the "inner club," "Establishment," or "priesthood of the House"—who might be expected to agree with one another across party lines.[28] We may be able to decide

---

[26]Reasoning based on this model has led us to look for general issue dimensions by studying the parties separately, rather than in combination. See also MacRae, *Dimensions of Congressional Voting*, p. 222.

[27]Coleman, *Community Conflict*.

[28]See White, *Citadel*; Clark, *The Senate Establishment*; MacNeil, *Forge of Democracy*.

which of these possible meanings of partisanship best applies in a given legislative body, at a particular historical period, if we can measure differing degrees of partisanship among the members of each legislative party and relate them to the activities of various leadership groups.[29] A further basis for choice among these definitions would be provided by the assignment of degrees of partisanship to roll calls, corresponding to the slopes of the cutting lines in Figure 6.4.

It also follows from this model that the measurement of partisanship and of ideological positions may be somewhat interdependent. For if the members of a party became more similar to one another in their positions on issues, there would be a corresponding increase in almost any indicator of partisanship that we have considered. We can thus measure changes in partisanship from one roll call to another in the short run for the same set of legislators, provided that their relative ideological positions do not change rapidly. But changes in the same index over the long run will not tell us so easily whether it is party solidarity or ideological distributions that have changed. Similarly, differences in values of a partisanship index between two distinct sets of legislators cannot so easily be attributed to differences in group solidarity as against ideological distributions.

Various other possible indices can also be used to characterize the partisanship of a roll call, based on the corresponding fourfold table. We have already discussed Yule's Q, and noted in Chapter 3 that there is a family of indices that are ordinally equivalent to Q; all of these generate the same lines of constant partisanship as Q, though for different constant values. We have also referred to ϕ, and implicitly to ϕ/ϕ_{max} and the tetrachoric coefficient, as well as to the percentage difference, whose absolute value is the Rice index of difference.[30]

A particularly interesting type of index is one that can be generalized to multiparty systems or other multicategory classifications of legislators. A simple example of this type is a generalization of the index we proposed above as a modification of Rice's index of difference: $(p_{+1} - p_{+2})^2$. Let

$p_{+i} =$ the proportion of positive votes in party or category i on a given roll call,

[29]A possibility not indicated in Figure 6.4.

[30]A modification of the percentage difference, to take account of the lesser variance of extreme proportions, is the arc sine transformation; see Dixon and Massey, *op. cit.*, p. 183.

and

$\bar{p}_+$ = the average of these proportions over all categories of legislators under consideration (we ignore the numbers of legislators in individual categories).

We may then define an index of intercategory difference in voting

$$\sum_i (p_{+i} - \bar{p}_+)^2$$

For convenience we may wish to take the square root of this index, or to multiply it by a constant such as the reciprocal of the number of categories. In the two-party case, if we multiply it by 2 we shall recover the index proposed earlier. (Exercise: show this.)

Another index of this type, which considers the number of legislators in each group, is related to the proportion of variation in the vote accounted for by the division of legislators into subsets. We shall derive this for the case of k subsets of legislators, then specialize to the case $k = 2$. Consider the $2 \times k$ table, for a given roll call,

n_{+1}	n_{+2}	.	.	.	n_{+k}	n_+
n_{-1}	n_{-2}	.	.	.	n_{-k}	n_-
n_1	n_2	.	.	.	n_k	N

where

n_{+j} = the number of legislators in subset j who vote positively

n_{-j} = the number in subset j who vote negatively

n_j = $n_{+j} + n_{-j}$ = the total number of legislators in subset j

n_+ = the total number of legislators who vote positively

$\quad = \sum_j n_{+j}$

n_- = the total number who vote negatively

$\quad = \sum_j n_{-j}$

N = the total number of legislators in the table

$$p_+ = \frac{n_+}{N}, \quad p_- = \frac{n_-}{N}, \quad p_{+j} = \frac{n_{+j}}{n_j}, \quad p_{-j} = \frac{n_{-j}}{n_j}, \quad p_j = \frac{n_j}{N}$$

For this table we wish to express the total variation among legislators in their votes on the roll call in question, and the variation that would be observed if each legislator were simply assigned the mean value for his subset. The proportion of the total which the latter constitutes is the index we wish.

The total variation among responses on the roll call is Np_+p_-, while the variation between subsets is $\Sigma n_j(p_{+j} - p_+)^2$. The desired index is then the variation between subsets, divided by the total variation:

$$\frac{\Sigma n_j(p_{+j} - p_+)^2}{Np_+p_-} = \frac{\Sigma p_j(p_{+j} - p_+)^2}{p_+p_-}$$

It can be shown that the variation within subsets, summed over all subsets, constitutes the remaining fraction of the total variation for the roll call.[31] (Exercise: show this.) We have thus defined an index of the proportion of total variation attributable to differences between these sets of legislators, which varies between 0 and 1. Unlike Q, however, it attains unity only when all the legislators in each subset vote alike. In the two-party case (a fourfold table), the proposed index can be shown[32] to be equal to ϕ^2. (Exercise: show this.)

The index of variation among subsets of legislators, discussed above, can be used to study the difference not only among legislative parties, but also among groups such as district or regional delegations. It has been used for this latter purpose in a study of district voting on various types of issues in the French National Assembly.[33]

It is also of interest to inquire whether an index of partisan opposition can be constructed in such a way that it cumulates elements attributable to each pair of legislators on each roll call, following the reasoning we used in considering the cohesion of a single party. Such an index is possible, but it does not resemble closely those that we have discussed above. For consider the fourfold table

[31]This index bears a relation to the intraclass correlation coefficient; see Steel and Torrie, *Principles and Procedures of Statistics*, pp. 191–193. It is also equal to χ^2/N; see Wallis and Roberts, *Statistics: A New Approach*, pp. 433–435; Kendall and Stuart, *The Advanced Theory of Statistics*, vol. 2, p. 504.

[32]For the equivalence see Walker and Lev, *Statistical Inference*, p. 272. The chi-square coefficient was also used as a measure of partisanship by Turner in *op. cit.*, pp. 29–31. However, this usage confuses tests of significance with estimation of parameters, and prevents the comparison of chambers having different numbers of members.

[33]MacRae, *Parliament, Parties, and Society*, p. 302, fn. 3.

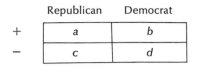

	Republican	Democrat
+	a	b
−	c	d

and let us count the number of agreements and disagreements across party lines. The agreements are $(ab + cd)$, the disagreements $(ad + bc)$, and the total of cross-party pairs is their sum, $(a + c)(b + d)$. We might then take as an index of disagreement between members of the parties

$$\frac{(ad + bc) - (ab + cd)}{(a + c)(b + d)} = \frac{(a - c)(d - b)}{(a + c)(b + d)}$$

This index is unity if $b = c = 0$ or if $a = d = 0$; it is −1 if the vote is unanimously positive or negative; and it is 0 is either party is divided evenly between + and − votes. It has no simple relation to the indices of association that we have considered.

It is also possible to construct indices of interlegislator agreement which weight unequally votes in the majority and minority on a given roll call. These and other indices may also be summed over cross-party pairs of legislators, to give indices of interparty agreement. Some indices of this sort for individual pairs of legislators will be discussed in the following chapter.

Another procedure for measuring intergroup differences among legislators, based on the relations between individual pairs, has been used by Truman, as a by-product of cluster-bloc analysis. While Truman's main analysis in *The Congressional Party* was aimed at the discovery of intraparty blocs on the basis of votes alone, he also carried out an interesting auxiliary analysis that made use of predetermined membership lists in order to examine the voting properties of the state delegations and committee delegations within each party in the House of Representatives.[34] For each member of such a group (e.g., a state delegation), he arranged that member's agreement indices with all his party colleagues in rank order. The positions of fellow members of the state delegation could then be examined as to their position in that ranking. Truman devised a procedure for aggregating measures of cohesion within each such group, and concluded that state

---

[34]Truman, *The Congressional Party,* chap. 7. Truman's method of bloc analysis will be discussed in the following chapter.

delegations were considerably more cohesive than committee delegations, within a given party.[35]

TIME SERIES OF PARTISANSHIP
IN CONGRESS

An extensive literature exists concerning the condition for partisan opposition in American legislative bodies, both state and national. Among the conditions that have been considered are the issue involved, the social and economic characteristics of particular states, the formal arrangements for representation (e.g., the upper vs. lower chamber), and the historical period.[36]

There is, however, a tendency to concentrate these investigations in recent periods, and to generalize about the party system without sufficient reference to historical data. One finding of this type is that party voting in the last few decades has been greatest in the industrialized and urbanized states.[37] Figures presented by Lowell for a few states in the 1890s, however, indicate that this relation has not always held.[38] This possible change in the correlations of party voing in the states will be relevant to a hypothesis developed below in relation to historical changes in congressional partisanship.

A major problem to which indices of partisanship are relevant is that of tracing and explaining variations in partisanship over time. We shall consider first the long-term variations in partisanship in the U.S. House of Representatives since pre-Civil-War times, and then the shorter-term variations in the post-World-War-II period.

A time series showing changes in party voting from 1835 to 1968, for periods for which data are available, is presented in Figure 6.5, which shows the percent of Lowell-type party votes in the House of Representatives in various years. It is clear that partisanship fluctuated considerably over this period. In the years following 1949, no session had as many as 10 percent party votes. The proportion in earlier

---

[35]*Ibid.*, pp. 257–258, 273–274. The procedure used does not provide a test of significance, however.

[36]This literature has been reviewed in Jewell and Patterson, *op. cit.*, chap. 17; and in Dye, "State Legislative Politics."

[37]Jewell and Patterson, *op. cit.*, p. 422.

[38]Lowell, *op. cit.*, pp. 538–541.

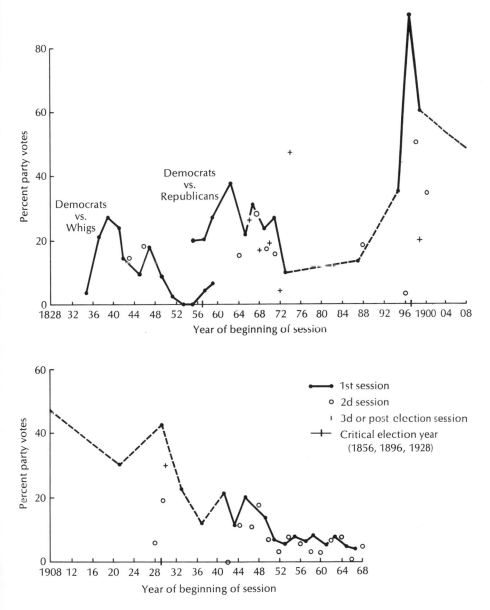

FIGURE 6.5. Party Voting in the US House of Representatives, 1835–1968. *Sources of data:* 1845, 1846, 1863, 1864, 1887, 1888, and 1897–1900 are from Lowell, "The Influence of Party upon Legislation in England and America"; the remaining points, 1835–1860, are from Alexander, *Sectional Stress and Party Strength,* Part II (based on selected roll calls); 1865–1874 are from unpublished data furnished by John L. Mc-Carthy; 1921, 1928, 1930–31, 1933, 1937, and 1944 are from Turner, *Party and Constituency,* p. 24; the remaining points, 1941–45, are from Young, *Congressional Politics in the Second World War,* Appendix B; 1895, 1896, 1929, 1930, and 1946–1968 are from calculations made under the direction of the author. The base for the proportion of party votes is the number of nonunanimous votes, in Lowell's sense, except for 1865–1874.

years, however, often exceeded this value, reaching its height in 1897 when 30 of the 35 roll calls in that year were party votes. A similarly high proportion were partisan in 1899. And in the second (lame-duck) session of the 43rd Congress, beginning in December 1874, nearly half the roll calls were party votes. In November 1874, the Democrats had gained control of the House; but before the new Congress could take office the sitting Republican majority hastened to pass its legislative program.[39]

Not only can a postelection session of Congress give rise to changes in partisanship, but so too can the difference between the first and second ordinary sessions. Points for the respective first sessions are indicated in Figure 6.5 by solid points, connected by solid lines (for consecutive Congresses) or dashed lines (where missing data intervene). Points for the second sessions are indicated by open circles, which lie for the most part below the lines connecting the solid points, indicating lesser partisanship in the second sessions than in the neighboring first sessions. Possibly the approach of an election year induces a greater sensitivity to constituency influences and a correspondingly lower partisanship.

Among the numerous variables that may account for these historical fluctuations in partisanship, one is the periodic occurrence of major electoral reorientations, or critical elections.[40] Three such elections have occurred in the period under study—in 1928, 1896, and probably in 1856—the last involving the demise of the Whig party and its replacement by the Republican party in presidential politics. The graph of Figure 6.5 suggests that partisanship fell to a low point before each of these elections and rose to a much higher value shortly thereafter. Conceivably the reorientation of the electorate was associated with a heightened expression in Congress of the new issues brought forth in the critical presidential election—issues which had previously been hindered from attaining clear partisan expression in Congress as well as in national campaigns.[41] A clear test of this hy-

[39]See Blaine, *Twenty Years in Congress,* pp. 563–565.

[40]See Key, "A Theory of Critical Elections"; MacRae and Meldrum, "Critical Elections in Illinois: 1888–1958"; and MacRae and Meldrum, "Factor Analysis of Aggregate Voting Statistics." This relation between congressional partisanship and critical elections has been suggested in Shannon, *Party, Constituency and Congressional Voting,* pp. 42–44.

[41]The action of the party system as a selective "gateway" for issues is hypothesized, for example, in Berelson, Lazarsfeld, and McPhee, *Voting,* pp. 209–212.

pothesis, however, awaits the addition of more points to the graph, as well as a closer study of the possible mechanisms by which partisanship changed. Data available from several studies of partisanship in the Senate tend to confirm the rise in partisanship after 1896, but fail to show a clear upsurge after 1928.[42]

We turn now to closer examination of year-by-year series for the period since 1940. With these series we may compare various indices of partisanship, as well as examine fluctuations in the importance of party in a single year or between Congressional sessions. Figure 6.6 presents series for three indices of partisanship, for Senate and House separately: the proportion of party unity votes (majorities opposing), the average index of difference, and the proportion of party votes (90 percent of one party opposing 90 percent of the other).

The series shown bear some relation to one another within each chamber, though they are not perfectly correlated. Their interrelations may be summarized by correlation coefficients in the absence of pronounced temporal trends; and if these series together with that for the average absolute value of Q are compared, the results indicate that those series using more of the information in the roll calls are more closely associated with one another.[43]

We may also compare Senate and House in terms of the series in Figure 6.6. Those years about which we can make the most confident interpretations are those for which all three series (for a given chamber) move in the same direction. For both chambers there was a decline in partisanship in 1942, probably reflecting a temporary wartime unity between the parties. All six of the series show a dip in 1946, perhaps reflecting the expectation of a swing toward the Republicans and a corresponding tendency for congressmen to run on district issues rather than in relation to President Truman's position. All but one rise in 1947, reflecting the intense partisanship of the Republican-controlled 80th Congress.

The Senate and House series are by no means identical, however;

---

[42]See Clubb and Allen, "Party Loyalty in the Progressive Years." J. B. Johnson, Jr., "The Extent and Consistency of Party Voting in the United States Senate," also provides data which on reanalysis support this conclusion. The proportions of Senate party votes given by Lowell, op. cit., however, reach a peak in the 50th Congress (1887–1888) after a trough in the 38th (1863–1864).

[43]The average index of difference and average $|Q|$ are correlated .94 for the Senate and .83 for the House. In each chamber the proportion of party unity votes is more closely associated with these two than is the proportion of party votes.

SENATE

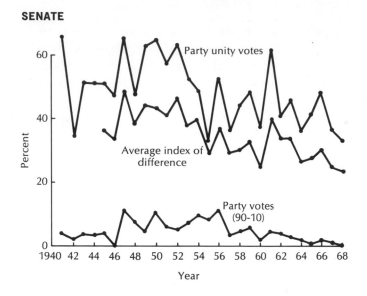

HOUSE OF REPRESENTATIVES

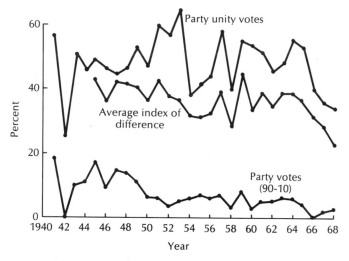

FIGURE 6.6. Indices of Partisanship for U.S. Congress, 1941–1968. Percent of party votes is based on all roll calls. Percent of party-unity votes (those on which majorities of the two parties were opposed) is based on all roll calls, following the practice of the *Congressional Quarterly,* which was used as a source for 1947–1968. Average index of difference between the two parties is also based on all roll calls. Data for 1941–1945 are based on graphs in Roland Young, *Congressional Politics in the Second World War,* Appendix B. Average indices of likeness and proportions of party unity votes were calculated with the aid of a computer program written by Leo M. Snowiss and modified by Daniel R. Graves.

correlations between series across chambers are generally lower than those within the same chamber.[44] One possible explanation of this difference is suggested by a closer examination of conditions under which the two series move in opposite directions. In 1950 the Senate series show a peak and the House series a trough, but in 1951 the opposite effects occur. To a certain extent this alternation continues through 1958, with the House becoming relatively less partisan in election years. In 1959, however, all six series move upward, and a new sort of alternation sets in, with the Senate as well as the House becoming more partisan in odd years, less partisan in even. One interpretation of these facts relates congressional partisanship to the expected influence of the Presidency in the coming election. When a strong President is in office and is expected to run again, as in 1948 and 1964, partisanship in the House may be maintained in election years. Under Eisenhower, a weaker or less partisan President, the biennial House elections may have been an occasion to appeal to districts rather than to party: House partisanship dropped sharply in 1954 and 1958. And when a presidential transition was expected, as in 1952 or 1960, House partisanship declined notably—though in the latter year, Senate partisanship also declined. We are thus led to hypotheses about constituency influence on the House and about the anticipation of presidential influence, both of which deserve further study.

The study of partisanship in relation to the pressures of election years is of particular interest in relation to general theories of representation. In the United States system, congressional representation (in contrast with presidential) seems to occur through appeals to the diverse aspects of the constituencies, unless the symbol and program of the Presidency draw the congressional campaigns together. The fragmentation that apparently occurs in election years in the absence of this presidential unifying influence is analogous to the weekend pressures toward fragmentation that occurred under weak premiers in the French National Assembly during the Fourth Republic.[45] This latter fragmentation, also a response to electoral and

[44]The correlations of indices across chambers are considerably lower, only one of the sixteen exceeding .6.

[45]MacRae, *Parliament, Parties and Society*, p. 312; Williams, *Crisis and Compromise*, p. 232 n.

constituency pressure, occurred along partisan lines in the French multiparty system, rather than within the parties as in the United States. But both these types of fragmentation militated against the "ideal type" of representative government (sometimes identified with Britain) in which two parties present candidates throughout the nation, all running on a single set of issues.

Another problem to which these data relate is the comparison of partisanship in the two chambers. In the proportion of 90–10 party votes, the House exceeds the Senate in 19 out of 28 years, but in party unity votes it exceeds in only 12 of 28, and in the index of difference, 13 of 24. These data do not fully confirm the widespread belief that the House is more partisan, since the result of the comparison depends on the index used. The problem deserves more careful study.

The study of partisanship in the Senate, and its difference at certain times from the degree of partisanship in the House, also raises the question whether the differences are substantive or are due to the relative ease of taking roll calls in the Senate. In general, several hypotheses as to the difference between upper and lower chambers may be suggested:

1. Different systems of districting permit different interests and coalitions to predominate.
2. A smaller chamber allows a greater degree of consensus among members of the body, so that the conditions for this consensus do not vary so clearly with constituency interests.
3. The terms and (for the U.S. Senate) years of election of the members make them less sensitive to constituency influences.
4. The smaller size of the upper chamber permits a larger number of roll calls, so that the meaning of proportions of roll calls in terms of an economy of legislative time is less clear.

Finally, we must again recall that different types of hypotheses have been used for interpretations in the long and short run. Over a single Congress, we expect neither the membership nor the members' positions on issues to change; we have thus related changes in votes or partisanship to external influences such as the nearness of an election or the symbolic significance of the Presidency. These influences, in turn, are considered to bear on the social cohesion of the legislative parties or to conflict with it by activating diverse constituency pressures. In the longer run, or in the contrast between two different legislative bodies, we expect differences in these same indices to reflect the configuration of interests in the political system, the corresponding attitudes and ideologies of the legislators, and the structural organization of the parties outside as well as inside the legislature. This latter type of hypothesis is more relevant to historical electoral reorientations or the contrast between urban and rural state legislatures in partisanship. Thus again we are forcibly reminded that a single index or operational definition can correspond to more than one concept, depending on the hypothetical model in which it is used.

This concludes the examples we shall give of time-series analysis of partisanship, but we also deal elsewhere with many of the themes treated here. The influence of the Executive on Congress is reflected not merely by partisanship but also by changes in the rank order of Congressmen on scales as the Presidency changes hands. The converse, constituency orientation, may well be reflected in differing sensitivity of the "in" and "out" parties to constituency influences, especially in relation to the closeness of their expected electoral contests. The structure of cleavage within the parties also varies from one Congress to another, as revealed by cluster analysis. And finally, the error rate in cumulative scales varies from one Congress to another, as well as between issues.[46]

[46]Changes in rank order of congressmen are treated in the two Kesselman articles *op. cit.* Differences in constituency relations were analyzed in MacRae, *Dimensions* . . . , chap. 4. Differences between the parties in internal issue structure were analyzed in MacRae, "A Method. . . ." And fluctuations in "error rate" have been reported in L. F. Anderson, "Variability in the Unidimensionality of Legislative Voting."

7.
BLOC ANALYSIS:
THE IDENTIFICATION OF FACTIONS

I N the last chapter we considered the difference in voting between sets of legislators, assuming that we knew in advance who was in each set. We turn now to the problem of identifying such sets or groupings from their votes, without advance knowledge as to their membership.[1]

The most frequent approach to this problem by political scientists has been to compute indices of similarity in voting between pairs of legislators, arrange these indices in a square matrix, and group together those sets of legislators whose votes most resemble one another. The procedures used to form these sets are similar to those discussed in Chapter 3 in connection with cluster analysis of roll calls. The resulting sets of legislators (justices, etc.) are typically referred to as "blocs," and the method as "cluster-bloc analysis"; we shall review these procedures below.

The procedure of grouping persons together by means of a matrix of pairwise relations has also been used by sociologists in sociometric analysis.[2] In that field, however, the matrix elements

---

[1]We set aside the question of identifying part of a group, knowing the remainder of its membership. This question is most likely to arise in historical studies, and the methods for approaching it may be analogous to the use of the discriminant function; see M. G. Kendall and Stuart, *The Advanced Theory of Statistics*, vol. 3, pp. 314–322. An analogous problem is the identification of the authorship of certain of the *Federalist* papers from their style; see Mosteller and Wallace, "Inference in an Authorship Problem."

[2]Numerous articles on this topic appear in *Sociometry*.

more clearly involve *relationships* between persons, e.g., friendship choices or reciprocated choices of this sort. The similarity between two legislators in their votes is a different sort of datum, as it describes their common orientation or behavior toward an external object (e.g., a bill or motion) rather than toward one another. And while we might well expect this common orientation to result from personal interaction, or to enhance interaction, it is a logically and conceptually distinct variable.

Specifically, the agreement between two legislators in their votes may result from similarity in their constituencies, ideologies, or other causes, without interaction or consultation between the legislators; and disagreement may result from causes other than personal hostility. If this is so, the similarity in their voting is an imperfect indication of their joint membership in any interacting social group in the legislature or elsewhere. We therefore risk an error of "misplaced concreteness," or of naive operationalism, if we completely identify the blocs found from such a matrix with interacting social groups.

To infer the existence of interacting social groups from agreement in voting, we must therefore try to control or set aside the effects of other variables that might also contribute to voting agreement. One approach to this problem, which we shall use in Chapter 8, is to try to measure legislators' ideological positions independently of their group affiliations, and to control these ideological positions while measuring group loyalty. A second approach involves the hypothesis that group influences alter over a shorter period than ideological positions. If this hypothesis is true, then *changes* in agreement between legislators, between roll calls, or between periods involving different degrees of group relevance, might provide a more valid indication of group interaction than would raw indices of similarity at a given time.

BLOC ANALYSIS BASED
ON FREQUENCY OF AGREEMENT

With this caution, we proceed to review the methods that have been used to identify blocs on the basis of similarity in voting. The earliest statistical work aimed at reconstructing blocs of legislators on the basis of their votes was that of Rice and Beyle.[3] Their general approach

[3]Rice, *Quantitative Methods in Politics,* chap. 16; Beyle, *Identification and Analysis of Attribute-Cluster-Blocs.*

Matrix of agreement scores (only the annotation labels "Bloc", "Independent Nucleus", "Fringe", and "Bloc" appear overlaid on the empty regions of the matrix):

	Neely, W. Va.	Kilgore, W. Va.	Humphrey, Minn.	Magnuson, Wash.	McMahon, Conn.	Lehman, N. Y.	Green, R. I.	Murray, Mont.	Anderson, N. M.	Myers, Pa.	Chavez, N. M.	Douglas, Ill.	Leahy, R. I.	Lucas, Ill.	Hill, Ala.	Sparkman, Ala.	McClellan, Ark.	Holland, Fla.	George, Ga.	Hoey, N. C.	Stennis, Miss.	Russell, Ga.	Chapman, Ky.
Neely, W. Va.		68	65	63	62	61		60	58														
Kilgore, W. Va.	68		64	60	59	58	58	59	61		60												
Humphrey, Minn.	65	64		63	62	65	62	62		60		60	60										
Magnuson, Wash.	63	60	63		60		59							Bloc									
McMahon, Conn.	62	59	62	60		58				60				58									
Lehman, N. Y.	61	58	65		58		58					58	59										
Green, R. I.		58	62	59									59										
Murray, Mont.	60	59	62		58																		
Anderson, N. M.	58	61																					
Myers, Pa.			60		60																		
Chavez, N. M.		60																	Fringe				
Douglas, Ill.			60			58																	
Leahy, R. I.			60			59	59									Bloc							
Lucas, Ill.					58																		
Hill, Ala.						Independent Nucleus										63							
Sparkman, Ala.															63								
McClellan, Ark.																		67	60	60	63	58	59
Holland, Fla.																	67		59	62	59		60
George, Ga.																	60	59		63	59		
Hoey, N. C.																	60	62	63				
Stennis, Miss.																	63	59	59			63	61
Russell, Ga.																	58				63		
Chapman, Ky.																	59	60			61		

FIGURE 7.1. Matrix of Agreement Scores Between 23 Democratic Senators in 81st Congress, 2nd Session. Only agreement scores of 58 or higher, on 74 selected roll calls, are shown. (David B. Truman, *The Congressional Party,* Wiley, 1959, p. 46)

has been followed more recently by Truman.[4] The method used by each of these writers was to prepare a matrix of agreement indices between pairs of legislators; the index used was either the number of roll calls on which a pair of legislators voted alike, or this number expressed as a fraction of the number of roll calls on which both voted. Blocs were then defined as subsets of legislators within which

[4]Truman, *The Congressional Party.* This method has also been used in unpublished studies by Lee F. Anderson.

every pair had at least a minimum specified index of agreement. In this respect the procedure is very similar to that presented in Chapter 3 for the binary matrix, although the corresponding index (the "proportion of similar responses or agreements" in Chapter 3) is not used for clustering roll calls.

An example of Truman's clustering procedure is shown in Figure 7.1. In this figure, 23 Democratic Senators in the 81st Congress are compared with one another with respect to their votes on 74 selected roll calls. Agreement scores of 58 or greater (the number of votes in agreement) are shown in the figure, other elements being left blank. At this threshold (corresponding to a binary matrix), a cluster of five non-Southern Democrats, another of four Southerners, and a pair from Alabama are found. Other Senators are designated as belonging to the fringe of a bloc if they have agreement scores as great as the threshold value with at least half the members of that bloc.[5]

Note that while the Senators are arranged in order as the rows and columns of Figure 7.1, the binary data of the figure provide no clear indication of this order, or of the order of the three groupings found. We shall return to this problem when we compare other findings from Truman's research with those of scale analysis.

While the procedures used by Truman and others for clustering the binary matrix of similarities between legislators are similar to those discussed in Chapter 3, they differ in detail. First, many of the indices discussed earlier are different from the one Truman used. Second, it has been customary in clustering legislators to identify fringes of particular blocs, either by considering a lower threshold of agreement or by listing legislators who agreed with some, but not all, members of a bloc. Third, some overlap between blocs has been permitted. Fourth, Beyle also distinguished votes on the prevailing and nonprevailing sides, clustering them separately; this practice was used subsequently in analyses of the Supreme Court. And Beyle used as a threshold of significant agreement the value of 25 percent, a criterion which has been shown not to be an adequate indicator of chance expectation.[6]

[5]Truman, *op. cit.*, pp. 46–47. Closer inspection of Figure 7.1 will also show that there were ties or alternative clusters in the binary matrix, and that the actual numbers of agreements had to be considered to arrive at the clusters shown.

[6]Hayes, "Probability and Beyle's Index of Cohesion." But Hayes' argument is based on indices of association for fourfold tables comparing pairs of legislators, an approach we shall criticize below.

This general type of bloc analysis has been developed rather independently for different types of legislative or deliberative bodies—legislatures, courts, and the United Nations General Assembly. We wish here to compare methods systematically, however, and shall therefore bring together treatments of different bodies by similar methods. Our primary basis for classifying these studies will be the type of index of similarity used. Among the studies that use each such type of index, we shall then point out differences in procedures for analyzing the matrix of similarities.

Indices similar to those of Beyle, Rice, and Truman have been used in the study of blocs on the U.S. Supreme Court, beginning with the work of Pritchett and continued by Schubert and others. Pritchett's bloc analysis was based on a count of the number of times that a pair of justices voted together; this number (or the corresponding percentage) was entered in one cell of a 9×9 matrix, and furnished the criterion for identifying blocs. Some of his analyses were based only on agreements in dissent, rather than majority opinions. This distinction has been much more characteristic of judicial analysis than of legislative, but we shall also discuss below some methods of assessing legislators' agreement which count minority agreements more heavily. This general approach has also been described in detail by Schubert.[7] One difference that has been observed between the findings based on agreements in dissent, and those based on agreement in the majority, is that the former tend to reveal blocs at the extremes of the ideological spectrum, while the latter reveal blocs in the center. A variation on this procedure, among the methods used by Schubert, is to analyze matrices of agreements of this type by successively joining together the pairs with highest agreement, to form a tree-like structure.[8]

This type of analysis has also been applied by Ellis Levin in an unpublished study of votes in the Chicago City Council. In 1951–

[7]See Pritchett, *The Roosevelt Court,* chaps. 2, 9; and *Civil Liberties and the Vinson Court,* chap. 9; also Schubert, *Quantitative Analysis of Judicial Behavior,* chap. 3.

[8]Schubert used McQuitty's "hierarchical syndrome analysis" for this purpose; see *ibid.,* pp. 112, 119, 144–158, 167–170. McQuitty's methods were considered in Chapter 3 above. A related method of McQuitty's was applied to Senate votes to produce a tree-like structure; see Wrigley and Fitch, "Patterns of Voting by United States Senators." This method is feasible for interlegislator scores, which rarely attain the value of 1.

1955, during the mayoralty of Martin H. Kennelly, this 50-man body was frequently divided on roll calls. The 124 roll calls that had at least three dissident votes were selected, and from them an index of agreement between each pair of aldermen was computed, equal to the proportion of agreement on the roll calls on which both voted. A tree-type clustering routine was used to combine pairs of aldermen, starting with those whose agreement was highest. When a pair was combined, its average agreement score with other legislators was used to replace the individual agreement scores in the matrix; when two such groups were averaged together, each group's agreement scores were weighted in proportion to the number of elements in the group.

The resulting grouping is shown in Figure 7.2. The two main subgroups largely separate Democrats and Republicans (the latter in CAPITALS). A few deviant cases were aldermen who later ran for office with different party affiliation—for example, Robert Merriam, who ran for mayor in 1955 as a Republican. Another interesting feature of the diagram is the lesser cohesion of the Republicans, who were in the minority and tended to cohere at lower levels of agreement than did the Democrats, as indicated by the longer horizontal lines to their junctions in the lower part of the diagram.

As we pointed out in Chapter 3, the ordering of legislators in a diagram such as Figure 7.2 does not follow in every detail from the process of combining branches. For while branches are not permitted to cross one another, any two legislators or groups that are combined at a branch point may be interchanged. Thus for a determinate sequence to be printed out by the computer, additional criteria must be specified to determine the sequence; this may depend, for example, on the input sequence of legislators, or on the similarities of legislators to one or more who are designated as reference points.

A variant of this type of index has been proposed by Lijphart to take account of abstentions in voting in the United Nations General Assembly.[9] Here, to measure the extent of agreement between two states, it seems desirable to include the effects of three categories of voting, one of which (abstention) presumably lies between the other two. To do this, Lijphart begins with the number of complete agreements, in any of the three categories, and adds to it one-half of the

---

[9]Lijphart presents this index in "The Analysis of Bloc Voting in the General Assembly," p. 910.

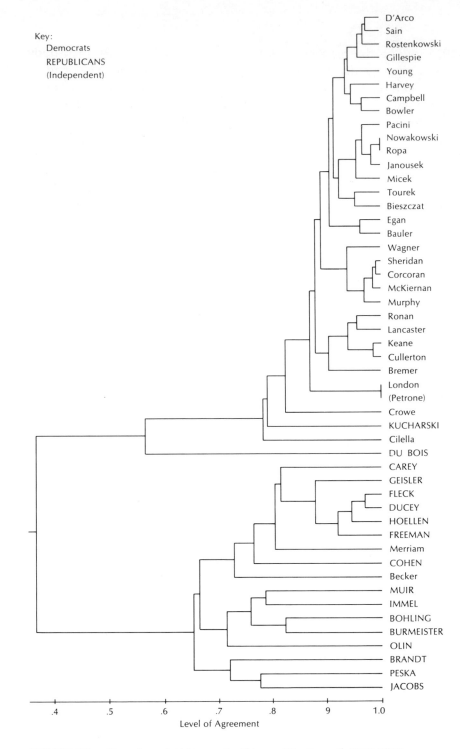

Key:
Democrats
REPUBLICANS
(Independent)

D'Arco
Sain
Rostenkowski
Gillespie
Young
Harvey
Campbell
Bowler
Pacini
Nowakowski
Ropa
Janousek
Micek
Tourek
Bieszczat
Egan
Bauler
Wagner
Sheridan
Corcoran
McKiernan
Murphy
Ronan
Lancaster
Keane
Cullerton
Bremer
London
(Petrone)
Crowe
KUCHARSKI
Cilella
DU BOIS
CAREY
GEISLER
FLECK
DUCEY
HOELLEN
FREEMAN
Merriam
COHEN
Becker
MUIR
IMMEL
BOHLING
BURMEISTER
OLIN
BRANDT
PESKA
JACOBS

.4   .5   .6   .7   .8   9   1.0

Level of Agreement

FIGURE 7.2. Clustering of Aldermen in Chicago City Council, 1951–1955.

Table 7.1 Fourfold tables of agreement and disagreement

| | | Justice (legislator) 1 | |
		+	−
Justice (legislator) 2	+	a	b
	−	c	d

partial agreements—i.e., the votes on which one nation votes in favor or against, and the other abstains. This combined total is then divided by the total number of votes on which both participated, and converted to a percentage. A matrix of indices of this type was constructed, and bloc configurations were examined at a succession of threshold values, each lower than the preceding.

The procedure of counting agreements between legislators may also be modified to produce a corrected count which takes into consideration the likelihood that each legislator will enter into agreements. This modification was used in one of Schubert's earlier studies of the Supreme Court. Each agreement score between two justices was divided by the "chance expectation" of their agreement. For this purpose one may imagine a fourfold table like Table 7.1, in which the elements counted are not individual votes but individual pair-agreements; one vote can thus enter into several agreements. In cell a would appear the number of agreements between justices 1 and 2 (the same as $a + d$ in Table 7.1); in cell b, the agreements of justice 1 with justices other than 2; and in cell c, the agreements of justice 2 with others than justice 1. Cell d would then be a count of all agreements in which neither justice 1 nor justice 2 was involved. The total of all agreements between all pairs of justices would be the total $(a + b + c + d)$. If one computes the marginal sums in the conventional manner, then Schubert's procedure is as follows:

In the margin of each table are entered the number of pairs in which each justice participated. Similarly, we have computed a total number of pairs for the entire table. "Expectations" were then computed in the conventional manner: for each pair of justices, the product of row and column marginals was divided by the grand total.[10]

The ratio of actual number of agreements (a) to chance expectation was then used as the entry in a matrix of agreements, and clusters

[10]Schubert, op. cit., pp. 169–170.

were found by McQuitty's Hierarchical Syndrome Analysis. Schubert did not use this index in subsequent work because of its lack of boundedness, the problem of measuring a justice's self-agreement, and the fact that its sampling distribution was unknown.

It is also possible to form indices of agreement based only on agreements on a specified side of each roll call or partition of legislators; this possibility was mentioned above in connection with Pritchett's use of dissenting agreements. But certain data that formally resemble roll calls create partitions with an even more obvious asymmetry. An example of such data is the division of a set of nations into members and nonmembers of a particular international organization. Russett has used data of this kind in studying international groupings.[11] He studied the memberships of 115 states in 163 international organizations; the number of members of an organization varied from 3 to 113, and the number of shared memberships for pairs of nations varied from 0 to 76. Russett constructed a square matrix whose entries were the number of joint memberships of the row and column nations, divided by the maximum value of 76, with values of unity on the diagonal. He then computed the principal components of this matrix, rotated them by the normal Varimax procedure (which corrects for disparities in the communalities, as they affect the rotation), and interpreted the resulting factor loadings or eigenvector elements. Factors corresponding to various recognizable regional groupings were found.

An interesting feature of Russett's procedure is that while membership in an international organization divides the nations in question into two subsets, agreement *as members* is treated differently from agreement *not* to be members. The partition of the "legislators" into two groups is now regarded as asymmetrical, in that more interaction is presumed to occur on one side than on the other.

Another index treating partitions of legislators asymmetrically, but also involving correction of the number of agreements, was used by Paul R. Brass and the author, in an unpublished study of legislators' positions in the Indian Lok Sabha (lower national chamber). For the period under study (late 1959), party discipline was so high on roll-call votes that these votes seemed useless for revealing detailed ideological differences. We therefore examined the joint questions

---

[11]Russett, *International Regions and the International System*, chaps. 6, 7. This volume also contains the results of United Nations voting analysis, originally published in Russett, "Discovering Voting Groups."

submitted by legislators, on the assumption that those legislators who joined together in submitting a question thereby revealed some ideological or group affinity. The reasoning here is analogous to that in Russett's use of membership in international organizations, and could of course be applied to joint sponsorship of bills, as in the U.S. Senate.

In the period from November 30 through December 11, 1959, during the Ninth Session of the 1957 parliament, a total of 411 joint questions were asked in 10 legislative days. The number of sponsors on the individual questions considered ranged from 2 to 24. Each question may be considered analogous to a roll call, dividing the chamber into two parts, but with a very one-sided vote. Moreover, the participation of M.P.s in these questions was far from uniform; of 505 members, only 133 participated in the joint questions examined. For convenience, we restricted our analysis to the 64 M.P.s who entered into 6 or more joint questions; the number of joint questions among this group was as high as 136 for one M.P. and 81 for another. It therefore seemed desirable to correct the indices of agreement for these disparities in tendency to submit questions.

This study, however, used the number of joint questions asked by a given legislator, rather than his number of agreement-pairs, as the basis for correction. If we refer again to Table 7.1, we can see a closer correspondence to this procedure, for the cell entries are now numbers of questions (pseudo-roll calls). The index used was

$$\frac{a}{\sqrt{(a+b)(a+c)}}$$

i.e., a, the number of agreements, divided by the geometric mean of the total numbers of joint questions asked by the two legislators, with or without one another.

We chose this index because it makes the self-agreement of each legislator unity, and simplifies the results of a factor analysis which was performed on the matrix of similarity indices. These properties can be shown more easily if we introduce a matrix notation such as that of Chapter 5, which will also be used in the next section.

Let us treat each joint question as a column in a data matrix, each legislator as a row, and let the entry in this vote-matrix be 1 if the legislator entered into the joint question for that row and column, 0 otherwise. Call this matrix **M,** and its entries m_{ij}. Then the matrix of agreements, if we were simply to count joint sponsorships without any correction, would be **MM'**. This matrix, multiplied by a constant but with different diagonal elements, was used by Russett. If, however, we apply the proposed correction, we should convert **M** to another data matrix **X,** whose elements would be defined by

$$x_{ij} = \frac{m_{ij}}{\sqrt{n_i}}$$

where

$$n_i = \sum_j m_{ij}$$

= the number of 1's in row i of **M,** or the total number of joint questions into which legislator i entered

The matrix of agreement based on **X** would then be **XX'**, and the index of agreement between legislators i and j would be

$$(\mathbf{XX'})_{ij} = \sum_k \frac{m_{ik}}{\sqrt{n_i}} \frac{m_{jk}}{\sqrt{n_j}} = \frac{\sum_k m_{ik} m_{jk}}{\sqrt{n_i n_j}}$$

For $i = j$, the self-agreement of any legislator will be unity, as the sum in the numerator is simply equal to n_i, the number of joint questions in which he participated, and the denominator is also equal to n_i. An additional simplification due to this type of correction is that the factor loadings for each legislator have a sum of squares that cannot exceed unity.[12]

Two further features of this index are of interest for comparison with others treated in this section. First, it is essentially based on dissenting votes; for if each question is treated as a hypothetical roll call, only the agreements in the minority are considered in the index of agreement, and no attention is paid to agreement *not* to sponsor a question. This decision relates in part to the low proportion of the legislature that sponsored each question; for if the list of names were a discharge petition in the U.S. House of Representatives, we might well prefer to treat the two subsets into which it divided the chamber as equal in importance.

Second, this index of agreement (like the one used by Russett) is

[12]See MacRae, "Direct Factor Analysis of Sociometric Data," p. 357 n. The procedures described in that article were carried out with the Lok Sabha data, and yielded clusters of legislators showing some similarity within clusters in party, region, and ideology.

one of those discussed by Sokal and Sneath in their treatment of taxonomic procedures, and is of a type that we rejected for cluster analysis of roll calls.[13] It is not an index of association, has no well-defined zero point, and thus does not tell us when the two legislators' votes are independent of one another. But this condition, which seemed so essential for measures of association between roll calls, may not be so reasonable for legislators. It may not be coincidental that a number of attempts to base indices of interlegislator agreement on a "zero" or "chance" standard for comparison have since revealed difficulties: Beyle's 25 percent criterion, Schubert's index described above, and (we shall argue) the use of indices such as ϕ based on fourfold tables comparing pairs of legislators.

We also required in Chapter 3 that an index of association between two roll calls change only its sign when the polarity of a roll call was altered. A related requirement for indices of legislator agreement (to which we shall return below) is that they be unchanged by polarity reversal of roll calls. This index, however, would not be the same if we singled out for attention those legislators who did *not* sponsor each question. A possible justification for our violating this condition is that the initiative taken by legislators to place themselves in a small minority divides the legislature asymmetrically. But the same approach has been used by Russett for international organizations in which a considerable majority of the nations studied were members. There may, therefore, be some other justification for methods that are sensitive to polarity reversal. Perhaps another relevant test concerns whether another item (joint question, international organization, discharge petition) may be imagined that joins together the legislators who were previously nonparticipants. In the formation of groups to sponsor questions or to join international organizations, such a supposition seems generally unreasonable; an association formed of all the nonmembers of a given association, or a question put by all the nonsponsors of a given question, is ordinarily hard to imagine. Similarly, in pre-Gaullist France, a cabinet coalition formed by all the opponents of a given cabinet was usually unlikely. On the other hand, a vote uniting all the nonsigners of a discharge petition in the U.S. House is more easily imagined, and resembles a reversed-polarity roll call such as often occurs.

An alternative basis for correcting the observed frequency of agree-

[13]See Chapter 3, fn. 10.

ment might be to consider the effect of the one-sidedness of the roll calls used; for the more nearly unanimous a roll call, the greater likelihood that any two legislators will agree on it. If the proportions of yeas and nays on roll call i are p_i and q_i respectively, then the expected proportion of agreements among all pairs of legislators on roll call i will approach $p_i^2 + q_i^2$ as the number of legislators increases.[14] An average of the values of this expression over all roll calls under consideration would provide an estimate of the proportion of agreement expected by chance.

COMPARISON OF LEGISLATORS BY FOURFOLD TABLES

In contrast to the above methods based on frequencies of agreement, Schubert and others have measured the agreement between pairs of justices or legislators by means of indices of association based on fourfold tables comparing their votes (see Table 7.1). In studies of the Supreme Court using this procedure, each justice's vote is classified as positive if it agrees with the majority decision, negative if opposed. From the resulting fourfold tables, values of ϕ are computed and factor analyzed. An early use of this procedure was made by Thurstone and Degan, who factor analyzed Supreme Court data but were unable to interpret the results; Schubert interpreted them in a subsequent article.[15] The comparison of legislators by fourfold tables, a procedure which we shall criticize below, was not used in an earlier article by Thurstone, who suggested that blocs could be identified by associations between roll calls rather than legislators, with computation of factor scores to reveal individual legislators' positions.[16]

Several analyses based on fourfold tables comparing justices have also been presented by Ulmer, who has analyzed them by means

---

[14]This expectation is expressed more generally, for the case of three alternative choices on a roll call and a finite universe, in Brams and O'Leary, "An Axiomatic Model of Voting Bodies."

[15]Schubert, *The Judicial Mind*, pp. 49–75. Schubert also compared ϕ with other possible coefficients for the fourfold table. Thurstone and Degan, "A Factorial Study of the Supreme Court"; Schubert, "A Solution to the Indeterminate Factorial Resolution of Thurstone and Degan's Study of the Supreme Court."

[16]Thurstone, "Isolation of Blocs in a Voting Body by the Voting Records of Its Members."

of one of McQuitty's techniques, known as linkage analysis.[17] This procedure identifies a pair of justices each of whom has his highest index of similarity (ϕ) with the other, and then searches for others whose own highest index is with one of the previously selected. The result is a grouping of justices and a set of numbers similar to factor loadings, indicating the relation of each justice with a group or type.

A closely related method has been used in a factor analysis by Grumm of votes in the Kansas legislature, and differs from Schubert's factor analysis only in that different choices of polarity are made and different rotational criteria employed. Grumm classifies the categories of the fourfold table according to the yeas and nays rather than the prevailing and dissenting sides. Using data on the lower house of the Kansas legislature, he finds Republicans and Democrats to occupy distinct regions in the factor space.[18]

Grumm has also applied to this legislature a tree-type clustering procedure akin to McQuitty's methods.[19] For the Kansas Senate, three clusters were defined, one of which combined members of both parties. For the House, however, "Two clusters were defined and they almost completely coincided with the two party groups."[20] Grumm uses a method based on the cardinal matrix, each entry being a ϕ coefficient computed from the fourfold table of yeas and nays. When a pair of items are combined to form a composite item, the new ϕ coefficient between the composite item and each other item is computed as a weighted average of the coefficients between the two members of the pair and the other item:

$$\phi_{(i+j),k} = \frac{\phi_{ik} + \phi_{jk}}{\sqrt{2 + 2\phi_{ij}}}$$

[17]Ulmer, "The Analysis of Behavior Patterns of the United States Supreme Court," and "Toward a Theory of Sub-Group Formation in the United States Supreme Court." McQuitty's linkage analysis is described in his "Elementary Linkage Analysis for Isolating Orthogonal and Oblique Types and Typal Relevancies." A number of other researches on the Supreme Court have also been based on fourfold tables; citations are given in Ulmer, "Pairwise Associations of Justices and Legislators," p. 107 n.

[18]Grumm, "A Factor Analysis of Legislative Behavior."

[19]Grumm, "The Systematic Analysis of Blocs in the Study of Legislative Behavior." The method used, devised for biological taxonomy, is described in Sokal and Michener, "A Statistical Method for Evaluating Systematic Relationships."

[20]Grumm, "The Systematic Analysis of Blocs," p. 360.

FACTOR SCORES AND OTHER METHODS

A third major approach to the grouping of legislators into blocs is used by Alker and Russett in their study of the United Nations General Assembly.[21] In keeping with Thurstone's initial suggestion for legislative analysis, they factor-analyze the votes in the Assembly and then plot the factor *scores* of individual states. While this does not at first glance appear to fall within the category of cluster-bloc techniques, we shall show in a later section that it is nearly equivalent to factoring a matrix of coefficients of agreement of a special type, whose elements are proportional to those of **ZZ'**. Russett has subsequently analyzed correlations between nations based on their votes in the General Assembly, a procedure more nearly similar to that of Schubert or Grumm.[22]

By analogy with our treatment in Chapter 5 of clustering roll calls in the factor space, we might also consider the clustering of legislators. This is in effect what Alker and Russett do when they plot factor scores and locate blocs in terms of neighboring sets of points. But the procedure could also be systematized if we wished, by computation of a matrix of interlegislator distances based on factor scores and application of clustering procedures to this distance matrix. A less systematic application of this line of reasoning will be made in Chapter 8, when we consider the locations of congressmen in the factor-score space.

Finally, we have suggested in Chapter 3 another method of identifying blocs or factions, which at first glance bears no relation to the pairwise methods discussed here. This is to find scale clusters using a Q-matrix and then to examine the distribution of p_+ in major clusters. When the values of p_+ are concentrated in one or more narrow intervals, we have some reason to suspect that such intervals mark off blocs that are distinguished from one another on the roll calls of that cluster.[23]

Though this method seems distinct from the approaches based on pairwise comparisons of legislators, it is actually similar in prin-

---

[21]Alker and Russett, *World Politics in the General Assembly.*

[22]Russett, "Discovering Voting Groups in the United Nations."

[23]MacRae, "A Method for Identifying Issues and Factions from Legislative Votes."

ciple to the methods based on factor-score similarity. Placement of legislators on cumulative scales is analogous to assignment of factor scores after factor analysis; in either case, the numerical values obtained describe the positions of legislators on continua corresponding to attitudes or group allegiances. When such a distribution separates two known groups such as legislative parties, or when it has intervals of lower density, we infer in either case that meaningful social groupings are being separated. A procedure for finding the best division of such a unidimensional distribution into subintervals has been proposed by Fisher.[24]

CRITICAL EVALUATION

The methods of bloc analysis that we have discussed fall largely into three types, apart from their particular subject matter. The first is cluster analysis based on an index such as the percent of agreeing votes between a pair of legislators; this is represented by Rice, Beyle, Truman, Lijphart, and Pritchett. The second is factor analysis based on coefficients of association computed from fourfold tables comparing pairs of legislators; this has been used by Schubert, Ulmer, and Grumm. The third is a type exemplified by the factor analysis of roll calls, and comparison of legislators in terms of factor scores; this has been used by Alker and Russett, and a related method will be presented in Chapter 8.[25] Each of these types tends to combine a particular index of association with a corresponding procedure for analysis; but a wider variety of combinations have been used and still others will be considered below.

One question that can properly be addressed to all these methods concerns the conceptual models with which they are to be used. In many of the cluster-bloc studies, there has been too close an identification of a particular means of identifying blocs with a quasi-sociological notion of a group. Both critics and users of this method have pointed out that indices of group membership or cohesion reflect multiple variables; but the research that is needed to separate these

24Fisher, "On Grouping for Maximum Homogeneity."

25A relation between direct factor analysis and indices of agreement is suggested in MacRae, "Indices of Pairwise Agreement Between Justices or Legislators," p. 140–141; but this method now seems inferior to the conventional factor-score approach.

variables, and to compare rival indices, still remains largely undone.[26]

The relevance of questions about conceptual models is more apparent if we consider the ways in which these models enter into interpretations of the findings. Some such interpretations are illustrated by Truman's *The Congressional Party,* which may be contrasted with the author's *Dimensions of Congressional Voting,* since both studied the House of Representatives in the 81st Congress.

Both these studies present arrays of congressmen that conform to a familiar left–right dimension. Both require information other than the matrix of votes alone in order to connect this array with ideological positions. Without such information, the scale scores alone could not tell us which position was left and which was right, or even whether the dimension in question conformed to this familiar distinction. But to present an array of blocs from left to right requires still further information. For the type of cluster analysis carried out in Chapter 3 gave rise to no obvious ordering of the clusters, except perhaps in size. They were later related to one another by coefficients of association between legislators' scale scores, but the array that resulted (if we had tried to make one) might well have been multidimensional.[27]

Truman's arrangement of blocs along a continuum must therefore come from some additional sort of information. One source of this information is our commonsense knowledge of legislators and their issue positions. But a more systematic source of information might be the overlaps between the fringes of blocs; a proper array of the blocs relative to one another would then place near one another those blocs that had the most overlap. By arranging blocs in a matrix whose entries were overlapping proportions (or average agreement across blocs), we might permute rows and columns to move the high proportions of overlap near the principal diagonal, and obtain a structure analogous to Guttman's simplex.

Though this method would be successful in arranging most of the blocs Truman found, it would be less so for one particular group of House Republicans. Six congressmen, from Iowa and Nebraska, are placed at the extreme right end of one array of blocs, but overlap

---

[26]A recent expression of this line of criticism, with reference to earlier literature, is Clausen, "The Measurement of Legislative Group Behavior."

[27]A series of linked clusters among Republican domestic votes in the 84th Congress was shown, however, in MacRae, "Cluster Analysis of Congressional Votes with the BC TRY System."

with no other blocs; while in another diagram of the same blocs, they are placed nearer the center but somewhat off to the side.[28] A similar nonoverlapping bloc also appears in a following analysis of the House Republicans, and Truman recognizes the difficulty of placing such groups clearly on left or right, that results from differing alignments of legislators on different issues.[29]

Thus while blocs can be ordered intuitively, it is better to order them by explicit procedures; and while a best ranking can presumably be found along a single continuum, the adequacy of such a ranking is an empirical question, just as the adequacy of a single factor to account for variance in a data matrix is an empirical question. This same problem has existed in the literature of sociometry, where it was thought at one time that the dimensionality in which social groups should be arranged could be limited to a single continuum, or to the two dimensions in which sociograms were plotted.[30]

It appears, therefore, that the sets of legislators found by cluster-bloc analysis are grouped together sometimes by social interaction but at other times by ideological similarity. The conditions under which one or the other of these bases of agreement is more important require closer attention. And when an array is found, its dimensionality should remain an empirical question.

A second critique that relates particularly to methods based on fourfold tables comparing two legislators or justices, is that these methods depend somewhat on the polarities chosen for the roll calls. Whether positive and negative votes are defined by yea and nay, liberal and conservative, or majority and minority, can move the agreements or disagreements of legislators from one cell in the four-fold table to the diagonally opposite one, and thus alter the coefficients of association.[31] Different choices of polarity have in fact been proposed by researchers working in different fields. In the study of the

---

[28]Truman, *op. cit.*, pp. 175, 173.

[29]*Ibid.*, pp. 177–180.

[30]Two stages in the development of this spatial model are represented in Coleman and MacRae, "Electronic Processing of Sociometric Data for Groups up to 1,000 in Size," and MacRae, "Direct Factor Analysis."

[31]This problem is a general one, applying to the "Q-technique" of factor analysis as well (factor analysis in which standard scores are computed for respondents rather than questions). M. G. Kendall writes, "If we reverse the sign of a given variable, for example (and there is no reason why we should not), we obtain a completely different set of correlations." See his "Discrimination and Classification," p. 181.

Supreme Court the practice has been uniformly to classify votes according to majority or dissenting position. Grumm's work on legislative analysis has made use of the yea and nay classification provided in the raw data. Lijphart has suggested that in the analysis of UN voting, clustering be done for "one coherent set of questions at a time," and that votes be then classified as favorable or unfavorable on this issue; a similar suggestion has been made by Davis with regard to comparing subjects on attitude tests.[32] Whatever justification there might be for these different choices in relation to the subject matter, they clearly hinder the comparison of results across fields.

Insofar as we wish to use indices that are invariant under polarity changes, the earlier indices such as Rice used are superior in this respect; they were based only on the total agreements $(a + d)$ and disagreements $(b + c)$, which were unaffected by changes in polarity. One might even imagine another index in which polarities were assigned at random to the items; in this case the expected values of the agreement cells would each be $(a + d)/2$, and of the "disagreement" cells $(b + c)/2$.[33] The usual coefficients of association could then be calculated, and Y would have a particularly simple value: the proportion of agreement minus that of disagreement.

ROLL-CALL–LEGISLATOR DUALITY

A more general treatment of indices of agreement between legislators, and their relation to associations between roll calls, may be given with the aid of the matrix concepts presented in Chapter 5. We saw there that factor loadings and factor scores were very closely related— that both emerge from a single procedure of factoring the data matrix. And regardless of whether they are computed in this way, or by initial factoring of a matrix $X'X$ or XX', they retain a close relation to one another, permitting a more detailed interpretation of either set of numbers (loadings or scores) if they are considered together.

Let us first consider this relationship for the case of orthodox factor analysis, as used by Alker and Russett.[34] If Z is the data matrix of

[32]Grumm, "A Factor Analysis," p. 341 n.; Lijphart, "The Analysis of Bloc Voting," 905; Davis, "On Criteria for Scale Relationships," p. 378. Ulmer has contended that particular choices of polarity are appropriate for particular subject matter, in "Pairwise Associations."

[33]This approach was suggested by Jonathan Pool.

[34]Op. cit.

standard scores corresponding to legislators' positions on roll calls, the procedure is to factor $Z'Z/N = R$. The factor scores are then given by equation (5.14), $F = ZA(A'A)^{-1}$. But we also showed that the matrix of factor scores F could be obtained by factoring the matrix ZZ'/N; for if we let $X = Z/\sqrt{N}$, direct factor analysis of this data matrix yields a matrix V whose rows are the eigenvectors of $X'X$, and a matrix U whose columns are the eigenvectors of XX', as in (5.7) and (5.8). The conventions of factor analysis require that the squared magnitude of each v vector be set to λ, and that of each u vector be set to unity.

The matrix XX', from which we could get the factor scores directly, can be considered as a matrix of interlegislator agreements. In the particular case $X = Z/\sqrt{n}$, each element in XX' is an average of products for a pair of legislators, each product being that of the two legislators' standard scores on a roll call. The average takes place over all roll calls and the sum of products is thus divided by n, the number of roll calls. If two legislators vote alike on a roll call, the product of their standard scores will be positive; if they disagree, it will be negative. But in addition, this method weights more heavily those agreements that occur on the minority side, and those on roll calls with extreme divisions, whose standard scores will be higher. The resulting index may be expressed as an element of XX':

$$(XX')_{ij} = \frac{(ZZ')_{ij}}{n} = \frac{\sum\limits_{k} z_{ik} z_{jk}}{n} = \frac{1}{n} \sum\limits_{k} \frac{(m_{ik} - \overline{m}_k)(m_{jk} - \overline{m}_k)}{s_k^2} \qquad (7.1)$$

where

i, j	= indices of the two legislators being compared
k	= roll-call index, over which summation occurs
z_{ik}, z_{jk}	= standard scores of legislators i and j on roll call k, with $z_{ik} = \dfrac{(m_{ik} - \overline{m}_k)}{s_k}$
m_{ik}	= number representing the vote of legislator i on roll call k
$(m_{ik} - \overline{m}_k)$	= deviation score of legislator i's vote from the mean vote, on roll call k
s_k	= sample standard deviation of votes of all legislators on roll call k

The index defined by (7.1) has several useful properties for measuring agreement between legislators. It is independent of the alteration of polarity of individual roll calls, for this changes the signs of both deviation scores for legislators i and j, but not that of their product. It gives a higher weight to votes that are cast in a small minority, as the deviation score is numerically greatest for such votes. If the initial matrix entries are 1 and 0 for yea and nay, and if the proportion of 1's is $\overline{m}_k = p_k$, then subtraction of this mean will yield entries of $(1 - p_k)$ and $-p_k$ respectively, each being proportional to the number of responses in the opposite category. In addition, those roll calls with extreme marginals are weighted more heavily by the division by s_k^2.

We may illustrate the properties of this index of agreement by means of the two numerical examples presented in Chapter 5.[35] The first used a data matrix **M** for five legislators and three roll calls. The matrix **Z** which was presented there is shown again in Table 7.2. We next compute the matrix $\mathbf{ZZ'}/n$, which has as its elements the agreement indices between the hypothetical legislators. (Exercise: compute this matrix.)

The eigenvalues of $\mathbf{ZZ'}$ are the same as those of $\mathbf{Z'Z}$; but since we previously factored $\mathbf{R} = \mathbf{Z'Z}/N$—dividing by the number of legislators—and are now factoring $\mathbf{ZZ'}/n$ (n being the number of roll calls), the eigenvalues of the matrix of legislator agreements are N/n (in this example, 5/3) times as great.

The 5×2 matrix of normalized eigenvectors shown in Table 7.2 will thus reproduce the matrix we factored, $\mathbf{ZZ'}/3$, within rounding errors. This is not precisely the matrix of factor scores, however; the latter is shown below it (as it appeared in Chapter 5), and differs from it in that the factor scores are standard scores, and thus the column sums of squares (designated $|\mathbf{f}|^2$) must each be equal to N (5 in this case). But if we are interested in the configuration of legislators' positions, as might be displayed by plotting factor scores in two dimensions, these two sets of coordinates differ only by a stretching of one axis relative to the other. The eigenvectors, normalized so that their sums of squares equal the eigenvalues, reproduce the matrix $\mathbf{ZZ'}/3$, while the factor scores do not.

The highest value of the index of agreement, 2.75, is the self-agreement of the top legislator, who was alone in the minority on two

---

[35]See the section in Chapter 5 on "Numerical Examples."

Table 7.2 Factor scores and indices of agreement: Numerical example (5 X 3)

$$
Z = \begin{bmatrix}
2.0 & 2.0 & .5 \\
-.5 & -.5 & .5 \\
-.5 & -.5 & .5 \\
-.5 & -.5 & .5 \\
-.5 & -.5 & -2.0
\end{bmatrix}
\qquad
\frac{ZZ'}{3} = \frac{1}{3}
\begin{bmatrix}
8.25 & -1.75 & -1.75 & -1.75 & -3.00 \\
-1.75 & .75 & .75 & .75 & -.50 \\
-1.75 & .75 & .75 & .75 & -.50 \\
-1.75 & .75 & .75 & .75 & -.50 \\
-3.00 & -.50 & -.50 & -.50 & 4.50
\end{bmatrix}
$$

The factors that will reproduce $ZZ'/3$ are:

$$
U'U = \begin{bmatrix}
1.65 & .21 \\
-.30 & -.40 \\
-.30 & -.40 \\
-.30 & -.40 \\
-.74 & .98
\end{bmatrix}
\begin{bmatrix}
1.65 & -.30 & -.30 & -.30 & -.74 \\
.21 & -.40 & -.40 & -.40 & .98
\end{bmatrix}
$$

$$
= \begin{bmatrix}
2.75 & -.58 & -.58 & -.58 & -1.00 \\
-.58 & .25 & .25 & .25 & -.17 \\
-.58 & .25 & .25 & .25 & -.17 \\
-.58 & .25 & .25 & .25 & -.17 \\
-1.00 & -.17 & -.17 & -.17 & 1.50
\end{bmatrix}
$$

$$
|\,u\,|^2 = \frac{5}{3}\,\lambda_1 \quad \frac{5}{3}\,\lambda_2
$$

$$
= 3.52 \quad 1.48
$$

The corresponding factor scores from the previous analysis are

$$
F = \begin{bmatrix}
1.96 & .39 \\
-.36 & -.73 \\
-.36 & -.73 \\
-.36 & -.73 \\
-.88 & 1.80
\end{bmatrix}
$$

$$
|\,f\,|^2 = \quad 5 \qquad 5
$$

---

of the three roll calls; the lowest self-agreement is that of the three legislators in the middle, who were in the majority on all three roll calls. The three in the middle have a small negative index value with the bottom legislator, even though they voted alike on two roll calls.

Several features of Table 7.2 deserve closer attention. First, the index of agreement between legislators, given in (7.1), can exceed unity. For while it superficially resembles a correlation coefficient, it is actually a sum across *rows* in the data matrix, of products of *column*-standard scores. The constraints that held r between +1 and −1 are thus not operative. Second, and for the same reason, the factoring carried out here is not the same as what has been called "Q" factor analysis (a symbol unrelated to Yule's Q-coefficient). This term has been applied to factor analysis that interchanges the rows and columns of the data matrix, computes standard scores on the new columns (formerly rows), derives correlation coefficients from them, and continues according to the standard procedures.[36] This sort of inverse factor analysis corresponds to the second of our three types of bloc analysis, which uses (for dichotomies) correlations based on fourfold tables each of which compares two legislators. For roll-call analysis this type seems inferior to the other two considered, because it is sensitive to polarities and because it has no precise duality or correspondence to the factors obtained from the more orthodox type of factor analysis of roll calls.[37]

A third feature of Table 7.2 is that the results are sensitive to duplication of roll calls. The first and second columns of Z (and of M) are identical, and the symmetry between the first and last legislators is thereby destroyed.

The second numerical example from Chapter 5 is shown in Table 7.3. As in the previous example, the self-agreements vary from values approaching 3 for the extreme legislators, to small values for the more central legislators. The index of agreement is again -1 for legislators whose patterns of response are exact opposites. This can be shown to be the largest possible negative value of the index. (Exercise: show this.) Again the factor loadings that result from factoring ZZ'/n are proportional in each column to the factor scores that were found from factoring $Z'Z/N$ (Table 5.1), but differ numerically because their sums of squares for columns must be different.

The loadings of legislators on the first factor arrange them in the same order as the scale scores that would have been assigned by counting the number of 1's in the rows of the vote-matrix M, in Table 5.1. The adjacent loadings are slightly more distant from one another at the extremes of the scale than at the middle, because of the additional weight given by standard scores to extreme responses

---

[36]See Cattell, *Factor Analysis*, pp. 90 ff.; Grumm, "A Factor Analysis"; and Russett, "Discovering Voting Groups."

[37]The results obtained by this method nevertheless seem reasonable, and it is possible that for some practical purposes they can still be used.

Table 7.3 Factor scores and indices of agreement: Numerical example (10 X 5)

$$
Z = \frac{1}{6}
\begin{bmatrix}
18 & 12 & 6 & 3 & 2 \\
-2 & 12 & 6 & 3 & 2 \\
-2 & -3 & 6 & 3 & 2 \\
-2 & -3 & 6 & 3 & 2 \\
-2 & -3 & 6 & 3 & 2 \\
-2 & -3 & -6 & 3 & 2 \\
-2 & -3 & -6 & 3 & 2 \\
-2 & -3 & -6 & 3 & 2 \\
-2 & -3 & -6 & -12 & 2 \\
-2 & -3 & -6 & -12 & -18
\end{bmatrix}
$$

$$
\frac{ZZ'}{5} = \frac{1}{180}
\begin{bmatrix}
517 & 157 & -23 & -23 & -23 & -95 & -95 & -95 & -140 & -180 \\
157 & 197 & 17 & 17 & 17 & -55 & -55 & -55 & -100 & -140 \\
-23 & 17 & 62 & 62 & 62 & -10 & -10 & -10 & -55 & -95 \\
-23 & 17 & 62 & 62 & 62 & -10 & -10 & -10 & -55 & -95 \\
-23 & 17 & 62 & 62 & 62 & -10 & -10 & -10 & -55 & -95 \\
-95 & 55 & -10 & -10 & -10 & 62 & 62 & 62 & 17 & -23 \\
-95 & 55 & -10 & -10 & -10 & 62 & 62 & 62 & 17 & -23 \\
-95 & 55 & -10 & -10 & -10 & 62 & 62 & 62 & 17 & -23 \\
-140 & -100 & -55 & -55 & -55 & 17 & 17 & 17 & 197 & 157 \\
-180 & -140 & -95 & -95 & -95 & -23 & -23 & -23 & 157 & 517
\end{bmatrix}
$$

$$
=
\begin{bmatrix}
2.86 & .87 & -.13 & -.13 & -.13 & -.53 & -.53 & -.53 & -.78 & -1.00 \\
.87 & 1.09 & .09 & .09 & .09 & -.31 & -.31 & -.31 & -.56 & -.78 \\
-.13 & .09 & .34 & .34 & .34 & -.06 & -.06 & -.06 & -.31 & -.53 \\
-.13 & .09 & .34 & .34 & .34 & -.06 & -.06 & -.06 & -.31 & -.53 \\
-.13 & .09 & .34 & .34 & .34 & -.06 & -.06 & -.06 & -.31 & -.53 \\
-.53 & -.31 & -.06 & -.06 & -.06 & .34 & .34 & .34 & .09 & -.13 \\
-.53 & -.31 & -.06 & -.06 & -.06 & .34 & .34 & .34 & .09 & -.13 \\
-.53 & -.31 & -.06 & -.06 & -.06 & .34 & .34 & .34 & .09 & -.13 \\
-.78 & -.56 & -.31 & -.31 & -.31 & .09 & .09 & .09 & 1.09 & .87 \\
-1.00 & -.78 & -.53 & -.53 & -.53 & .13 & -.13 & -.13 & .87 & 2.86
\end{bmatrix}
$$

The factor loadings from **ZZ'/5** are:

$$
\begin{bmatrix}
1.34 & .95 & -.35 & .20 & .15 \\
.75 & .15 & .31 & -.49 & -.42 \\
.22 & -.37 & .36 & .10 & .17 \\
.22 & -.37 & .36 & .10 & .17 \\
.22 & -.37 & .36 & .10 & .17 \\
-.22 & -.37 & -.36 & .10 & -.17 \\
-.22 & -.37 & -.36 & .10 & -.17 \\
-.22 & -.37 & -.36 & .10 & -.17 \\
-.75 & .15 & -.31 & -.49 & .42 \\
-1.34 & .95 & .35 & .20 & -.15
\end{bmatrix}
$$

$|u|^2 =$ 4.99 2.65 1.16 .63 .57

The corresponding factor scores from **Z'Z/10** are:

$$
\begin{bmatrix}
1.90 & 1.84 & -1.02 & .79 & .61 \\
1.05 & .30 & .92 & -1.98 & -1.74 \\
.31 & -.71 & 1.02 & .40 & .73 \\
.31 & -.71 & 1.02 & .40 & .73 \\
.31 & -.71 & 1.02 & .40 & .73 \\
-.31 & -.71 & -1.02 & .40 & -.73 \\
-.31 & -.71 & -1.02 & .40 & -.73 \\
-.31 & -.71 & -1.02 & .40 & -.73 \\
-1.05 & .30 & -.92 & -1.98 & 1.74 \\
-1.90 & 1.84 & 1.02 & .79 & -.61
\end{bmatrix}
$$

$|f|^2 =$ 10 10 10 10 10

(those in a small minority). Had we assigned scale scores on the basis of average ranks, the legislators in the middle would have been more widely separated because each of the two middle scale categories is represented by three legislators.

If we knew in advance that the data in question represented a single cumulative scale, we could perhaps base scale scores on the first factor and ignore the rest. But if our task is to discover multiple scales from a matrix of associations, the subsequent factors that will be generated by conventional factor analysis for each individual scale are likely to confuse our search for other scales, as suggested in Chapter 5.

We have shown in these two examples that legislators' factor scores, as they emerge from conventional factor analysis, may also be considered as the results of factoring a matrix of interlegislator-agreement indices of the type given in (7.1). The only difference between the two is in the constants of proportionality by which the individual factor entries are multiplied.

But conventional factor analysis is actually only a single case of the more general correspondence, or duality, between a class of legislator-agreement indices and roll-call similarity indices. Moreover, it is by no means the simplest case of this correspondence; we presented it first only because it is better known to some readers. We shall now consider other simpler indices for which this correspondence exists.

A second index of interlegislator agreement of this type, proposed earlier by the author, is based on a matrix $\mathbf{X}$ which is formed from the original vote-matrix $\mathbf{M}$ simply by subtracting the column means.[38] For a matrix of this kind a typical element (after division by n) is

$$\frac{1}{n} (\mathbf{XX'})_{ij} = \frac{1}{n} \sum_k (m_{ik} - \overline{m}_k)(m_{jk} - \overline{m}_k) \tag{7.2}$$

the same expression as in (7.1) but without s_k^2 in the denominator. If for this matrix $\mathbf{X}$ we form $\mathbf{X'X}/N$, and if there are no absences on the roll calls in question, index (7.2) generates entries in the matrix $\mathbf{X'X}/N$ that are equal to the cross-product considered in Chapter 3, i.e., to $(ad - bc)/N^2$. This result will be proved below when we ex-

---

[38]MacRae, "Indices of Pairwise Agreement." This index is criticized in Ulmer, "Pairwise Association."

amine the relation between indices of agreement between legislators and the corresponding indices between roll calls. But because this method gives rise to the cross-product as an index of association between roll calls, and because that index is even more sensitive than ϕ to variations in p_+ among roll calls, this method seems inferior to the use of conventional factor scores for the placement of legislators.

In (7.2) the deviation scores again have the effect of weighting each vote (yea or nay) in proportion to the number of votes in the opposite category, as we indicated in the discussion of (7.1). Thus (7.2), like (7.1), gives additional weight to agreements by members of the minority on a given vote. This is analogous to counting only "dissenting agreements," as is done in studies of the Supreme Court. Still another way of weighting minority agreements higher is to divide by the number of legislators in the category in question; this procedure has been followed by Lingoes in a method proposed for analyzing multicategory items.[39]

Some still simpler examples of this roll-call–legislator duality are provided by those instances in which the entries in the matrix **X** consist only of $+1, 0$, and -1. Let the number of roll calls (columns) be n, and the number of roll calls on which legislators i and j cast meaningful votes (e.g., excluding absences) be n_{ij}'.

If "prevailing" or "majority" votes are represented by 1's, and the rest by 0's, the elements of **XX'** will be agreements on the prevailing side. If "dissenting" or "minority" votes are represented by 1's (or by -1's), and the rest by 0's, the elements of **XX'** will be numbers of agreements in dissent. Converted to proportions, they will correspond to one of the types of matrices used by Pritchett. Division by n, which can be expressed in matrix terms, will give the proportions based on all roll calls in the matrix; division by n_{ij}' will give proportions based on those roll calls on which both legislators cast meaningful votes.

The matrix **XX'** also has a dual matrix, **X'X**, whose entries are numbers of dissenting votes shared by two decisions or cases. Conceivably this matrix could be factored; if it were, its factor scores would correspond to the factor loadings from the matrix of "agreements in dis-

---

[39]The method is "multivariate analysis of contingencies"; see Lingoes, "The Multivariate Analysis of Qualitative Data."

sent." The same reasoning could be applied to any other dichotomization of votes, such as a liberal–conservative division.

Another variation of this type is to allow all votes of one polarity (e.g., yeas or prevailing votes) to be represented by 1's in **X**, those of the opposite polarity by −1's, and intermediate votes or absences by 0's. In this case, the matrix **X′X** would have as its elements the number of agreements minus the number of disagreements for each pair of legislators. If there were no 0's these entries would be a linear transformation of the agreement counts in Truman's matrices and would yield precisely the same blocs on clustering of the binary or ranked matrix. We showed this relation between the two agreement indices in Chapter 3 when discussing the "proportion of similar responses or agreements"; for if the total agreement is I_1 and the net agreement I_2, then $I_2 = 2I_1 - 1$.

If there were zeros, we should still have a count of agreements minus disagreements. And if we used n_{ij}' as the basis for calculating the net proportion of agreement, this proportion would still be twice the total proportion of agreement, minus one. The elements of **X′X** in this case would measure the net similarity between pairs of roll calls, i.e., the number of legislators who voted alike on a pair minus the number who opposed one another. If there were 0's in **X,** and if we counted the net proportion of agreement using n as the denominator, the result would resemble the index proposed by Lijphart.[40]

The interesting feature of these indices is that they all may be factor analyzed, and all have dual sets of factor loadings obtainable from factoring **X′X.** Because of this correspondence, the information available from factoring **X′X** is useful in interpreting the factors of **XX′,** as we shall show in Chapter 8.

Let us now consider more systematically the sorts of indices of association or similarity between roll calls that can correspond to indices of agreement between legislators. We wish to know more generally what this possible class of indices may be, and how many of the indices discussed in Chapter 3 might enter into this correspondence.

For this treatment we return to the restricted case in which the

[40]Lijphart, "The Analysis of Bloc Voting," p. 910. A matrix of agreement indices of this type for the artificial data of Figure 5.1 has been analyzed by James C. Lingoes by means of the Guttman-Lingoes "smallest space analysis," with results in reasonable agreement with that figure.

initial vote matrix **M** contains only two kinds of elements, e.g., 1 and 0. We may then transform these elements for each roll call, forming **X** from **M,** where $x_{ij} = f_j(m_{ij})$. The column of **X** for roll call j will then contain two types of elements, which we denote by f_{1j} and f_{0j} for the previous 1 and 0 respectively. A similar (but not necessarily identical) pair of values are assigned for column (roll call) k. The numbers of legislators who jointly have the four possible combinations of these values will be given by the entries in a fourfold table comparing the two roll calls. If in this table we let j correspond to the columns and k to the rows, then

$a =$ the number of legislators whose votes are transformed into f_{1j} and f_{1k}

$b =$ the number with f_{0j} and f_{1k}

$c =$ the number with f_{1j} and f_{0k}

$d =$ the number with f_{0j} and f_{0k}

The (j, k) entry in the matrix **X'X** will then be

$$(\mathbf{X'X})_{jk} = af_{1j}f_{1k} + bf_{0j}f_{1k} + cf_{1j}f_{0k} + df_{0j}f_{0k} \tag{7.3}$$

We first consider the simple case where the transformation $f(m_{ij})$ is the same for all roll calls. In this case we can write

$$f_{1j} = f_{1k} = f_1 \quad \text{and} \quad f_{0j} = f_{0k} = f_0$$

The (j, k) entry relating these two roll calls then becomes

$$(\mathbf{X'X})_{jk} = af_1^2 + (b + c)f_0f_1 + df_0^2$$

If $f_0 = 0$

$$(\mathbf{X'X})_{jk} = af_1^2$$

i.e., it is proportional to a, the number of votes in category 1 shared by both roll calls. Similarly, if $f_1 = 0$, $(\mathbf{X'X})_{jk}$ will be proportional to the number of shared votes in category 0.

If $f_0 = -f_1$,

$$(\mathbf{X'X})_{jk} = f_1^2(a - b - c + d)$$

proportional to the net number of agreements.

We next consider the more general case in which f_j may differ from one roll call to another. But we impose an additional restriction: that each column in **X,** corresponding to each roll call, have a mean of zero. This gives rise to the two equations

$$(a + c)f_{1j} + (b + d)f_{0j} = 0$$

$$(a + b)f_{1k} + (c + d)f_{0k} = 0$$

(7.4)

Equation (7.4) can then be used to eliminate f_{0j} and f_{0k} from (7.3), the result being

$$(\mathbf{X'X})_{jk} = f_{1j}f_{1k}\left[a - \frac{b(a+c)}{b+d} - \frac{c(a+b)}{c+d} + \frac{d(a+c)(a+b)}{(b+d)(c+d)}\right]$$

which simplifies to

$$(\mathbf{X'X})_{jk} = \frac{Nf_{1j}f_{1k}(ad - bc)}{(b+d)(c+d)}$$

If we convert this into an index of average similarity between the two roll calls by dividing by N, the result is simply

$$\frac{f_{1j}f_{1k}(ad - bc)}{(b+d)(c+d)}$$

If we let $f_{1j} = q_j = (b + d)/N$, and $f_{1k} = q_k = (c + d)/N$, the index of average similarity becomes the cross-product $(ad - bc)/N^2$. And if we let

$$f_{1j} = \frac{q_j}{\sqrt{p_jq_j}} \quad \text{and} \quad f_{1k} = \frac{q_k}{\sqrt{p_kq_k}}$$

it is equal to ϕ. (Exercise: derive the expression for ϕ.)

Since $(\mathbf{X'X})_{jk}$ involves $(ad - bc)$ in the numerator, it will necessarily be zero for two roll calls that are independent of one another. But it seems impossible to choose a function f_j that will produce an index that is unity for a perfect cumulative scale relationship. We might wish, for example, to have $(\mathbf{X'X})_{jk}$ equal to Q; but the denominator of Q (i.e., $ad + bc$), cannot be obtained by a product of functions that depend only on the individual roll calls separately, such as $f_{1j}f_{1k}$ would provide.

In a formal sense, all our observations about roll-call–legislator duality might be repeated with reference to indices of similarity between legislators rather than roll calls. Each row of the matrix **X,** under the conditions we have assumed, also contains only two kinds of elements, and the corresponding elements of **XX'** can thus be expressed in terms of the cell entries in corresponding fourfold tables comparing *legislators*. This duality holds at least until we remove the column means or otherwise treat the columns differently, whereupon the rows no longer consist of only two types of elements.

Thus in the simple case where f_1 and f_0 are the same for all columns, they are also the same for all rows; and the first class of indices we developed under these assumptions are truly symmetrical with respect to the exchange of roll calls and legislators. Whether they validly measure important concepts is another question, unanswerable at present because of the lack of research combining analysis of **X'X** and **XX'** for such indices.

The more complex case in which the column means are removed destroys this type of row–column symmetry; but one is then tempted to remove row rather than column means and work with fourfold tables comparing legislators, computing ϕ from these tables. We have already indicated that this procedure seems undesirable because of the sensitivity of the results to polarity alteration.

An alternative approach to the placement of legislators and roll calls in comparable spatial models—though it does not correspond to any simple index of pairwise agreement between legislators—is provided by the Guttman-Lingoes multidimensional scaling procedure, which locates both in the same space.[41]

FACTOR SCORES FOR THE Q-MATRIX

Both here and in Chapter 5 we have pointed to the dilemma between obtaining cumulative scales, on the one hand, and benefiting from the mathematical convenience of principal-component analysis and factor-score computation, on the other. A coefficient of association such as Q, which permits us to identify clusters of roll calls forming cumulative scales, fails to fit the model of nonnegative eigenvalues which holds for matrix products such as **X'X**.

Before we introduced the logic of factor analysis, however, we found clusters in the Q-matrix, made cumulative scales from them, and assigned scores to legislators. These latter scores were similar in some ways to factor scores. We must now ask how far it is possible

[41]See Lingoes, *op. cit.*

to extend this procedure toward placing legislators in multidimensional space.

We may first recall that when we cluster the Q-matrix, the addition of one more cluster does not necessarily entail the addition of a new dimension. A new cluster may involve simply a combination of previous ones, in the sense that factor loadings of roll calls or factor scores of legislators may be calculable as linear combinations of values for other clusters. Thus, while the assignment of scores on a set of scale clusters superficially resembles the assignment of coordinates in a multidimensional space, the corresponding space may have fewer dimensions than the number of clusters. Moreover, even if the clusters are linearly independent of one another, in the sense that there are as many dimensions as clusters, they will in general define a set of oblique rather than orthogonal coordinate axes.

If we compute principal components of the Q-matrix, the result will be a set of orthogonal coordinate axes corresponding to the eigenvectors and these will be interpretable in somewhat conventional terms as long as the corresponding eigenvalues are positive. They will satisfy the condition that $(\mathbf{A'A})$ is diagonal.

We must then ask whether coordinates of legislators, analogous to factor scores, can be meaningfully computed for the factors of a Q-matrix. In what sense could they be interpreted? One possible sense is that, given the matrix $\mathbf{A}$ of factor loadings of the Q-matrix, we might look for another matrix $\mathbf{F}$ which when postmultiplied by $\mathbf{A'}$ will yield the best least-squares approximation to a data matrix $\mathbf{X}$. This would mean that for each set of factor loadings in $\mathbf{A}$ we should seek a corresponding set of numbers for legislators, so that when these numbers are combined with factor loadings (as though they were factor scores), the result would approximate the data (e.g., votes) as closely as possible.[42] This requirement would be expressed by the equation

$$\hat{\mathbf{X}} = \mathbf{FA'} \tag{7.5}$$

a modification of equation (4.35).

While in orthodox factor analysis the factor scores or columns of $\mathbf{F}$ were also eigenvectors, this is not in general true in the present case. But the problem is very similar to the one we encountered in deriving

[42]This relation is given in Horst, *Factor Analysis of Data Matrices*, pp. 478–479.

equations (5.5). Again we wish to approximate **X** optimally, in a least-squares sense, as a product of two matrices. We consider the case of one factor, i.e., **a** and **f** as column vectors.

In the notation of Chapter 5, we now know the vector **v** (which may be an eigenvector of **Q**, or any vector of nonzero magnitude) and wish to find the corresponding **u**. We thus begin with the same expression for the residual sum of squares as we used in deriving (5.5), and now differentiate it only with respect to the u_i's, considering the v_j's as fixed. We obtain only the first of equations (5.5):

$$-2 \sum_j v_j(x_{ij} - u_i v_j) = 0$$

These equations in turn reduce to the matrix equation

$$\frac{\mathbf{Xv'}}{|\mathbf{v}|^2} = \mathbf{u}$$

which gives the vector **u** corresponding to any given **v**.

If as before we set $|\mathbf{v}|^2 = \lambda$, we can again compute factor scores by means of equation (5.13) or (5.14):

$$\frac{\mathbf{Xv}_p'}{\lambda} = \mathbf{u}_p \quad \text{or} \quad \mathbf{F} = \mathbf{XA(A'A)}^{-1} \tag{7.6}$$

provided that **A′A** is again a diagonal matrix. We have modified (5.14), replacing **Z** with **X**, to indicate that the present result holds for any data matrix, including the vote-matrix **M** itself.[43]

The convention of setting $|\mathbf{v}|^2 = \lambda$ permits us, as before, to approximate the matrix of associations as well as the data matrix. But when the associations are Q's or coefficients other than ϕ, however, there is a possibility of large negative eigenvalues, for which this convention will have no meaning.

We shall now illustrate the computation of factor scores based on a Q-matrix, first with a single dimension and then with two dimensions in the artificial numerical examples used. We begin with the two numerical examples used in Chapter 5 and in Tables 7.2 and 7.3 above.

---

[43]This method could also be used to generate "factor scores" corresponding to Kruskal's MDSCAL or the Guttman-Lingoes "smallest space analysis," based on the coordinates of roll call points and on the data matrix. A related possibility of going from roll-call points to legislator points has also been shown in Alker, "Statistics and Politics," Appendix.

Each of these two numerical examples began with a data matrix that constituted a perfect cumulative scale. Consequently, the corresponding Q-matrices, or matrices of any coefficients that attain unity for a perfect scale relationship, will have unities for all entries. When factored, each will reveal only one eigenvector, all of whose elements are 1's, and one eigenvalue equal to the order of the matrix—3 and 5 for the two respective examples.

Now suppose we wish to approximate the data matrix **M**, rather than the matrix of standard scores (let **X** = **M**), in the first of these examples. We can use the left-hand equation of (7.6) because there is only one eigenvector:

$$\frac{1}{3}\begin{bmatrix} 1 & 1 & 1 \\ 0 & 0 & 1 \\ 0 & 0 & 1 \\ 0 & 0 & 1 \\ 0 & 0 & 0 \end{bmatrix}\begin{bmatrix} 1 \\ 1 \\ 1 \end{bmatrix} = \frac{1}{3}\begin{bmatrix} 3 \\ 1 \\ 1 \\ 1 \\ 0 \end{bmatrix}$$

The right-hand column vector is the set of factor scores for the five legislators. Each score corresponds simply to the number of 1's among that legislator's responses. For a perfect cumulative scale, this procedure is therefore equivalent to one of the scale-scoring methods discussed in Chapter 2; but like the orthodox factor-score procedure, it gives additional weight to the duplicated roll call in the data matrix, setting the first legislator farther from the middle three than is the fifth. This possible artifact must be borne in mind when we use this procedure in Chapter 8. Another way to envision it—and the process of assigning factor scores in general—is to consider the effect of one roll call (one column of **X**) at a time. The first two roll calls each move the first legislator (row) away from the others; the third roll call moves the last legislator away from the first four.

While we have reproduced a set of scale scores by this method, and have accounted perfectly for the Q-matrix, the product **FA'** no longer accounts perfectly for the data matrix **X**. (Exercise: verify this numerically.) Moreover, the sum of squares of the elements in $\mathbf{u}\sqrt{N}$ (or **f**) is no longer equal to N, nor would it have been had we used **Z** instead of **M** for **X** in (7.6). And the orthogonality relation between factor scores, as expressed by (4.39), no longer obtains. Thus while we can compute "factor scores" from the Q-matrix or similar matrices, they do not have all the conventional properties of factor scores. If, however, we had subtracted column means to produce **X** from **M**, the means of the resulting "factor scores" would have also then have been zero—a property we shall use in Chapter 8. (Exercise: prove this.)

The second numerical example, shown in Tables 5.1 and 7.3, leads to similar conclusions. Again we apply the left-hand equation of (7.6):

$$\frac{1}{5}\begin{bmatrix} 1 & 1 & 1 & 1 & 1 \\ 0 & 1 & 1 & 1 & 1 \\ 0 & 0 & 1 & 1 & 1 \\ 0 & 0 & 1 & 1 & 1 \\ 0 & 0 & 1 & 1 & 1 \\ 0 & 0 & 0 & 1 & 1 \\ 0 & 0 & 0 & 1 & 1 \\ 0 & 0 & 0 & 1 & 1 \\ 0 & 0 & 0 & 0 & 1 \\ 0 & 0 & 0 & 0 & 0 \end{bmatrix} \begin{bmatrix} 1 \\ 1 \\ 1 \\ 1 \\ 1 \end{bmatrix} = \frac{1}{5}\begin{bmatrix} 5 \\ 4 \\ 3 \\ 3 \\ 3 \\ 2 \\ 2 \\ 2 \\ 1 \\ 0 \end{bmatrix}$$

The factor scores, or scale scores, are again sums of the 1's in the corresponding rows of **X**. Because no roll calls are duplicated, the top and bottom ends of **u** (or **f**) are symmetrical as regards their distances from the center items. Again the sum of squares is not equal to N.

We next consider the two-dimensional example presented in Figure 5.1, with 30 data points and 26 cutting lines. The artificial roll calls generated by that figure were converted into a Q-matrix, which was factored by means of principal components; the first three positive eigenvalues were 23.1, 5.0, and .8, indicating a two-dimensional space.[44] The first two eigenvalues were chosen for interpretation and were plotted in Figure 5.2. The right-hand equation of (7.6) was used for the computation of factor scores, except that the column means of the data matrix were subtracted before matrix multiplication. The resulting configuration of "legislator" points is shown in Figure 7.3.

The relative positions of the points in Figure 7.3 agree remarkably well with those of the data points in Figure 5.1; each row of points is distinct and the rows are nearly parallel. There is, of course, a rotation relative to the initial diagram, but this can be corrected to some extent by locating preferred axes, either from the configuration of points itself or from the location of the extreme clusters in the factor-loading diagram, Figure 5.2. For in spite of some departures from the orthodox factor-score model, our present procedure for computing

---

[44]Comparative data on the results of factoring matrices of other coefficients were given in Chapter 5, fn. 30.

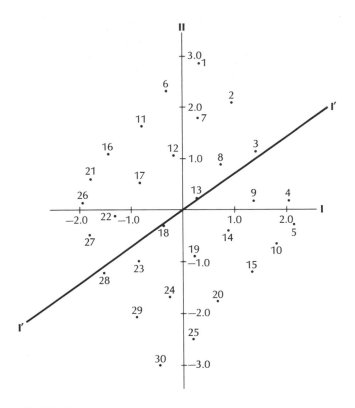

FIGURE 7.3. Two-dimensional Configuration of Points Recovered from Factor Scores Based on Twenty-Six Artificial "Roll Calls" (Computed by the equation $\mathbf{F} = \mathbf{XA(A'A)}^{-1}$, where $\mathbf{X}$ is the data matrix with column means removed).

"factor scores" still retains the property that factor scores and loadings rotate together, as shown in (4.38).

The initial array of points in Figure 5.1 has been transformed from a rectangle into an array approximating a parallelogram. Nevertheless, a set of cutting lines can be drawn in Figure 7.3 which will separate the points in exactly the same fashion as the lines in Figure 5.1; in this sense, the array of points in Figure 7.3 constitutes a perfect solution to the problem of reproducing the initial artificial roll-call data. There is, of course, an infinite family of solutions of this kind; any one perfect solution will give rise to an infinite subset of this family if we consider new coordinates, each of which is a linear transformation of the two initial axes, and which are linearly independent of one another.[45]

Even without this sort of transformation, there is also the variety of solutions that can be produced by moving the points (as long as they do not cross cutting lines), or by corresponding movement of the lines. In this sense the particular configuration we have found is one that has been accidentally selected among many. As the number of input roll calls and legislators increased, this additional freedom of movement would be limited, especially in parts of the space where lines and points were dense. But it is also possible that the alignment of points in our solution will provide information about the roll calls that were involved; a dense concentration of points will suggest a subset rarely divided on roll calls, and a line of points, a subset divided only on one particular type of issue. Close inspection of details of this kind may lead to more accurate interpretations of real roll-call data.

It might appear that by fitting cutting lines to the array of points in Figure 7.3, we have availed ourselves of too many degrees of freedom. The perfect reproduction of the initial data is also possible, however, if we allow the slopes of the cutting lines to be determined by the factor loadings plotted in Figure 5.2; for as we shall show in equation (8.3), an optimal separation of the legislator-points corresponding to yeas and nays on a given roll call is provided by a line perpendicular to the radius vector defined by the factor loadings of that roll call. The line must then be moved away from the origin by an appropriate distance. The possibility of doing this is illustrated by rotated axis I' in Figure 7.3, an axis defined by the cluster of roll-call points 22–26 in Figure 5.2. A set of lines perpendicular to this axis will perfectly separate the sets of points 1–5, 6–10, 11–15, 16–20, 21–25, and 26–30. Another axis could be drawn in the same direction as a line passing through the cluster 1–4 in Figure 5.2, and cutting lines perpendicular to it would also separate the sets of points 1-6-11-16-21 26, etc. The parallelogram configuration in Figure 7.3 is therefore due to the fact that these two axes were not orthogonal in the factor loadings of Figure 5.2.

[45]Among these transformations, those that do not preserve right angles will be referred to as *shearing* transformations. The simplest transformation of this type is $x' = x, y' = y + ax$. The points in Figure 7.3 can be moved into an approximately rectangular array by a transformation of this type.

The procedure we have used to reproduce the artificial roll-call data here will be applied in the next chapter to real roll calls. While it appears useful, its utility would be greatly enhanced by a rigorous theory that stated the conditions under which it could best be used, the types of error introduced by the model itself, and the possible transformations that gave rise to families of acceptable solutions. It would also be desirable, as in orthodox factor analysis, to have precise criteria as to the proper number of factors or dimensions to be interpreted.[46]

[46]For methods making fewer assumptions, see Lingoes, *op. cit.*; and Coombs, *A Theory of Data*. The present method is preferred because it can be programmed for large data matrices at the present time.

The method of scale scoring proposed in Chapter 2, for assignment of precise rank scores, cannot easily be extended to two dimensions because the assumption of a bivariate distribution, analogous to the rectangular distribution of ranks, constrains the solutions excessively.

8.
LEGISLATORS' PARTY
OR GROUP ALLEGIANCE

W E have dealt so far with methods that purported to identify issues, on the one hand, and factions, on the other, both from the same roll-call data. Matrices of relations between pairs of roll calls were said to reveal issues, while matrices of relations between legislators were said to reveal blocs or factions. Yet when we analyze these two types of matrices, we see that they often correspond very closely to one another, as do the indices used to summarize them. One indication of this correspondence is the fact that factor loadings and factor scores are measured on the same coordinate axes. The naming of these axes then requires us to apply the same concepts to groupings of roll calls and groupings of legislators.

We have preserved the distinction between the study of issues and that of factions partly by our choice of examples. The votes of Republicans in the House of Representatives furnish a good example of multiple divisions on distinct issues. Had we used the Democrats' votes, or the votes of both parties together, the same procedures would have been more likely to reveal general clusters of roll calls reflecting conflict between groups or parties.

Some indices that are used to measure the partisanship of individual legislators, or their positions on issues, also suffer from this ambiguity. The same general procedures can be used, for example, to produce indices that are considered to measure party loyalty and liberalism-conservatism. Such indices are likely to combine both elements in unknown proportions, and the elements need to be separated.

Several indices that purport to measure legislators' partisanship make use of an initial selection of roll calls that presumably involve partisanship, followed by a count of the frequency with which a given legislator votes with his party on them. This approach can be applied either by selecting a subset of roll calls for computation of the index, or by weighting various roll calls differently according to their presumed degree of partisanship.

The most widely used index of this kind is the *party unity index* of the *Congressional Quarterly,* also employed by Turner under the name of "index of party loyalty."[1] It is based on an initial identification of *party unity votes*—those on which majorities of the two parties oppose one another—and then computation of the percent of votes on which each legislator agrees with his own party. The resulting index for the Republicans is then 100 minus the corresponding index for a Democrat who voted identically (ignoring absences). A modification of this procedure, used by Mayhew, chooses roll calls according to their subject matter but without a requirement of party opposition, and then counts the proportion of a legislator's votes that are in accord with his own party's majority.[2] The same procedure was used by Truman, though without any initial subdivision of roll calls according to subject matter, to form a "party orthodoxy index." And the *Congressional Quarterly*'s indices of "Presidential support," "bipartisan support," and the like also use the same principle.[3]

That indices of this type have some validity is suggested by their associations with leadership position in Congress. Goodwin has shown, for example, that over a series of recent Congresses the President's floor leaders in House and Senate scored higher than their party colleagues on indices of both party unity and presidential support. But on an index of "anti-internationalism," presumably more closely related to issues than to party loyalty as such, Farnsworth has

---

[1]Turner, *Party and Constituency,* p. 78.

[2]Mayhew, *Party Loyalty Among Congressmen,* p. 10.

[3]Truman, *The Congressional Party,* pp. 326–327. The *Congressional Quarterly* publishes its indices for every Congress; for the 89th Congress, for example, values of the indices were given in the issues of December 16, 23, and 30, 1966.

also shown differences between Senate Foreign Relations Committee members and others.[4] Without closer examination, therefore, we cannot be sure whether the difference between leaders and followers is based on group loyalty or issue positions.

Thus while these indices of party loyalty may well involve loyalty to the legislative party as an ingredient, we cannot be sure that they do not also measure ideological leanings. For the party unity index is also highly correlated with cumulative scales measuring major intraparty divisions.[5] While it may involve a greater degree of partisanship than an index based on all roll calls, we cannot say that it excludes ideological or issue variables. Whether it should do so is in part a matter of definition, but for our purposes it is desirable to distinguish the two variables.

The party unity index also fails to distinguish adequately those legislators who are so extremely loyal to their party leaders or positions that they sometimes oppose the party majority. It is difficult, of course, to imagine that a lone deviant from the rest of his party is taking that position as a result of party loyalty; but the difference between voting with 51 percent of one's party and 49 percent is so slight that these situations should perhaps not be classed differently. And insofar as the party unity index measures ideological positions, it tends to ignore the votes of extreme ideologues in either party.

The same general type of selection procedure has also been used for construction of indices alleged to measure ideological positions or attitudes on issues: The *New Republic* index, for example, is based on the proportion voting "liberal" (usually the same polarity as Democratic) on a selected set of roll calls considered to involve liberalism. We criticized this procedure in Chapter 2 on the ground that multiple issues might be involved in such an index; but we must now raise the question whether such roll calls might also involve an admixture of party loyalty as well.

Following the reasoning of Chapters 2 and 3, one might try simply to select roll calls that measure pure partisanship, and to construct cumulative scales measuring this dimension. This has been done in a study of the Massachusetts legislature. And different sets of roll calls

---

[4]Goodwin, "The Seniority System in Congress," p. 427; Farnsworth, "A Comparison of the Senate and Its Foreign Relations Committee on Selected Roll-Call Votes."

[5]MacRae, *Dimensions of Congressional Voting*, pp. 304–306.

have been distinguished approximately according to their concern with issues or with allegiance to a cabinet faction in a study of the French National Assembly.[6] But this latter type of distinction is less clearly available in Congress, and the only roll calls that are clearly completely partisan are perfect party votes such as those on the choice of the Speaker of the House. The problem is to distinguish degrees of partisanship on different roll calls and to use this information to measure the degrees of partisanship of individual legislators.

GROUP ALLEGIANCE
AND ATTITUDES ON ISSUES

When terms such as "party loyalty" and "liberalism" are used to refer to similar and closely correlated indices, we must be sure that the distinction between the two concepts is clear. This clarification is to be sought not only through more intensive statistical analysis, but also by systematic reflection on the meanings of the concepts involved, their relation in possible models of behavior, and the possible range of indicators that might be devised to measure each concept.

We wish to distinguish the concepts "group allegiance" (with party as the principal group in question), and "attitudes on issues."[7] By "group allegiance" we mean a solidarity or sympathy for fellow members of a group, or for its leaders and symbols, which is substantively diffuse, i.e., which can be brought into play legitimately on a wide variety of concrete matters.[8] By an "attitude on an issue" we mean in the present context a predisposition to favor or oppose some outcome of legislation, or some symbol involved in the proposed legislation. The two concepts are not completely distinct by definition, for if a proposed law favors or disadvantages a legislator's group, he will be predisposed for or against it by group allegiance. Conversely, if one of his group's central symbols is involved in the content of a bill—and such symbols may well be those of political ideologies—he may again

[6]MacRae, "Roll Call Votes and Leadership"; MacRae, *Parliament, Parties and Society in France 1946–1958*, chaps. 4–7.

[7]Related distinctions are suggested in MacRae, in "Some Underlying Variables in Legislative Roll Call Votes," and in *Dimensions of Congressional Voting*, p. 360.

[8]The term is akin to Parsons' "specificity-diffuseness," but we refer here only to diversity of subjects of legislation, not to interactions outside the legislative role. See Parsons, *The Social System*, p. 66 and *passim*.

be predisposed for or against it by a direct connection between group allegiance and the content of the bill.

The possible independent variation of group allegiance and issues is illustrated, however, by a change of meaning that often occurs in Congress and other legislative bodies. A bill may have come to the floor for action, and members may be generally aware of its provisions, when the majority leader will rise and state that it is an important party issue, or that the President wants it passed. The symbols of party and party allegiance then become connected with the bill to a degree that they had not been before. A similar change takes place in a parliamentary regime when the premier makes a bill a question of confidence in his cabinet—in France, this has been said to change the question from a "technical" to a "political" one.[9] In either case, the verbal content of the bill or motion is not in itself sufficient to connect it in this way with party or with the cabinet coalition. It is true, of course, that words are continually subject to interpretation, selection, and emphasis; indeed, the majority leader, the premier, or others in the ensuing debate are likely then to call attention to words or provisions in the bill, or to label and categorize it, in ways that connect it positively or negatively with party and group interests. This connection can of course take place at various stages in the consideration of a bill, sometimes long before it comes to the floor.

Group allegiance is thus reflected by a predisposition, partly independent of the content of a bill, which may be linked to the bill by the actions of persons in the name of the group. Alternatively, it can be linked with a bill by the presentation of counter symbols, e.g., a negative position taken by an opposing party. This distinction is an instance of a more general one which is widely observed in sociology and social psychology. Though we cannot review this literature thoroughly here, several examples will illustrate the prevalence of the distinction.

Probably the closest analogy to our proposed distinction is that between "party identification" and "issue orientation," made in the studies of the University of Michigan Survey Research Center.[10] Ex-

[9]See MacRae, *Parliament, Parties and Society*, p. 68. The various means used by leaders in the House of Representatives to make party positions effective are described in Ripley, *Party Leaders in the House of Representatives*, chap. 5.

[10]See A. Campbell, et al., *The American Voter*, chaps. 6–8.

tensive research has demonstrated the value of this conceptual distinction; and if the ordinary voter has an identifiable party allegiance, professional politicians might be expected to have even more of it.

Another approach to the study of citizens' voting emphasizes the changing importance of primary-group allegiance during a political campaign. Berelson, Lazarsfeld, and McPhee in *Voting* pointed out the mobilization of these groups in a campaign, and the presumed increase in relevance of certain issues to these groups as the campaign progressed. They also demonstrated the connection between Catholicism and Democratic preference in the United States—a connection by no means intrinsic to Catholic doctrine, as the political correlates of Catholicism in other countries indicate.[11] Here both primary groups and a major religious–ethnic group, while they may have had "essential" or "constitutive" attitudes, also served somewhat as empty bottles into which particular political choices could be poured.

Also illustrative of the mobilization of social solidarities in support of new political issues—not intrinsic to these groupings at the start—is the model of community conflict proposed by Coleman. As conflict develops, previously separate groups coalesce on one side or the other, and distinct issues become organized into an ideological pattern. Still another example of the separability of group allegiances from positions on particular issues is provided by a typology of issues in Lipset *et al.*, *Union Democracy*. Among the types of political issues distinguished there were "ins-and-outs" issues—those on which a given party was likely to take different stands depending on whether it controlled the government.[12]

A different perspective that leads to the same distinction is provided by the study of social movements. Heberle, in referring to the various ideas that are combined in the ideology of a social movement, writes,

Some of these may be regarded as specific and essential to the movement; these are the really integrating ideas. Others may be of mere accidental

---

[11]Berelson, Lazarsfeld, and McPhee, *Voting*, chaps. 6, 7. An attempt to verify their polarization hypothesis for a smaller group was not entirely successful; see MacRae and Kilpatrick, "Collective Decision and Polarization in a 125-Man Group." For the reference to Catholicism, see Berelson *et al.*, *op. cit.*, pp. 64–71.

[12]Coleman, *Community Conflict*; Lipset, Trow, and Coleman, *Union Democracy*, pp. 291–296. Turner, in *Party and Constituency*, p. 70, also noted a change in party positions on issues, related to party control of the Presidency.

significance for this particular movement. The former may be called the *constitutive* ideas, since they form the spiritual-intellectual foundation of group cohesion or solidarity.[13]

There are several possible ways to distinguish between the constitutive and accidental ideas of a given group. As Heberle suggests, one way concerns the function of ideas for the group and their contribution to group cohesion. A second relates to the life history of the movement. At its genesis, a movement may reflect a particular demand, the interest of persons in a social category, or a social strain. Later it may develop allegiances or enmities with other groups because of the relation of their views to its own on central issues, and may adopt other positions of these groups (or their opposites) as parts of its own ideology. These latter beliefs appear less essential to the group's position. Also later in its development, such a group may become more concerned with organizational interest as such, and may thus be led to take new positions on particular issues.[14]

The solidarity of a group—its cohesion, its members' allegiance to the group and its symbols as well as their positive feelings for one another—may be maintained or increased by the group's support of particular political positions.[15] It is in this sense that Heberle singles out certain ideas as constitutive or integrating. In small groups, communication about particular matters may also promote solidarity, while other subjects divide the group. All these possibilities of course exist for political parties and their members in a legislature.

Our assertion here, however, is the converse: that group solidarity can influence positions on issues. For some ideas, the solidarity of the group may be mobilized by its leaders, or by the action of external influences such as opposition, to influence members' attitudes on an issue that is not constitutive. But just how many ideas, and which ones, are constitutive is an empirical question; some groups are more concerned with ideology than others.

[13]Heberle, *Social Movements*, p. 13. See also Smelser, *Theory of Collective Behavior*, pp. 359–361.

[14]This type of change was referred to by Weber as "routinization of charisma" in *The Theory of Social and Economic Organization*, pp. 363–373. It has been observed in organizations as well as social movements. Banfield refers to the "maintenance and enhancement needs" of organizations in *Political Influence*, p. 263. Blau and Scott refer to organizations' "preoccupation with administrative problems" in *Formal Organizations*, p. 228.

[15]See Weber, *op. cit.*, pp. 136–139; Parsons, *op. cit.*, pp. 97–98.

Legislative parties sometimes conform to the model of community conflict as they did before the American Civil War or during the European revolution of 1848.[16] They then show an increasing polarization, sometimes resulting in the disruption of a preexisting party, and the range of nonconstitutive or accidental ideas becomes correspondingly narrower. At other times, parties may show a gradual decline in ideological concern and thus take positions on new issues more for bargaining power or organizational survival than in terms of the substance of the issues.

But in the United States Congress in the period after World War II from which our data are drawn, we do not expect to see a pronounced temporal trend in the relevance of issues to party. The time series shown in Figure 6.6, and the hypotheses presented in that chapter, suggest rather that the congressional parties in that period experienced fluctuations in the relevance of party to particular issues without a major increase or decrease. There may indeed have been a greater partisanship on certain issues than others (e.g., less on foreign aid); but we should also be able to observe differences in partisanship among roll calls on a given substantive issue, in relation to leaders' acts and party symbols. This period, and the parties in it, had several of the requisites for separation of party allegiance from issues. The parties were old organizations and had not recently absorbed major movements of protest; they were cadre rather than mass parties and did not depend on the ideological mobilization of large numbers of members; and the active members of state parties often depended on material rather than ideal rewards for their membership.[17]

In analyzing the two-party system in the United States Congress, we are concerned with the opposition between the parties on various issues. We typically relate the group relevance of an issue to the degree of opposition between the two parties on that issue; this in turn may be measured by some of the indices considered in Chapter 6, as well as others to be proposed here. The literature on voting behavior and social movements that we have reviewed tends to consider the cohesion of a group by itself on an issue, independently of

[16]Both have been studied by statistical analysis of roll-call votes. See Alexander, *Sectional Stress and Party Strength;* Silbey, *The Shrine of Party;* and Mattheisen, "A Scale Analysis of the Prussian National Assembly of 1848."

[17]The "mass vs. cadre" distinction is that of Duverger, in *Political Parties,* p. 63. The atypicality of ideal rewards is pointed out in Wilson, *The Amateur Democrat.*

the group's opposition to its environment; but we shall not attempt to measure the cohesion of individual parties separately.

The model with which we proceed is thus one in which individual legislators are endowed to varying degrees with a diffuse "party loyalty." And while this loyalty may be connected with central issues that are important to the party, we also expect it to be mobilized to different degrees on different votes, in a way that is not completely determined by the substance of the proposals in question.

STATISTICAL CONTROL OF "LIBERALISM" TO MEASURE PARTISANSHIP

The conceptual distinction between group allegiance and attitudes on issues has been made in the development of two indices of partisanship, both of which are in this respect superior to the other indices we have discussed. Matthews, wishing to measure the "party effort" of individual Senators independently of their general liberalism or conservatism, used the method of residuals from a regression line to make this separation. He first plotted the party unity index values, for the Senators of a given party, against their conservatism–liberalism scores based on domestic roll calls selected by the *New Republic*.[18] He then used the residuals of "party unity," after the contributions of "liberalism" had been controlled or removed by a regression equation, as a purer index of partisanship. The reasoning underlying this procedure is as follows:

. . . The unity which the parties display in the Senate is far more a result of the similarity of members' attitudes than of either "pressure" or persuasion from party leaders. . . . However, the unity within each party in the Senate cannot be explained entirely on this basis. . . . Some senators have higher party unity scores, given their ideological position, than others. . . . The difference between how often a senator actually votes with his party and how often he would be expected to on the basis of his over-all ideological stance, we shall call party effort.[19]

Matthews' reasoning suggests a line of investigation which still remains promising, and which we shall use: the study of partisanship by multidimensional approaches. No single roll call or selection of roll calls can be guaranteed to reflect partisanship in pure form. Es-

[18]Matthews, *U.S. Senators and Their World*, pp. 133 ff., 276 f.
[19]*Ibid.*, pp. 133–135.

pecially in Congress, ideology or issue content is always a possible factor in the vote. But by extending the principle used by Matthews, we may be able to measure partisanship more accurately and separate it from ideology.

The validity of Matthews' index was supported by its associations with Senators' committee assignments, seniority, and the electoral cycle.[20] Similar relations may be used as criteria for testing alternative indices of partisanship.

A related index has been proposed by Dempsey: the difference between the proportions of votes on which a legislator agrees with his party's typical ideological position on "party" as against "non-party" roll calls.[21] He defines the former type of roll call as one on which majorities of the two parties are opposed (i.e., a party unity vote), and the latter as one on which the majorities of both parties agree. On nonparty roll calls he uses a method analogous to factor analysis to set polarities. This index appears to give consistent values for the same Senators over successive sessions. But while it exemplifies a useful line of reasoning, it is liable to artifacts. For suppose both parties could be arrayed on separate continua, as in the Guttman scale model (see Figure 6.4, lower diagram). Suppose further that all the roll calls considered were derived from this model, but with the more partisan roll calls cutting off only small proportions of liberal Republicans and conservative Democrats. Then Dempsey's index would reveal as most partisan the conservative Republicans and liberal Democrats, even though the model included no intraparty differentials in partisanship over and above the ideological differences within each party.[22] Closer examination of the index values given by Dempsey for various Senators shows that this is the case: liberal Democrats and conservative Republicans, as identified by their positions on nonparty issues, tend uniformly to have the lowest "loyalty shift scores." This result leads us to view Dempsey's index with caution, as well as to recall this possible artifact when we examine other indices.

[20]*Ibid.*, pp. 135–138. Additional tests of the index with House data, however, have shown difficulties due to skewed distributions.

[21]Dempsey, "Liberalism-Conservatism and Party Loyalty in the U.S. Senate."

[22]Another problem suggested by the model concerns roll calls with "negative partisanship." Presumably Dempsey's index for "party" roll calls was identical with the party unity index; but on the occasional negatively partisan vote, it would ignore the coincidence of ideological deviance and partisan conformity.

Both Matthews' and Dempsey's indices may be related to a general problem concerning the measurement of factor scores on a single factor by means of indices that involve that factor only in combination with others. Suppose that we had two approximate measures of partisanship and liberalism, expressed by the standard scores z_{i1} and z_{i2} respectively for the ith legislator. Suppose further that each of these approximate measures could be expressed as a combination of two exact measures of partisanship and liberalism, whose factor scores were F_{i1} and F_{i2} respectively. Then the relation between the approximate measures and the factor scores could be expressed as a special case of equations (4.26):

$$z_{i1} = F_{i1}a_{11} + F_{i2}a_{12} + e_{i1}$$
$$z_{i2} = F_{i1}a_{21} + F_{i2}a_{22} + e_{i2}$$

(8.1)

Because the standard scores z_{i1} and z_{i2} are approximate measures of the variables F_{i1} and F_{i2} respectively, we expect a_{11} and a_{22} to be the largest of the factor loadings. If the a's were known, we could find a linear combination of z_{i1} and z_{i2} that eliminated F_{i2}, thus involving only F_{i1} and error terms; this would be an estimate of partisanship uncontaminated by ideology.[23]

If we start only with the two approximate measures, however, we do not know the a's. Matthews' method, modified by the use of standard scores, would be to compute the regression of z_{i1} (party unity index) on z_{i2} (liberalism index). If z_{i2} is a pure measure of liberalism ($a_{21} = 0$), and if the error terms can be ignored, the residuals will involve only the partisanship factor. (Exercise: verify this.) If, however, the z's are imperfect measures with error terms, and if the liberalism index involves some element of partisanship, then the residuals will no longer be completely free of liberalism.

Dempsey's method involves computing two different indices that play the part of z_{i1} and z_{i2}, and subtracting the second from the first. It must be presumed that the loadings a_{12} and a_{22} are equal if this subtraction is to produce a pure measure not involving F_{i2}. In other words, our choice of two sets of roll calls, more and less partisan,

---

[23]This procedure is carried out by Matthews for one party at a time, in which case the difference between the parties is not measurable. The combination of equations (8.1) is similar to the use of "suppressor variables"; see Guilford, *Fundamental Statistics in Psychology and Education*, pp. 403–408.

must not involve any accidental concomitant difference between the two sets in the ideological factor (by $a_{12} \neq a_{22}$). The same problem would exist if we distinguished between roll calls of high and low partisanship by some index of partisanship, such as Q; it also exists for a rank difference between legislators' positions on two scales, to be discussed below.

The party unity index measures only one variable, z_{i1}, but raises the coefficient a_{11} of F_{i1} somewhat by using only votes on which the two parties oppose one another. While application of the two-factor model shows the inadequacy of the party unity index, it also suggests (as does Dempsey's method) another approach. This alternative procedure, which is guided by the models of (8.1), is to find the factor loadings by factor analysis, provided we can identify the "partisanship" and "ideology" factors adequately among the various possible rotated axes. We shall now attempt to do this.

FACTOR SCORES, ISSUES, AND PARTISANSHIP

Another procedure for distinguishing legislators' issue positions from their party or factional loyalty is to locate them in a multidimensional factor space and to try to identify particular rotated axes that correspond to partisanship and to the various aspects of issues. We shall carry out such an analysis for the votes of the House in the first session of the 87th Congress, chosen because it permits comparison with other studies of the same data.

We use the 108 roll calls in the first session of the 87th Congress (1961) on which there were one or more dissenting votes.[24] A Q-matrix between all pairs of these roll calls, for Democrats and Republicans together, was computed. It is believed that the results would be very similar if any of several other coefficients fitting the cumulative-scale criterion had been used.[25]

---

[24]The use of roll calls with only one or two dissenting votes leads occasionally to loadings and communalities as high as 1.5, but by including all roll calls with any dissent we need not choose an arbitrary threshold for the inclusion of roll calls. When all contested roll calls are included in this way, however, the capacity of the Q-matrix program permits the study of only one annual session at a time.

[25]See MacRae, "Partisanship and Issues in Congressional Voting," for a parallel analysis using r_t.

All the eigenvalues were computed and factor loadings were computed for the six principal components with largest positive eigenvalues. The eigenvalue fourth largest in magnitude was negative, but difficulty-factor loadings that had resulted from the use of ϕ in a previous analysis were reduced. Our subsequent analysis will be limited to the first two factors. Although it might be improved by consideration of other factors, this procedure yields simpler and more intelligible results.[26]

Figure 8.1 shows the distribution of loadings of roll calls on the first two factors, indicated as I and II. The signs of the loadings of some roll calls have been reversed so as to locate all points in the right half-plane; this corresponds to a polarity adjustment made after the factor analysis.

In the lower right corner of Figure 8.1, on the axis marked I', is a point marked $+$, corresponding to the vote on the Speakership— a perfect party division on which only 7 of the 435 members were absent. One way to locate a preferred axis in this space is to pass it through this point. This rotated axis is shown as axis I', and an axis orthogonal to it is indicated as II'. We shall use axis I' to define a dimension of partisanship. As we shall show below, the coordinates or projections of legislator points on this axis for the two parties in the factor-score diagram are necessarily more completely separated than they would be on any other axis. Nevertheless, the actual degree of separation of the parties (in Figure 8.2 below) is remarkably good and serves further to confirm our choice of this axis.

It is also conceivable that preferred axes could be located from the distribution of points in Figure 8.1 without knowledge of the content or the partisanship of particular roll calls. The procedure most often used for this purpose is Varimax rotation, which might yield new orthogonal axes similar to I' and II', spanning most of the roll-call points in a 90° arc. Though a few points lie outside this arc, it may be possible to define an arc of greatest density of points, perhaps spanning less than 90°. The boundaries of such a region are not precise, however, and it is not clear from the data presently available that such a concentration of points will always occur. For this reason, we

[26]The computer programs were written by Brian F. Sherry. The five eigenvalues largest in magnitude were 79.9, 14.6, 8.5, −7.9, and 6.8. The Speakership vote had loadings of .92 and .56 on factors 1 and 2, but less than .08 on factors 3–6, suggesting that for these data two dimensions provide an adequate description of partisanship.

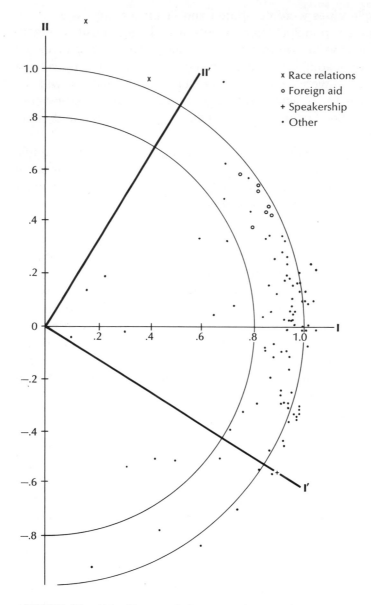

FIGURE 8.1. U.S. House of Representatives, 1961: Factor Loadings for 108 Roll Calls, Based on Q-Matrix, for Democrats plus Republicans.

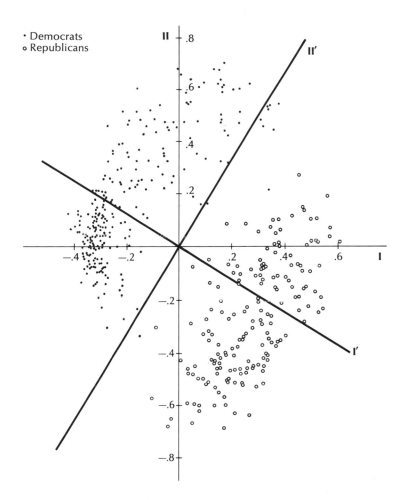

FIGURE 8.2. Unrotated Factor Scores for 1961 House, Based on Q-Matrix.

choose to pass axis *I'* through a purely party division, which always occurs for the Speakership in odd years in contemporary Congresses, and can be added to the data matrix for other years.

We hypothesize (as a first approximation) that axis *I'* measures pure partisanship and that axis *II'* measures pure ideology, independent of the influence of party. This hypothesis gains some support from the substantive content of the roll calls whose points fall near the two axes; several votes on foreign aid, indicated by open circles in

Figure 8.1, fall near axis II' in keeping with the generally lower partisanship on foreign aid. Two roll calls on race relations appear at the top of the diagram, corresponding to the negative partisanship often observed on votes of this kind.[27]

A related indication of the way in which axis I' measures partisanship is provided by the direct association between the votes on each roll call and party. For each point in Figure 8.1 we could compute a value of Q measuring the association between party and the votes on that roll call; such values actually were computed between the Speakership vote and all others as part of the Q-matrix. These values of Q, if they were shown in the figure, would vary systematically as we proceeded around the outer circle in the figure. Before doing so, we first set aside the points within the innermost of the two circles shown, of radius (h) .8. For the four points nearest the origin, the values of Q with party ranged from .02 to .30, and for the other seven within this circle, from .28 to .72.

We then focus our attention on those points outside the inner circle in clockwise order. At the very top of the diagram are two (marked ×) dealing with the transfer of the Freedmen's Hospital to Howard University, and with an appropriation for the Civil Rights Commission. The values of Q with party for these two roll calls are −.80 and −.51 respectively, relative to polarities set by factor I; both show negative partisanship in this way as well as in their position relative to axis I'. Just to the right of axis II' is another roll call whose value of Q is −.21; as in Figure 5.2, axis II' does not pass exactly through those points whose roll calls have zero association with those defining axis I'.

Moving clockwise from axis II', we find seven roll calls on foreign aid, indicated by open circles, with Q's ranging from .09 to .58. The four other roll calls in the same area of the figure have values from .13 to .63. The lowest of these eleven values are for the two points lying closest to axis II'. Between the lowest of the foreign-aid votes and axis I, values of Q range from .59 to 1, and between axes I and I', from .84 to 1. Below axis I', the values of Q decline again, that for the very lowest point in the figure being only .6.

[27]See Figure 6.2, above, and the accompanying discussion. The fact that foreign-aid votes are here interpreted as nearly pure liberalism–conservatism, devoid of partisanship, runs counter to our interpretation of foreign aid, in Chapter 3, as a distinct issue. We also encounter this problem below, in interpreting the votes of isolationist congressmen from agrarian–radical areas as showing low partisanship.

The values of Q are thus very approximately equal to the projections of the points on axis I'. If the individual variables were quantitative rather than dichotomous, we should expect this relation to hold more exactly. But for these data, it is possible for a roll call to divide only one of the two parties, thus having $Q = 1$ with party, while the corresponding point did not lie on axis I'. The reason for this is that the divided party may be split along ideological as well as along partisan lines—a possibility we shall see more clearly when we consider the congressmen's factor scores.

We next proceed to compute factor scores for the congressmen, approximating the data matrix X as in equation (7.5). We choose to approximate X rather than Z because the former is simpler and involves fewer assumptions; it is possible, however, that variations on this method will yield improvements.[28] The corresponding distribution of factor scores is shown in Figure 8.2. The axes I, II, I', and II' in this figure correspond to those in Figure 8.1, for as we showed in (4.38), factor scores and factor loadings may be rotated together to preserve the approximation of $\hat{X}$. But while the coordinates are the same in the two figures, the two spaces do not correspond exactly and cannot be superimposed; if the scale of one is increased, and that of the other decreased correspondingly, the approximation of $\hat{X}$ will be unaltered. For this reason we shall speak of the "factor-loading space" and the "factor-score space" separately.[29]

The most striking finding of this analysis is the nearly complete separation of the legislators of the two parties by axis II'. This separation provides further evidence that axis I' measures the partisanship of legislators as well as of roll calls. And while other conventional indices, such as the party unity index, liberalism index, or Administration-support index, effect a substantial separation of the parties,

---

[28]Factor scores were computed according to equation (7.6). In the matrix X, column means were subtracted, however, and each congressman's coordinates were divided by the proportion of roll calls on which he voted. These last two modifications were intended to correct for absences, and to prevent the points for members with low attendance from clustering near the origin. Further variations of this procedure need to be compared carefully, including the use of other coefficients of association, other threshold levels for dissidence, and the use of X or Z. The inclusion of roll calls with only one dissenting vote, together with the use of Z, gave rise to extreme outlying points in the distribution of factor scores, and these were deemed undesirable.

[29]Other models, however, such as the Lingoes MSA-II, place legislators in the same space as points corresponding to yea and nay on roll calls.

none appears to separate them as completely as axis I'.[30] We shall examine below whether differences within each party, as well as differences between them, are consistent with the hypothsis that axis I' measures partisanship.

Because of this separation of the parties, which has been observed in numerous studies of both House and Senate (using various coefficients of association), we might alternatively have chosen preferred axes on the basis of the factor-score diagram and transferred them to the factor-loading diagram. The clear division of the legislator-points into two subsets for the two parties suggests several possible bases of choice of axes. The result of such rotation not only seems to give a clearer meaning to "partisanship" than many other indices, but also resembles the model put forward earlier in Figure 6.4.

This method of choosing axes, while useful, would be unconventional in two respects: it would center the choice of new axes on the factor-score diagram, rather than the conventional factor-loading diagram; and instead of seeking to maximize near-zero loadings, it would seek to *minimize* the number of such loadings on the rotated partisanship axis.

The most frequent approach to the selection of preferred axes in factor analysis has derived from Thurstone's notion of "simple structure." He contended that axes corresponding to simple and meaningful concepts were those on which some of the variables had zero or near-zero loadings.[31] The rotation of axes to attain this condition, or to approximate it as closely as possible, was done graphically by early investigators; but more recently, a series of efforts have been made to perform the operation objectively and automatically by means of computer routines. The most widely used routines of this kind have performed orthogonal rotations, but others have been developed to identify preferred axes at oblique angles to one another. In all the well-known procedures of this kind, however, the simple-structure criterion is used.

The inadequacy of the simple-structure approach for the present problem relates to one of the central themes of this book: that we must often tailor our techniques of research and measurement to

[30]See MacRae, *Dimensions of Congressional Voting*, pp. 305–306; Key, *Public Opinion and American Democracy*, p. 484; and Truman, *op. cit.*, p. 284.

[31]See Harman, *Modern Factor Analysis*, pt. III; Horst, *Factor Analysis of Data Matrices*, pt. V; Thurstone, *Multiple Factor Analysis*, chaps. 14, 15; and above, Chapter 4, last section.

the requirements of the substantive problems at hand, rather than devising them in the abstract or adapting them only to the *form* of the data. Simple structure and corresponding oblique axes may be relevant to the analysis of issue dimensions from a single party's votes, as in Chapter 5, but they are less useful in the study of partisanship.

Other procedures for finding preferred axes from the factor-score diagram may also be imagined, and must be compared with the one we have chosen. If the two party clusters are parallel, one might pass a best straight line through each, minimizing the sum of squares of distance *perpendicular* to the line; the average slope of the two intraparty lines might then be used to define an axis orthogonal to the partisanship axis. If the two intraparty lines diverged in slope from one another, distinct party axes might be defined; at least one Senate analysis, as well as a study by Grumm, suggest that this may occur.[32]

A second method for finding preferred axes would be to maximize the effective discrimination between the two parties. Computation of a discriminant function for several dimensions would identify that combination of dimensions that best separated the two parties; this could then be taken as the partisanship axis.[33]

A third method might also be used, which would not depend on advance knowledge of the party membership of the legislators. This would be an analytic rotation that had, in a sense, the opposite criterion from the Varimax. Instead of maximizing the variance of squared factor loadings on the rotated axes it would minimize it, with the aim of defining a partisanship axis on which intraparty homogeneity was maximized within each party. In two dimensions, this rotation would be just 45° away from the Varimax solution.[34] Such a procedure, though closely related to an existing solution, would not be completely optimal; for ideally only the variance along the rotated partisanship axis should be minimized, and this should be done within the parties separately.

We also hypothesize (as a first approximation) that axis *II'* meas-

[32]Grumm, "A Factor Analysis of Legislative Behavior," p. 353. The type of analysis used was based on correlations between legislators, a procedure we have criticized in Chapter 7 in the section on "Critical Evaluation."

[33]For the definition of the discriminant function, see M. G. Kendall and Stuart, *The Advanced Theory of Statistics,* vol. 3, pp. 314–322.

[34]See Chapter 4, last section, and Kaiser, "Computer Program for Varimax Rotation in Factor Analysis."

ures pure ideology, aside from the effects of partisanship. Examination of the array of legislators within each party supports this hypothesis, since those at the lower left in each party are generally more liberal and those at the upper right more conservative; this evidence will be considered in detail in connection with the following figures. But Figure 8.2 presents another problem with respect to ideology: the most liberal Republicans are farther to the left on axis II' than the most liberal Democrats. This departure from our commonsense expectations calls for careful analysis; we therefore proceed to examine the properties of the factor space.

PROPERTIES OF THE FACTOR SPACE

Because the space in Figure 8.2 has been created by procedures that are somewhat unorthodox for factor analysis, and because even the orthodox factor loadings might have properties that would influence our interpretations, we must examine our results closely for artifacts. We have done this already for artificial data, in connection with Figures 5.1, 5.2, and 7.3, and some of the interpretations made there can be transferred to our real congressional data.

We have seen, for example, that right angles in the initial space containing the artificial legislator-points were not transferred precisely into right angles in the factor-loading or factor-score spaces. More precisely, a pair of items that are independent of one another in the Q-matrix, or two sets of items that have this property, seem to give rise to points in the factor-loading space that are approximately, but not exactly, at right angles to one another with respect to the origin. We also observed that in the analysis of the artificial data, any shearing transformation of these points and cutting lines, transforming rectangles into parallelograms, would have given rise to the same "roll calls" and therefore to the same factor loadings and scores. This revealed an indeterminacy in the solution, which relates also to some of our problems of interpreting the congressional data.

Let us begin by considering the relation between the factor-loading space and the factor-score space. We have shown that the two rotate together. The next correspondence that we wish to consider is that between points in the factor-loading space and *cutting lines* (or hyperplanes) in the factor-score space. Suppose we wish to locate a line in the factor-score space that best separates the legislators who voted yea on a particular roll call from those who voted nay. We might try to find the direction numbers of such a line by solving for the regression coefficients in the equation

$$x_{ij} = b_1 F_{i1} + b_2 F_{i2} + e_{ij} \qquad (8.2)$$

where

b_1, b_2 = regression coefficients, to be determined, for line j

F_{i1}, F_{i2} = factor scores of legislators on axes I and II

e_{ij} = an error or residual term

The intercept in (8.2) may be assumed to be zero because the mean of x_{ij} is 0, for every j, if we ignore corrections for absences; for we have made the column means of **X** equal to 0, and the columns of **F** also have zero means, being linear combinations of the x's. But then (8.2) is identical in form with equation (7.5), which we used in justifying the computation of the factor scores, $\hat{X} = FA'$, a variant of (4.26) or (8.1), a fundamental equation of factor analysis. We need only replace the b's in (8.2) by the corresponding factor loadings to obtain the equivalent of (7.5). The factor loadings for the roll call in question therefore provide a solution for (8.2), exact when no corrections for absence are made.

Equation (8.2) thus defines a regression plane that approximates the dichotomous variable corresponding to votes on the roll call. The intersection of this plane with the I–II plane is given by setting the left-hand side of (8.2) to zero and omitting the error term. It then defines a line passing through the origin

$$0 = a_{11} F_{i1} + a_{12} F_{i2} \qquad (8.3)$$

The direction numbers of this line are the factor loadings of the roll call. But they define a vector such that for factor-score points on that line, the projection of the factor-score vector on the vector **a** is zero, or the two vectors are orthogonal. Thus the line separating the two sides on any roll call in Figure 8.2 must be at right angles to the corresponding radius vector in Figure 8.1.

There is thus a determinate relationship between the angular positions of points in Figure 8.1, relative to the origin, and the angular positions of cutting lines that might be drawn in Figure 8.2. The cutting lines defined by (8.3) pass through the origin, but actual lines that optimally separated legislators voting yea and nay on a given roll call would in general have some nonzero value on the left-hand side of the equation, and would not pass through the origin. Cutting lines for roll calls with extreme values of p_+ would thus be farthest from the origin. The goodness of fit of the cutting-line model might then be evaluated by the proportion of votes that it reproduced correctly, a generalization of the coefficient of reproducibility.

Equation (8.3) may be applied to the special case of a pure party vote, such as that on the Speakership. A cutting line orthogonal to axis I' must be the one that best separates the parties, or the yeas and nays on such a vote, in the sense of (8.2). The sense in which it is best is not identical with reproducibility, however, as the latter takes no account of distances from the cutting line. The cutting line that best separates the parties need not pass through the origin, however, as axis II' does. Since in the 87th Congress the Democrats outnumbered the Republicans, we should expect that a cutting line parallel to axis II' but displaced toward the Republicans would separate them better, as it would in Figure 8.2.

Another application of (8.3) might be to a vote involving no partisanship at all, arraying the legislators entirely in terms of their ideological or liberal–conservative positions (provided we could identify such a vote). Clearly, a vote having zero association with party (e.g., $Q = 0$) would correspond to a cutting line perpendicular to the radius vector to the corresponding point in the factor-loading space. This would be a cutting line near to, but not coincident with axis I', and would divide the two parties in nearly equal proportions. The use of such a cutting line would correspond to our measurement of legislators' ideological positions along an axis similar to axis II'.

We know, however, that such a definition of an ideological axis does not correspond to our commonsense notions of party ideology or our conceptual description of party cohesion. To define "ideology" as orthogonal to partisanship in this way would artificially require that the median liberalism of the two parties be the same. This would run counter to our knowledge of their ideologies, and prejudge an empirical question. As we have argued above, it seems more reasonable to define a completely nonpartisan roll call as one corresponding to some value of Q (vote, party) greater than zero, if we can identify such a value. In this case, there might be an ideological difference between the parties even when the group ties and symbolic allegiances of the legislative parties were not mobilized on the vote in question.

If an axis measuring pure ideology exists, however, how can it be found? Our identification of axis I' as a partisanship axis does not answer this question, as the ideology axis need not be orthogonal to it; indeed, it does not give entirely reasonable results to use axis II' as the ideology axis. We must choose among all possible axes oblique to axis I'—a choice equivalent to that among shearing transformations that preserve axis I' and define a new axis as a linear combination of I' and II'. We cannot make this choice in terms of goodness of fit to the model to the data alone; if, for example, the data constitute a perfect two-dimensional scale, like our artificial data, then *any* shearing transformation of a perfect solution is also a perfect solution. Some additional information is thus necessary if we are to choose an ideology axis among these possibilities.

This additional information could come from one of two sources. We might examine the distribution of factor-loading points in Figure 8.1, and place the pure-ideology axis near the upper limit of the dense cluster of points, just above the open circles representing votes on foreign aid, if this could be justified by an objective procedure. Alternatively, we could use information about the resort to party symbolism in the debates, or estimate the partisan relevance of roll calls from interviews or related sources.

Whatever information of this kind is used, it is clear that only a limited range of shearing transformations of the space in Figure 8.2, and a correspondingly limited range of oblique axes, will be allowed. We do not expect the ideology axis to be closer to axis I' than a line in Figure 8.1 passing through the foreign-aid roll calls. A cutting line orthogonal to such an axis would pass through the middle of the Democrats' distribution in Figure 8.2, leaving about two-thirds of the Democrats but only one-third of the Republicans to the liberal side. Cutting lines parallel to this one, if moved to the liberal and conservative extremes of the cluster of points, would define an approximate envelope which together with two additional lines parallel to axis II' would enclose the entire parallelogram-shaped configuration of points. If we then compared Republicans and Democrats on this liberalism axis, we should conclude that the two most liberal Republicans (Lindsay and Halpern) were just as liberal as the most liberal Democrats—though they differed greatly in partisanship, which was correlated with liberalism. Perhaps coincidentally, the points for the Whips of the two parties would also correspond to similar degrees of liberalism in these terms. And even though we have not specified precisely how this axis should be located, we may still proceed to analyze the configurations of legislator-points within the parties, knowing that the range of possible shearing transformations is limited.

A further feature of the distribution of legislator points (which will appear more clearly in Figure 8.4) is that they appear in some areas of the figure to be arrayed nearly in straight lines. If the existence of this feature can be verified, it may be due to subsets of legislators voting together on large numbers of issues, but being separated from one another on one or more sets of votes that had similar factor loadings but different cutting points. In this respect one of the features of our artificial data would be duplicated in actual roll calls.

INDIVIDUAL DIFFERENCES WITHIN THE PARTIES

The following two figures show further detail of the distributions of factor scores for Democrats and Republicans respectively; they are simply larger-scale graphs of the individual parties' points shown in Figure 8.2. Figure 8.3 shows that the Democrats at the upper right— those most positive on axis II'—were all from the South (open circles in the figure). Some of the better-known members of this group are indicated by name: Howard W. Smith (Va.), then chairman of the Rules Committee; William Colmer (Miss.) also of Rules; and John Bell Williams, subsequently elected Governor of Mississippi. As we move from the upper right corner toward the center of the distribution, we find occasional non-Southerners, the three most conservative being Democrats from Missouri.

The dense cluster of points near the lower left corner of Figure 8.3 includes urban Democrats from all regions of the country other than the South. This cluster corresponds as nearly as any group in the diagram to a disciplined party of the European type. At the left edge of this cluster are a few members of the party who took still more liberal stands—James Roosevelt (Calif.), William Fitts Ryan (N.Y.), Edith Green (Ore.), and others.[35]

[35]The use of Z rather than X for computing factor scores would place these members at the extreme negative end of the party's distribution on axis II'; this did not occur in the orthodox (ϕ-matrix) factor analysis procedure. The use of Q or a similar index gives full loadings on factors I and II to those roll calls with a small minority of liberal dissenters.

○ South
+ Rules, Ways & Means
x Whip, Majority Leader
· Other

FIGURE 8.3. Democrats, 1961 House: Factor Scores Based on Q-Matrix for Both Parties.

Figure 8.3 may also be used to examine the validity of axis I' as a measure of differences in partisanship within the party. Those Democratic congressmen who occupied positions of leadership, either in the congressional party or in relations with the Presidency, can be singled out for attention. John W. McCormack (Mass.), the Majority Leader in 1961, is indicated in the figure by an $\times$ near axis I. His position on axis I' is more negative (more opposed to the Republicans) than that of most Democrats, though it is not atypical for legislators near his position on axis II'. The Whip, Carl Albert (Okla.), who subsequently became Majority Leader, is also represented by an $\times$, near axis I'; his position on this axis corresponds to high partisanship. His fellow members in the whip organization did not, however, occupy extreme positions on axis I', and are not identified in the figure.[36]

The members of two major committees—Rules and Ways and Means—are indicated by $+$ signs, and aside from Southern Democrats, seem to have particularly high partisanship, i.e., to be more opposed to the Republican position on axis I' than other Democrats. These include Hale Boggs (La.), the present Whip; Wilbur Mills (Ark.), who in spite of his conflicts with President Johnson has substantial support in Congress; and Carl Elliott (Ala.) and James W. Trimble (Ark.), known to be reliable party supporters, who were appointed to the Rules Committee in 1961. The members of these two major committees have generally higher partisanship scores on axis I' than do their fellow Democrats. The only outstanding exceptions to this feature were Smith and Colmer of Rules, and Harrison (Va.) and Herlong (Fla.) of Ways and Means. In contrast to these Southerners, it is noteworthy that Ikard and Thornberry of Texas joined Elliott, Trimble, Boggs, and Mills in high partisanship.

Closer inspection of the data suggests that the Northern members of these major committees were accompanied by their state delegations in their partisanship. It is quite possible, however, that they influenced their delegations as well as being influenced by them.

A conspicuous example of low partisanship among the Democrats, combined with a liberal ideological stand, was Otis G. Pike (N.Y.), whose point appears at the very bottom of the diagram. Pike's campaigning style has been very nonpartisan. In the 87th Congress he

[36]Democratic assistant whips are appointed by the state delegations, not the party leadership; see Ripley, *op. cit.*, p. 40.

opposed the administration's farm program and included in a news-letter to his constituents a complaint about excessive pressure from the executive, which was later quoted by Republican leader Hal-leck.[37] Pike had been elected as a freshman in 1960 by a margin of less than 1 percent, with a lead of 7.5 percent over Kennedy in his district.[38] Clearly, he had needed Republican votes and might well need them again. Thus for Pike the pure-partisanship index appears to reflect not merely relations with House colleagues, but constituency relations as well. A similar relation held for Haley (Fla.), whose district had gone over 60 percent Republican for President in 1956 and 1960.

Figure 8.4 permits a similar examination of the meaning of axes I' and II' for the Republicans. At the liberal extreme (lower left corner) are John Lindsay and Seymour Halpern (N.Y.) and Florence Dwyer (N.J.). At the upper right, in contrast, are James B. Utt (Calif.), Bruce Alger (Tex.), and Noah Mason (Ill.), known conservatives. On the conservative side (just above Taber and St. George of New York) are also the three California congressmen who were members of the John Birch Society.

Members of the Rules and Ways and Means Committees are again indicated by + signs, and tend to have somewhat higher than average values on the partisanship axis, I'. In addition, high partisanship was shown by William E. Miller (N.Y.), then Chairman of the Republican National Committee and later candidate for Vice-President with Goldwater; and by Gerald Ford, subsequently Minority Leader. Anomalous positions are occupied by Charles Halleck (Ind.), and Leslie Arends (Ill.), the Minority Leader and Whip respectively; both are near the center of their party's distribution on axis I'. Halleck's position is unexpected in view of his reputation for opposition, but perhaps his position and Arends' can be related to intraparty factionalism.[39]

---

[37]See Hadwiger and Talbot, *Pressures and Protests*, p. 199. An account of one of Pike's later campaigns is given in R. Harris, "Reporter at Large."

[38]Data on the presidential vote by congressional districts are given in the *Congressional Quarterly Almanac*, vol. 17 (1961), pp. 1033–1075. A detailed analysis of differences between the congressional and presidential vote appears in Cummings, *Congressmen and the Electorate*.

[39]See Ripley, *op. cit.*, pp. 106–109; Peabody, "Party Leadership Change in the United States House of Representatives," pp. 683–686.

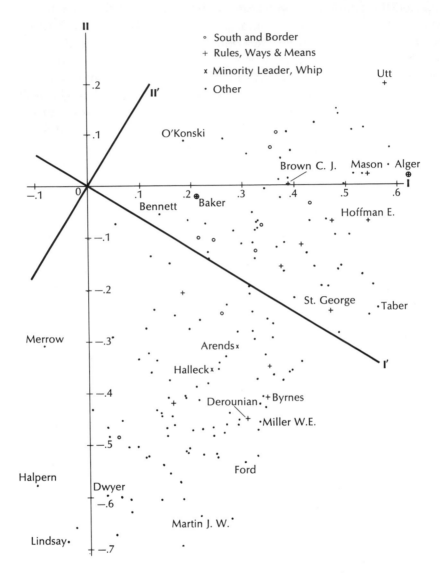

FIGURE 8.4. Republicans, 1961 House: Factor Scores Based on Q-Matrix for Both Parties.

Generally less than average in partisanship are the Republicans from the South and Border states, indicated by open circles, and two members with a substantial third-party tradition in their districts: Bennett (Mich.) and O'Konski (Wis.).[40] The placement of these congressmen again suggests that the lesser partisanship of their district campaigns may be associated with their low partisanship in Congress. All these congressmen had been elected from districts that would have been close or Democratic on the basis of the presidential vote alone; most of them led their presidential ticket; and apparently their need for Democratic votes at home had some relation to their nonpartisan behavior in the House.

We thus hypothesize that the pure-partisanship scores relate, at least for points near the boundary between the parties, to district conditions as well as to relations in Washington. This hypothesis gains some support from comparison of Figure 8.2 with a similar diagram for the 86th Congress; in the latter case, just before a presidential election year, the sets of points for the two parties interpenetrated somewhat. One may imagine that those congressmen who feared the effects of a presidential swing were doing whatever they could to generate a district vote cast for them personally rather than on party grounds.[41] The incidence of this threat to electoral security would seem to vary, not only among congressmen and districts, but also between presidential years and off years.

It is also desirable to test whether the higher partisan opposition

[40]The Border states in question are Kentucky, Missouri, Oklahoma, and West Virginia. The agrarian radicalism of Michigan and Wisconsin was reflected in domestic liberalism combined with isolationism. The ideological positions of Bennett and O'Konski in the 81st Congress are shown in MacRae, *Dimensions of Congressional Voting*, p. 248. See also Waldman, "Liberalism of Congressmen and the Presidential Vote in Their Districts."

[41]A study of congressional districts over time in the postwar period shows that while it is rare for the proportion of the major-party vote cast for a first- or second-term nonsouthern Congressmen in a presidential year to differ from the corresponding presidential vote by more than a few percent, the congressman's lead can rise as high as 15 percent or more as he acquires seniority. In this study an adjustment was made in the 1956 presidential vote, the percent Democratic being raised by 5 points to compensate somewhat for the extensive ticket splitting in favor of Eisenhower in that year. See A. Campbell and Miller, "The Motivational Basis of Straight and Split Ticket Voting." The capacity of an incumbent to become known in his district is demonstrated in Miller and Stokes, "Constituency Influence in Congress," p. 54.

shown by party leaders and members of major committees in 1961 was shown in other years. In 1953, for example, in the Republican-controlled 83rd Congress, both Rayburn and Boggs showed less than average partisanship. And a study of the 84th Congress, still under Eisenhower but controlled by the Democrats, showed substantial defection by major committee leaders on the Democratic side, more than on the Republican. An example was a conspicuous vote by O'Neill of Rules, with several of his Massachusetts colleagues, against the Democratic farm program, because of the price of peanuts used by the candy industry in his district. Perhaps the anticipation of another Eisenhower landslide in 1956 led even major Democratic figures to vote in a nonpartisan fashion. Thus the relations we have found may be conditional on the differences between Presidential and off-year elections, or majority and minority, or the party that expects to ride the presidential coattails and the one that expects to lose if too closely tied to the presidential race. It seems likely, however, that these problems of conditional validity and multiple causation are common to all indices of partisanship based on the general reasoning we have followed, and are not peculiar to rotated factor scores.

The conceptual validity of our measure of partisanship also depends on whether we expect the leaders of opposing parties to oppose one another more in voting than the rank and file, or to co-operate more. We shall return to this question below.

A final problem in the relation between the concept "partisanship" and its measurement derives from the possibility that we are measuring a variable correlated with, but not identical with, this concept. One such variable might be the lack of visibility of a particular roll call to potential issue publics. Conceivably there are some roll calls on which interest groups are deeply involved; which develop slowly and permit these groups to mobilize; and which can be portrayed simply to the voters, stripped of the obscurities of parliamentary tactics and congressional careers. These may be the ideological roll calls, while the less visible may tend to be the partisan ones. The congressional party may be more united when pursuing interests of its own, somewhat separate from broad ideological issues. Whether the covert character of these struggles is an essential accompaniment of partisanship, or an accidental and loosely correlated feature, remains to be determined. But among those legislators whose electoral positions are least secure in terms of the partisan vote in their districts, perhaps there is greater concern that their votes will be publicized; thus on votes that most of their colleagues consider intrachamber matters, they may still feel constrained to take positions that conform to district interests.

RELIABILITY AND VALIDITY

We have been continually concerned with the relation between concepts and measurements, and nowhere is this concern so important as in our factor-score index of partisanship. In analyzing the properties of the factor space, and the positions of legislative party leaders in it, we have thrown some light on this relation; but we need to probe Its validity by as many methods as are available to us. For while we have made a plausible case for the correspondence of axis I' to partisanship, we must test it more rigorously before we can accept it as a measure of this concept. Our proposed oblique axis for ideology also requires testing, but it can be checked against indices computed for the parties separately, such as those developed in Chapter 3. All the types of criticism we have earlier directed at other indices, must be directed at these rotated factors. In particular, we should like to test whether they contain artifacts of the methods used, and whether they genuinely correspond to the concepts in question.

Problems of this kind are conventionally treated under the rubrics of "reliability" and "validity."[42] The former of these two terms, in application to psychological tests, often refers to the correlation between test scores on the same persons when a test is readministered. More generally, high reliability corresponds to invariance of a measure of a concept under minor and presumably irrelevant modifications of the conditions of observation, such as a short lapse of time. In the case of roll calls, we can rarely examine two successive votes on the same question; rather, we shall be concerned with the results of treating the same data by means of different procedures aimed at measuring the same concept. Alternatively, we may examine different sets of roll calls, closely resembling one another, and see whether legislators are assigned similar scores by reapplication of the same statistical procedures.

To examine the *validity* of our measures, we examine "the success

[42]See Kaplan, *The Conduct of Inquiry*, pp. 76–77, 198–206.

with which the measures obtained in particular cases allow us to predict the measures that would be arrived at by other procedures and in other contexts."[43] We thus examine the relations between measures based on roll-call votes alone, and indicators of the same concepts based on other sorts of data. In doing so, we are considering the relations of one measure with others that differ progressively more and more from it. Eventually we pass the outer limit of the initial concept, and find ourselves comparing measures of two different concepts. Such comparisons are still relevant to the assessment of the initial measure; but they can fail because of the inadequacy of the empirical hypothesis linking the two concepts, and thus are not ordinarily considered tests of validity.

We thus consider first the variability between alternative measures of issue positions and partisanship obtained from the *same* roll-call data by different procedures. Ideally, the properties of such alternative methods should be established by logical and mathematical analysis. In the absence of such analysis, however, we shall attempt to show that the results have some constancy or invariance among methods of analysis which vary considerably in assumptions and procedures.

The degrees of partisanship involved in the factor loadings of particular roll calls appear very similar when we compare results from factoring matrices of coefficients that preserve the cumulative-scale relation—Q, Y, r_t, ϕ/ϕ_{max}. On the other hand, the angular position of factor-loading points can vary as much as 20° between these results and those from factoring ordinary ϕ-matrices. A comparison of these methods using the artificial data of Figure 5.1 showed that the factor-loading points for roll calls in each set of parallel cutting lines diverged from one another by as much as 50°. The angular separations that result from analyses based on $(ad - bc)$ resemble those from ϕ in this respect.

Legislators' degrees of liberalism and conservatism in Figure 8.2 can be compared with similar positions computed from factor analysis of the data for one party at a time. For this purpose we use legislators' coordinates on rotated axis II', which measures ideological differences within each party orthogonal to partisanship. We expect that the analysis of one party at a time will reveal as a first principal com-

[43] *Ibid.*, p. 199.

ponent the single dimension along which maximal intraparty difference exists, and that this will not reflect partisanship. This principal
component actually correlates .92 with values on axis II' for the
Democrats in 1961, and .90 for the Republicans.

Positions on axis II' may also be related to scale positions based on
analysis of the parties separately. For the Democrats, the ranking
provided by the dominant scale correlates .88 (r) with their ordering
on axis II'; for the Republicans, whose scales are more distinct in
relation to subject matter of legislation, the correlation with the leading scale is .87.

The invariance of legislators' positions on the partisanship axis (I')
is harder to demonstrate, since we have no clear measure of this
variable from our previous analyses. One which we have proposed
is the rank difference between legislators' positions on two scales,
of high and low partisanship respectively. This possibility was discussed in connection with the scales in Figure 6.3. Such a measure
is imperfect as a standard of comparison, because the two scales in
question may also differ in their degree of association with the liberalism factor, and there may be variation among the roll calls in each
scale as to the degree of partisanship or liberalism they involve. If
the roll calls from 1961 in the two scales are identified among the
points in Figure 8.1, those in Scale 2 lie almost entirely above those in
Scale 1. If a radial line were drawn from the origin, 12° above the
horizontal axis, all the points of Scale 1 would lie below it, and all
but two of Scale 2 above it. Thus the roll calls in the two scales have
hardly any overlap in their degrees of partisanship. Each scale contains
considerable internal variation in this respect; the points in Scale 1
range downward as far as axis I', while Scale 2 includes several of
the foreign-aid votes indicated in that figure.

The distribution of points in Figure 6.3 corresponding to the roll
calls in the two scales suggests that these scales provide very little
information about the placement of the liberal Democrats, as there
are very few points for values of p_{+D} greater than .5. But for the Republicans the distribution of cutting points covers the entire range of
p_{+R}, and we may thus use the two scales to illustrate this approach to
the measurement of partisanship. If the two scales differed only in
partisanship, we should expect the difference in rank between them,
for a given legislator, to indicate his partisanship.

We shall use the method for rank scoring of cumulative scales, described in the last section of Chapter 2, in order to use as much as possible of the information provided by the roll calls in the two clusters. Rank scores were constructed for the Republican congressmen for the two scales, and the difference between rank scores on the two scales was computed for each congressman.

When we compare individual Republican congressmen's positions on the partisanship axis, with the rank difference based on these two scales for the same Congress, the result is a moderate degree of association (.48), suggesting some degree of intermethod reliability, but also some discrepancies. A number of the departures of one index from the other appear for values of rank shift near zero, and may be due to the fact that relatively small shifts in rank from scale to scale occur for congressmen near the extremes of their liberalism distribution. This problem has been observed before in connection with Dempsey's loyalty-shift scores. And as we suggested for Dempsey's index, the best combination of the two rankings is not a simple difference; if Scale 2 is given a weight of $-.61$, the multiple R becomes .60.

Another possible comparison of measures obtained by different methods from the same data is that between analyses of both parties together and of the individual parties separately. These two approaches to factor analysis would correspond perfectly if one could give rise to the same matrix of associations as the other. Conceivably a matrix of partial associations, with party controlled, would resemble the average of the two matrices computed for Democrats and Republicans separately. But as we have seen in the discussion of Table 4.2 and equation (7.3), this requirement apparently cannot be met by indices that at the same time conform to the cumulative-scale model. We do not attempt, therefore, to obtain a perfect logical relation between analyses for both parties combined and those for the parties separately, but simply point to correlations for typical data.

Our comparison of results from these two types of analysis—parties together and parties separate—does, however, suggest that the intra-party variations in partisanship that we have found might also enter to some degree into results for the parties separately. Thus while we have centered our attention in single-party analyses on the search for issue clusters, we might also conceivably find that partisanship contributes in a limited degree to the structure of voting within a given party.

A second aspect in which the variation of index values can be examined relates to changes in the sample of roll calls used. Such changes may of course involve substantive differences in the concepts being measured; but we wish here to examine whether changes in the sample that are presumably irrelevant to a given concept, will leave the value of an index of that concept unaffected.

One such type of alteration in the sample, with which we have been concerned in evaluating other methods, is the addition of roll calls that duplicate one or more in the initial sample. It appears that this change in the sample would not affect the rotated factor loadings, though it would cause the first unrotated principal component to pass nearer the duplicated roll call. For factor scores, on the other hand, duplication of a roll call would magnify the separation of legislators produced by that particular roll call, relative to others. Thus if a large number of purely party votes were cast, the gap between the parties would be increased in comparison with intraparty variation along axis I'.

We may also make empirical comparisons of the values of the partisanship-factor scores for different sets of roll calls. It seems less reasonable with political data than with psychological data, however, to assume that different sets of roll calls can be used as alternative measures of the same underlying universe of attitudes. Division of the roll calls of a given Congress into even and odd halves, conventional in the split-half comparisons of psychological testing, has apparently been done for legislative votes only by psychologists.[44] In a test of this type of invariance for the 87th Congress, the correlations between partisanship coordinates for even and odd roll calls were .78 for the Democrats and .68 for the Republicans.

Comparison of the partisanship scores of the same legislators from one session of a given Congress to another, or from one Congress to another, is of interest; but the correlations are lower, and we are led to explain them in substantive terms rather than simply as unreliability. Between 1961 and 1962, these correlations dropped to .59 for the Democrats and .58 for the Republicans, and between the 84th and 87th Congresses both were equal to .55. Study of deviant cases in the corresponding scattergrams suggested that meaningful changes in partisanship were occurring, affecting entire state delegations, and were related to the allocation of leadership positions within the parties. The fact that these associations are lower than those for liberalism

[44]Dempsey, *op. cit.*; Fitch, "Predicting Votes of Senators of the 83rd Congress."

(compare Table 3.5) may be a substantive finding about the two variables; but it may also result in part from the truncation of the distribution of partisanship, initially defined by the contrast *between* the parties.

Let us now consider the validity of the partisanship axis in terms of its relations with indicators of partisanship based on information other than roll-call votes. We must rely here on two types of information: characteristics of roll calls and characteristics of legislators. In either case we compare the partisanship loadings or scores with values of another variable expected to measure this concept.

Consider first those characteristics of *roll calls* that are associated with the mobilization of partisanship. We look to the situation in which a given roll call was conducted, and not simply to the content of the legislation in question. For this purpose, the words or actions of party leaders can serve as indicators of the partisanship of a roll call. Information of this sort may come from legislative debates, from the President's State of the Union message, from the judgments of members of the whip organization or the legislative liaison staff of the White House. Certain types of votes that involve the Executive, such as the effort to override a veto, the confirmation of an appointment, or the approval of a reorganization plan, clearly involve a particular aspect of partisanship. The general judgment that partisanship is higher on closely contested critical amendments than on votes on final passage, may also be relevant.

Another relevant condition is the possession of the Presidency, or of the congressional majority, by one party or the other. The orientation of the parties on foreign aid, for example, has changed between Democratic and Republican presidencies in recent years. This change should be reflected in a different set of factor loadings for roll calls on comparable subjects under Democratic and Republican presidents.

One obvious indication of increased partisanship is the action of legislative party organizations in mobilizing support. One step in this process is the counting of prospective votes by the whip organizations. For the 1962 House session, there were seven roll calls on which the Democratic whip organization carried out polls.[45] If the points corresponding to these roll calls are located on a diagram for 1962

---

[45]Ripley, "The Party Whip Organizations in the United States House of Representatives," pp. 569–570 n.

similar to Figure 8.1, they occupy an arc of about 50°, from near the partisanship axis (I') almost to the set of roll calls on foreign aid shown there. Their average angular position in the diagram corresponds approximately to *unrotated* axis I. This result suggests that partisanship, as reflected in the actions of the Democratic whip organization, corresponds to a combination of axes I' and II' and not to the issue-free partisanship we have discussed so far. The positions of the Whip himself (Albert), and of his successor, Boggs, however, are nearer to rotated axis I' in Figure 8.3.

The House Republican Policy Committee also took positions on nineteen roll calls in 1961, all dealing with domestic matters.[46] The distribution of their points occupied an arc similar to that for the Democrats' whip polls, centered slightly below axis I. While conceivably the Republicans might have had different criteria for judging party positions—and their choice of bills was largely different—in the 87th Congress they apparently agreed with the Democrats as to the location in Figure 8.1 of votes on which party positions were taken. The positions of the Republican Whip, Arends, and of Chairman Byrnes of the Policy Committee in Figure 8.4, however, are nearer to axis I' than I, like the positions of Albert and Boggs.

We also expect certain characteristics of the *legislators* to be related to their partisanship. We have discussed the relations between partisanship and certain House leadership positions, as well as an inverse relation with the need for cross-party support in the congressman's district. There are, however, many other characteristics of legislators that may be used for this purpose. Frequent use of party symbols, or deliberate use of nonpartisan terminology, may indicate that party is more or less important to a legislator. Systematic measurements of this variable have been made in interview studies of state legislatures.[47]

Occupancy of leadership positions may also be associated with partisanship, as we have suggested; and Matthews has shown that Senators moving "prematurely" into choice committee posts also in-

---

[46]Listed in Jones, *Party and Policy-Making*, pp. 93–94.

[47]See, for example Ferguson and Klein, "An Attempt to Correlate the Voting Records of Legislators with Their Attitudes Toward Party." Legislators' reports as to the partisanship of roll calls were also used in Crane, "A Caveat on Roll-Call Studies of Party Voting."

creased in their "party effort."[48] But there is also an extensive literature that suggests that the partisanship of leaders will be less, rather than greater, than that of the rank and file of their parties. These studies have contended that some legislative bodies (including Congress) contain a bipartisan inner circle of leaders who understand one another and maintain the norms of the institution.[49] Moreover, Fenno describes the muting of partisanship by the norms of the House Appropriations Committee.[50] And in our data the members of the two parties on this committee are less separated in partisanship than those of Rules or Ways and Means. Further study is needed to reconcile these divergent notions of partisanship and to show the conditions under which each is valid.

Another criterion with which partisanship scores may be compared is the judgment of informed observers. One observer close to the Speaker and the whip organization during the Rayburn era particularly cited Representative Trimble (D., Ark.) as willing to cooperate with the leadership when votes were needed. Trimble was among the highest on the partisanship dimension, even though not among the most liberal group.

To test such a relationship systematically, we require many judgments as to individual Representatives' partisanship. A set of judgments of this kind for the Democrats was obtained from an informed Washington observer. His ratings of partisanship were then analyzed in relation to the two rotated factor scores by means of multiple regression. The result was a multiple correlation of .89, but primarily attributable to the predictive power of axis II', "liberalism." The partial correlation coefficient for scores on axis I' was only .67 as great.[51] One interpretation of this finding might be that allegiance to the Presidency, as measured by these judgments, has a substantial

---

[48]*U.S. Senators and Their World*, p. 136.

[49]For example, MacNeil, *Forge of Democracy*, chap. 5; Clark, *The Senate Establishment*; and MacRae, *Parliament, Parties and Society*, chap. 7.

[50]Fenno, *The Power of the Purse*, chap. 5.

[51]On a five-point scale of "their willingness to give something extra when requested by the House leadership or the White House." The rater was a person in Washington who worked closely with Congress during the Eisenhower, Kennedy, and Johnson administrations. The analysis was repeated for North, Border, and South separately, and in each case the partial correlation for partisanship was .8 to .9 times that for liberalism; the multiple correlation ranged from .7 to .8 for the three regions.

ideological or issue-related component, and is by no means the same thing as Congressional partisanship as it relates to committee leaders. The partisanship of the elective leaders of the congressional parties may be intermediate between the two, while the positions of committee leaders in the two parties may be least divergent from one another in ideology or liberalism. Consideration of the disparate axes found by different validating measures might thus lead to the conclusion that partisanship is not a unitary concept. Huitt has in fact pointed out a divergence among meanings of the term in criticizing the indices of "party votes":

The curious thing is that our model of the party in the basic texts is much more sophisticated. . . . A reasonably competent student in the freshman course can write that the major party "is a federation of state and local parties." Why is not this model carried over into research and Congress? Suppose that two members bearing the same party designation split their votes on a roll call. Might it not be that one is voting with the national committee party, the other casting an opposing vote *with* a state or local party which bears the same name . . . ?[52]

The same question could be raised about the presidential and congressional parties.

There remains another aspect in which legislators' positions in the factor-score space require comparison with direct observation: the legislators' perception of that space. We have alluded to their placement of themselves and one another with respect to issue positions and partisanship. This placement, however, is most accurate and most likely to be reported when it deals with the the legislator's own party. We have contended, in fact, that one reason for the entry of partisanship into our model as an additional dimension is the fact that legislators place themselves on issues with respect to their party colleagues, but do so far less precisely with respect to the opposing party. In this respect, the factor-score space corresponds only partly to legislators' perceptions; rather, it is a composite of various spaces, each being defined not by the entire membership of the chamber, but by members of one party. This superposition of different perceptual spaces has been observed in attitude studies, in that persons tend to recognize finer distinctions near their own position than far from it. Additional research on legislators' perceptions of one another's positions would clarify the significance of the dimensions we have found.

[52]Huitt, "Congress, The Durable Partner," p. 26.

OTHER FACTORIAL STUDIES

The separation of parties or voting blocs in a space such as that of Figure 8.2 has also been observed in other studies. In a Q-type factor analysis of the Kansas legislature, Grumm found a clear separation between the parties. And in a study of the United Nations General Assembly, Alker and Russett used factor scores based on matrices of ϕ-coefficients to locate voting blocs; while they found meaningful separations between blocs, there was apparently no dimension corresponding closely to partisanship.[53] Our main interest here, however, is in factorial studies of Congress.

In two recent studies of Congress, the Varimax criterion has been used to rotate factor loadings, and one of the resulting axes has been interpreted in terms of partisanship. Senate voting in the 87th Congress was studied by Anderson, Watts, and Wilcox, again using the ϕ coefficient.[54] Their results may be compared with ours, because the angular positions of roll-call points are not radically altered by the use of ϕ as against Q when the range of marginal proportions among the roll calls is not extreme. These writers preselected roll calls in terms of Riker's coefficient of significance, which eliminated highly one-sided roll calls from their sample.[55]

In factor-loading diagrams presented by these authors, two roll calls with high communality but very low associations with party can be located, and an axis similar to II' in Figure 8.1 passed through them.[56] This axis does not correspond to one of the first two principal components, but it does correspond almost exactly with their rotated factor 2. This correspondence appears coincidental rather than a result to be expected generally from Varimax rotation. The fact that the axis perpendicular to the zero-partisanship axis separates the parties well suggests that if a diagram similar to Figure 8.2 were made

---

[53]Grumm, op. cit.; Alker and Russett, World Politics in the General Assembly, p. 38 and numerous figures. See also Alker, "Statistics and Politics."

[54]Anderson, Watts, and Wilcox, Legislative Roll Call Analysis, pp. 144–169.

[55]Riker, "A Method for Determining the Significance of Roll Calls in Voting Bodies."

[56]Anderson, Watts, and Wilcox, op. cit., pp. 162–163. The roll calls are nos. 01 and 20. The associations between roll calls and party were computed with the aid of auxiliary data on the yea–nay divisions for the two parties.

for these Senate data, the separation would be even more complete at a dividing value other than zero.[57] The presence of a large Democratic majority in that Congress, together with the necessity that standard scores have a zero mean, forces the Democratic distribution to extend nearer to the origin than the Republican.

The second study for which we may compare rotation criteria is one by Marwell, dealing with the 81st, 82nd, and 83rd Congresses.[58] Comparison with this earlier period is complicated by the fact that foreign-aid votes seem to have been more nearly independent of domestic issues at that time.[59] We shall consider roll calls that have high communality on Marwell's first two rotated factors. Again we use the association between party and the vote to locate an axis of zero partisanship. For the 81st Congress the two roll calls with lowest association with party dealt with Mexican labor and postal services.[60] Although their communalities are not high, their similar angular position suggests that if Factor I is reflected (as later in the article), a counterclockwise rotation of 17° would bring it into correspondence with a zero partisanship axis.[61] It thus appears that Marwell's rotated axes I and II correspond roughly with *un*rotated principal components I and II in Figure 8.1. And while he achieves pure loadings for civil rights issues on his factor II, he thereby fails to pass the orthogonal axis precisely through pure partisanship, but rather passes it through a combination of ideology and partisanship.

Marwell's factor loadings for the 82nd Congress permit a second application of our rotation criterion. Here the two roll calls with lowest association with party concern beef prices and the investigation of tax-exempt foundations.[62] Taken together, they suggest that rotated

[57]*Ibid.*, p. 165.

[58]Marwell, "Party, Region, and Dimensions of Conflict in the House of Representatives."

[59]Marwell finds a separate rotated factor for foreign-aid roll calls. Such a factor does exist in our 1961 data, but the loadings of foreign-aid votes on it are typically no greater than .2. It is possible that the distinctness of the foreign aid issue decreased after the 83rd Congress; see MacRae, "A Method for Identifying Issues and Factions," pp. 919–923; Rieselbach, *The Roots of Isolationism*, p. 37.

[60]In Marwell's numbering these are 61527 and 65467.

[61]Computed as $\tan^{-1}(.3)$ on the basis of the average of loadings for the two roll calls.

[62]Nos. 75368, 82965 in Marwell, *op. cit.*

axis II is within 3° of being a zero partisanship axis, and consequently that axis I is equally near a partisanship axis. Marwell suggests that a 17° rotation would bring the axes for the 82nd Congress into correspondence with those for the 81st; but if our procedure is followed, a similar rotation in the opposite direction would be performed on the factor loadings for the 81st. This is consistent with the fact that Marwell's factor scores for factor I are more highly associated with party in the 82nd than in the 81st.[63]

We suggest, therefore, that there is no clear justification for the use of the Varimax criterion for rotation of roll-call factor loadings if a pure-partisanship axis is sought. The legislative circumstances of the Senate or the House in a particular session determine the distribution of points in the factor space. Inspection of a number of these plots suggests that the points often fall largely into one 90° sector of the two-space, but that they do not always do so. The presence of an isolated cluster of roll calls with a given degree of partisanship may indeed justify attention to that axis as defining a particular issue. For the location of a pure-partisanship axis, however, other procedures seem more appropriate.

CONCLUSION

It appears that for analysis of issues within the contemporary American congressional parties, some variety of cluster analysis together with precision scale scoring will exploit the data as fully and accurately as any other available method. This approach makes fewer assumptions than factor analysis, stays close to the data, and requires little mathematical preparation to learn. It may, however, have the disadvantage that it neglects those less ideological issues that combine various considerations in nonscalable form; for these issues, some form of multidimensional analysis may be necessary.

Multidimensional analysis is forced on us much more strongly, however, by the problem of measuring partisanship. Among the models of this type now available for processing large data matrices, we

[63] *Ibid.*, p. 393; the associations are .81 and .91 respectively. We do not extend the comparison to the 83rd Congress because no suitable roll calls were found in Marwell's sample with sufficiently low party associations to locate axis II'. In this comparison we use the term "zero partisanship" to refer to a zero association between vote and party, and not to zero mobilization of group loyalty.

have the difficult choice between conventional ϕ-matrix factor analysis, which is rigorous mathematically but inadequate to the data, and other methods that violate some of the assumptions of factor analysis but fit the data better. We choose the latter because methods are developed, after all, to solve empirical problems. However elegant the standard methods of factor analysis may be, they do not yield single clear-cut dimensions for identifiable issue clusters, and they fail especially in this respect when extreme divisions are analyzed. In order to understand Congress, we need to be able to identify members who take extreme positions on general issues. There is undoubtedly much more that can be learned from roll-call votes, and which may be concealed by the methods we choose. But at least this one aspect of the data becomes clearer when we examine factor scores from matrices of Q or similar coefficients.

The choice among methods of measurement is a continuing process. In data domains that permit precise measurement, the refinement of measures is an important aspect of that process. Here again, the particular data with which we are concerned make a difference. The assumption has been widespread in analysis of interview and questionnaire data that very precise measurement is unjustified because of the imprecision of the data. The approximate invariance of factors when the index of association is changed, the relative irrelevance of a few extreme cases, and the possibility of framing attitude questions in form other than that of dichotomies, have made it less necessary in attitude research to refine the procedures for analyzing dichotomous data.

When a vein of potentially rich but impure ore exists, however, more effort and expense must be devoted to mining and refining it. The vein in question consists of the documentary records of legislative voting over considerable historical periods, now existing for the United States and other countries. Our capacity to generalize rigorously about the working of political systems is strongly limited by the shortage of extensive time series; and in addition to generating such series by systematic observation in the future, we can profit from the full exploitation of those that are available for the past.

GLOSSARY

B-coefficient a coefficient used in cluster analysis: the ratio of the average intercorrelation among the variables in a cluster, to their average correlation with variables outside

binary expressed in terms of dichotomies; e.g., the *binary matrix*, a matrix each of whose elements can be either 0 or 1

cardinal numbers numbers that can be added, subtracted, multiplied, or divided, in distinction to ordinal data, which cannot. A *cardinal matrix* has cardinal numbers as elements

central value a statistic such as the mean or median, based on a distribution of values of a variable, that indicates where the distribution as a whole is located with respect to that variable (also known as *location*)

chi-square a statistic which may be computed for a contingency table, to measure the statistical significance of the departure of the relation between two variables from independence

cluster-bloc analysis a method of analyzing matrices of voting similarity, to find sets of legislators with similar voting patterns

cluster analysis the family of procedures that may be used to discover sets of similar elements in a larger set of elements, for each of which there are observations of a number of variables

communality (h^2) in factor analysis, the proportion of the variance of an item which is accounted for by a set of factors

contingency table the table resulting from cross-tabulation of two polytomies

control, statistical a procedure for setting aside the effects of one or more variables while examining the effects of others

covariation the sum of products of deviation scores of two variables: the covariation of X and Y is $\Sigma(X - \overline{X})(Y - \overline{Y}) = \Sigma xy$

covariance the covariation of two variables divided by the sample size, i.e., $\Sigma xy/N$

cross-product for a fourfold table with entries a, b, c, d, the index of association $(ad - bc)/N^2$

cumulative scale a set of dichotomous items having patterns of response which can be arranged in a single ordered sequence

data matrix a rectangular array of data values, typically with persons as rows, items as columns

derivative in calculus, the rate of change in one variable with respect to an infinitesimal change in another

determinant a square array of numbers giving rise to a single number by the operation of specified rules; e.g., the determinant of a fourfold table is $ad - bc$

deviation score for a variable X, the new variable $x = X - \overline{X}$ created by subtracting the mean

diagonal matrix   a square matrix all of whose elements off the principal diagonal (elements other than a_{ii}) are zero

dichotomy   a classification into two categories

difference, Rice's index of   for two sets of legislators voting on a given roll call, the absolute value of the difference in percentages voting yea (or nay) in the two groups

direction numbers   a set of numbers characterizing the direction of a straight line in Cartesian coordinates, the cosines of the angles between the line and the respective axes

discriminant function   that linear combination of a set of variables which best separates two classes of the entities for which the variables are observed

eigenvalue   a number λ characteristic of a square matrix, **M**, entering into the equation $\mathbf{v}\mathbf{M} = \lambda\mathbf{v}$ or its equivalent

eigenvector   a vector **v** characteristic of a square matrix **M**, entering into the equation $\mathbf{v}\mathbf{M} = \lambda\mathbf{v}$

factor   one of a set of underlying variables accounting for or summarizing a set of observed variables

factor analysis   one of several procedures for simplifying data matrices or matrices of associations; extended here to include principal component analysis

factor loading   in factor analysis, the correlation between an observed variable and an underlying factor, known as the loading of that variable on that factor; by extension, an element of an eigenvector of a matrix of associations

factor score   in factor analysis, the value of a factor for a person, legislator, or row in the data matrix

fourfold table   the table produced by cross-tabulating two dichotomies

gamma (γ)   a coefficient of association applicable to the cross-tabulation of two sets of ranked categories (polytomies). If the two sets of categories can be combined into a single cumulative scale, gamma will attain one of its limiting values, $+1$ or -1

geometric mean   the square root of the product of two numbers

Gramian matrix   a square matrix none of whose eigenvalues is negative; formed by the multiplication of a matrix by its transpose

hyperplane   the generalization of a plane to more than three dimensions; a surface having the equation $\Sigma a_i x_i = k$

identity matrix   a diagonal matrix all of whose diagonal elements are unity. When multiplication by such a matrix is allowed, the product is the same as the other multiplier matrix

increasing function (increasing transformation) a function $y = f(x)$ such that whenever x increases, y increases

intercept the value of a linear function when $X = 0$; for the line $Y = a + bX$, a is the intercept, i.e., the value of Y at which the line intersects the Y-axis

invariant unchanged when some other condition varies, e.g., a function that is invariant under a transformation of one of its defining variables

inverse of a square matrix another matrix which, when multiplied by the first in either sequence, gives as a product an identity matrix

iteration one of a series of similar operations that may be performed in a long sequence, e.g., by a computer

least squares a criterion for the fit of various statistical models to data, i.e., that the sum of squared deviations between observed and estimated values, $\Sigma(Y - \hat{Y})^2$, be a minimum

likeness, Rice's index of for two sets of legislators voting on a given roll call, 100 minus the index of difference, or $100(1 - |p_{Y1} - p_{Y2}|)$

linear combination of two or more variables a new variable obtained by multiplying each of the initial variables by a corresponding constant and adding ($w = \Sigma a_i x_i$)

linear dependence a variable is linearly dependent on a set of other variables if it can be expressed as a linear combination of the others

linear transformation a transformation of the form $x_2 = a + bx_1$, or $\mathbf{B} = \mathbf{AT}$ where $\mathbf{T}$, the transformation matrix, is any matrix with real elements

location (see *central value*)

marginals in a cross tabulation of two polytomies, the row totals or column totals, commonly presented in the margins of the table

matrix a rectangular array of numbers, characteristically subject to specified rules for addition and multiplication (see also *diagonal, identity*)

monotone, monotonic increasing or remaining the same as another variable increases, as a monotone transformation

normalize to adjust the values of a set of numbers (e.g., the elements of a vector) by multiplying by a constant, so that the sum of their squares equals a desired value

oblique not perpendicular; in multidimensional space, not orthogonal

order (of a square matrix) the number of rows or columns

ordinal variable a variable whose values may be arranged in rank order, but may not legitimately be added or multiplied

orthogonal in two or three dimensions, perpendicular; in any number of dimensions, two vectors are orthogonal if $\Sigma a_i b_i = 0$

partial derivative the derivative of one variable with respect to another, taken when one or more additional variables are held constant

partition   a division of a set into subsets, such that each element of the initial set is a member of exactly one subset

party vote   in a two-party legislature, a roll-call on which more than a specified proportion of one party is opposed to more than the same proportion of the other. For Lowell, the proportion required is more than 90 percent

party unity index   the proportion of all party unity votes on which a legislator agrees with the majority of his party

party unity vote   in a two-party legislature, a roll call on which majorities of the two parties are opposed

Pearson correlation (r)   a coefficient of association between two quantitative variables, ranging from $+1$ to -1, given by the equation $r = \Sigma z_x z_y / N$, where N is the number of cases on which variables X and Y are observed, and z_x, z_y are the standard scores of X and Y

phi (ϕ)   a coefficient of association between two dichotomies, equivalent in this case to r, given for a fourfold table by

$$\phi = \frac{(ad - bc)}{\sqrt{(a + b)(a + c)(b + d)(c + d)}}$$

pivot item   an item, in a matrix of associations, chosen as the initial basis for forming a cluster or computing a factor

polarity   the relation between votes (yea or nay) on a roll call and directions ($+$ or $-$) on an underlying variable; the relation may be direct or reversed

polytomy   a variable that can assume a discrete set of values equivalent to a classification into multiple categories. For a *ranked* polytomy the sequence or ranking of these values or categories is specified. For two and three categories the corresponding terms are *dichotomy* and *trichotomy*

positive semidefinite (Gramian)   a square matrix is positive semidefinite if all its eigenvalues are real and none is negative

postmultiplication   multiplication of a matrix by another on its right

premultiplication   multiplication of a matrix by another on its left

principal component   a new variable formed by linear combination of a set of observed variables, which contributes a maximum to their total variance

product–moment correlation   (see *Pearson correlation*)

Q   a coefficient of association between two dichotomous variables, given for the corresponding fourfold table as $(ad - bc)/(ad + bc)$

radius vector   the vector from the origin of coordinates to a point

regression line (plane, equation)   a linear function (linear combination of variables plus a constant) that best predicts a quantitative variable from a set of quantitative predictors, according to the criterion of least squares

reproducibility   a coefficient measuring the adequacy of a cumulative scale, equal to 1.0 minus the proportion of error responses

residual   the remaining value of a variable after a predicted value (as from regression or factor analysis) is subtracted

sample standard deviation (s)   for a variable X, $s = (\Sigma x^2/N)^{\frac{1}{2}}$, where x is the deviation score of X and N the sample size. To be distinguished from the estimate of the standard deviation for the universe from the same sample, which divides by $N - 1$ rather than N (the latter estimate is not used in this book)

scalar   a cardinal number, as distinguished from a matrix or vector

set   any collection or list of elements, e.g., legislators, roll calls, clusters, values of a variable

shearing transformation   a transformation of a space in which straight lines remain straight, i.e., any transformation in which the resulting variables are linear combinations of the initial ones, but in which orthogonality is not preserved

slope of a straight line   the increase in Y per unit increase in X; b in the equation $Y = a + bX$

specification   for an association between two variables, the identification of a value (range) of a third variable for which the association between the first two is most pronounced

standard deviation   for a sample, $s = (\Sigma x^2/ N)^{\frac{1}{2}}$ (see *sample standard deviation*); for an infinite universe, the limit of this value as N increases, estimated from a sample by

$$\sqrt{\Sigma x^2/(N-1)}$$

standard score (z)   for a value of a variable X from a specified distribution, the deviation score x divided by the sample standard deviation, i.e., $z_x = x/s_x$

submatrix   a matrix obtained by selecting from an initial matrix only those elements in specified rows and specified columns

subset   a set that is part of another set (including, in rigorous usage, either the entire initial set or the empty set)

symmetric matrix   a square matrix $\mathbf{M}$ such that $m_{ij} = m_{ji}$ for all i, j

tau (τ)   a coefficient of rank correlation based on the numbers of consistent and inconsistent pairwise rankings provided by two ordinal variables

tetrachoric correlation   the value of r that would have obtained in a bivariate normal distribution from which a given fourfold table could be obtained by converting X and Y into dichotomies

trace (of a square matrix)   the sum of diagonal elements Σa_{ii}

transformation   a function of a single variable, or a set of functions of a set of variables, carrying a point into another point or a vector into a vector

transpose (of a matrix)   another matrix whose rows are the columns of the first and vice versa

tree method of clustering   a procedure for analyzing a matrix of similarities, that joins two most similar items (branches), forms a composite item from them, and repeats iteratively

variation   the sum of squares of deviation scores of a variable, e.g., Σx^2

variance the square of the standard deviation; for a sample (as used here), $s^2 = \Sigma x^2/N$

vector a set of numbers that may be treated by the rules of matrix addition or multiplication as a one-row or one-column matrix; also may be considered as a set of coordinate values in a multidimensional space, defining a directed line segment

Y a coefficient of association between two dichotomous variables, given for the corresponding fourfold table as $(\sqrt{ad} - \sqrt{bc})/(\sqrt{ad} + \sqrt{bc})$

BIBLIOGRAPHY

Alexander, Thomas B., *Sectional Stress and Party Strength*, Nashville, Tenn., Vanderbilt University Press, 1967.

Alker, Hayward R., Jr., *Mathematics and Politics*, New York, Macmillan, 1965.

Alker, Hayward R., Jr., "Statistics and Politics: The Case for Causal Measurement," paper presented at September, 1967 meeting of the American Political Science Association, Chicago.

Alker, Hayward R., Jr., and Bruce M. Russett, *World Politics in the General Assembly*, New Haven, Yale University Press, 1965.

Anderson, Lee F., "Individuality in Voting in Congress: A Research Note," *Midwest Journal of Political Science, 8*, no. 4 (November, 1964), 425–429.

Anderson, Lee F., "Variability in the Unidimensionality of Legislative Voting," *Journal of Politics, 26*, no. 3 (August, 1964), 568–585.

Anderson, Lee F., Meredith W. Watts, Jr., and Allen R. Wilcox, *Legislative Roll-Call Analysis*, Evanston, Ill., Northwestern University Press, 1966.

Anderson, T. W., *Introduction to Multivariate Statistical Analysis*, New York, Wiley, 1958.

Arrow, Kenneth, *Social Choice and Individual Values*, New York, Wiley, 1963.

Aydelotte, William O , "Voting Patterns in the British House of Commons in the 1840's," *Comparative Studies in Society and History, 5*, no. 2 (January, 1963), 134–163.

Banfield, Edward C., *Political Influence*, New York, Free Press, 1961.

Barber, James David, *The Lawmakers: Recruitment and Adaptation to Legislative Life*, New Haven, Yale University Press, 1965.

Belknap, George M., "A Method for Analyzing Legislative Behavior," *Midwest Journal of Political Science, 2*, no. 4 (November, 1958), 377–402.

Berelson, Bernard R., Paul F. Lazarsfeld, and Wiliam N. McPhee, *Voting*, Chicago, University of Chicago Press, 1954.

Beyle, Herman C., *Identification and Analysis of Attribute-Cluster-Blocs*, Chicago, University of Chicago Press, 1931.

Blaine, James G., *Twenty Years in Congress*, Norwich, Conn., The Henry Bill Publishing Co., 1893, vol. 2.

Blau, Peter M., and Richard Scott, *Formal Organizations*, San Francisco, Chandler, 1962.

Bodewig, E., *Matrix Calculus*, 2nd ed., New York, Interscience, 1959.

Bogue, Allan G., "Bloc and Party in the United States Senate, 1861–1863," *Civil War History, 13*, no. 3 (September, 1967), 221–241.

Bonner, Raymond E , "On Some Clustering Techniques," *IBM Journal of Research and Development, 8*, no. 1 (January, 1964), 22–32.

Borgatta, Edgar F., "Difficulty Factors and The Use of r_{phi}", *Journal of General Psychology, 73*, no. 2 (October, 1965), 321–337.

Borgatta, Edgar F., "An Error Ratio for Scalogram Analysis," *Public Opinion Quarterly, 19*, no. 1 (Spring, 1955), 96–100.

Brams, Steven J., and Michael K. O'Leary, "An Axiomatic Model of Voting Bodies," paper presented at the September, 1969 meeting of the American Political Science Association, New York City.

Brimhall, Dean R., and Arthur S. Otis, "Consistency of Voting in our Congressmen," *Journal of Applied Psychology, 32*, no. 1 (February, 1948), 1–14.

Campbell, Angus, Philip E. Converse, Warren E. Miller, and Donald E. Stokes, *The American Voter,* New York, Wiley, 1960.

Campbell, Angus, and Warren E. Miller, "The Motivational Basis of Straight and Split Ticket Voting," *American Political Science Review, 51,* no. 2 (June, 1957), 293–312.

Campbell, Donald T., and Donald W. Fiske, "Convergent and Discriminant Validation by the Multitrait-Multimethod Matrix," *Psychological Bulletin, 56,* no. 2 (March, 1959), 81–105.

Campbell, Peter, "Discipline and Loyalty in the French Parliament During the Pinay Government," *Political Studies, 1,* no. 3 (September, 1953), 247–257.

Canon, Bradley C., "Voting Behavior in Collegial Decision-Making Bodies: The Case of the FCC," paper presented at meeting of the Midwest Political Science Association, Chicago, May 3, 1968.

Carroll, John B., and Harry Levin, "A Method for Determining the Polarity of Behavior Items," *Child Development, 27,* no. 4 (December, 1956), 427–438.

Cattell, Raymond B., *Factor Analysis,* New York, Harper & Row, 1952.

Cattell, Raymond B., "A Note on Correlation Clusters and Cluster Search Methods," *Psychometrika, 9,* no. 3 (September, 1944), 169–184.

Cattell, Raymond B., and Malcolm A. Coulter, "Principles of Behavioural Taxonomy and the Mathematical Basis of the Taxonome Computer Program," *British Journal of Mathematical and Statistical Psychology, 19,* pt. 2 (November, 1966), 237–269.

Chesire, Leone, Milton Saffir, and L. L. Thurstone, *Computing Diagrams for the Tetrachoric Correlation Coefficient,* Chicago, University of Chicago Bookstore, 1933.

Chilton, Roland J., "A Review and Comparison of Simple Statistical Tests for Scalogram Analysis," *American Sociological Review, 34,* no. 2 (April, 1969) 238–245.

Clapp, Charles L., *The Congressman: His Work as He Sees It,* Washington, D.C., Brookings, 1963.

Clark, Joseph S., et al., *The Senate Establishment,* New York, Hill and Wang, 1963.

Clausen, Aage R., "Measurement Identity in the Longitudinal Analysis of Legislative Voting," *American Political Science Review, 61,* no. 4 (December, 1967), 1020–1035.

Clausen, Aage R., "The Measurement of Legislative Group Behavior," *Midwest Journal of Political Science, 11,* no. 2 (May, 1967), 212–224.

Clubb, Jerome M., and Howard W. Allen, "Party Loyalty in the Progressive Years: The Senate, 1909–15," *Journal of Politics, 29,* no. 3 (August, 1967), 567–584.

Coleman, James S., *Community Conflict,* New York, Free Press, 1957.

Coleman, James S., *Introduction to Mathematical Sociology,* New York, Free Press, 1964.

Coleman, James S., and Duncan MacRae, Jr., "Electronic Processing of Sociometric Data for Groups up to 1,000 in Size," *American Sociological Review, 25,* no. 5 (October, 1960), 722–727.

Congressional Quarterly Almanac, Washington, D.C., Congressional Quarterly Service, annual.

Coombs, Clyde H., *A Theory of Data,* New York, Wiley, 1964.

Crane, Wilder, Jr., "A Caveat on Roll-Call Studies of Party Voting," *Midwest Journal of Political Science, 4,* no. 3 (August, 1960), 237–249.

Cummings, Milton C., *Congressmen and the Electorate,* New York, Free Press, 1966.

Cureton, Edward E., "Note on ϕ/ϕ_{max}," *Psychometrika, 24,* no. 1 (March, 1959), 89–91.

Dahrendorf, Ralf, *Class and Class Conflict in Industrial Society,* Stanford, Calif., Stanford University Press, 1959.

Davis, James A., "On Criteria for Scale Relationships," *American Journal of Sociology, 63,* no. 4 (January 1958), 317–380.

Davis, James A., "A Partial Coefficient for Goodman and Kruskal's Gamma," *Journal of the American Statistical Association, 62*, no. 317 (March, 1967), 189–193.

Dempsey, Paul, "Liberalism-Conservatism and Party Loyalty in the U.S. Senate," *Journal of Social Psychology, 56*, no. 2 (April, 1962), 159–170.

Dixon, Wilfrid J., and Frank J. Massey, Jr., *Introduction to Statistical Analysis*, 2nd ed., New York, McGraw-Hill, 1957.

Dogan, Mattei, and Stein Rokkan, eds., *Quantitative Ecological Analysis in the Social Sciences*, Cambridge, Mass., M.I.T. Press, 1969.

DuBois, Philip H., *Multivariate Correlational Analysis*, New York, Harper & Row, 1957.

Duverger, Maurice, *Political Parties*, 2nd ed., B. and R. North, trans., New York, Wiley, 1959.

Dye, Thomas R., "State Legislative Politics," in Herbert Jacob and Kenneth N. Vines, eds., *Politics in the American States*, Boston, Little, Brown, 1965.

Easton, David, *A Systems Analysis of Political Life*, New York, Wiley, 1965.

Edwards, A. W. F., "The Measure of Association in a 2×2 Table," *Journal of the Royal Statistical Society, A, 126*, no. 1 (1963), 109–114.

Edwards, A. W. F., and L. L. Cavalli-Sforza, "A Method for Cluster Analysis," *Biometrics, 21*, no. 2 (June, 1965), 362–372.

Farnsworth, David N., "A Comparison of the Senate and Its Foreign Relations Committee on Selected Roll-Call Votes," *Western Political Quarterly, 14*, no. 1 (March, 1961), 168–175.

Farris, Charles D., "A Method of Determining Ideological Groupings in the Congress," *Journal of Politics, 20*, no. 2 (May, 1958), 308–338.

Fenno, Richard F., Jr., *The Power of the Purse*, Boston, Little, Brown, 1966.

Ferguson, LeRoy C., and Bernard W. Klein, "An Attempt to Correlate the Voting Records of Legislators with Their Attitudes Toward Party," *Public Opinion Quarterly, 31*, no. 3 (Fall, 1967), 422–426.

Finer, S. E., H. B. Berrington, and D. J. Bartholomew, *Backbench Opinion in the House of Commons, 1955–59*, Long Island City, N.Y., Pergamon Press, 1961.

Fisher, Walter D., "On Grouping for Maximum Homogeneity," *Journal of the American Statistical Association, 53*, no. 284 (December, 1958), 789–798.

Fitch, David J., "Predicting Votes of Senators of the 83rd Congress: A Comparison of Similarity Analysis and Factor Analysis," Doctoral Dissertation, University of Illinois, 1958.

Fortier, J. J., and H. Solomon, "Clustering Procedures," in Paruchuri R. Krishnaiah, ed., *Multivariate Analysis*, New York, Academic Press, 1966, pp. 493–506.

Friedman, H. P., and J. Rubin, "On Some Invariant Criteria for Grouping Data," *Journal of the American Statistical Association, 62*, no. 320 (December, 1967), 1159–1178.

Froman, Lewis A., Jr., *Congressmen and Their Constituencies*, Chicago, Rand McNally, 1963.

Froman, Lewis A., Jr., and Randall Ripley, "Conditions for Party Leadership: The Case of the House Democrats," *American Political Science Review, 59*, no. 1 (March, 1965), 52–64.

Fruchter, Benjamin, *Introduction to Factor Analysis*, Princeton, N.J., Van Nostrand, 1954.

Gage, N. L., and Ben Shimberg, "Measuring Senatorial Progressivism," *Journal of Abnormal and Social Psychology, 44*, no. 1 (January, 1949), 112–117.

Gerson, Elihu, and Peter J. Kassan, "A Measure of Association Based on the Analysis of Uncertainty," unpublished MS, University of Chicago, 1967.

Gibson, W. A., "A Latent Structure for the Simplex," *Psychometrika, 32*, no. 1 (March, 1967), 35–46.

Good, I. J., *The Estimation of Probabilities,* Cambridge, Mass., M.I.T. Press, 1965.

Goode, William J., and Paul K. Hatt, *Methods in Social Research,* New York, McGraw-Hill, 1952.

Goodman, Leo A., "Partial Tests for Partial Taus," *Biometrika, 46,* pts. 3 and 4 (December, 1959), 425–432.

Goodman, Leo A., "Simple Statistical Methods for Scalogram Analysis," *Psychometrika, 24,* no. 1 (March, 1959), 29–43.

Goodman, Leo A., and William H. Kruskal, "Measures of Association for Cross Classifications" (I), *Journal of the American Statistical Association, 49,* no. 268 (December, 1954), 723–764.

Goodman, Leo A., and William H. Kruskal, "Measures of Association for Cross Classifications II: Further Discussion and References," *Journal of the American Statistical Association, 54,* no. 285 (March, 1959), 123–163.

Goodwin, George, Jr., "The Seniority System in Congress," *American Political Science Review, 53,* no. 2 (June, 1959), 412–436.

Green, Bert F., "A Method of Scalogram Analysis Using Summary Statistics," *Psychometrika, 21,* no. 1 (March, 1956), 79–88.

Greenstein, Fred I., and Alton F. Jackson, "A Second Look at the Validity of Roll Call Analysis," *Midwest Journal of Political Science, 7,* no. 2 (May, 1963), 156–166.

Grumm, John G., "A Factor Analysis of Legislative Behavior," *Midwest Journal of Political Science, 7,* no. 4 (November, 1963), 336–356.

Grumm, John G., "The Means of Measuring Conflict and Cohesion in the Legislature," *Southwestern Social Science Quarterly, 44,* no. 4 (March, 1964), 377–388.

Grumm, John G., "The Systematic Analysis of Blocs in the Study of Legislative Behavior," *Western Political Quarterly, 18* no. 2, pt. 1 (June, 1965), 350–362.

Guilford, J. P., *Fundamental Statistics in Psychology and Education,* New York, McGraw-Hill, 1965.

Guttman, Louis, "The Cornell Technique for Scale and Intensity Analysis," *Educational and Psychological Measurement, 7,* no. 2 (Summer, 1947), 247–280.

Guttman, Louis, "A General Nonmetric Technique for Finding the Smallest Coordinate Space for a Configuration of Points," *Psychometrika, 33,* no. 4 (December, 1968), 469–506.

Guttman, Louis, "A Generalized Simplex for Factor Analysis," *Psychometrika, 20,* no. 3 (September, 1955), 173–192.

Guttman, Louis, "A New Approach to Factor Analysis: The Radex," in P. F. Lazarsfeld, ed., *Mathematical Thinking in the Social Sciences,* New York, Free Press, 1954.

Hadwiger, Don F., and Ross B. Talbot, *Pressures and Protests: The Kennedy Farm Program and the Referendum of 1963,* San Francisco, Chandler, 1965.

Halmos, P. R., *Finite-Dimensional Vector Spaces,* 2nd ed., New York, Van Nostrand, 1958.

Harman, Harry H., *Modern Factor Analysis,* 2nd ed., Chicago, University of Chicago Press, 1967.

Harris, Chester W., "On Factors and Factor Scores," *Psychometrika, 32,* no. 4 (December, 1967), 363–379.

Harris, Richard, "Reporter at Large: How's It Look?" *New Yorker,* vol. 43 (April 8, 1967), pp. 48–137.

Hartigan, J. A., "Representation of Similarity Matrices by Trees," *Journal of the American Statistical Association, 62*, no. 320 (December, 1967), 1140–1158.

Hayes, Samuel P., Jr., "Probability and Beyle's Index of Cohesion," *Journal of Social Psychology, 9*, no. 2 (May, 1938), 161–167.

Heberle, Rudolf, *Social Movements*, New York, Appleton-Century-Crofts, 1951.

Hendrickson, Alan E., and Paul O. White, "Promax: A Quick Method for Rotation to Oblique Simple Structure," *British Journal of Statistical Psychology, 17*, pt. 1 (May, 1964), 65–70.

Henry, Andrew F., and Edgar F. Borgatta, "A Consideration of Some Problems of Content Identification in Scaling," *Public Opinion Quarterly, 20*, no. 2 (Summer, 1956), 457–469.

Horst, Paul, *Factor Analysis of Data Matrices*, New York, Holt, Rinehart & Winston, 1965.

Hotelling, Harold, "Analysis of a Complex of Statistical Variables into Principal Components," *Journal of Educational Psychology, 24*, no. 6 (September, 1933), 417–441.

Huitt, Ralph K., "Congress, The Durable Partner," in Elke Frank, ed., *Lawmakers in a Changing World*, New York, Prentice-Hall, 1966.

Hyman, Herbert H., *Survey Design and Analysis*, New York, Free Press, 1955.

Jacob, Herbert, and Kenneth N. Vines, *Politics in the American States*, Boston, Little, Brown, 1965.

Jewell, Malcolm E., and Samuel C. Patterson, *The Legislative Process in the United States*, New York, Random House, 1966.

Johnson, John Bockover, Jr., "The Extent and Consistency of Party Voting in the United States Senate," Doctoral Dissertation, University of Chicago, 1943.

Johnson, Stephen C., "Hierarchical Clustering Schemes," *Psychometrika, 32*, no. 3 (September, 1967), 241–254.

Jones, Charles O., *Party and Policy-Making*, New Brunswick, N.J., Rutgers University Press, 1964.

Jouvenel, Robert de, *La République des camarades*, Paris, Grasset, 1914.

Kaiser, Henry F., "Computer Program for Varimax Rotation in Factor Analysis," *Educational and Psychological Measurement, 19*, no. 3 (Autumn, 1959), 413–420.

Kaiser, Henry F., "Formulas for Component Scores," *Psychometrika, 27*, no. 1 (March, 1962), 83–88.

Kaiser, Henry F., "Scaling a Simplex," *Psychometrika, 27*, no. 2 (June, 1962), 155–162.

Kaplan, Abraham, *The Conduct of Inquiry*, San Francisco, Chandler, 1964.

Keefe, William J., "Party Government and Lawmaking in Illinois General Assembly," *Northwestern University Law Review, 47*, no. 1 (March-April, 1952), 55–71.

Kemeny, John G., and J. Laurie Snell, *Mathematical Models in the Social Sciences*, Boston, Ginn, 1962.

Kendall, M. G., *A Course in Multivariate Analysis*, New York, Hafner, 1957.

Kendall, M. G., "Discrimination and Classification," in Paruchuri R. Krishnaiah, ed., *Multivariate Analysis*, New York, Academic Press, 1966.

Kendall, M. G., and A. Stuart, *The Advanced Theory of Statistics*, vol. 2: *Inference and Relationship*, New York, Hafner, 1961; vol. 3: *Design and Analysis, and Time Series*, New York, Hafner, 1967.

Kendall, Patricia L., and Paul F. Lazarsfeld, "Problems of Survey Analysis," in Robert K. Merton and Paul F. Lazarsfeld, eds., *Continuities in Social Research: Studies in the Scope and Method of "The American Soldier,"* New York, Free Press, 1950.

Kenney, J. F., *Mathematics of Statistics*, New York, Van Nostrand, 1939, pt. 2.

Kesselman, Mark J., "Presidential Leadership in Congress on Foreign Policy," *Midwest Journal of Political Science, 5,* no. 3 (August, 1961), 284–289.

Kesselman, Mark J., "Presidential Leadership in Congress on Foreign Policy: A Replication of a Hypothesis," *Midwest Journal of Political Science, 9,* no. 4 (November, 1965), 401–406.

Key, V. O., Jr., "A Theory of Critical Elections," *Journal of Politics, 17,* no. 1 (February, 1955), 1–18.

Key, V. O., Jr., *Public Opinion and American Democracy,* New York, Knopf, 1961.

King, Benjamin, "Step-Wise Clustering Procedures," *Journal of the American Statistical Association, 62,* no. 317 (March, 1967), 87–99.

Kossack, Carl F., "Statistical Analysis, the Computer, and Political Science Research," in Joseph L. Bernd, ed., *Mathematical Applications in Political Science, II,* Dallas, Southern Methodist University, Arnold Foundation Monographs, *XVI,* 1966.

Kruskal, J. B., "Multidimensional Scaling by Optimizing Goodness of Fit to a Nonmetric Hypothesis," *Psychometrika, 29,* no. 1 (March, 1964), 1–27.

Kruskal, J. B., "Nonmetric Multidimensional Scaling: A Numerical Method," *Psychometrika, 29,* no. 2 (June, 1964), 115–129.

Lazarsfeld, Paul F., "Interpretation of Statistical Relations as a Research Operation," in Paul F. Lazarsfeld and Morris Rosenberg, eds., *The Language of Social Research,* New York, Free Press, 1955.

Lazarsfeld, Paul F., and Neil W. Henry, *Latent Structure Analysis,* Boston, Houghton Mifflin, 1968.

Lazarsfeld, Paul F., ed., *Mathematical Thinking in the Social Sciences,* New York, Free Press, 1954.

Libby, Orin G., "A Plea for the Study of Votes in Congress," *Annual Report of the American Historical Association,* Washington, D.C., Government Printing Office, 1896, vol. 1, pp. 323–334.

Lijphart, Arend, "The Analysis of Bloc Voting in the General Assembly: A Critique and a Proposal," *American Political Science Review, 57,* no. 4 (December, 1963), 902–917.

Lingoes, James C., "Multiple Scalogram Analysis," *Educational and Psychological Measurement, 23,* no. 3 (Autumn, 1963), 501–524.

Lingoes, James C., "The Multivariate Analysis of Qualitative Data," *Multivariate Behavioral Research, 3,* no. 1 (January, 1968), 61–94.

Lingoes, James C., "New Computer Developments in Pattern Analysis and Nonmetric Techniques," in *Proceedings, IBM Symposium, Uses of Computers in Psychological Research, November, 1964,* Paris, Gauthier-Villars, 1966.

Lipset, Seymour Martin, Martin Trow, and James S. Coleman, *Union Democracy,* New York, Free Press, 1956.

Lorr, Maurice, ed., *Explorations in Typing Psychotics,* Long Island City, N.Y., Pergamon Press, 1966.

Lowell, A. Lawrence, "The Influence of Party upon Legislation in England and America," *Annual Report of the American Historical Association,* Washington, D.C., Government Printing Office, 1901, vol. 1, pp. 319–541.

Lowi, Theodore J., "American Business, Public Policy, Case-Studies, and Political Theory," *World Politics, 16,* no. 4 (July, 1964), 677–715.

Mac Lane, Saunders, and Garrett Birkhoff, *Algebra,* New York, Macmillan, 1967.

McMurray, Carl D., "A Factor Method for Roll-Call Vote Studies," *American Behavioral Scientist, 6,* no. 8 (April, 1963), 26–27.

MacNeil, Neil, *Forge of Democracy*, New York, McKay, 1963.

McQuitty, Louis L., "A Conjunction of Rank Order Typal Analysis and Item Selection," *Educational and Psychological Measurement, 25*, no. 4 (Winter, 1965), 949–961.

McQuitty, Louis L., "Elementary Factor Analysis," *Psychological Reports, 9*, no. 1 (August, 1961), 71–78.

McQuitty, Louis L., "Elementary Linkage Analysis for Isolating Orthogonal and Oblique Types and Typal Relevancies," *Educational and Psychological Measurement, 17*, no. 2 (Summer, 1957), 207–229.

McQuitty, Louis L., "Improved Hierarchical Syndrome Analysis of Discrete and Continuous Data," *Educational and Psychological Measurement, 26*, no. 3 (Autumn, 1966), 577–582.

McQuitty, Louis L., *A Method of Pattern Analysis for Isolating Typological and Dimensional Constructs*, Lackland Air Force Base, San Antonio Texas, USAF Personnel Training and Research Center Research Report, 1955, no. 55–62.

McQuitty, Louis L., "Multiple Rank Order Typal Analysis for the Isolation of Independent Types," *Educational and Psychological Measurement, 26*, no. 1 (Spring, 1966), 3–11.

MacRae, Duncan, Jr., "Cluster Analysis of Congressional Votes with the BC TRY System," *Western Political Quarterly, 19*, no. 4 (December, 1966), 631–638.

MacRae, Duncan, Jr., *Dimensions of Congressional Voting* (University of California Publications in Sociology and Social Institutions, vol. 1, no. 3), 1958, pp. 203–390.

MacRae, Duncan, Jr., "Direct Factor Analysis of Sociometric Data," *Sociometry, 23*, no. 4 (December, 1960), 360–371.

MacRae, Duncan, Jr., "Indices of Pairwise Agreement Between Justices or Legislators," *Midwest Journal of Political Science, 10*, no. 1 (February, 1966), 138–141.

MacRae, Duncan, Jr., "A Method for Identifying Issues and Factions from Legislative Votes," *American Political Science Review, 59*, no. 4 (December, 1965), 909–926.

MacRae, Duncan, Jr., *Parliament, Parties and Society in France 1946–1958*, New York, St Martin's, 1967.

MacRae, Duncan, Jr., "Partisanship and Issues in Congressional Voting," paper presented at September, 1968 meeting of the American Political Science Association, Washington, D.C.

MacRae, Duncan, Jr., "Roll Call Votes and Leadership," *Public Opinion Quarterly, 20*, no. 3 (Fall, 1956), 543–558.

MacRae, Duncan, Jr., "The Sociology of Legislatures," *Il Politico, 32*, no. 3 (September, 1967), 578–589.

MacRae, Duncan, Jr., "Some Underlying Variables in Legislative Roll-Call Votes," *Public Opinion Quarterly, 18*, no. 2 (Summer, 1954), 191–196.

MacRae, Duncan, Jr., and Dee M. Kilpatrick, "Collective Decision and Polarization in a 125-Man Group," *Public Opinion Quarterly, 23*, no. 4 (Winter, 1959), 505–514.

MacRae, Duncan, Jr., and James A. Meldrum, "Critical Elections in Illinois: 1888–1958," *American Political Science Review, 54*, no. 3 (September, 1960), 669–683.

MacRae, Duncan, Jr., and James A. Meldrum, "Factor Analysis of Aggregate Voting Statistics," in Mattei Dogan and Stein Rokkan, eds., *Quantitative Ecological Analysis in the Social Sciences*, Cambridge, Mass., M.I.T. Press, 1969.

MacRae, Duncan, Jr., and Susan B. Schwarz, "Identifying Congressional Issues by Multidimensional Models," *Midwest Journal of Political Science, 12*, no. 2 (May, 1968), 181–201.

Marvel, R. D., "The Nonpartisan Nebraska Unicameral," in Samuel C. Patterson, ed., *Midwest Legislative Politics*, Iowa City, University of Iowa Institute of Public Affairs, 1967, pp. 89–120.

Marwell, Gerald, "Party, Region, and Dimensions of Conflict in the House of Representatives," *American Political Science Review, 61,* no. 2 (June, 1967), 380–399.

Mattheisen, Donald, "A Scale Analysis of the Prussian National Assembly of 1848," unpublished paper.

Matthews, Donald R., *U.S. Senators and Their World,* Chapel Hill, University of North Carolina Press, 1960.

Mattson, R. L., and J. E. Dammann, "A Technique for Determining and Coding Subclasses in Pattern Recognition Problems," *IBM Journal of Research and Development, 9,* no. 4 (July, 1965), 294–302.

Mayhew, David R., *Party Loyalty Among Congressmen,* Cambridge, Mass., Harvard University Press, 1966.

Mellor, D. H., "Inexactness and Explanation," *Philosophy of Science, 33,* no. 4 (December, 1966), 345–359.

Menzel, Herbert, "A New Coefficient for Scale Analysis," *Public Opinion Quarterly, 17,* no. 2 (Summer, 1953), 268–280.

Merton, Robert K., and Paul F. Lazarsfeld, eds., *Continuities in Social Research: Studies in the Scope and Method of "The American Soldier,"* New York, Free Press, 1950.

Miller, Warren E., and Donald E. Stokes, "Constituency Influence in Congress," *American Political Science Review, 57,* no. 1 (March, 1963), 45–56.

Mood, Alexander M., and Franklin A. Graybill, *Introduction to the Theory of Statistics,* 2nd ed., New York, McGraw-Hill, 1963.

Monsma, Stephen V., "Interpersonal Relations in the Legislative System: A Study of the 1964 Michigan House of Representatives," *Midwest Journal of Political Science, 10,* no. 3 (August, 1966), 350–363.

Mosteller, Frederick, "Association and Estimation in Contingency Tables," *Journal of the American Statistical Association, 63,* no. 321 (March, 1968), 1–28.

Mosteller, Frederick, and David L. Wallace, "Inference in an Authorship Problem," *Journal of the American Statistical Association, 58,* no. 302 (June, 1963), 275–309.

Munger, Frank, and James Blackhurst, "Factionalism in the National Conventions," *Journal of Politics, 27,* no. 2 (May, 1965), 375–394.

Nering, Evar D., *Linear Algebra and Matrix Theory,* New York, Wiley, 1963.

Overall, John E., "Cluster Oriented Factor Solutions: Oblique Powered Vector Factor Analysis," *Multivariate Behavioral Research, 3,* no. 4 (October, 1968), 479–488.

Parsons, Talcott, *The Social System,* New York, Free Press, 1951.

Patterson, Samuel C., "Patterns of Interpersonal Relations in a State Legislative Group: The Wisconsin Assembly," *Public Opinion Quarterly, 23,* no. 1 (Spring, 1959), 101–109.

Peabody, Robert L., "Party Leadership Change in the United States House of Representatives," *American Political Science Review, 61,* no. 3 (September, 1967), 675–693.

Peabody, Robert L., and Nelson W. Polsby, eds., *New Perspectives on the House of Representatives,* Chicago, Rand McNally, 1963.

Pearson, Karl, "On the Correlation of Characters Not Quantitatively Measurable," *Philosophical Transactions of the Royal Society, 195* (1901), 1–47.

Prewitt, Kenneth, *The Recruitment of Political Leaders: A Study of Citizen-Politicians,* Indianapolis, Bobbs-Merrill, 1970.

Pritchett, C. Herman, *Civil Liberties and the Vinson Court,* Chicago, University of Chicago Press, 1954.

Pritchett, C. Herman, *The Roosevelt Court: A Study in Judicial Politics and Values, 1938–1947*, New York, Macmillan, 1948.

Rasch, Georg, *Probabilistic Models for Some Intelligence and Attainment Tests*, Copenhagen, Danmarks Pedagogiske Institut, 1960.

Rice, Stuart A., *Quantitative Methods in Politics*, New York, Knopf, 1928.

Rieselbach, Leroy N., *The Roots of Isolationism*, Indianapolis, Bobbs-Merrill, 1966.

Riker, William H., "A Method for Determining the Significance of Roll Calls in Voting Bodies," in John C. Wahlke and Heinz Eulau, eds., *Legislative Behavior*, New York, Free Press, 1959.

Riley, Matilda W., John W. Riley, and Jackson Toby, *Sociological Studies in Scale Analysis*, New Brunswick, N.J., Rutgers University Press, 1954.

Ripley, Randall B., *Party Leaders in the House of Representatives*, Washington, D.C., Brookings Institution, 1967.

Ripley, Randall B., "The Party Whip Organizations in the United States House of Representatives," *American Political Science Review, 58*, no. 3 (September, 1964), 561–576.

Rosenau, James N., "Senate Attitudes Toward a Secretary of State," in John C. Wahlke and Heinz Eulau, eds., *Legislative Behavior*, New York, Free Press, 1959.

Rothman, David J., *Politics and Power: The United States Senate 1869–1901*, Cambridge, Mass., Harvard, 1966.

Russett, Bruce M., "Discovering Voting Groups in the United Nations," *American Political Science Review, 60*, no. 2 (June, 1966), 327–339.

Russett, Bruce M., *International Regions and the International System*, Chicago, Rand McNally, 1967.

Schubert, Glendon, *The Judicial Mind: Attitudes and Ideologies of Supreme Court Justices, 1946–63*, Evanston, Ill., Northwestern University Press, 1965.

Schubert, Glendon, *Quantitative Analysis of Judicial Behavior*, Bureau of Social and Political Research, Michigan State University, 1959.

Schubert, Glendon, "A Solution to the Indeterminate Factorial Resolution of Thurstone and Degan's Study of the Supreme Court," *Behavioral Science, 7*, no. 4 (October, 1962), 448–458.

Shannon, W. Wayne, *Party, Constituency and Congressional Voting*, Baton Rouge, Louisiana State University Press, 1968.

Silbey, Joel, *The Shrine of Party*, Pittsburgh, University of Pittsburgh Press, 1967.

Smelser, Neil J., *Theory of Collective Behavior*, New York, Free Press, 1962.

Sokal, Robert, and Charles Michener, "A Statistical Method for Evaluating Systematic Relationships," *University of Kansas Science Bulletin, 38* (March 20, 1958), 1409–1438.

Sokal, Robert R., and Peter H. A. Sneath, *Principles of Numerical Taxonomy*, San Francisco, Freeman, 1963.

Solomon, Herbert, "A Survey of Mathematical Models in Factor Analysis," in H. Solomon, ed., *Mathematical Thinking in the Measurement of Behavior*, New York, Free Press, 1960.

Somers, Robert H., "A New Asymmetric Measure of Association for Ordinal Variables," *American Sociological Review, 27*, no. 6 (December, 1962), 799–811.

Spaeth, Harold J., and Scott B. Guthery, "The Use and Utility of the Monotone Criterion in Multidimensional Scaling," *Multivariate Behavioral Research, 5* (1970; in press).

Steel, Robert G. D., and James H. Torrie, *Principles and Procedures of Statistics*, New York, McGraw-Hill, 1960.

Stewart, Frank M., *Introduction to Linear Algebra*, Princeton, N.J., Van Nostrand, 1963.

Stone, Philip J., Dexter C. Dunphy, Marshall S. Smith, and Daniel M. Ogilvie, *The General Inquirer*, Cambridge, Mass., M.I.T. Press, 1966.

Stouffer, Samuel A., et al., *Measurement and Prediction*, volume IV of *Studies in Social Psychology in World War II*, Princeton, N.J., Princeton University Press, 1950.

Thurstone, L. L., "Isolation of Blocs in a Legislative Body by the Voting Records of Its Members," *Journal of Social Psychology, 3*, no. 4 (November, 1932), 425–433.

Thurstone, L. L., *Multiple Factor Analysis*, Chicago, University of Chicago Press, 1947.

Thurstone, L. L., and J. W. Degan, "A Factorial Study of the Supreme Court," *Proceedings of the National Academy of Sciences, 37*, no. 9 (September, 1951), 628–635.

Toby, Jackson, and Marcia L., "A Method of Selecting Dichotomous Items by Cross-Tabulation," in Matilda W. Riley, John W. Riley, and Jackson Toby, *Sociological Studies in Scale Analysis*, New Brunswick, N.J., Rutgers University Press, 1954.

Torgerson, Warren S., *Theory and Methods of Scaling*, New York, Wiley, 1958.

Truman, David B., *The Congressional Party*, New York, Wiley, 1959.

Tryon, Robert C., "Domain Sampling Formulation of Cluster and Factor Analysis," *Psychometrika, 24*, no. 2 (June, 1959), 113–135.

Tryon, Robert C., *Theory of the BC TRY System: Statistical Theory*, Berkeley, 1964, (dittoed).

Tryon, Robert C., and Daniel E. Bailey, *Cluster Analysis*, New York, McGraw-Hill, 1969.

Turner, Julius, *Party and Constituency: Pressures on Congress* (The Johns Hopkins University Studies in Historical and Political Science, series 69, no. 1) Baltimore, Johns Hopkins Press, 1951.

Ulmer, S. Sidney, "The Analysis of Behavior Patterns of the United States Supreme Court," *Journal of Politics, 22*, no. 4 (November, 1960), 629–653.

Ulmer, S. Sidney, "Pairwise Associations of Justices and Legislators: Further Reflections," *Midwest Journal of Political Science, 11*, no. 1 (February, 1967), 106–115.

Ulmer, S. Sidney, "Toward a Theory of Sub-Group Formation in the United States Supreme Court," *Journal of Politics, 27*, no. 1 (February, 1965), 142–151.

VanDerSlik, Jack R., "Constituencies and Roll Call Voting," Doctoral dissertation, Michigan State University, 1967.

Wahlke, John C., Heinz Eulau, William Buchanan, and LeRoy C. Ferguson, *The Legislative System*, New York, Wiley, 1962.

Waldman, Loren K., "Liberalism of Congressmen and the Presidential Vote in Their Districts," *Midwest Journal of Political Science, 11*, no. 1 (February, 1967), 73–85.

Walker, Helen M., and Joseph Lev, *Statistical Inference*, New York, Holt, Rinehart & Winston, 1953.

Wallis, W. Allen, and Harry V. Roberts, *Statistics: A New Approach*, New York, Free Press, 1956.

Warburton, Frank W., "Analytic Methods of Factor Rotation," *British Journal of Statistical Psychology, 16*, pt. 2 (November, 1963), 165–174.

Ward, Joe R., Jr., "Hierarchical Grouping to Optimize an Objective Function," *Journal of the American Statistical Association, 58*, no. 301 (March, 1963), 236–244.

Webb, J., Eugene, Donald T. Campbell, Richard D. Schwartz, and Lee Sechrest, *Unobtrusive Measures*, Chicago, Rand McNally, 1966.

Weber, Max, *The Theory of Social and Economic Organization*, A. M. Henderson and Talcott Parsons, trans., New York, Oxford University Press, 1947.

Weisberg, Herbert F., "Dimensional Analysis of Legislative Roll Calls," doctoral dissertation, University of Michigan, 1968.

White, William S., *Citadel*, New York, Harper & Row, 1957.

Williams, Philip M., *Crisis and Compromise*, Hamden, Conn., Archon Books, Shoe String Press, 1964.

Wilson, James Q., *The Amateur Democrat*, Chicago, University of Chicago Press, 1962.

Woodbury, Max A., and W. Siler, "Factor Analysis with Missing Data," *Annals of The New York Academy of Sciences, 128,* art. 3 (January, 1966), 746–754.

Wrigley, Charles, and David J. Fitch, "Patterns of Voting by United States Senators," paper presented at American Psychological Association, San Francisco, Sept. 7, 1955.

Young, Roland, *Congressional Politics in the Second World War*, New York, Columbia, 1956.

Yule, G. Udny, "On the Association of Attributes in Statistics," *Philosophical Transactions of the Royal Society, 194* (1900), 275–319.

Yule, G. Udny, *Introduction to the Theory of Statistics*, London, Griffin, 1911.

Yule, G. Udny, "On the Methods of Measuring the Association Between Two Attributes," *Journal of the Royal Statistical Society, 75* (1912) 570–642.

INDEX

Association (*Continued*)
  and cross-product ratio, 46
    threshold, 75
  partial, 99
  partisan in voting, 59, 99 f., 190
  secular decline in, 73 f.
    See also Matrix; Similarity
Asymmetry, in partisanship indices, 183
  in partitions of legislators, 216
  of roll calls and legislators, 20
    See also Symmetry
Attitude(s), to issues, 191, 245 ff., 248 ff.
  measurement of, 16, 32
  methods of study, vs. legislative roll
    calls, 32
  research, 2
  scaling, random component in, 29
  space, 283
  systems as issues, 191
    See also Frame of reference; Leg-
      islators
Attributes, universe of, 24
Axelrod, Robert, 57
Axes, and correlation coefficient, 111
  in factor analysis, 128, 259
  oblique, for ideology, 275
    See also Rotation
Aydelotte, William O., 3, 43

B-coefficient, in clustering, 87
BC TRY system, *see* Noncommunality
  cluster analysis
Belknap, George M., 18, 24
Bennett, Charles E., 273
Berelson, Bernard R., 203, 250
Beyle, Herman C., 209, 211–212, 223
Bills, legislative stages of, 4
Binary, *see* Dichotomous variables; Matrix
Binormamin, oblique rotation method,
  155
Biology, cluster analysis in, 45, 218 f.,
  221 n.
Bipartisan action, *see* System
Birkhoff, Garrett, 128, 133
Bloc analysis, 208 ff.
  binary matrix in, 211
  vs. cluster analysis, 211
  evaluation, 223 ff.
  of legislators' votes, 208 f.
  procedures, 211
  vs. scaling, 224
  vs. sociometry, 208 f.
Blocs, arrangement of, 224
  extreme, phi-factors, 152, 157
    Q-factors, 157
  fringe of, 211
  identification from cutting points, 66

multidimensionality, 224
Truman's continuum, 224
Boggs, Hale, 270, 274, 281
Bonner, Raymond E., 54, 69, 88–89
Border states, *see* Regional groupings
Borgatta, Edgar F., 24, 158
Brams, Steven J., 123, 220
British House of Commons, 43
Byrd, Harry F., 20
Byrnes, John W., 281

Campaign, political, group mobilization,
  250
Campbell, Angus, 250, 273
Campbell, Donald T., 12
Campbell, Peter, 178–179
Cardinal matrix, 86 ff.
    See also Matrix
Cartesian coordinates, factor loadings as,
  111
  naming, 245
Categories, of coalitions, 74
  ideological, 14
  of issues, 12, 14 f.
  legislators' 2, 12, 14, 21, 41, 52
  multiplicity of, 13
    See also Classifications; Frame of
      reference
Catholicism, and votes of electorate, 250
Cattell, Raymond B., 54, 59, 230
Centroid factoring, 136
Chance expectation, *see* Expectation
Characteristic root, *see* Eigenvalues
Chi-square statistic, 42, 198 n.
Chicago City Council, Republican cohe-
  sion in, 212 f.
Circumplex, 87
Civil rights, partisanship on, 188, 190, 260
  vote structure, 40
Clark, Joseph S., 195, 282
Classification, in clustering, 57
  of issues, 12, 14 f.
    See also Categories
Clausen, Aage R., 70, 73, 189, 224
Cleavages, in community conflict, 250
  in parties, 71, 205, 207, 252, 257
  pluralistic, 181
  superimposed, 181
Cluster analysis, 24, 28 ff., 51 ff.
  BC TRY technique, 106 f.
  binary matrix in, 54, 57
  in biology, 40 f., 45 n., 218 f., 221 n.
  cardinal matrix, 54
  corrected phi in, 48
  cross-product, 45
  definition of, 41, 54
  error decisions in, 89, 155

Eisenhower (*Continued*)
  liberalism under, 188
  party relations under, 188
  vote shifts under, 190
Elections, critical, 202
Electorate, Catholicism and votes of, 250
  issues among, 202
    See also Constituency
Elliott, Carl, 270
Error, in association index, 48 f.
  in cluster analysis, 155
  in identifying clusters, 89
  measurement, 48 f.
  in Q-matrix factoring, 170
  in rank reversals, 36
  in a scale, 23, 29, 37, 40
  uncorrelated terms, 115
"Establishment" and partisanship, 195 f.,
    282
    See also Leadership
Examples, numerical, computation of fac-
    tor scores, 229
  factoring, correlation matrix, 135, 146
    ff., 150
    data matrix, 229, 231
    perfect scale, 240 f.
    two-dimensional scale, 164, 241
  principal-component analysis, 146 ff.
Executive branch of government, influ-
    ence of, 4, 249
  in France, 249
  on partisanship, 195
    See also Presidency
Expectation, chance, correction of agree-
    ment indices for, 211, 215 ff., 220

Factions, cohesion of, 175 ff.
  definition, 175
  identification, 11 ff., 208 ff., 222
  and issues, 245
  membership measures, 175
  as social groups, 6, 248
    See also Groups; Party
Factor(s), control in partisanship measure,
    255
  definition, 103
  as dimensions of clusters, 110, 238
  as variables, quantitative, 91
    See also Rotation
Factor analysis, 91 ff.
  of agreement indices, 163, 179 ff., 217
    f., 220 f., 234
  axes in, 128, 259
  vs. cluster analysis, 40, 52, 91 ff., 129
  of congressional issues, 286
  of data matrix, 138 ff.
  dichotomous variables, 151 ff.

difficulty factor, 257
  direct, 45, 138 ff.
  eigenvectors, 140, 153
  inverse, 230
  iterative procedures, 141
  matrices in, 123 ff.
  normalization, 140, 143
  one-factor case, 92, 104 f., 113 f.
  pairwise relations, 40
  party separation by, 221, 284
  phi in, 46, 48, 284
  principal, 131 n.
  of Q-matrix, 113, 154, 159, 230, 256 ff.
  residuals in, 88, 110 ff.
  square-root method, 104 n.
  stopping factoring, criteria for, 126,
    135, 257
  tetrachoric correlation coefficient vs.
    Q-matrix, 159
  trial vector, 134, 136, 141
  two-factor case, 111, 115 ff.
  Y vs. Q, 159
    See also Factoring; Principal-com-
      ponent analysis
Factor loadings, artificial data, 168
  as Cartesian coordinates, 111
  from clusters, 105 f.
  from coefficients, 276
  cutting line, orthogonality, 170, 264
    slopes, 243, 265
  distance matrix from, 160, 168
  in eigenvector, 135
  estimate of, 105 f.
  and factor scores, 138, 143 ff., 226, 261
  matrix of, 124
  orthogonality of, 117, 135, 170, 264
  and partisanship, 260
  reversal of signs, 137
  rotated, 126, 130
  and variance, 92, 115
Factor scores, for artificial data, 241
  for axis rotation, 118, 130, 261 f., 264
  in bloc analysis, 222 ff.
  computation, 144 ff., 149, 227, 229
  for congressmen, 161 f., 220, 227, 260,
    268
  data matrix factoring, 142
  definition, 113
  and factor loadings, 138, 143 ff., 226,
    261
  fine structure of, 268
  and ideology, 276
  and issues, 256 ff.
  liberalism and, 264, 266, 271
  measurement, 255
  orthogonality, 113 ff., 115 ff., 130, 145,
    149

Matrix (*Continued*)
   transposition, 118 f., 123
   vote, 123
     See also Data matrix; Q-matrix
Matthews, Donald R., 253 f., 281
Mayhew, David R., 184, 246
MDSCAL, computer procedures, 78 f., 81
   coordinates and factor analysis, 92
   separation of clusters, 82 ff.
     See also Nonmetric multidimensional scaling
Meaning, *see* Interpretation
Measurement, 6
   of attitudes, 16, 32
   in bloc analysis, 223
   and concepts, 6, 207, 209, 245, 248, 262, 275 f.
   error in, 23 f.
   of factor scores, 255
   of ideology, 259 f., 266, 276
   invariance and reliability, 275
   of membership, 176
   of partisanship, 191, 253, 257, 260, 287
   problems of, 14
   procedure of, 2
   of similarity, 41 ff., 198 n.
Meldrum, James A., 138, 202
Membership lists, measures based on, 176
Merriam, Robert E., 213
Mexican labor, 285
Miller, William E., 271
Mills, Wilbur, 270
Minorities, index of agreement and, 199, 212, 218, 228, 233
Minority Leader, 270, 271
Minres solution, in factor analysis, 132 n.
Moment, *see* Product-moment
Mosteller, Frederick, 46, 208
MSA-II, 170 n.
Multidimensional measurement, 287
   vs. cluster analysis, 83 f.
   model, 163 f.
Multidimensional space, axis rotation in, 112
Multiple dimensions, criterion of nearness in, 87
Multiplication, matrix, 122
     See also Postmultiplication; Premultiplication
Multivariate analysis of contingencies, 233

Noncommunality cluster analysis, 88, 106 f., 110
   communality estimates, 115
   pivot items, 117
     See also Variance

Nonmetric multidimensional scaling, 75–84
Nonvoting, *see* Absences
Norm, of vector, 132
Normalization, of eigenvectors, 134 f., 137, 140, 143, 147
   in Q-factor scores, 239
   in Varimax procedure, 129
   vector magnitude, 133
Notation, *see* Symbols
Numerical examples, *see* Examples

Objectivity in scaling, 29, 39
O'Konski, Alvin E., 68, 70, 283
O'Leary, Michael K., 123, 220
O'Neill, Thomas P., Jr., 274
Operationalism, naiveté in, 209
     See also Definition
Opposition, bipartisan, 177, 182 ff.
Order, of matrices, 119
Ordering, in tree diagram, 213
Ordinal matrix, *see* Ranked matrix; Cluster analysis
Organizations, and ideology, 251
     See also Committee; Majority; Minority; Whip
Origin, distance from, 125
Orthogonality, of cutting lines, 264
   of eigenvectors, 135
   of factor loadings, 117, 135, 170, 264
   of factor scores, 113–117, 130, 145, 149
   nonorthogonality, 146, 240
   in rotation, 118, 127, 130
   of vectors, 135
     See also Matrix
Overall, John E., 107

Pairwise relations, matrices of, 51, 119
   and positive proportion, 58
   in rank reversals, 36
   roll-call comparison, 39 f.
   of scale items, 25
   and Yule's Q, 49
Parsons, Talcott, 243, 251
Partial relationships, 99
Partisanship, on agriculture, 270, 274
   analysis, 197, 247 f.
   axis rotation, 192, 262, 286
   civil rights, 188, 190, 260
   concepts of, 195, 248 f.
   cutting lines, 193, 196, 266
   definition, 5, 283
   and Establishment, 195 f., 282
   fluctuations, 202, 205, 273
   on foreign aid, 190, 260, 281
   graphing, 185 ff.
   historical series, 200

Proportion (*Continued*)
  and cross-product, 46
  and cutting lines, 266, 285
  difficulty factors, 158
  faction identification, 222
  in index of difference, 183
  and pairwise comparisons, 58
  and phi, 152, 158
  in ranking of legislators, 30
  roll-call scalability, 191
  zero-box criterion, 42
Proxy voting in France, 178
Prussian National Assembly (1848), 252 n.
Psychological testing, 40 f., 158, 279
Public opinion, congressional appraisal, 71

Q, *see* Yule's Q
Q-matrix, for artificial data, 166, 241
  clusters from, 161 f., 169
  vs. distance matrix, 84 f., 160, 162, 169
  eigenvalues, 166–168, 241
    negative, 143, 151, 155, 159 n., 168, 237, 239
  factor analysis, 113, 154, 156 f., 159, 230, 237 ff., 257, 284
  factor scores, nonorthogonality of, 146, 240
  not Gramian, 151
  of House Republicans, 60
  information in, 84, 86, 161, 170
  least squares in, 238
  perfect-scale factor, 84, 151, 240
  vs. phi, 109, 153 f.
  principal-component analysis of, 151, 238
  residuals in, 107, 151, 159
  threshold in, 56, 58, 82
  tree diagram with, 85 f.
  vote selection by, 53

Race relations, *see* Civil rights
Rank order typal analysis, 76
Rank, reversals, 35 f.
  scores, 30 f., 256, 278
Ranked matrix, 54, 75–78
Ranking, 37 n., 50, 54, 75, 87 f.
Ratings by observer, 282
Rayburn, Sam, 274, 282
Rearrangement, of matrices, 16, 21, 63, 224
Reed, Daniel A., 68, 70
Regional groupings, in House, 268, 273
  in India, 218
  international, 216

in Senate, 211
Regression, 142
  equation, 93 f., 95 f. 102 f., 113 f., 253
  linear and dichotomies, 93 n.
Reliability, 275
Religion, *see* Catholicism
Representation, congressional vs. presidential, 205
Reproducibility, coefficient of, 23, 264, 266
  See also Adequacy
Republican National Committee Chairman, 271
Republicans in Congress, 58, 245, 280 f.
  cluster analysis of, 64, 70, 78, 82–85, 108
  division on issues, 144
  liberalism and conservatism among, 66, 188, 264, 266 f., 271
  partisanship, 99 f.
  phi-factors, 152, 156 f.
  Q-factors, 156 f.
  scaling, 64, 67, 72 ff.
  Senators, 18, 22, 26, 52
  votes, 19, 22, 26, 52 f., 67, 245 f.
Residuals, computation of, 126
  in correlation matrix, 103, 107, 135, 138, 146
  in data matrix, 139, 141
  in factor analysis, 88, 111, 113 ff.
  in Q-matrix 107, 151, 159
  from regression line, 95 f., 102, 253, 255
  space produced by, 110
  uncorrelated, 114 f.
Reversal, in indices, 45, 50
  of polarity, 45
  of rank, 32 ff.
  of signs, 137
Reversibility, criterion for indices, 45, 50
Rice, Stuart A., 5, 179–182, 188, 192, 196, 203, 209, 212, 223, 226
Rieselbach, Leroy N., 74, 155, 285
Riker, William H., 178, 284
Ripley, Randall B., 4, 249, 273, 280
Roll-call votes, artificial data, 168, 170, 244
  classification of, 12 f.
  clustering, 159 f., 168, 211
  comparisons, split-half, 279
  cutting line slopes, 196, 265
  disadvantages, 4 f.
  dissidence criteria, 59
  duality with legislators, 20, 27, 142, 149, 226, 236
  duplicated, 117, 230, 240, 279
  factor loadings, 138, 260, 276, 279